Organisational Behaviour

D0335516

ORGANISATIONAL BEHAVIOUR
AN INTRODUCTION

Edited by

CHRISTINE CROSS

RONAN CARBERY

© 2016 Christine Cross and Ronan Carbery

Individual chapters © 2016 Individual contributors

All rights reserved. No reproduction, copy or transmission of this publication may be made without written permission.

No portion of this publication may be reproduced, copied or transmitted save with written permission or in accordance with the provisions of the Copyright, Designs and Patents Act 1988, or under the terms of any licence permitting limited copying issued by the Copyright Licensing Agency, Saffron House, 6–10 Kirby Street, London EC1N 8TS.

Any person who does any unauthorized act in relation to this publication may be liable to criminal prosecution and civil claims for damages.

The authors have asserted their rights to be identified as the authors of this work in accordance with the Copyright, Designs and Patents Act 1988.

First published 2016 by
PALGRAVE

Palgrave in the UK is an imprint of Macmillan Publishers Limited, registered in England, company number 785998, of 4 Crinan Street, London, N1 9XW.

Palgrave Macmillan in the US is a division of St Martin's Press LLC, 175 Fifth Avenue, New York, NY 10010.

Palgrave is a global imprint of the above companies and is represented throughout the world.

Palgrave® and Macmillan® are registered trademarks in the United States, the United Kingdom, Europe and other countries.

ISBN 978–1–137–42944–5   paperback

This book is printed on paper suitable for recycling and made from fully managed and sustained forest sources. Logging, pulping and manufacturing processes are expected to conform to the environmental regulations of the country of origin.

A catalogue record for this book is available from the British Library.

A catalog record for this book is available from the Library of Congress.

Library of Congress Cataloging-in-Publication Data

Names: Cross, Christine, editor. | Carbery, Ronan, editor.
Title: Organisational behaviour : an introduction / Christine Cross, Ronan Carbery.
Other titles: Organisational behaviour (Palgrave Macmillan)
Description: London : New York, NY : Palgrave Macmillan, 2016. | Includes index.
Identifiers: LCCN 2015043146 | ISBN 9781137429445 (pbk.)
Subjects: LCSH: Organizational behavior.
Classification: LCC HD58 . 7 .O668734 2016 | DDC 658—dc23
LC record available at http://lccn.loc.gov/2015043146

Printed in China

SHORT CONTENTS

CONTENTS

LIST OF FIGURES

LIST OF TABLES

ABOUT THE EDITORS

Dr Christine Cross is Senior Lecturer in Human Resource Management and Organisational Behaviour and Head of the Department, Personnel and Employment Relations at the Kemmy Business School, University of Limerick. Prior to joining the University of Limerick she worked for a number of multinational organisations in both management and human resource management roles. This experience has led to a wide range of research, consultancy and publication interests covering areas such as the workforce experiences of immigrants, training and development in call centres, and investigating the glass ceiling. She is co-editor of *Human Resource Management: A Concise Introduction* (2013) and *Human Resource Development: A Concise Introduction* (2015), both published by Palgrave.

Dr Ronan Carbery is Senior Lecturer in Management in the School of Management and Marketing at University College Cork. Ronan is co-editor of the *European Journal of Training and Development*. His research interests include career development, talent management and participation in human resource development (HRD) activities. Ronan was awarded the University of Limerick Teaching Excellence award in 2013. He is co-editor of *Human Resource Management: A Concise Introduction* (2013) and *Human Resource Development: A Concise Introduction* (2015), both published by Palgrave.

ABOUT THE CONTRIBUTORS

Dr Vivienne Byers is a Lecturer in the College of Business at the Dublin Institute of Technology and teaches organisational behaviour and change, as well as public sector management. She also lectures as adjunct faculty at University College Dublin in the area of public sector management and leadership, and has carried out consultancy in the health sector. She has a background in communications development, having practised as a speech and language therapist for many years. Her research interests include organisational behaviour, communication, change and leadership in the public sector.

Dr Colette Darcy is Vice Dean for Postgraduate Studies and Research within the School of Business and a Senior Lecturer in Human Resource Management at the National College of Ireland. She is a former Government of Ireland Scholar and was awarded the European Foundation for Management Development/Emerald Outstanding Doctoral Thesis Award for her research examining employee fairness perceptions and claiming behaviour. Her research interests extend to organisational justice and work–life balance. She has published her work in a number of academic journals including

the *European Journal of Industrial Training* which awarded her the Outstanding Paper Award Winner at the Literati Network Awards for Excellence in 2008.

Dr Michelle Hammond is a Lecturer in organisational behaviour at the University of Limerick. She is also course director for the MSc in Work and Organisational Psychology. Michelle's research focuses on leadership, work–life balance, and creativity and innovation. In addition to authoring *An Integrative Theory of Leader Development: Connecting Adult Development, Identity, and Expertise*, she has published in journals such as the *Journal of Managerial Psychology, Journal of Vocational Behavior* and *Human Resource Management Review*.

Dr Jennifer Hennessy is a lecturer in Human Resource Management in the School of Business at the Waterford Institute of Technology. Her areas of interest include person–organisation fit, career management, work–life interaction strategies and employee engagement. She has presented her work at a number of international conferences. Jennifer is a senior researcher with RIKON (a service innovation centre based at the School of Business, Waterford Institute of Technology). She is a reviewer for the *European Journal of Training and Development* and holds Chartered CIPD membership. Prior to this she was employed as a human resource management (HRM) generalist in a multinational high technology organisation where she managed a redundancy and career development outreach programme.

Dr Gráinne Kelly is a Lecturer in Human Resource Management at Queen's University Belfast. She is a former Government of Ireland Scholar (IRCHSS) and was awarded a University of Limerick Advanced Scholarship to conduct her PhD studies. She has presented her research at numerous academic and professional conferences and has published articles in such journals as the *Human Resource Management Journal*, *International Journal of Human Resource Management*, *Work, Employment and Society* and *Personnel Review*. She is an External Examiner for Carlow Institute of Technology and a Char-

tered Member of the Chartered Institute of Personnel and Development (MCIPD). Gráinne is a reviewer for journals such as the *International Journal of Human Resource Management*, *Journal of Managerial Psychology* and *Personnel Review*. Her research focuses on employee perspectives of HRM in knowledge intensive firms, knowledge management and international HRM.

Dr Jean McCarthy lectures in the areas of human resource management, organisational behaviour and human resource development in the Department of Personnel and Employment Relations at the Kemmy Business School, University of Limerick. She is also a Global Research Associate with the Sloan Center on Aging and Work at Boston College, and a former Fulbright Scholar at Colorado State University. Jean is co-director of the Age in the Workplace Research Network (AWR-net), which is an international, interdisciplinary network of researchers concerned with advancing knowledge on age-related issues at work. Her other research interests include the social psychology of prejudice and strategic HRM. Jean has extensive experience in teaching at undergraduate, postgraduate and post-experience levels, as well as working with community-based and youth reach education and training programmes.

Dr Paul McGrath is a Lecturer in the areas of organisational behaviour, organisational theory and change management in the University College Dublin Michael Smurfit School of Business. He has a PhD from the Warwick Business School. Paul worked for 11 years in the Irish civil service and has engaged in a range of consulting and training assignments in the Irish public, private and voluntary sectors. He has published his research in a number of international journals and regularly presents his work at international conferences. His current research interests include the changing dynamics of organisational design, in particular the shift towards cellular or holographic modes of organising; the difficulties organisations face in investigating and learning from mistakes; and the challenges of managing risk in dynamic and high-risk work contexts. He has received awards for both his teaching and research.

Dr Caroline Murphy researches and lectures in the Department of Personnel and Employment Relations at the Kemmy Business School, University of Limerick. Caroline is a former IRRT-funded research scholar. She completed her PhD in 2011 in the area of trade union organising and collective representation in the workplace. She also holds a Masters in International Tourism from the University of Limerick. She lectures in industrial relations, human resource management and organisational behaviour. Caroline has extensive experience in teaching at undergraduate, postgraduate and post-experience levels, and in the delivery of courses to specific industry groups. Her current research interests include employee representation, female labour market participation and progression, and precarious work practices.

Jill Pearson is a Lecturer in work and organisational psychology, organisational behaviour and research methodology at the Kemmy Business School, University of Limerick. She was inaugural course director of the University of Limerick's MSc in Work and Organisational

Psychology/Behaviour. Prior to joining the University, she worked in HR in both the public and private sectors and she studied and taught at the London School of Economics and the London Business School. Her primary area of research focuses on careers and career success. Jill is a member of the International Careers Research Project that is conducting comparative, longitudinal research on the careers of graduates internationally. Her research also includes 360-degree feedback, absenteeism, customer incivility, aging and gender.

Dr Lorraine Ryan lectures in employment relations and human resource management at the University of Limerick. She is a former IRCHSS Government of Ireland scholar. Her research interests include employment relations, workplace bullying, working time, annual hours agreements, workplace partnership, collaborative bargaining and mutual gains. She was previously part of an international consortium of researchers examining employment relations in the airline industry and is currently part of a research team for a study commissioned by the Irish government looking at the prevalence of zero hours and low hours contracts and their impact on employees. Lorraine has presented papers at a number of national and international

conferences and has published in the *International Journal of Human Resource Management* and *European Management Journal.* She is a member of the Irish Academy of Management and the International Association on Workplace Bullying and Harassment.

Dr Deirdre O'Shea is a Registered Work and Organisational Psychologist and Lecturer at the Kemmy Business School, University of Limerick. Deirdre's research interests include psychological resource-based interventions, emotions and emotion regulation, self-regulation, work motivation, proactive behaviour, occupational health psychology, the psychology of entrepreneurship, and voice and silence in the workplace. She has published in both national and international peer-reviewed journals, and regularly presents at international conferences. She is currently involved in a number of national and international collaborative research projects investigating these topics and has received research funding from the Irish Research Council (2014), Enterprise Ireland (2008, 2009), and European Association of Work and Organisational Psychology (2013), among others. She has also received funding from the National Forum for the Enhancement of Teaching and Learning (2014).

Dr Ultan Sherman lectures in organisational behaviour and human resource management in the Department of Management and Marketing at University College Cork. His research interests lie broadly in the relationship between work and psychology with specific focus on the psychological contract and knowledge circulation in organisations. He has published in *Group and Organization Management*, a leading international journal in the organisational behaviour field. A Registered Psychologist with the Psychological Society of Ireland, Ultan has worked with major multinational companies in the areas of employee development, selection and team dynamics.

FOREWORD

Organisations are changing dramatically as we move to a fully post-industrial society in which the service economy has risen significantly. There is now a tremendous emphasis on knowledge sharing and collaboration in organisations as firms try to extract the competitive advantage that resides in the intellect of employees. Managers have had to adjust to the rise of new organisational forms including the professional service model and virtually enabled networks, as well as the more traditional industrial forms we are accustomed to. Increasingly, organisations face the need to think not just about profits but also about people and the planet. Environmental awareness, once a thing of some curiosity, is now a real factor in the decision-making of giant corporations and governments who can see the tangible impact of climate change worldwide. Yet, even these values differ across countries and across organisational boundaries.

As a result, much management education needs to focus on creating global managers who are highly competent and capable of operating across borders. Management educators are now faced with generational and cultural differences in the classroom. They need to engage with the Facebook generation who are impatient with older technologies and 'me-too' textbooks. These students need to be stimulated with social media, internet-based resources, live cases, video clips and online quizzes. I am very pleased to say that all of these issues and approaches have been incorporated in the design and delivery of this textbook. I am sure it will act as a great introduction to the discipline of organisational behaviour for undergraduates and managers alike. It is written in an interesting way and will stimulate students to enquire further and delve deeper into the subject. Students will begin to question their own psychological make up and to become aware of their own decision-making biases. Additional assessments of their leadership, motivational style and personality will help them to become self-aware. Self-awareness is now the holy grail of leadership development for managers and it is great that students will become mindful of this topic at an early stage of their studies.

The authors are to be commended for writing an accessible, interesting and relevant textbook on organisational behaviour. I am sure that it will be well received and know that it will be highly effective in helping to develop the next generation of managers in the public and private sectors, to include NGOs and health services as well as those who work in the digital economy.

Professor Patrick Flood, FAcSS, FRSA,
Professor of Organisational Behaviour at Dublin City University

PREFACE AND EDITORS' ACKNOWLEDGEMENTS

While there are a large number of excellent organisational behaviour (OB) textbooks available, the impetus for writing this came from the fact that there are few which provide material for an introductory one-semester taught course, which include information from contexts all over the world, including the UK, US, Ireland, Middle East and Europe. This book has been written primarily for first and second year undergraduate students who are taking OB modules for the first time, and the concepts discussed in this book are relevant to students from any discipline.

We have written this book in easy to understand language and have presented the material in such a way as to highlight the practicality of the issues involved in work and employment. There is a strong emphasis on skills development throughout each of the thirteen chapters, with key features such as up to date news pieces, active case studies, discussion activities, highlighted key terms and video interviews with experienced OB and HR professionals.

We would like to acknowledge the help we received with writing this text. Ursula Gavin, Lauren Zimmerman, Georgia Walters and Amy Grant at Palgrave provided incredible assistance and support from the initial proposal stage to the design and layout of the final text. The anonymous reviewers of each of the chapters provided excellent feedback for which we are very grateful. In addition to the contributors to the textbook, we would like to thank colleagues at the University of Limerick, in particular, Patrick Gunnigle, Noreen Heraty, Jonathan Lavelle, Sarah MacCurtain, Juliet McMahon, Michelle O'Sullivan and Tom Turner who provided us with support and encouragement throughout the process.

We are particularly grateful for the time that the participants in the Spotlight on Skills video features gave us, and for their excellent insights into industry practice.

Finally, we would like to thank our families: Dave, Oisín and Luíseach Cross, and Michelle and Julie Carbery.

TOUR OF THE BOOK

Learning Outcomes

A set of learning outcomes are identified at the start of each chapter. After you have studied the chapter, completed the activities and answered the review questions, you should be able to achieve each of the objectives.

Key Terms

Each chapter contains an on-page explanation of a number of important words, phrases and concepts that you need to know in order to understand OB, its theoretical basis and its related areas.

Making Links

To allow you to see the interconnected nature of the topics in the field of OB, areas that link to topics and concepts in other chapters are identified.

POWER IN ORGANISATIONS

Power is everywhere in organisations and people are concerned with it – those who have it want to keep it and those who don't have it often want to get it. Yet power is a difficult concept to identify and is often confused with other concepts such as authority and leadership. For example, a manager may find it difficult to get employees to do what he wants them to do, even though he is in a position of authority. Someone else in the organisation may easily persuade others to do as she wants, but is not 'the boss'. So, who has more power in these two situations? Where does power come from and why are some people in organisations powerful, while others aren't? How do people in organisations use their power? To answer these questions, we must first understand what power is.

DEFINING POWER

Dahl's (1957) famous definition of power asserts that it exists where person A can get person B to do something that B would not otherwise do. A closely related concept is influence. Power often refers to the *potential* of one person to cause another to act in accordance with their wishes, whereas influence refers to the actual *behaviour* of that person (Somech and Drach-Zahavy, 2001). Definitions of power typically assume that the person with power and the person subject to it have incompatible objectives; influence, however, can be exerted collaboratively where goals are not mutually exclusive (Tjosvold et al., 1992). The essence of power therefore may be control over the *behaviour of others* or the ability to influence others. This may be achieved by bringing about change in others' beliefs or attitudes or by having the capacity to reward or punish others. In an organisational context, power can stem from those who have control over resources and the ability to make decisions around the allocation of those resources to others. Power can come in many different forms, but importantly, power is not absolute.

The extent of power is dependent on the amount of resistance to it. In other words, person A has more power over person B if he can get B to do something without B 'putting up a fight' or resisting doing it. The extent to which people will resist power or succumb to influence depends on a number of factors including personality ▶ Chapter 24 and culture. The cultural values of a society have a tremendous impact on the extent to which people readily accept others in positions of power. Hofstede's (1991) well-known model of culture identified power distance ▶ Chapter 12◀ as reflecting the extent to which employees welcome the idea that people in organisations rightfully have power. Japan typically has a high level of power distance, meaning people readily accept the role of management as power holders. Western cultures tend to have lower power distance, meaning that they do not accept management power as readily and value individuality and diversity. This makes them less susceptible to power influence. Dependency is also very important when examining power relationships. The more dependent one party is on another, the more they may be influenced by them.

power exists where person A can get person B to do something that B would not otherwise do.

In Reality

These short vignettes demonstrate that OB is not merely 'common sense', but based on rigorous research and evidence which often contradicts our assumptions.

50 ORGANISATIONAL BEHAVIOUR

IN REALITY

Have you ever heard the old adage 'what you see is what you get'? We tend to think that our perceptions are relatively stable and unfaltering and that what we perceive closely matches the real world. However, in fact, our perception can often be manipulated to change what we experience. Many companies invest significant marketing and advertising resources to try and create a certain perception of their product. In a study conducted by researchers at Columbia University and MIT, participants in a pub were asked to evaluate regular beer and an 'MIT brew' to which a few drops of balsamic vinegar had been added (Lee et al, 2006). The researchers discovered that disclosure of the additional ingredient of the balsamic vinegar significantly reduced people's preference for the MIT brew only when the disclosure took place prior to tasting. This suggests that participants' perceptions changed enough to influence how they experienced the subsequent tasting of the beer. What is also interesting is the fact that the addition of the balsamic vinegar can actually enhance the flavour of the beer, yet people's perception of the taste of vinegar produced a negative connection to its taste in the beer. This connection was strong enough to alter subjects' perception of what the beer would taste like!

This experiment demonstrates how our perception can be influenced to such a degree that it can change our subsequent experience of an event. Our perception of an event or experience is therefore subject to various influences and is not as objective as the old adage would lead us to believe.

Consider This ...

This feature is designed to stimulate critical thinking about a specific issue, idea or perspective related to the chapter topic.

EMOTIONS AND THE WORKPLACE   137

CONSIDER THIS...

Ashton-Jones and Ashkanasy (2008) showed how specific discrete emotions have different effects on our behaviour and actions. Consider the impact of the following emotions in these work-related contexts:

1   If moral emotions (for example, guilt, shame) have the effect of making us less likely to engage in unethical behaviour and acting on immoral decisions, why do people still engage in unethical and immoral acts?
2   If an employee has an angry exchange with his manager, how might this impact his trust of that manager? Are there other factors that this depends on?
3   What is the effect of fear versus anger during organisational change ▶ Chapter 13◀?

employee is very satisfied with their job, they have no reason to change or to try anything differently. Researchers have suggested that managers want *engaged* workers, rather than satisfied workers (Bakker and Oerlemans, 2011). Work engagement is associated with active positive emotions and so provides the motivational drive to strive for higher effort and performance.

Emotions can also help us to learn. By providing feedback, emotions may stimulate retrospective appraisal of actions, and in this way, conscious emotional states can promote learning and alter guidelines for future behaviour (Baumeister et al., 2007b). Furthermore, emotions amplify the nature of consequences and outcomes in terms of reward and punishment (Tice, 2009). Finally, emotions stimulate counterfactual thinking, which can enhance the prospects of improving behaviour by considering alternatives to events that have already occurred (Tice, 2009). Hence, emotions can lead to adaptive improvements in behaviour by improving learning. For example, Keith and Frese (2005) demonstrated that emotion control contributed to more effective learning when individuals were encouraged to make errors during training.

OB in the News

Each chapter contains an example of coverage of its main topic in the media. The aim here is to highlight how you can apply the constructs and concepts in the chapter to the management of people in the real world of the workplace. A set of questions accompanies each feature to assist with this application to a practical situation.

316 ORGANISATIONAL BEHAVIOUR

ASDA's Planned Strategic Change in Northern Ireland

In 2005, Britain's second-biggest supermarket, Asda, bought 12 Safeway supermarket stores in Northern Ireland from Morrisons for £73.6 million. Asda is owned by US retail organisation Walmart. Asda's leaders formulated a new strategy which involved changing perceptions of Safeway as a discount store targeting working-class customers to marketing itself to wealthier shoppers. However, one of the key problems with this strategy was that it was led by senior management who failed to draw upon the store managers' knowledge that existing customers were no longer visiting the stores, resulting in huge losses for the organisation.

Asda's executives learned that, for change implementation to stay on track, knowledge of whether interventions were working must be communicated upward and shared in a timely way with top management.

Other issues that the company faced involved the local community's fears about the implications of this change for indigenous farmers and producers. Asda reassured customers and promised to collaborate with all of Safeway's existing Northern Irish product suppliers. It also offered prices which mirrored those of its stores in the rest of the UK. Its prices were very competitive and resulted in savings for customers and significant investment in Northern Ireland through job-creation which initially amounted to 250 new jobs. After undergoing a successful change process, Asda's business went from strength to strength with a growing number of stores in Northern Ireland. The company also expanded its range of products to include books, movies, electronics, flowers, furniture, mobile phones, and insurance, photo and travel services.

IN THE NEWS

1   Consider what has happened in the retail industry since Asda came to Northern Ireland.
2   What other major changes have occurred since 2005, and what was the nature of these changes?

Source:
http://news.bbc.co.uk/1/hi/northern_ireland/4412261.stm (last accessed 26 August 2016).

LEWIN'S CHANGE MODEL

In the mid-20th century, psychologist Kurt Lewin identified three stages of change that are the basis of contemporary approaches to change management. In the aftermath of the Second World War, Lewin published two essays, 'Behaviour and Development as a Function of the Total Situation' (1946) and 'Frontiers in Group Dynamics' (1947) (see Lewin, 1951), which made important contributions to our understanding of organisational change and development. First, he highlighted the role that context plays in shaping individual behaviours.

Building Your Skills

This feature asks you to place yourself in the position of a line manager and to think about what you would do in the situation that has been presented to you.

Active Case Study

Short case studies at the end of each chapter provide the opportunity for you to link the material covered in that chapter to a real-life situation. Questions are posed at the end of the case studies, which can be answered either in class or as part of an assignment. Longer cases appear at the end of each section and demonstrate how multiple concepts, such as personality, perception and motivation, come together in practice.

Chapter Review Questions

Each chapter ends with questions that can be used as class exercises or for self-testing and evaluating your knowledge about the chapter topic.

Multiple Choice Questions:

In the interactive ebook these multiple choice questions test your understanding of the key points in each chapter.

Further Reading

The aim of these lists is to highlight a few specific texts and journal articles we believe can assist you in developing your understanding and furthering your knowledge of the many areas introduced in this book.

Useful Websites

An abundance of websites exist on topics related to OB. At the end of each chapter we have identified those we believe you will find most useful in furthering your knowledge and understanding of the discipline.

Spotlight on Skills: text and video feature

This feature aims to encourage you to develop your skills in OB by asking you to consider specific questions and activities. This gives you the opportunity to identify and diagnose problems and formulate possible solutions or actions in relation to the chapter topic. Each of these features is accompanied by a video interview with a professional that plays in your interactive ebook. The skills-related questions posed in the text feature are addressed by the practitioner in the video. To maximise this resource, you should first attempt to answer the questions in the book and then watch the video.

Companion Website

The book's companion website at www.palgrave.com/carbery-ob offers a number of resources for both lecturers and students, including PowerPoint slides, a comprehensive testbank of multiple choice questions and solutions to the Active Case Study questions.

DIGITAL RESOURCES

About the Interactive Ebook

Included free with each copy of *Organisational Behaviour* is access to an interactive ebook. Replicating the pages of the printed book and offering all the versatility of an ebook that you would expect, such as bookmarking and easy searching, the ebook also features a wealth of multimedia content:

- **Video interviews** with a range of business professionals, to accompany the Spotlight on Skills text feature. Once you've attempted the questions, click ▶ to watch the video.
- **Multiple choice quizzes** at the end of every chapter to test your understanding. Simply click ☑ to begin the quiz.
- The end-of-chapter **summaries in audio format** to help you revise. Click 🔊 to hear them.

The unique code included with your book gives you access to the ebook for a whole year. After the initial download, the ebook can be read offline, giving you freedom and flexibility to use it on campus, at home, even on the bus! For details on how to download your ebook, visit www.palgrave.com/carbery-ob with your individual code at the ready. You'll never find yourself falling behind on the reading your lecturer assigns, with the book accessible anytime and anywhere from your mobile device or laptop.

About the Website

In addition to the interactive ebook, a range of resources for both students and instructors is available at www.palgrave.com/carbery-ob.

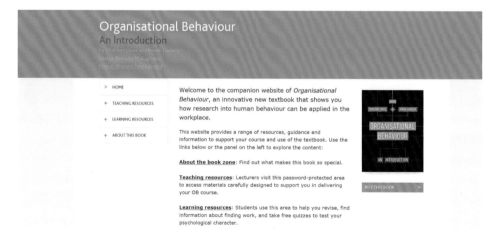

Resources for students:

- Flashcards to test your understanding of the key terms in OB
- Employability resources: links to additional information about finding work
- Links to free online quizzes to test your psychological character

Resources for instructors:

Instructors who adopt this book gain access to a selection of resources to help plan and deliver their courses:

- A testbank containing multiple choice questions for every chapter
- Chapter-by-chapter PowerPoint® slides to use in teaching
- Teaching notes to accompany all the Active Case Studies questions
- The Spotlight on Skills video interviews to play in class

ABOUT THE SPOTLIGHT ON SKILLS CONTRIBUTORS

There are 13 Spotlight on Skills features in this textbook, each linking to videos on the companion website. Background information about the practitioners and their experience is given below.

Chapter 1: Carla DiBenedetto, Cook Medical

Carla DiBenedetto has been employed by Cook Medical since 2005, working initially as part of the European HR team managing employees based in the UK, Italy, the Netherlands and Scandinavian countries. Carla is currently HR Manager for Cook Ireland & the Shared Service Centre. Carla holds a Bachelor of Civil Law Degree from University College Cork, and a Graduate Diploma in Business Administration and Master of Science in Human Resource Management from the University of Limerick.

Chapter 2: Fiona Clarke, Eurostar

Fiona Clarke has worked in HR for 13 years in a variety of industries – pharmaceuticals, medical devices, global distribution and retail – and in a variety of cultures, including American, Japanese, British and Irish. More recently, Fiona has been employed by Eurostar International Limited, initially as an HR Business Partner for Commercial and Corporate Services. In this role Fiona established a partnership approach with her internal client groups, supporting them in all aspects of HR. In June 2015, Fiona moved into a new role as Project Management Office (PMO) Manager within Eurostar, responsible for establishing the PMO function through a partnership approach with the business and for managing the quality of a portfolio of company-wide strategic projects.

Fiona holds an Honours Degree in Human Resource Management and Marketing from the University of Stirling, a Diploma in Project Management from Dublin Business School and a professional qualification from the CIPD (Chartered Institute of Personnel and Development).

Chapter 3: Gavin Connell, University of Limerick

Gavin Connell is the Head of Careers, Cooperative Education & Careers Division, University of Limerick. Gavin is Masters-qualified in work and organisational behaviour with a degree in Human Resources. He has 20 years of industrial experience in manufacturing, process engineering, learning and development, recruitment, and has HR experience in Ireland and also across Europe, the Middle East and Africa (EMEA).

Gavin currently supports students in developing employability skills and implementing their career plans, and is also responsible for engaging employers on all matters of graduate recruitment and employability. A significant element of this role is to influence policy formulation and planning within the University on issues relating to career development and employability, as well as graduate employment. He holds a Level A/B Psychological Society qualification in Psychometric testing/Profiling and is also MBTI certified.

Chapter 4: Melissa Challinor, Which?

Melissa Challinor has worked at Which? since 2006, initially as Training and Development Manager where she introduced City & Guilds qualifications for the Member Service Centre. Melissa is currently the Resourcing and Development Manager there, responsible for recruiting, onboarding and developing new employees, ongoing learning for existing employees and bespoke learning such as a 9-month programme for the Which? legal team. Melissa redesigned the assessment tools for Member Services for which she received a team Talent award. Melissa is a Chartered Member of the CIPD and holds MSc and BSc degrees from the University of Essex. She is also a British Psychological Society member and accredited in the use of the Hogan and Talent Q tools.

Chapter 5: Clare Hodder, Freelance Rights Consultant

Clare Hodder is a Rights and Licensing Consultant working with a broad range of publishers and service providers to help develop profitable licensing opportunities and establish compliant rights acquisition practices. Prior to embarking on a consultancy career Clare was the Associate Director of Rights for Palgrave Macmillan, having worked within various rights roles for the company over a 15-year period.

In addition she chaired the Publishers Association's Academic and Professional Division Copyright Committee for 9 years and remains an active participant in industry fora concerned with copyright and licensing issues.

Clare studied English at Southampton University and holds a Post Graduate Diploma in Publishing.

Chapter 6: Fiona Fennell, The Cregg Group

Fiona Fennell is a Director of Cregg Recruitment. Fiona is Masters-qualified in Business Systems and Innovation with a Degree in Business, both from the University of Limerick. She is currently completing her Yellow Belt Certification in Lean/Six Sigma. With 20 years' recruitment and HR experience in Ireland and Australia, Fiona works regularly to design recruitment process outsourcing (RPO) service delivery models for key accounts and leads a team of 20 consultants. She holds a Level B Psychological Society qualification in Psychometric testing/Profiling.

Chapter 7: Doug Howlett, Munster Rugby

Doug holds the record of being the all-time leading try scorer for the All Blacks Rugby team. He has been involved in professional sports teams for 20 years. Doug is Corporate Ambassador for Munster Rugby where he works alongside the Commercial Board, using some of his many talents to broaden Munster's business network and commercial opportunities. Doug continues to have a number of personal endorsements and business interests. He is currently undertaking an MBA at University College Cork.

Chapter 8: Joanna Moriarty, Green Park Interim & Executive Search

Joanna Moriarty was Publishing Director for SPCK until 2014, during which time she also developed leadership roles in the third sector. She now sits on the boards of several charities, including Feed the Minds, and is designated a National Leader of Governance by the National College for Teaching, supporting school heads and Governing Bodies. Joanna now combines her third sector and leadership experiences as an Associate Partner in the Charities and Social Enterprise practice at Green Park, providing consultancy and governance reviews, and recruiting for both board and executive positions.

Chapter 9: Declan Deegan, Milford Care Centre, Limerick

Declan Deegan has over 20 years' experience in the area of HR. He has worked for Wang, EMC and with Dell Computers in many roles, including Recruitment Manager, Senior Human Resources Manager and EMEA Business Ethics Manager. He was also the HR manager for the overseas facility in Poland. He is currently Head of Human Resources, Education and Learning and Development at Milford Care Centre in Limerick.

Chapter 10: Gina London, international communications expert; and Philippa Brown, Springer Nature

Gina London is an Emmy award-winning CNN correspondent and anchor with more than a decade of television, radio, internet and print experience. She is now an internationally recognised speaker and expert at helping professionals improve themselves and their companies through dynamic and powerful communications.

During her network television tenure, Gina covered a wide range of breaking news stories including the US President Bill Clinton scandal and the aftermath of the 9/11 terrorist bombings. She later served as Senior Vice President and strategist for one of the largest government affairs firms in the United States, where she led media and public outreach positioning for multi-million dollar development, transit and energy campaigns.

Gina has expertise in nearly every facet of communications from social media, branding and crisis communications to working with the media and presentation skills. She MC'd the first *Day of Peace* at the Disney Institute in Florida, which featured Nobel Peace Prize Laureates Oscar Arias and Archbishop Desmond Tutu. She has consulted and conducted seminars around the world for hundreds of high-profile clients including SAP, Wells Fargo, Deloitte, Daimler and the US Department of State.

Having lived and or worked in more than a dozen countries including Ireland, France, Germany, Italy, Jordan, UK, UAE, Israel, Macedonia, Romania, Tunisia, Nigeria, Ghana, Cambodia and Indonesia, Gina is passionate about promoting professional cultural awareness. In 2006, she served as the first resident country director for the International Republican

Institute in Egypt until newspapers falsely labelled her a spy and called for her assassination, which prompted her to flee the country.

A published author, her writing and interviews have appeared in *The Orlando Sentinel*, *The Denver Post*, *Le Notizie*, *Travel Girl* magazine and *Fast Company*.

Philippa Brown is Global Internal Communication Manager at Springer Nature and has eight years' experience of managing internal communications during periods of complex organisational change. She enjoys designing innovative and effective communication solutions to diverse business challenges and has most recently specialised in developing and implementing employee communication strategies to support merger and integration activities.

Philippa has a BSc (Hons) in International Business from the University of Warwick and a Postgraduate Diploma in Internal Communications Management from Kingston University.

Chapter 11: Jigna Patel, Springer Nature

Jigna Patel has been working for Springer Nature since 2013 within the International Higher Education business as Finance Manager, providing financial analysis and commercial support to the Management Team as well as working alongside the central finance teams. Prior to Springer Nature, Jigna has held finance positions at advertising and marketing companies, as well as at a professional services firm where she gained her Chartered Accountant qualification in 2008. Jigna graduated from University College London with a BSc degree in Mathematics with Management.

Chapter 12: Micheál Clancy, Kerry Group

Micheál Clancy is HR Manager for Kerry's Food Ingredients manufacturing facilities in Charleville and Carrigaline in Ireland. Micheál started his career with Kerry Group in 2003 as part of their Graduate Development Programme, joining directly from the University of Limerick's Kemmy Business School. He has worked in a variety of HRM roles within the organisation, having previously been based in Kerry's Corporate Head Office in Tralee as well as a number of its manufacturing facilities in Ireland and the Netherlands. A Bachelor of Business Studies graduate of the University of Limerick, Micheál also holds a Diploma in Employment Law, a Diploma in Management Practice from the Irish Management Institute and a MBS in Human Resource Management from the University of Limerick.

Chapter 13: Simon Shaw, Eurostar

Simon Shaw is the Head of Eurostar's Contact Centre which houses 220 employees. He is responsible for driving and enhancing multi-channel customer experience strategy and working across the wider Eurostar business to use customer insight in order to drive continuous improvement. Simon has also successfully delivered a department-wide change programme to create clearer accountability across all management levels and stronger succession plans and career opportunities for frontline teams. He has a Diploma in Management Studies from Leicester University.

ACTIVE CASE STUDY GRID

Chapter	Title	Industry	Location	Focus
1	Direct selling	Various	Worldwide	Sales workforce
2	BrewBite	Micro Brewery	UK	Recruitment, selection and organisational culture fit
3	Bridgewater	Manufacturing	Germany	Continuous improvement process and employee perceptions
4	Pulsate	Home entertainment	UK/Ireland	Employee attitudes to a company takeover
5	A Tale of Two Sports	Soccer and rugby	Spain and New Zealand	Team motivation
6	Doctors on Duty	Medical profession	Any country	Emotions and the medical profession
7	Quality Teamwork?	Manufacturing	USA and China	Developing teams
8	Leadership for a New Generation?	High-tech	USA	Impact of leadership styles
9	EngCo.: Power, Politics and Conflict in Action	Engineering	Middle East	Sources of conflict and power and political tactics
10	Communications and Growth at Version 1	IT services	Western Europe	Social media communications strategy
11	Organisational Redesign at Novartis	Pharmaceutical	Switzerland	Organisational redesign initiative aimed at enhancing productivity
12	Trouble Brewing?	Craft Beer	Japan	Impact of outside investment on organisational culture
13	Change at PharmaChem	Pharmaceutical distributor	Asia	Strategies for managing change
End of Section One		Computer manufacture	Germany, Japan	Motivation, personality, perception, emotions, attitudes, global organisations
End of Section Two		Health care	Australia	Communication, organisational culture, organisational change

BUILDING YOUR SKILLS

Most of you reading this textbook will be undertaking a third-level programme and are focused on gaining employment once you graduate. While you are no doubt taking an Organisational Behaviour module because it is required as part of your programme, there is much to be learned about the way in which people act, react and interact in the workplace which will benefit you once you begin work. As you will find out while reading this book the overarching goal of Organisational Behaviour is to help us to explain, predict and control the behaviour of others at work. Following from that, the aim of this textbook is to help you to better understand the workplace and the behaviour of those who work there. In order to help you gain an insight into the behaviour of people in the workplace, throughout this textbook you will find a series of features in each chapter designed to help you develop your skills in a number of key areas that are common to most workplaces.

This textbook is structured around sections and chapters, but this is just in an effort to help you to better understand each topic. In reality all topics are connected; for example, when you are hiring someone new for the organisation you will be searching for information on their personality in order to determine whether they will 'fit' into the organisation's culture; you will be interested in their motivation for wanting to work for your organisation and their intrinsic level of motivation; you will be interested in their ability to communicate with you and with others in a group situation. So, in effect you are searching for an understanding of how they might behave in your organisation.

As mentioned in the Tour of the Book, there are two features entitled 'Building your Skills' in each chapter. The interrelatedness of these skills will become apparent as you work through the textbook. At the heart of all chapters is the concept of the management of people at work. If we now examine the skills identified in each chapter and their connections this will become clear.

In Chapter 1 you become aware of the importance of taking an evidence-based approach to making decisions and why this is key in the management of people at work. Too often assumptions are made about issues that directly impact on workers' behaviour. For example, many managers work on the assumption that everyone is motivated by money, so to offer people more money will directly result in an increase in output levels. We learn, however, in Chapter 5 that the skill of motivating people is a multifaceted concept. Managers need to have an understanding of the theories of motivation in order to better understand why some people are driven by money and some by other factors, such as praise for a job well done or the necessity to 'fit' into their work group. The national culture in which the organisation operates will also have an impact on the level of motivation. Those undertaking repetitive jobs are more likely to be bored at work and a key issue for management is how to motivate them. The use of the job characteristics model is a key concept in the design of jobs and helping you to understand why people behave the way they do at work. Having knowledge of it will help a manager to design work in order to maximise employee motivation.

The workplaces of today are home to a diverse group of people. People of different ages, genders, race and ability are all expected to work together in a way that allows the organisation to perform effectively. However, diversity brings challenges and a manager needs to understand the issues that a diverse workforce can create. These include difficulties in group work; in differing perceptions of policies and in understanding different cultural contexts. Team working brings a specific set of challenges. You are likely to be familiar with social loafing. This is where a member of the group does not fully engage with the work to be completed by the group yet expects to get credit for the group's work. It is important that teams function effectively and Chapter 7 deals with issues of team composition and how you can use Belbin's Team Roles to better understand the roles people play in teamwork. The role of leadership is a key concept in organisational behaviour. There are many different approaches to leadership and the skills necessary to develop a team are important for organisational functioning.

Working in an organisation brings with it many challenges and one of these is dealing with conflict at work. There can be many different reasons for the existence of conflict which are identified in Chapter 9 with some of the possible ways of resolving conflict. The concept of conflict resolution is also linked to the issues raised in earlier chapters which deal with personality traits and attitudes, both of which have an influence on your conflict resolution style. This chapter also examines the sources of power you may have and how an awareness of this can assist with understanding the conflict management process.

Chapters 11 to 13 deal with skills related to the organisational context in which you may be working. Organisations are subject to change and operate in a culturally diverse context, leading to a series of challenges which you have to be aware of. The importance of communication is a key skill here.

Chapter	Building Your Skills	
1	Decision-making	Managing people
2	Managing diversity	Making tough decisions
3	The dangers of confirmation bias	Perceptual errors
4	Conflict management	Managing relationships
5	Pay as a motivator	Applying the job characteristics model
6	Enhancing positive emotions	Learning to reappraise
7	Understanding team roles	Team building
8	Leadership skills	Group leadership
9	Identifying sources of power	Conflict resolution
10	Presentation skills	Understanding information overload
11	Understanding organisational structure	Contingency analysis
12	Communicating organisation culture to employees	Appreciating national cultural diversity
13	Understanding resistance to change	Change management skills

The need to have strong presentation skills is an aspect of your coursework which you may not enjoy, but presenting information is a feature of everyday working life. Regardless of the industry sector or size of organisation you will work in, you will need to have the ability to present your ideas clearly and succinctly. This will often happen in a setting where you use a software program such as Microsoft® PowerPoint to provide an overview of the context and the key points. Increasingly, job vacancies also require you to make an oral presentation as part of the selection process. During your time in college it is very likely you will be asked to make a presentation as part of a module. In order to communicate your ideas and arguments cogently, we suggest that you think about your presentation as involving a number of stages which we outline below. We identify the main points you should consider which will enable you to develop this important skill, either through your coursework or after university in your work life.

Planning your presentation

- Be clear about what your core message is and repeat this at different stages during the presentation in order to increase its impact. Is it to inform? To sell your idea? To defend a position? To present a new idea? Whatever the answer, keep asking yourself this in different ways. What is the objective I want to achieve? What will I accept as evidence that my presentation has succeeded? What do I want the audience to think or feel at the end of the presentation?
- Analyse your audience. What are their expectations of your presentation? Do they expect to be informed? Persuaded? Have their existing ideas challenged? What do they already know? The key to a successful presentation is to know what your audience expects and ensure that you meet or exceed that expectation.
- Ensure you know how much time you have for your presentation. Be careful not to run over an allocated time slot as this will detract from its effectiveness.
- Think about what you look like. What should you wear? This may seem a little strange to include here; however, confidence is an important element in an effective presentation. You need to be comfortable and appropriately dressed to project the 'right' message.

Handling nerves

Many people find this the most difficult part of making a presentation.
- Be well-prepared and organised. Most people will feel nervous before a presentation. Knowing what you are going to say will reduce your level of nervousness. The first two minutes of any presentation are the most crucial. If you feel confident and clear about what you are going to say in the early stage of the presentation this will help alleviate your nerves for the remainder. Once you have passed the first two minutes and you have started to believe that the presentation is going well, you can then be more confident that it will be a success.
- Don't read directly from your notes – use visual aids. This means that the words and/or images you select should act as your 'prompt'. Do not try and look down at hard copy notes in your hand as they will just provide a false sense of security. If you lose your place in

the notes, or have learned them off by heart and then accidentally mix them up, your level of effectiveness in the eyes of the audience will be diminished.

- Rehearse in advance. Trial runs are an excellent method of preparation and allow you to establish how long your presentation will take. This also develops your self-confidence, which will help to reduce your nervousness.
- Pay attention to your 'mannerisms' and work to overcome them. Ask a friend or family member to highlight any repeated unconscious behaviours you might have, such as running your hands through your hair, shaking the change in your pocket, swaying from side to side or speaking too fast. These are very distracting for the audience.
- Practise deep breathing before you get to the place where your presentation is taking place. This will help to reduce the overall feeling of nervousness.
- Arrive in the room early so that you have plenty of time to check the equipment and ensure that, if you are using a software program, your presentation is working.
- Thinking positively means you are more likely to feel and behave positively.

Structuring your presentation

The golden rule is simple:

- Tell them what you are going to tell them (introduction)
- Tell them (main body)
- Tell them what you've told them (conclusion).

The introduction

- The introduction should comprise approximately ten per cent of your presentation. It should provide a map for the reader of what is going to come.
- Introduce the topic and yourself (if necessary).
- Start with an attention-grabbing hook – make a bold claim, present a striking fact/statistic, ask a question, use a quotation. If you have a suitable quote, surprising information or a visual aid, use it to gain the interest of your audience.

The main body – delivery and body language

- Speak clearly and audibly throughout. Vary the tone of your voice as this will hold the audience's interest in your message.
- Don't speak too fast as your message can get lost if the audience are unable to follow it.
- Project your voice out towards the audience. Do not speak down to your shoes!
- Face the audience, not the screen behind you or your laptop. Speak directly to the audience and make eye contact with people in the room. This demonstrates that you are paying attention to them and encourages them to pay attention to you.
- Show enthusiasm for the topic/issue/idea, as enthusiasm is contagious.
- Regard the presentation as an opportunity to shine.

The conclusion

- Remind the audience of what you set out to do at the start. That means stressing the main message behind or aim of your presentation.
- Briefly repeat the main points you made.
- End on an interesting note, as this will assist people in remembering your presentation.
- Thank the audience for listening and invite questions.

PUBLISHER'S ACKNOWLEDGEMENTS

The publisher and the authors would like to thank the organisations and people listed below for permission to reproduce material from their publications:

American Psychological Association, for permission to reproduce:

Figure 2.1 'Personality dimensions across the life course.' Adapted from B. W. Roberts, K. E. Walton & W. Viechtbauer (2006). Patterns of mean-level change in personality traits across the life course: A meta-analysis of longitudinal studies. *Psychological Bulletin*, 132(1), 1–25. Copyright © 2006 by the American Psychological Association.

Figure 4.3 'The relationship between job satisfaction and job performance.' From Judge, T. A., Thoresen, C. J., Bono, J. E., and Patton, G. K. (2001). The Job Satisfaction-Job Performance Relationship: A Qualitative and Quantitative Review. *Psychological Bulletin*, 127(3), 376–407. Copyright © 2001 by the American Psychological Association.

Figure 5.2 'Maslow's hierarchy of needs theory.' From Maslow, A.H. (1943). A theory of human motivation. *Psychological Review*, 50(4), 370–396. This material is now in the public domain.

Figure 5.3 'Job characteristics model.' Adapted from Hackman, J. R. and Oldham, G. R. (1975). Development of the Job Diagnostic Survey. *Journal of Applied Psychology*, 60(2), 159–170. Copyright © 1975 by the American Psychological Association.

Figure 6.2 'The two-dimensional structure of core affect.' From Feldman Barrett, L., and Russell, J. A. (1998). Independence and bipolarity in the structure of current affect. *Journal of Personality and Social Psychology*, 74(4), 967–984. Copyright © 1998 by the American Psychological Association.

Figure 9.1 'Influence model.' Adapted from Yukl, G., Kim, H. and Falbe, C. M. (1996). Antecedents of influence outcomes. *Journal of Applied Psychology*, 81(3), 309–317. Copyright © 1996 by the American Psychological Association.

Figure 13.3 'Three-step model of change.' Adapted from Lewin, Kurt (1997). *Resolving Social Conflicts and Field Theory in Social Science*. Washington, DC: American Psychological Association. Copyright © 1997 by the American Psychological Association.

The Positive and Negative Affect Scale in the Trait Affectivity – Test Yourself box. From Watson, D., Clark, L. A., and Tellegen, A. (1988). Development and Validation of Brief Measures of Positive and Negative Affect: The PANAS Scales. *Journal of Personality and Social Psychology*, 54(6), 1063–1070. Copyright © 1988 by the American Psychological Association.

All reproduced with permission. The use of APA information does not imply endorsement by APA.

American Sociological Association and Charles Perrow, for permission to reproduce and adapt Figure 11.6 'Categorising external environments' and Figure 11.7 'Types of technology.' From Perrow, C. (Apr. 1967). A Framework for the Comparative Analysis of Organizations. *American Sociological Review*, 32(2), Figure 1, pg. 196. Copyright © ASA 1967.

Kim S. Cameron, for permission to reproduce and adapt Figure 12.2 'The competing values framework.' From Cameron, K. S., & Quinn, R. E. (1999). Diagnosing and changing organizational culture. Reading: Addison-Wesley. Copyright © Kim S. Cameron 1999.

Elsevier, for permission to reproduce:

Table 2.2 'Measure yourself on the Big Five.' From Gosling, S. D., Rentfrow, P. J., and Swann, W. B. (2003). A very brief measure of the Big-Five personality domains. *Journal of Research in Personality*, 37(6), 504–528. Copyright © Elsevier 2003.

Figure 4.1 'Theory of planned behaviour.' From Ajzen, I. (1991) The theory of planned behaviour. *Organizational Behavior and Human Decision Processes*, 50(2), 179–211. Copyright © Elsevier 1991.

Figure 4.4 'Organisational commitment questionnaire.' From Mowday, R.T., Steers, R.M., and Porter, L.W. (1979). The measurement of organizational commitment. *Journal of Vocational Behavior*, 14 (2), 224–247. Copyright © Elsevier 1979.

Dr Sybil Eysenck (Personality Investigations Publications & Services), for permission to reproduce Figure 2.3 'Eysenck's personality types and associated traits.' From Eysenck, HJ (1965) *Fact and Fiction in Psychology*. Harmondsworth: Penguin. Copyright © Personality Investigations Publications & Services 1965.

The Free Press, for permission to reproduce and adapt Table 8.1 'Leader traits and skills.' From *The Bass Handbook of Leadership: Theory, Research, and Managerial Applications*, 4th edition by Bernard M. Bass with Ruth Bass. Copyright © 1974, 1981, 1990, 2008 by The Free Press. All rights reserved. Reprinted with the permission of The Free Press, a Division of Simon & Schuster, Inc.

Gill & Macmillan, for permission to reproduce and adapt Figure 9.3 'Dual concerns model.' From Wallace, J., Gunnigle, P., McMahon, G. and O'Sullivan, M. (2013). *Industrial Relations in Ireland*. Dublin: Gill & Macmillan. Copyright © Gill & Macmillan 2013.

Gulf Publishing Company, for permission to reproduce and adapt Figure 8.1 'The managerial grid.' From Blake, R. and Mouton, J. (1964). *The Managerial Grid: Key Orientations for Achieving Production through People*. Houston, TX: Gulf Publishing Company. Copyright © Gulf Publishing Company 1964.

Harvard Business Publishing, for permission to reproduce and adapt Table 13.1 'Kotter's 8-step process.' From Kotter, J. P. (March-April1995). Leading Change: Why Transformation Efforts Fail. *Harvard Business Review*, 73(2), 59–67. Copyright © 1995 by the President and Fellows of Harvard College.

Pierce Howard and Jane Howard, for permission to reproduce and adapt Table 2.1 'The Big Five Personality Dimensions.' From Howard, P.J. and Howard, J.M. (2001). *The Owner's Manual for Personality at Work: How the Big Five Personality Traits Affect Performance, Communication,*

Teamwork, Leadership, and Sales. Austin, TX: Bard. Copyright © Pierce Howard and Jane Howard 2001.

Institute for Social Research, for permission to reproduce and adapt Table 9.1 'Sources of power.' From French, J.R.P. and Raven, B. H. (1959). The Bases of Social Power. In D. Cartwright (Ed.), *Studies in Social Power* (pp.150–167). Ann Arbor, MI: Institute for Social Research. Copyright © Institute for Social Research 1959.

John Wiley & Sons, Incorporated, for permission to reproduce:

Figure 12.1 'Schein's model of organisational culture.' Adapted from Schein, E. H (1985). *Organizational culture and leadership*. San Francisco: Jossey-Bass Publishers. Copyright © 1985 John Wiley & Sons, Incorporated.

Figure 13.1 'Kotter's integrative model of organisational dynamics.' Adapted from Kotter, J. P. (1980). An integrative model of organizational dynamics. In E. E. Lawler, D. A. Nadler, and C. T. Cammann (Eds.), *Organizational assessment: perspectives on the measurement of organizational behavior and the quality of work life* (pg. 282). New York: John Wiley & Sons, Incorporated. Copyright © 1980 John Wiley & Sons, Incorporated.

Oxford University Press, for permission to reproduce and adapt Table 4.1 'Three forms of prejudice.' From Table 5.1 (p. 132), Glick, P. (2002). Sacrificial Lambs Dressed in Wolves' Clothing: Envious Prejudice, Ideology, and the Scapegoating of Jews. In L. S. Newman & R. Erber (Eds.), *Understanding Genocide: The Social Psychology of the Holocaust* (pp.113–142). Oxford: Oxford University Press. Copyright © Oxford University Press, Inc.

Palgrave, for permission to reproduce:

Figure 2.4 'A sample feedback report using Cattell's 16PF.' From Bratton, J. (2015) *Introduction to Work and Organisational Behaviour.* London: Palgrave. Copyright © Palgrave 2015.

Figure 13.4 'Factors affecting employee responses to change.' Adapted from Hayes, J. (2010) *The Theory and Practice of Change Management.* Basingstoke: Palgrave Macmillan. Copyright © Palgrave 2010.

Pearson Education, Inc., New York, for permission to reproduce:

Table 8.2 'LPC approaches.' From Fiedler, Fred E. and Chemers, Martin M. (1974). *Leadership & Effective Management*, 1ˢᵗ Ed. Pearson Education, Inc., New York: New York. Copyright © 1974 Pearson Education, Inc., New York.

Figure 11.2 'Mintzberg's model of organisational structure.' From Mintzberg, Henry (1979). *Structuring of Organizations*, 1ˢᵗ Ed. Pearson Education, Inc., New York: New York. Copyright © 1979 Pearson Education, Inc., New York.

Both printed and electronically reproduced by permission of Pearson Education, Inc., New York.

Profile Books Limited, for permission to reproduce and adapt Figure 13.2 'The McKinsey 7S framework.' From Peters, T. and Waterman, R. H. (2004). *In search of excellence: Lessons from America's best-run companies.* London: Profile Books Ltd. Copyright © 2004 Profile Books Limited.

Taylor & Francis, for permission to reproduce Figure 4.2 'Work centrality scale.' From Arvey, R., D., Harpaz, I., and Liao, H. (2004). Work Centrality and Post-Award Work Behavior of Lottery Winners. *The Journal of Psychology,* 138(5), 404–420. Copyright © Taylor & Francis Ltd 2004 (http://www.tandfonline.com).

The publisher and the authors would also like to thank everyone who has supplied images for the book. Please refer to individual credit lines for details.

1 INTRODUCING ORGANISATIONAL BEHAVIOUR

Michelle Hammond

LEARNING OUTCOMES

BY THE END OF THIS CHAPTER YOU SHOULD BE ABLE TO:

- Define organisational behaviour (OB) and discuss its goals as a field of study.
- Identify the major disciplines that contribute to understanding OB.
- Demonstrate evidence of the value of OB for individuals and companies.
- Identify the main methods used in OB research.
- Identify the major levels of analysis in OB and the interplay among them.
- Summarise contemporary issues facing the field of OB.

© ISTOCK.COM/RAWPIXEL LTD

THIS CHAPTER DISCUSSES...

IN REALITY

When faced with difficult problems, when in need of the next product, or when trying to improve processes in workplaces, businesses commonly establish working groups to brainstorm and come up with creative ideas. The perception is that this is the best way forward, but in reality nearly all research studies (Pauhus *et al.*, 1993) have found that group brainstorming leads to the generation of fewer ideas than comparable numbers of solitary brainstormers in both laboratory and organisational settings. Why might this be the case? First, sometimes people slack off in groups expecting other team members to take the lead. Most often it's the most extraverted person who shares their ideas, not necessarily the person with the most or best ideas. Quite often people are hesitant to share ideas for fear of saying something stupid – they worry they'll be judged by others. Other times people get blocked by what someone else said or only come up with ideas that are similar to those already proposed. Research suggests that brainstorming is most effective when individuals take time to process the problem or opportunity individually and bring their ideas to the group afterwards. If group brainstorming is to be used, groups need to make sure that the leader does not share his or her idea first but instead defers judgement, focusing on trying to come up with as many ideas as possible, regardless of their quality. Additionally, the use of trained facilitators, diversity in team members, and the creation of a 'playground' where members feel a sense of play and positive emotion while engaging in creativity may reduce some of the threats to group creativity (Thompson, 2003).

INTRODUCTION

What makes employees see their work in different ways? How do these differences affect their motivation and satisfaction with the job? Would they respond differently to rewards, different types of leadership or structures at work? How would they work together? If you have ever wondered about how people act and think the way they do in the workplace, you have been thinking about organisational behaviour (OB), probably without knowing it. By studying concepts and research in OB you will be able to understand and ultimately affect attitudes and behaviours at your current or future place of work.

This chapter provides an introduction and background to the field of OB. It is broken down into four important questions to consider when studying organisational behaviour:

1 What is OB?
2 Why does OB matter?
3 Where does OB knowledge come from?
4 Why is OB more important today than ever?

Addressing these questions will give you a solid basis for understanding the topics covered in the rest of the book.

WHAT IS ORGANISATIONAL BEHAVIOUR (OB)?

What is this business about 'organisational behaviour'? Do organisations really behave? Perhaps not, but people certainly do. The field of OB is really about understanding how people think, act and react in the workplace, and the influence of many factors on their behaviour. These factors include issues around individuals, their relationships with others such as their co-workers and boss, the group or department they are in, and the structure and culture of the organisations they work in. As a discipline, OB is ultimately concerned with using this information to promote certain desirable employee attitudes and behaviours, as well as the effectiveness of the organisation more broadly. Because these factors around people, their relationships, and the broader organisational context all affect how they act in the workplace, the field, then, is inherently *multi-level*. By multi-level we mean that individuals operate within groups, and groups operate within organisations, and likewise organisations operate within a larger environmental context. If we fail to take the contexts into consideration we are missing a key piece of the puzzle.

We cannot understand one employee in isolation. Individuals are part of a team and the team influences that individual. For example, if everyone in Bob's team is in a really grumpy mood that is likely to influence Bob and he'll probably be feeling the same way by the end of the day even though he woke up in a great mood. Likewise, Bob's input, personality, knowledge and so on, has an influence on his team. And we see that teams are part of departments and departments are part of organisations with their own history, values, culture, policies and so on. And finally, the whole organisation is all part of a larger environmental context including the market, economic situation, local, national and global regulations and national culture(s). These influences go from top down, for example from the environment or the organisation on the individual, or from bottom up, from the individual to the organisation (see Figure 1.1).

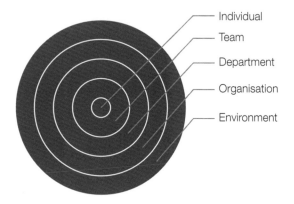

— Individual
— Team
— Department
— Organisation
— Environment

Figure 1.1 The multi-level nature of the field of OB

organisational behaviour is a field of study which seeks to understand and improve organisational effectiveness by examining factors such as individuals, teams, and organisational culture and structure and the way they interact

While studying OB, it's useful to take a systems thinking approach. This basically means that if we want to understand a problem, we need to keep in mind how that problem is part of an overall system. In the context of organisational behaviour, systems thinking helps us to realise that an organisation is made of different parts that affect and are affected by one another. Similarly the organisation interacts with its larger environment. Systems thinking has its roots in general systems theory, which was originally developed from the physical sciences. Ludwig von Bertalanffy (1968) and Kast and Rosenzweig (1972), who later brought this to the field of OB, suggested that a system is a complex structure of interacting elements which are open to, and interact with their environment. Systems theory suggests that the organisation is a system made of interrelated and interdependent parts. One can study each component in isolation, but when we do so, we fail to capture the essence of the whole.

As you read this chapter, be sure to keep in mind what level the material is focused on – is it the individual, the team, or the organisation? – and remember that they are all influenced by and influence other levels. Similarly, as you are reading each of the chapters in the textbook, it may feel as if they are independent and unrelated. Try to take a systems perspective and remind yourself that they do influence and are influenced by each other. If you have work experience, try to think of how these aspects of the workplace affected your own behaviour. For example, you might think about how your personality affected the way you worked with others on a team, and how that team operated within the larger culture of the organisation. If you don't have work experience, sport teams, schools and families operate in a similar way.

Just as OB involves a complex interplay across various levels of analysis the field itself draws from a variety of fields of research. In order to better understand individual-level phenomena such as personality and job performance, OB draws from work and organisational psychology, whereas research in cognitive psychology informs our discussion on perception. In order to understand groups and teams and emotions, OB draws from social psychology. At the organisational level, theories of sociology and anthropology help us to understand the structure of the organisation and inform our understanding of culture and values.

You are probably less familiar with interdisciplinary fields than with more traditional 'vertical' fields such as accounting, marketing, or finance. OB cuts across lots of other disciplines that provide us with some understanding of how people behave in different situations as well as information about work in general, bringing them together with the goal of understanding how and why people act the way they do at work. Additionally, there is a concern for both the employee – the person – and the workplace – the bottom line.

WHY DOES OB MATTER?

First of all, OB matters because the concepts within OB, and in this textbook, affect the success of companies and the experience of its employees working there. In a 2003 study, Fulmer *et al.* suggested that organisations that value the research outcomes within OB

systems thinking is an approach that considers the organisation as a system made of different parts that affect and are affected by one another. Similarly the organisation interacts with its larger environment

FlexJobs

FlexJobs promises to 'find the best telecommuting jobs, part-time professional jobs and other flexible jobs in over 100 career categories, all hand-screened and legitimate.' FlexJobs was founded by Sarah Sutton Fell after she was made redundant from her position as VP of Operations and Sales for an online beauty company. She was in her early thirties and eight months pregnant with her first child at the time, and was looking for career options that offered flexibility to balance work and her growing family. She found it very difficult to sort the get-rich-quick-while-working-from-home scams from the valid job posts. Her frustrations with the difficulty in finding legitimate flexible or part-time opportunities, paired with her entrepreneurial spirit, became the motivation to start FlexJobs.

OB IN THE NEWS

She launched the company when her son was just 3 months old.

For a small fee, jobseekers can access thousands of legitimate flexible jobs including telecommuting (also known as remote working) part-time, contract and others in a variety of industries. The site also offers advice on making flexible job arrangements work. FlexJobs has placed roles with big companies such as Google, IBM, Xerox, AT&T and American Express, and has over 25,000 members. It has been featured on a number of media sources and Fell was named a '2011 Game Changer' by *Workforce Management*.

According to their website, FlexJobs is a resource for:

- Parents wanting to be more flexible for their kids and families.
- Someone looking for a second job or supplemental income that utilises their skills and education in a professional way.
- Military spouses who need the flexibility to work from anywhere, in case their spouses are re-stationed.
- People with physical or health issues trying to find flexible work and telecom-muting jobs to suit their needs.
- Retirees looking to stay professionally active and to earn some income.
- Competitive athletes want-ing a professional job that will fit around their training and competition schedules.

©COMSTOCK

- And anyone else who would appreciate a job that fits with their life, not a life that fits with their job! (www.flexjobs.com/About.aspx: last accessed on 6 August 2015)

The mission of FlexJobs stands in stark contrast to the 2013 decision by Yahoo's CEO, Marissa Mayer, to cut all telecommuting in the company. Mayer had previously worked for Google and was instrumental in creating the well-known culture which landed Google at the top of the 100 Best Companies list. Many criticised this decision, saying it was a step backwards in workplace flexibility, that it would more negatively impact women than men, and that it created an environment where face time was more important than productivity. Marissa commented that 'people are more productive when they're alone but they're more collaborative and innovative when they're together. Some of the best ideas come from pulling two different ideas together.' (http://tech.fortune.cnn.com/2013/04/19/marissa-mayer-telecommuting/: last accessed on 6 August 2015) 'When you look at things like the Yahoo! Weather app, that wouldn't have happened if those two people hadn't run into each other.' She added, 'You needed someone from Flickr to say, "Hey, I've got these geo-tagged photos, and I know where these photos were taken and we can probably detect whether or not there [are] faces in them or whether they're a scene" and them running into someone from Weather who says, "Hey, could we make our app more beautiful?"

"I sort of call it the Reese's Peanut Butter Cups effect," she added. "The chocolate and peanut butter taste great together, but that only happens when people really say, 'What happens when we combine these things?'"' (www.inc.com/jill-krasny/marissa-mayer-twitter-telecommuting-policy.html#ixzz30Xri2KLR: last accessed on 6 August 2015)

Questions

1 Do you agree more with Marissa Mayer's point of view or with the mission of FlexJobs?
2 What types of employees or managers might be most attracted to flexible work arrangements?
3 What are some advantages and disadvantages of telecommuting and flexible work for employees?
4 What sorts of challenges does managing a telecommuting workforce bring?

Sources

www.flexjobs.com/ (last accessed on 6 August 2015).

http://archive.9news.com/money/story.aspx?storyid=179738&catid=531 (last accessed on 6 August 2015).

www.forbes.com/sites/laurashin/2014/01/17/work-from-home-the-top-100-companies-offering-flexible-jobs-in-2014/ (last accessed on 6 August 2015).

www.workingmother.com/best-company-list/146788 (last accessed on 6 August 2015).

www.forbes.com/sites/learnvest/2012/12/04/having-a-baby-and-a-startup-how-flexjobs-was-born/ (last accessed on 6 August 2015).

outperform their counterpart organisations. The study compared the 100 Best Companies to Work For in America with organisations matched for size and industry. The results showed that not only did employees from the 100 best companies have more positive attitudes towards their workplaces, but also these organisations outperformed their counterparts financially. Furthermore, businesses which took a more systematic approach to making changes in their organisation, following good OB practice (called organisational behaviour modification) experienced a 17 per cent increase in performance (Stajkovic and Luthans, 1997). This practice involved identifying, measuring, analysing, intervening in and evaluating employees' behaviours in contrast to changes made more haphazardly. These studies highlight the importance of not only the content of OB but also its systematic approach.

While this is all well and good, you might be asking yourself, why does OB matter to *me*, personally? Here are a few reasons why understanding OB may matter to you, regardless of where your career takes you.

1 It will provide you with a better understanding of the world of work:

Chances are you will have a job at some point in your life, and it will be likely to make up a significant percentage of your waking hours. Insights coming from OB can help you to work better, to promote more positive relationships with your co-workers and boss, and even know when quitting your job might be the best move for you. Because OB is the study of why people behave as they do in work settings, it is probably the most applicable material to any job. The content that we will cover has to do with all human behaviour in the workplace and often more generally – it'll give you insights into working with other people, managing stress, and structuring jobs and companies.

Many people are promoted into management positions based on technical expertise, with little understanding of people – how to manage them, who to hire, how to work through conflict and what motivates people. Even if you don't pursue a job in human resources or management, the knowledge and skills you learn in this OB module will be useful.

2 It promotes self-insight and personal growth:

In addition to improving your skills in working with others, studying OB can be a bit like pointing a microscope at yourself. Because the field is about understanding people in the workplace, it is personally relevant to *you*. When you study personality ▸**Chapter 2**◂, you might consider dimensions of your own personality and how they may impact the way you behave and how others respond to you. By studying perception ▸**Chapter 3**◂, you might consider the way you accurately (or inaccurately) categorise events or the factors that shape how you see yourself and the world. In studying attitudes and values ▸**Chapter 4**◂, especially in relation to organisational structure ▸**Chapter 11**◂ and culture ▸**Chapter 12**◂, you might have a better understanding of the kind of workplace where you might find the most meaning and satisfaction. Through an understanding of leadership ▸**Chapter 8**◂ and power and politics ▸**Chapter 9**◂ you might consider what type of boss inspires you and what type of leader you might like to be. And considering emotions and stress ▸**Chapters 5 and 6**◂ may give you insights into how to maintain and promote your own psychological health. Finally, understanding team dynamics ▸**Chapter 7**◂ and communication ▸**Chapter 10**◂ might help you to make sense of how people speak to you and what they mean, and how to avoid and learn from conflict.

3 It gives you the ability to speak with others from various disciplines:

One of the most useful things about having a background in OB is that you are able to talk to different people about their jobs. If you have friends in diverse fields – engineering, medicine, music, journalism, education – you will be able to talk to all of them about what they do because you have an understanding of people at work. After studying OB, you might not understand the *content* of their work, but you will be able to get to grips with the *context* of the workplace.

BUILDING YOUR SKILLS

Decision-making

Imagine your company is hiring a new operations manager and you are on a selection panel. One candidate received top marks in his degree, has relevant work experience, scored very highly on the pre-screening test and answered the questions very well in the interview. However, you just get a bad feeling about this person. You are annoyed by some of his mannerisms and some things he says make you feel vaguely uncomfortable. What do you do? What do you base your selection decision on: your intuition, or his credentials and performance in the interview?

WHERE DOES OB KNOWLEDGE COME FROM?

People are familiar territory, and it has been said before that psychology is the science of the obvious. As OB draws heavily on psychology, you may feel this also applies here. Granted, there will be some new terms and words you've never heard before, but for the most part, you may have some notion as to what OB involves from your own lives, experience and prior reading. However, a grave mistake students make is opening their books and thinking 'I know this stuff.' Just because it may seem more straightforward than other subjects at first, this does not mean it is purely intuitive either. As OB is a social science, it is based on rigorous research. Sometimes the research might coincide with your own thoughts on these topics, but at other times it might cause you to rethink your ideas.

Using your intuition and experiences, note down which of the following statements you believe to be true and which you think are false. You can then check your answers on the companion website at www.palgrave.com/companion/carbery-ob.

1   You can read a person's emotional state by watching their facial expressions closely.
2   Taller people are more successful than shorter people.
3   Better decisions are made without emotions.
4   Organisations that treat their employees fairly and with respect are more profitable than others.

So how did you do? These statements will give you an idea of some of the fascinating topics that are part of OB as well as showing that although OB may seem like common sense, the feeling that something is just 'common sense' is often evoked *after* we have gathered all the facts and made sense of them. This is referred to as hindsight bias in psychology and means that you overestimate the accuracy of your intuition, believing that you 'knew it all along.' This tendency comes from a desire to make sense of our lives; to be able to understand – and anticipate – events in our world.

Managers might fall into the same hindsight bias trap in making sense of the accuracy of their own intuition or personal feeling on a decision. One way to prevent this is to balance the use of intuition in decision-making with evidence-based practice. Through evidence-based practice, managers become more scientific about how they think about organisational problems and changes (Rousseau, 2006). They rely on information from social science and OB research to make decisions. The criminologist Lawrence W. Sherman summed it up well when he said, 'We are all entitled to our own opinions, but not to our own facts' (2002, p. 223).

So how and where do we get this evidence?

RESEARCH METHODS IN OB

Within OB, evidence comes from systematic research. Scientific research is 'the systematic study of phenomena according to scientific principles.' It is important to note here the two phrases 'systematic' and 'according to scientific principles.' This means that there is a method

hindsight bias refers to the tendency, after an event has occurred, to overestimate our ability to have foreseen the outcome

evidence-based practice grounds decisions on the best presented scientific evidence

scientific research is the systematic study of phenomena according to scientific principles

to what we do and some scientific guidelines governing the quality of the subsequent research. It's not just haphazard observation or testing. It's more than that, as we saw in the 'In Reality…' box above. The scientific process includes stages of:

1 Description – the accurate portrayal or depiction of a phenomenon.
2 Explanation –understanding why the phenomenon exists and what causes it.
3 Prediction – anticipating an event prior to its occurrence.
4 Control – manipulating antecedents to change behaviour.

You might consider OB an applied science. As a field, the goal of OB is both to know and to improve; that is, it has a practical focus. OB researchers use scientific methods in order to build the body of knowledge, but seek to do so in order to improve the working world.

In general, research in OB and other social sciences involves developing and testing theories. Theories are collections of statements that specify how and why variables are related, as well as the conditions in which they should (or should not) be related. However interesting or logical the theories are, they are only useful when they have stood up to testing. Verification of theories is necessary to show that they are indeed accurate and applicable. There are different methods of conducting OB research for the development and verification of theory, including:

● Quantitative survey research – This methodology involves the use of surveys of a population and attempts to quantify a phenomenon (that is, to numerically represent something such as performance or attitudes). The data gathered is analysed using statistics to find trends in behaviour across individuals, groups or organisations. Survey research is often very useful to theory testing.
● Laboratory studies or experiments – Experiments involve the manipulation of certain variables in controlled environments. In OB research, experiments are often conducted with samples of university students. They provide precision but are often limited in their generalisability to a real-life situation.
● Qualitative interviews and focus groups – Interviews provide an in-depth understanding of phenomena through interviewing one individual at a time or in groups. Interviews range from unstructured to highly structured and researchers analyse the data for themes in responses.
● Case studies – A case study involves a very in-depth study of one individual, group or organisation. Case studies may include observation over a period of time, analysis of historical records, and interviews. Case studies provide rich understanding of phenomena and are realistic, but they often have limited generalisability to other settings or contexts.
● Meta-analyses – A meta-analysis involves the statistical compilation of a previous body of quantitative research on a particular topic. While they can often account for some limitations within any given study such as small sample size, results of meta-analyses are only as good as the studies that are included.

theories collections of assertions that specify how and why variables are related, as well as the circumstances in which they should and should not be related

Scholars and practitioners within OB take a contingency approach. Like a systems thinking approach, the contingency approach suggests that organisational and individual behaviour is contingent, or depends, on a number of interacting factors. The contingency approach highlights that there is no 'one best approach' that works for every company in every situation. There are fewer clear cut answers – although, when it comes to the exams, there will clearly be 'correct' answers! However, in general, the context is important. So a lot of things we learn will be dependent on different situations. In OB there are no 'laws' that apply to all contexts like the laws of physics. People are less predictable than gravity, but there are basic trends. We might not be able to predict any one person's behaviour at one given point in time, but as humans, we are united in some common experience, and have a tendency to act in similar ways. Similar types of people may act similarly in similar situations. There are important lessons to be learned and there is real value in learning about people in work.

 **CONSIDER** THIS...

Moneyball, the 2011 sport drama starring Brad Pitt and Philip Seymour Hoffman, presents the true story of how the Oakland A's baseball team used a sophisticated analytic approach involving statistics (which they call 'sabermetrics') to assemble a team on a budget. Watch the trailer from this film (available on YouTube) now in light of your understanding of evidence-based management. Specifically, focus on the use of information to make decisions. Contrast the information used historically by the scouts with data used as suggested by Peter Brand and Billy Beane. How did others react to this new approach?

© GETTY IMAGES/FUSE

HISTORICAL PERSPECTIVES OF OB

When trying to understand where we are in a field and where we are going, it's often helpful to consider where we have been. It is easy to think that there has always been an acknowledgement of the importance of understanding workplaces and human behaviour within them, but the history of OB is actually relatively short. The systematic study of behaviour of people at work really only began a little over a hundred years ago. Below are some VIPs (Very Important People) and VIR (Very Important Research) in the history of OB.

SETTING THE SCENE

Let's go back in time. You were very inspired as a child in 1900 when Marconi successfully completed the first transatlantic radio transmission and now, as a young adult in 1920, you

contingency approach suggests that organisational and individual behaviour is contingent, or depends, on a number of interacting factors

believe you have developed a very efficient and clear radio receiver. Now that radio broad-casting is becoming more and more popular you think every household should buy your product. The Great War is over and you have great expectations for positive change. You have just received a patent for producing the radio receiver and come up with enough capital to start your plant. However, since this is new technology you need workers with a variety of skills to produce your radio. The ideal candidate is someone who is skilled in electrical wiring and welding for the radio receiver, and woodworking for the beautiful exterior. You can only find a few people with all of these qualifications and because of their varied skills, you would have to pay them considerably more than they are making in their current jobs. You had envisioned selling your radios for a reasonable price. Unfortunately for you, study in the fields of management and organisational behaviour is just beginning, and 'Google' is a long way off, so you cannot just research best practices.

- What are you going to do to set up your plant?
- How will you distribute the work?
- What will you do to make sure your radio is affordable?
- What will you offer your employees?

We will now go through several of the ways of thinking about organising work that became popular around that era. As we go through these, think about what similarities each approach has with your own imagined journey back to 1920. What could this approach offer that you may have been missing? What is missing in each approach? What are the pros and cons of each?

SCIENTIFIC MANAGEMENT

If you were Fredrick Taylor, you would have focused on hiring good managers in addition to finding skilled workers. These managers might know a little about how to make radios, but they would be particularly skilled in monitoring others' work. They would have all the responsibility in the plant and the workers would be accountable to them. Before beginning production you would have analysed each component of the jobs for each of your workers. You would also have very specific instructions on each intermediary step. Additionally, you would have discovered the optimal timing for everything, including breaks. You would then train all of your workers on this procedure. You may have also found that electricians can easily learn to do the woodworking on the exterior of the radios, but woodworkers have a difficult time with the electrical wiring. As such, you hire electricians and teach them woodworking. Finally, you and your managers carefully monitor the whole process. Are the workers follow-ing your exact specifications? Are breaks timed properly? You would reward your employees financially based on their levels of production.

Scientific management, also referred to as Taylorism, was one of the first attempts to put the scientific method into practice to improve efficiency and productivity in the workplace. Frederick Winslow Taylor (1856–1915) conducted a number of experiments mostly in manu-facturing contexts around the best way to perform tasks and the optimal timing of breaks. These experiments are referred to as 'time-and-motion studies.' These studies broke down each job into its component parts, timed and analysed each part separately, and attempted to combine the most appropriate physical tasks and movements in the most efficient way. Taylor did this by careful observation of the best performers, studying how they carried out their tasks, timing everything, and alternating various job factors to see which worked best. He also advocated higher levels of compensation for employees who were more productive as part of his 'fair day's work' perspective.

Despite this perspective on adequate monetary compensation, Taylor's approach was highly criticised for treating people as if they were machines, which was partly responsible for the dehumanisation of factories. Although he is often blamed for failing to take the human aspects into consideration, some of Taylor's legacy is felt today. While reading about the time-in-motion studies, did it remind you of training techniques for athletics – trying to analyse your body's movements to beat the clock? Taylorism might be considered one of the first inroads towards the process and operations management and improvement practices we see today, such as Six Sigma and Lean Manufacturing. The major aim of these practices is similar to Taylor's goal: to improve efficiency and productivity while maintaining consistency in the quality of work. However influential they were, Taylor's practices are not continued in the same manner today.

SPOTLIGHT ON SKILLS

There has been a lot of discussion about using evidence-based management. Why is it important for organisations? How do you or would you look for information and evidence to make decisions in your organisation?

To help you answer these questions, in your ebook click the play button to watch the video of Carla DiBenedetto from Cook Medical talking about evidence-based management.

FORDISM

If you were Henry Ford, who was influenced by Frederick Taylor, you would have set up your plant similarly, yet with a few important distinctions. While Taylor analysed each job indi-vidually, Ford analysed the whole process of production. Rather than hiring one person with all the required skills, or hiring an electrician and training him as a woodworker, you came up with an ingenious solution: the assembly line. Before starting actual production, you would have carefully worked out the best way to make radios. Perhaps you discovered that it is best to create the exterior first, varnish the front before adding the electronic components, then complete the main receiver, and finally do the wiring and assemble it all. You would have discovered that you can break down the manufacturing of the radio into many small stages that require very little skill. It's very easy to train workers to do their one specific job and pass the piece on to the next person to complete the next part. By the end of the line you have a perfectly complete radio. At first, your plant is a huge success. You can mass produce excellent (and affordable) radios. But after a while, your employees seem to get incredibly bored.

Henry Ford (1863–1947) is best known for founding the Ford Motor Company and the assembly line. His principles, referred to as Fordism, were grounded in the goal of producing standardised, low-cost goods. Through standardisation of a product his customers could be guaranteed quality and consistency. This changed the ways things were made. No longer were skilled craftsmen responsible for creating their work: machines were largely responsible for doing it. These machines and the specialisation of tasks allowed low-skill workers to fill the factories with very little training. Like Taylor, Ford believed it was important to offer adequate pay for his employees – often so they could afford to purchase a Ford Model T car for themselves! He originally offered $5 a day to his employees, which was double the prevailing wage. As mentioned above, one of the criticisms of Fordism is that it led to the erosion of craftsmanship, unfulfilling and meaningless work for employees, and that it overemphasised money as a motivator. Ford was accused by some of an 'overbearing paternalism' in both positive (taking care of the workers) and restrictive (forbidding employees to smoke, even away from the work premises) ways. Fordism was very successful and the assembly line is still alive and well today in many manufacturing companies, but at what cost?

MAX WEBER AND BUREAUCRACY

If you were Max Weber, you would have also focused on efficiency like Ford and Taylor, but especially at the administrative level. You would have instituted a well-defined division of administrative labour among persons and offices, with set rules and regulations that everyone must follow, regardless of their status. This included a personnel system with consistent patterns of recruitment and stable linear careers based on expertise. There would be a hierarchy among offices, such that the authority and status were differentially distributed among employees and management, and formal and informal networks that connected organisational actors to one another through flows of information and patterns of cooperation. And most importantly there would be a written trail of all rules, regulations, meetings and events.

Max Weber was a German sociologist, who advocated bureaucracy as a universal way to organise workplaces. The overarching goal of bureaucracy was administrative efficiency. According to Weber (1947), bureaucracies, in order to function well, must have the following characteristics:

- *Formal rules and regulations* which included written guidelines to govern behaviour.
- *Impersonal treatment* which involved an avoidance of favouritism and special treatment.
- *Division of labour* in which all duties were divided into specialised tasks which were performed by the most appropriately-skilled individuals.
- *Hierarchical structure* where positions were ranked clearly by level.
- *Authority structure* which specified that decisions would be made based on hierarchy and rank.

There are certainly some advantages to bureaucracies. For example, employees can expect to be treated similarly (impersonal treatment) which may be perceived as fair. They should have a clear understanding of what is expected of them and where they stand in the organisation. Weber also advocated considering employees as a permanent lifelong obligation of the organisation, offering a strong sense of job security. However, bureaucracies are often criticised for their 'red tape' or excessive regulation or rigid conformity to formal rules that may squelch innovation. Also all decisions are made at the top, giving employees little voice or room for individual creativity.

HUMAN RELATIONS MOVEMENT — HAWTHORNE STUDIES

If you were part of the Human Relations Movement, you would have challenged some of the ideas of Weber and Ford. You would have focused not so much on demanding performance from your employees for monetary rewards, but by thinking about other forms of motivation such as supportive supervision, a consideration of relationships at work and of the emotional needs of employees. You would have strongly criticised and rejected the view of employees as machines which you perceived your predecessors in scientific management to hold.

The Human Relations Movement came out of a response to criticisms of Weber and Ford. The movement is often attributed to Elton Mayo's famous Hawthorne Studies which were a collection of investigations at the Western Electric Company's Hawthorne Works in Illinois in the late 1920s and early 1930s. The primary goal of these studies was to examine the effects of working conditions on productivity, including lighting, length of rests and duration of the working week. The results of the analysis at the time showed that productivity increased following just about any change they made, including increasing the levels of light very minimally. Further, productivity remained high even when the conditions returned to normal. This has created what is referred to as the Hawthorne Effect. It is thought to have caused production to increase, not because there was a change in the working conditions, but because management showed interest in making improvements. It gave workers the feeling that they were part of a team and they gained a sense of belonging. While there is some debate around the interpretation and replication of the Hawthorne effect, it is important to be aware that attention, interpersonal relations, and group norms are important predictors of performance; ability does not explain it all.

Other research conducted as part of the Hawthorne Studies included interviews with employees which revealed that some people deliberately kept their performance low. Group norms also existed to keep these base rates low and employees who out-performed were punished by their co-workers. They were afraid that if they raised the level of their output, management would come to expect more. These findings highlighted the importance of group norms and social factors – especially relationships with supervisors – in predicting behaviour at work and that the workplace is a social system made up of many interdependent parts. Out of the Hawthorne Studies came the Human Relations Movement that emphasised involvement and support at work, interpersonal relationships and emotional and social needs. This was really a very new way of thinking about behaviour at work at the time.

POSITIVE ORGANISATIONAL BEHAVIOUR

The positive organisational behaviour approach came out of the positive psychology movement and is often attributed to Fred Luthans whose pioneering work began around the turn of the 21st century. Historically psychology had a tendency to focus on the diagnosis of problems and treatment. Psychologists typically followed a medical model of figuring out what was wrong with a patient and trying to treat him or her. This approach was also trickling into the field of OB and into the workplace. Addressing concepts within OB seemed to happen only when things were going poorly or management perceived something to be wrong with their employees. Obviously it's important to be looking for what is going wrong and trying to fix problems, but a primary focus on what is wrong is limiting. At the end of the last century and beginning of this century, there has been a movement to look at what is right and to play to those strengths. The goal then is to prevent problems rather than just fix them. While research in positive organisational behaviour is still in its early stages, this body of work seeks to put a positive spin on many of the core concepts in OB. For example, research might focus on redesigning work to emphasise employees' strengths to encourage them to be their 'best selves.'

As you can see, despite its relatively short history, the field of OB has come a long way. The first systematic studies were just over a hundred years ago, but were limited in many ways as discussed above. Further, you might argue that the context of work a hundred years ago was quite different than it is today. It is important to understand the history, learn from it where possible, and adapt as a field.

BUILDING YOUR SKILLS

Managing People

You are managing a six person team. There is one member of the team who has a great attitude, lifts the spirits of the team when faced with difficulties and is often referred to as 'the heart' of the team. However, this person is failing to perform at an acceptable level despite your efforts at providing training and coaching for them. What do you do to effectively manage the situation? If you fired this employee for poor performance, what effect might that have on the team? How important is this?

WHY IS OB MORE IMPORTANT TODAY THAN EVER?

So how is the world of work different for you today than it was for your great-grandparents? What are the implications of these changes for the field of OB? Several factors affecting what, where and how we work and their implications for OB are described below.

GLOBALISATION

The global economy is continuing to change rapidly due to technological innovations, economic fluctuations and the rise of service and knowledge work, among other reasons. Globalisation has meant that goods, services, and capital frequently flow across borders and so organisations need to move beyond a local focus. This also means that the context where many people complete work and craft their careers has changed as well. It can be argued that globalisation has changed the job of a manager. Now, managers are more likely to experience the following:

1 Working with people from different cultural backgrounds.

As a manager, you are likely to be responsible for managing people with very different backgrounds from your own. Your communications, ideas for motivating and recognising others, and even your mannerisms may be interpreted very differently from your intentions. Similarly this miscommunication may be happening among members of your team. How do you ensure everyone is working towards the team's goal and getting on well?

2 Increased foreign assignments.

As he was leaving General Electric (GE), Jack Welch said: 'The Jack Welch of the future cannot be like me. I spent my entire career in the United States. The next head of GE will be somebody who spent time in Bombay, in Hong Kong, in Buenos Aires. We have to send our best and brightest overseas and make sure they have the training that will allow them to be the global leaders who will make GE flourish in the future' (Mor Barak, 2014). What factors might affect the success of a foreign assignment? A manager might be trying to lead a workforce with very different needs, beliefs, expectations, and practices from his or her own, while facing his or her own issues with being away from home.

3 Managing across time zones and managing virtual teams.

Even if a manager is not on a foreign assignment some of the same issues may arise at home. Because of globalisation, many companies are multi-national and are spread across many different countries, many have clients or customers in other countries, and others involve collaborations with or outsourcing from other companies across borders. Consider managing a team which is located across the globe. How (and when) do you communicate?

It is important to take the cultural context into consideration when studying concepts and theories in OB. Did you notice that many of the historical studies mentioned above took place in companies in the US? What effect might that have on the field? Considering the cultural dimensions is consistent with taking a systems thinking and contingency approach as mentioned before. Let's say you learned all about the importance of rewards and recognition for employees and from this you develop a scheme to motivate your employees that involves giving a weekly bonus to the best worker in each work group. It works brilliantly in Ireland. You tell your manager friend in the US. It works brilliantly there. Then you are transferred to Japan and set up the same system, and it is a total flop. Why? The cultural differences. Japan is a much more collectivistic culture and employees do not like to be singled out for individual attention, because this goes against group norms and values. Therefore, it's important to see how the larger environment affects the individual (systems thinking) as well as how one theory works in one situation but not another (contingency approach).

CHANGING WORKPLACE DEMOGRAPHICS

There have been a number of changes to the demographic makeup of the workplace, particularly in the following three ways:

1 There has been an increase of women in the workforce. The increase of women and dual-earner couples has triggered a desire for more family-friendly practices and flexibility. Additionally, many men are expressing a desire to reduce time spent at work in favour of increased engagement at home.
2 With the rise of globalisation, emigration, and global careers, the workforce is becoming more diverse. It is very common for individuals to work in some capacity with others of a different race or cultural background. For example, within the United States, the Hispanic population is growing exponentially faster than the White population. In fact, minority groups now outnumber the traditional majority group members in California and New Mexico.
3 People are living and continuing to work longer than ever before. In some countries, such as the US, individuals over 85 are the fastest growing segment of the population. In many countries the mandatory retirement ages are becoming older and mandatory retirement limits do not exist in many countries.

So why would the changing demographics of the workplace be important in understanding OB? In most countries, legislation exists to prevent discrimination in a wide range of employment and employment-related areas. These include recruitment and promotion, pay, working conditions, training or experience, dismissal and harassment. This legislation often defines discrimination as treating one person in a less favourable way than another person based on any of several grounds which may include gender, marital or family status, sexual orientation or religion. Employers need to be mindful that their practices are in line with the law.

Additionally, while diversity has the potential to bring about more perspectives, greater innovations, and better decision-making, these things do not happen on their own (Stahl *et al.*, 2010). When people are different from one another there are added challenges that need to be overcome and this has implications in the workplace as well. For example, gender differences in communication ▶**Chapter 10**◀ may need to be tackled in order to promote effective communication in the workplace; teams comprising diverse members may pose added challenges ▶**Chapter 7**◀; individual stereotypes and perceptual biases ▶**Chapter 3**◀, attitudes and values ▶**Chapter 4**◀ and cultural differences ▶**Chapter 12**◀ may affect the ability for individuals to work together to achieve organisational goals while maintaining personal well-being ▶**Chapters 5 and 6**◀

 THIS...

In many countries, a mandatory retirement age is in effect. As the population ages, this issue comes to the forefront. Do you think employees should be forced to retire when they reach a certain age? What are the implications of these employees leaving their workplaces? What might the experience be like for the employee? How can retirements be managed most appropriately to facilitate both the retiree and the company?

TECHNOLOGICAL GROWTH

It is clear the last few centuries have seen tremendous technological growth. This has changed the nature of work and this has implications for personal privacy and work–life balance. Through technological growth, we have seen the decrease of the manufacturing sector and the huge growth of the services and information industries. Furthermore, this has polarised workforce needs. For example, think about the technology now in place when you go to an airport. In many airports, there are touch screens where you check in for your flight. You can also check in from home and print off your boarding pass. Highly technical jobs are needed to set up and monitor those systems (therefore there is an increase in high-skill jobs), but the mid-level jobs which involve the technical aspect of checking you in, confirming seats and dealing with issues are now handled electronically. However, someone is still needed to do the manual job of putting the baggage claim tickets on the baggage and lifting it onto the conveyor belt. Furthermore, there are growing needs for employees to have competence in both technical skills and service skills. Technicians often interact directly with the customers and customers are allowed, even encouraged, to influence the design process.

Currently, being creative and innovative is of utmost importance in order to compete. Companies have to continually reinvent themselves, adapting their products or services to changing customer needs and demands. Furthermore, as an employer, job applicants and employees have access to much more information than before about your company. For example, websites such as www.glassdoor.com provide reviews of companies and CEOs, and even include a place for applicants to post the questions they were asked at interview. Similarly, employers have more access to information about their employees through social media sources such as LinkedIn and Facebook. Additionally, technological advances have opened opportunities for employees to be accessible to their employer just about 24 hours a day, 7 days a week. This brings issues around work–life balance to the forefront. Where is the line between open information exchange and privacy?

Direct Sales: The Way Forward or Peddling of the Past

'Join the Party' (It Works!)

'Take charge of your future' (Amway)

'Making money is unlimited, so go ahead and dream big!' (Avon)

'Join the sisterhood that empowers you' (Thirty-One Gifts)

'Love what you do. Start your success story today' (Mary Kay)

The promises above have all appeared on the websites of companies that operate through direct sales. Direct sales companies seem to be popping up everywhere. Rather than having a set retail property, direct sales companies operate sales from person to person. Distributors might conduct business through sales parties in someone's home, one-on-one demonstrations or online. The customer experience may involve sitting in the comfort of a friend's house, nibbling on tasty morsels and checking out the latest merchandise. Distributors may experience benefits from

ACTIVE CASE STUDY

working from home, being around one's friends and social contacts, and earning income and discounts. Remuneration through direct sales companies is based on either personal product sales or also on the product sales of other representatives that the distributor attracted to the company (referred to as multi-level compensation plans).

Direct sales appear to be big business. The World Federation of Direct Selling Associations (WFDSA) reported global direct sales of $182 billion in 2014 with a 6.4% three-year cumulative growth rate for the industry. Products include cosmetics and personal care (34%) through companies such as Mary Kay and Avon; wellness and nutrition supplements (29%) such as Herbalife, Isagenix, BeachBody; and household goods (17%) such as Amway, Pampered Chef, Tupperware and Vorwerk.

Direct sales have a long history. It can be argued that

this was the original method of selling. The Direct Selling Association boasts, 'Early direct sellers – hawkers, peddlers, traders, itinerant merchants and caravans – are part of an ancient tradition that originated in man's basic need to exchange goods and to communicate.' More recent history includes door-to-door sales and in-home gatherings. Despite the retro image of stay-at-home mothers awing over Tupperware, this form of sales may be the way of the future as technological changes have expanded the manner and scope of sales in modern times. *Direct Selling News* quotes Alessandro Carlucci, CEO of Natura Cosméticos and Chairman of the WFDSA: 'The opportunity this industry has to really be even more powerful is in taking advantage of the fact that we are living in a moment in our society when technology is reinforcing relationships and allowing us to do more and better business' (Tortora, 2014). He suggests that technological changes, including access to analytics, targeted marketing, and social media, have created a perfect environment in which direct marketing will thrive into the future. Because direct selling often begins with one's personal contacts, relationships are exceptionally important. Social media, especially, allows for immediate information to spread very quickly with little investment. Such messages can also be targeted, based on client demographics and preferences.

Many direct sales companies have strong cultures in which members feel highly committed

© CAMACANUL

and personally connected. For example, an in-depth study into Amway, one of the largest direct sales companies, revealed some of the tactics the company uses to encourage members to personally identify with the company and its products (Pratt, 2000). Tactics include encouraging members to question their previous way of life (seeing oneself as an overworked and underpaid employee who was not fully utilising one's talents), urging them to build a new dream (financial freedom, working from home, a new car and so on) and building up how the company can help the individual reach his or her dreams. This process might also include a mentor or coach, motivational conferences, attractive rewards for performance and regular encouraging communications. While there are many loyal members of such companies, others have different opinions of some direct sales companies. For example, websites offer support to those who attempt to leave direct sales companies, including (www.pinktruth.com: Pink Truth: Facts, Opinions, and the Real Story behind Mary Kay Cosmetics) and Ex-cult (www.ex-cult.org/: Amway distributors). It seems that many people either love or hate direct sales companies.

Questions

1 Despite a long history, why do you think direct sales are increasing so rapidly? How does technological growth impact this? Do you think direct selling will continue to grow?

2 What demographic group would be most attracted to working in direct sales? Why?

3 Why do you think employees/ ex-employees experience such strong feelings (whether positive or negative) towards their companies?

4 Do you see any ethical concerns with direct sales companies and multi-level compensation plans? List all potential ethical issues that might be involved in direct sales.

Sources

www.directselling411.com/about-direct-selling/history-of-direct-selling/ (last accessed on 21 August 2015).

www.marykay.com/en-US/BeABeauty Consultant/Pages/Default.aspx (last accessed on 21 August 2015).

www.myitworks.com/locate/join/ (last accessed on 21 August 2015).

www.thirtyonegifts.com/join/ (last accessed on 21 August 2015).

www.wfdsa.org/about_wfdsa/?fa= globalStats (last accessed on 21 August 2015).

www.youravon.com/REPSuite/ become_a_rep.page?siteid=avon&p= BaRMid&c=BaRMid&s=BaRMid (last accessed on 21 August 2015).

Pratt, M.G. (2000). The good, the bad, and the ambivalent: Managing identification among Amway distributors. *Administrative Science Quarterly*, 45(3), 456–493.

Tortora, A. (2014) Billion Dollar Markets. *Direct Selling News*, 1 October. Available at: http://directselling-news.com/index.php/view/billion_dollar_markets#.VcsVX3FViko (last accessed on 21 August 2015).

 SUMMARY

 IN THE EBOOK, CLICK TO HEAR AN AUDIO SUMMARY

The field of OB is really about understanding how people think, act and react in the workplace, and the influence of many factors on their behaviour. The field is concerned with the well-being of employees as well as the performance of the organisation. It is important to remember that OB is multi-level and to consider workplaces through a systems thinking approach. Try to keep this in mind when reading through the following chapters. Remember each topic cannot be considered in isolation, as each is really affected by the others, so try to see connections across the chapters. When reading the 'In Reality' sections, keep in mind the importance of evidence-based practice and consider the methods used in the research. Within this chapter, several historical perspectives on OB were presented including Scientific Management, Fordism, Bureaucracy, the Human Relations Movement and Positive Organisational Behaviour. Be sure you can identify the main points of each and see how the field progressed historically. Finally, as you read this textbook consider both the history of OB and the contemporary issues that make OB more important now than ever before, such as globalisation, changing workplace demographics and technology growth. These issues are discussed as we move through the chapters in this textbook.

CHAPTER REVIEW QUESTIONS

1   In what ways is the field of OB different from other fields of study within business and the social sciences? In which ways is it similar to them?
2   How might courses on organisational behaviour be useful for someone entering the field of management? Or for someone in a technical field such as engineering or medicine?
3   Describe the roles of evidence-based management and intuition in organisational decision-making. What are the strengths and weaknesses of each approach?
4   Distinguish between qualitative and quantitative methods.
5   Briefly summarise how classical perspectives (Scientific Management, Fordism, Bureaucracy) influence our understanding of the workplace today. How are these perspectives limiting?
6   How are employment relationships changing currently? How might this affect how you prepare yourself for your career?
7   What are opportunities that come from increased globalisation and diversity?

MULTIPLE CHOICE QUESTIONS

In your ebook, click to take a multiple choice quiz to test your understanding of this chapter.

FURTHER READING

Denscombe, M. (ed.) (2010) *The Good Research Guide for Small-scale Social Research Projects*, 4th edn. Maidenhead: Open University Press.

Grey, C. (2012) *A Very Short, Fairly Interesting and Reasonably Cheap Book About Studying Organizations*, 3rd edn. London: Sage.

Pugh, D.S. and Hickson, D.J. (2007) *Writers on Organizations*, 5th edn. London: Penguin Books.

ⓦⓦⓦ USEFUL WEBSITES

www.careers.org/

Here is a great site for many career-related issues. There is also a good deal of advice about surviving and prospering in organisations.

http://pessoal.sercomtel.com.br/assis/English/Glossaries%20&%20Resources/Miscellanea/Virtual%20Desk/1netiq/Netiq.html

This is the site of Business Netiquette International that provides a quick-hit guide to online manners for international travellers.

www.trade.gov

This is the site of the International Trade Administration, packed with resources to help US business succeed globally.

www.glassdoor.com

Pick a company and read a few reviews. What do they reveal about OB constructs?

2 PERSONALITY

Jill Pearson

LEARNING OUTCOMES

BY THE END OF THIS CHAPTER YOU SHOULD BE ABLE TO:

- Explain the two sides of the nature–nurture debate.
- Distinguish between nomothetic and idiographic theories of personality.
- Describe each of the Big Five personality characteristics and map the behaviour of individuals onto these characteristics.
- Distinguish between traits that are good for all jobs and those that are important only for some jobs.

- Discuss how and why organisations measure individual personality characteristics.
- Identify problems with using self-report instruments in the selection process.
- Identify bright and dark personality characteristics beyond the Big Five that are important in understanding individual-level behaviour at work.

© IMAGESOURCE

THIS CHAPTER DISCUSSES

IN REALITY

Did you know that first impressions don't always last? While personality is considered to be stable over time, the impressions we gain about people, based on their personality, can change as we get to know them better. Furthermore, personality characteristics that are typically considered to be an advantage in many situations also have a 'dark side', which will be discussed in more detail at the end of the chapter. Extroversion, for example, has long been considered an advantage in many aspects of life. Extroverts are more successful at job interviews; they earn more money and tend to be happier in their jobs and careers. Extroversion is also considered important for leadership positions as well as for success in jobs like sales and teaching. Additionally, it is considered to be particularly important for group work and team performance. When groups first come together, team members form initial impressions of each other. Because of extroverts' tendency to express enthusiasm, confidence and dominance they are perceived to be highly competent at the outset and often get selected for leadership positions.

However, recent research has found that those initial good impressions can change for the worse as the team works towards their interdependent goals (Bendersky and Shah, 2013). Extroverts seem to disappoint their fellow group members as time goes on by not delivering on what was initially expected. It's not clear whether the extroverts 'promised' too much or whether their fellow group members simply expected too much. Interestingly, this research also found that individuals with a high need for emotional stability (that is, high in neuroticism) have a 'bright side' that has been given little attention until recently. As the task groups progressed, neurotics surprised their fellow group members by exceeding expectations and therefore their status within the group increased. It's nice to know that 'bad' first impressions don't always last.

INTRODUCTION

Have you ever wondered why your best friend wants to be alone so much of the time while you really like to be with other people, even when studying? Or why your friend can always seem to get her work done ahead of schedule while you are working like mad, even staying up all night and missing lectures, just to get your assignments finished? Perhaps you are the one who wonders why your gregarious friends struggle to meet deadlines. Chances are that you and your friend have different personality characteristics. Although you are taking the same subjects at university and have the same interests, maybe you wonder whether you are suited to different types of jobs after you graduate because of these personality differences.

Organisations are interested in the concept of personality because they believe, and indeed research has shown, that personality differences impact on behaviour at work. Personality affects motivation, communication, team interaction, and performance in both positive and negative ways. The focus of this chapter is to explore this relationship. Personality theories are examined and the issue of assessing personality for organisation-based decisions is outlined. We begin by defining personality and discussing the extent to which our genes versus our environment influence the type of personality we have. We then discuss alternative theoretical approaches to understanding personality before focusing on five specific personality characteristics on which people differ (called the Big Five or the Five-Factor Model) and their implications for behaviour in organisations. This leads us on to the important issue of if, when and how employers should assess personality when hiring and managing employees. We finish off by discussing alternative lenses to the Big Five including what might be termed 'ugly' personality traits.

WHAT IS PERSONALITY?

We all have a notion of what personality is. A friend tells you that she's met someone new and she thinks you'll like him. She immediately goes on to tell you what he's like:

> 'He's got a great personality, so much energy. He's fun and funny. He tells the best stories and really likes to have a good time. But he works hard too; you can tell that he wants to do something with his life.'

What she is describing is his social reputation, which is the way that we all – friends, family, neighbours, co-workers and supervisors – perceive other people. While social reputation isn't the same thing as personality, someone's social reputation is influenced by their personality. So what exactly is personality? While there is no universally accepted definition, we can think about someone's personality as their mental make-up. **Personality** is typically defined as the relatively stable set of psychological characteristics that can distinguish one individual from another and can provide generalised predictions about a person's behaviour. There are three important points relating to this definition that need to be emphasised.

1 Stability implies consistency over time and in different situations. We describe someone as being warm and kind if they are like this most of the time and in diverse life situations.
2 People differ in terms of how they think, feel and act. These **individual differences** are psychological ways in which people differ from each other and include factors such as intelligence, personality, and emotionality, and mean we can describe people according to their different personality characteristics.
3 While someone's behaviour is influenced by their personality, behaviour is also influenced by the social context. Some situations are described as **strong situations** in that everyone, regardless of their personality, behaves in the same way. For example, personality is likely to have less influence on behaviour in the armed forces, where the rules are clearly defined and the consequences for not following them are severe, than it might do in an organisation such as Google.

There is another interesting point about the personality–behaviour link. As the definition indicates, by knowing someone's personality characteristics, we can make reasonable predictions about their behaviour. Psychologists have studied ways to accurately measure personality

personality the relatively stable set of psychological characteristics that can distinguish one individual from another and can provide generalised predictions about a person's behaviour

individual differences are psychological ways in which people differ from each other and include factors such as intelligence, personality, and emotionality, and mean we can describe people according to their different personality characteristics

strong situations those in which the rules and expectations of the social context control the behaviour of people regardless of their personality

and used this information to determine the impact of different personality characteristics on a wide range of behaviours within and beyond organisations, and this will be covered in more detail later in the chapter. However, for most of us in day-to-day life, the inference goes the other way. Instead of knowing someone's personality and using it to predict their behaviour, we tend to infer someone's personality by observing what they do, as well as what they say and by what others say about them (that is, their social reputation). This is because we cannot measure personality directly. These observations and assessments may or may not be accurate, but they do influence the impressions and judgements we make about other people.

BUILDING YOUR SKILLS

Making Tough Decisions

You are a line manager and your HR manager is recommending the use of personality tests to improve hiring decisions. Even if the tests have good predictive validity, you are worried about how the tests would be perceived by job applicants. Do some research yourself; ask some people you know if they have encountered such tests when applying for jobs and if they were concerned about them. What's your view now? Has it changed? How will you respond to the HR manager?

NATURE–NURTURE DEBATE

Where does our personality come from? Is it from the genes that our parents pass on to us or is it influenced by our environment? This question basically summarises what is known as the nature–nurture debate. Imagine that you are quite imaginative and creative and your parents are too. It's possible that they've passed on an 'openness to experience gene' and/or an 'artistic gene' to you. This supports the nature side of the argument. However, it is also likely that you observed and imitated your parents' behaviour as you were growing up. Perhaps they're artists or musicians. Furthermore, your parents not only tolerated your creative pursuits, but they actively encouraged and rewarded them. The presence of these environmental conditions supports the nature side of the debate. So how do we separate them to understand the role of nature and nurture in the formation of personality?

The answer comes in part from studying twins who are raised apart. Behavioural scientists have conducted studies of twins who have been adopted by different sets of parents to try to disentangle these two influences. If identical twins (that is, those who share 100 per cent of their genetic makeup) have the same personality traits, even when they grow up in different environments, then there is strong support for the nature side of the debate. Researchers at the University of Minnesota have been carrying out such studies for several decades and have found that genes do in fact have a significant impact on personality. After reviewing several studies of twins and personality, Loehlin (1992) concluded that genes can explain between one-third and one-half of the variance in different personality traits.

Another research approach to understanding the influence of genes on personality is to examine personality traits over time (called life course research). Participants of these studies complete personality assessments several times throughout their life. Since people's environments are different at different points in their life, it could be inferred that personality has a strong genetic component if people's personality profiles are reasonably stable throughout their lives. Roberts *et al.* (2006) reviewed 92 life course studies that included over 50,000 people. As can be seen from Figure 2.1, some traits are reasonably stable while others change quite a bit over time. For example, openness to experience is quite stable once people become young adults. (It seems that teenagers are much less open to new experiences – no doubt reflecting the cliché you might have heard your parents recite when you were in secondary school: 'You think you know everything!') On the other hand, people become more conscientious as they age. Interestingly, life course studies show that relative positions between people tend not to change on the various traits. In other words, while you and your best friend are both likely to become more conscientious as you get older, if your friend is more conscientious than you are now, it is likely that she will continue to be into your old age.

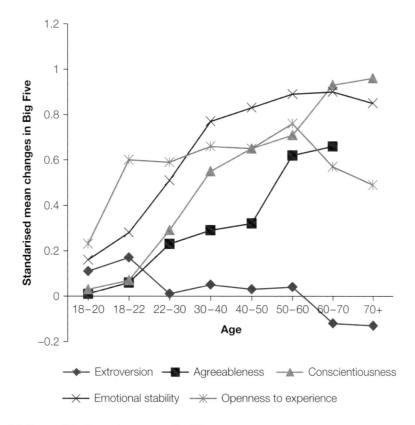

Figure 2.1 Personality dimensions across the life course

Source: Adapted from Roberts et al. (2006).

While heredity clearly plays a major part in determining one's personality, environmental factors are important too. People's personalities develop in part because they internalise their surroundings. Social, cultural and situation factors all have an effect on personality.

- *Social factors:* Interactions with parents, siblings, peers and others influence our personality and behaviour through a process of socialisation. Although socialisation takes place throughout our lives, early socialisation (for example, as the result of birth order) is particularly influential in the development of personality.

- *Cultural factors:* Socialisation also happens at the societal level and some researchers (for example, Heine and Buchtel, 2009) believe that cultures actually provide societies with their own unique personalities. A large study of more than 50 cultures found variation in the dominance of certain personality traits. For example, people from China, India, Nigeria and Iran tend to be more introverted than people from Iceland, Spain, Australia and Estonia. Of course this doesn't mean that there are no extroverts in China and no introverts in Iceland; these country differences are merely averages (McCrae *et al.*, 2005) ▶Chapter 12◀.

- *Situational factors:* Specific situations or experiences also play a role in the development of personality. Traumatic events, such as surviving 9/11 or experiencing bullying as a child, teenager or adult can change a person, often in dramatic ways.

THEORIES OF PERSONALITY

There are a great number of theories of personality that attempt to explain how personalities develop and/or why people differ. These theories can be categorised as either idiographic or nomothetic. The idiographic approach tries to understand the essence of someone's personality and believes that all aspects of someone's personality are unique to that person

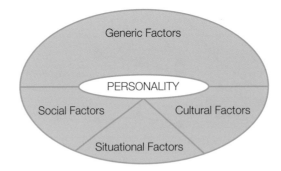

Figure 2.2 Influencing factors on personality

socialisation the process of learning how to think, feel and behave by conforming to and imitating influential others within social settings

idiographic an approach which describes personality in terms that are unique to the individual

nomothetic an approach which describes personality in terms of specific dimensions that vary across people

alone. It also links someone's personality with their perceptions and attitudes in an attempt to understand their behaviour. Idiographic theories tend to have their roots in clinical psychology and are largely concerned with issues like helping people to cope with their everyday demands.

SPOTLIGHT ON SKILLS

Organisations want to hire the person who has the best knowledge, skills and abilities for any job they are trying to fill. They also want someone who will fit well into the job, work group and organisational culture ▶ **Chapter 12** ◀. Sometimes the applicant that fits the best is lacking in one or more competencies and sometimes the person with the best skill set doesn't seem quite right in terms of their personality or fit for the job or organisation.

1 Which is more important, skills or fit? Why?

2 How much reliance should you place on psychometric tests and assessments when making selection decisions?

3 How should you go about integrating a new employee who has the right skills but might not be a clear fit?

To help you answer these questions, in your ebook click the play button to watch the video of Fiona Clarke from Eurostar talking about personality.

IDIOGRAPHIC APPROACHES

FREUD'S PSYCHODYNAMIC THEORY

No doubt you have heard of Sigmund Freud. His psychodynamic theory is probably the most famous of the idiographic approaches to personality. Freud believed that our personalities are made up of three interacting parts called the id, the ego and the superego. The **id**, which is something that we're born with, is an unconscious part of our personality and drives us to seek immediate gratification. The **ego** operates at a conscious level; its function is to think, control and organise. The ego decides when to give in to the impulses of the id and when to succumb to the demands of reality. The **superego** is the moral regulator of personality. It is culturally influenced and tells us what we should and shouldn't do. Furthermore, it punishes us with guilt when we do the wrong thing. It is the ego's job to manage the ongoing tension between the impulses of the id and the moral judgement of the superego. Imagine the anxiety you might feel if you were to get a last-minute ticket to the sporting event of the year on a day that your boss needs you to chair an important meeting. Freud's theory focused on how an individual's personality develops, starting in early childhood. When people are well-adjusted, their ego is able to manage the id–superego conflict. However, when the ego can't cope, it develops defence mechanisms such as **repression** to protect itself.

Despite Freud's prominence, there are a number of reasons why his psychodynamic theory in particular, and idiographic approaches in general, have had limited impact on organisations. Their origins in clinical psychology mean that the focus has been largely on 'abnormal' rather than normal populations. Their idiosyncratic perspective means that measures of personality dimensions have not been developed and there is no real mechanism for comparing the personalities of different people. Furthermore, Freud's theories have come under particular scrutiny because it is not possible to test them using scientific methods.

NOMOTHETIC APPROACHES

In contrast, theories adopting the nomothetic approach focus on identifying dimensions of personality that can be used to measure similarities and differences between people. They assume that personality characteristics are relatively stable within people over time. These theories are typically subdivided into **trait theories** and **type theories**. While there are many similarities between trait and type theories – including in some cases the dimensions on which theorists believe people vary – trait theories measure personality dimensions on a continuum from low to high whereas type theories classify people typically using dichotomies of opposites. Two influential, nomothetic theories were developed by Eysenck (1965) from the 1940s and by Cattell (1965).

EYSENCK'S TYPE THEORY

Eysenck identified two key dimensions on which he believed that people vary: extroversion and emotional stability which resulted in four distinct personality types:

- Emotionally Stable Extroverts (Sanguine Types)
- Emotionally Stable Introverts (Phlegmatic Types)
- Emotionally Unstable Extroverts (Choleric Types)
- Emotionally Unstable Introverts (Melancholic Types)

While Eysenck's theory is considered a type theory, he believed that specific traits stem from each of the four types. For example, Emotionally Stable Extroverts (known as Sanguine Types), tend to be sociable, outgoing, lively and carefree. Details of the traits associated with each of the four types are shown in Figure 2.3.

repression a defensive mechanism in which anxiety-producing thoughts are pushed into the unconscious

trait theories theories that describe people in terms of enduring personality characteristics

type theories theories that place individuals into predetermined categories thereby identifying them as a particular personality type

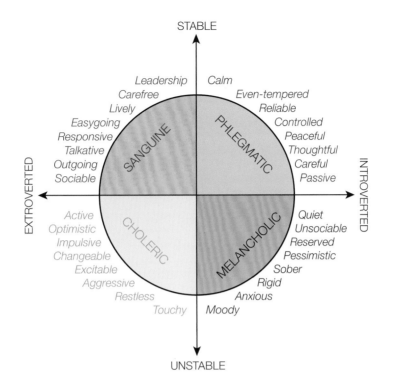

Figure 2.3 Eysenck's personality types and associated traits

Source: Eysenck (1965).

CATTELL'S TRAIT THEORY

Cattell (1965) believed that a distinction should be made between surface traits, which are observable through someone's behaviour, and source traits, which cause behavioural tendencies. He called source traits the fundamental building blocks of personality and through extensive testing with thousands of people he refined his theory and measurement instrument into a scheme of 16 source traits. Cattell's Sixteen Personality Factor Questionnaire (known as the 16PF) is widely used in organisations for selection, career development, team building, leadership assessment and other purposes. A sample feedback report with the continuum of the 16 source traits is shown in Figure 2.4.

THE FIVE-FACTOR MODEL (OR BIG FIVE)

There has been a lot of debate among researchers about how many traits are needed to comprehensively describe an individual's personality. You can see from our discussion that Eysenck and Cattell disagreed as to the correct number. Over three-quarters of a century ago, Allport and Odbert (1936) identified several thousand words in the dictionary that

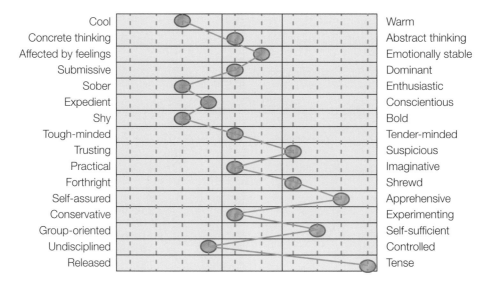

Figure 2.4 A sample feedback report using Cattell's 16PF

Source: Bratton (2015).

describe normal everyday personality characteristics. They challenged the psychological research community to figure out exactly how many clusters of personality synonyms are needed to distinguish human behaviour from one individual to another. While researchers will continue to deliberate on this topic, most agree that a winner was declared in the 1980s with the emergence of the Five-Factor Model (FFM) known widely as the 'Big Five' (McCrae and Costa, 1987). Most individual differences in personality can be classified into five broad domains or dimensions which, importantly, are theoretically independent. That means that someone's level on one of the five dimensions is completely unrelated to their level on the other dimensions.

The five personality dimensions included in the model are: Openness to experience, Conscientiousness, Extroversion, Agreeableness and Need for emotional stability. (This last factor is traditionally known as Neuroticism, but many have changed the label to 'Emotional stability' or 'Need for emotional stability' because 'neuroticism' has such negative connotations.) OCEAN is a useful acronym to help you remember the five dimensions although you can also use CANOE.

Each of the dimensions can be thought of as a continuum so, for example, someone could be high or low on extroversion. Think back to the chapter introduction in which two friends differed in how much time they liked to spend with other people. The friend who likes to spend a lot of time on her own is likely to be low on extroversion so would be an introvert. Because it is a continuum, someone may also be in the middle. The term 'ambivert' has started to gain popularity as a label for those who fall somewhere in the middle. Table 2.1 provides a brief description of the five personality dimensions and Table 2.2 provides you with a chance to score yourself on a shortened version of the Big Five.

BUILDING YOUR SKILLS

Managing Diversity

You are a project manager in a multinational company and you are putting together a group of experts to work on a high profile project. The team will be quite diverse in that the members will all work in different jobs and will all come from different countries. Should you also consider personality when designing the team? What would be the most desirable traits you would look for in future team members?

© ROYALTY-FREE/CORBIS

Table 2.1 The Big Five Personality Dimensions

		High		Low
O	Open to experience	**Explorer** Like to learn about new ideas and experience new things; tend to be inquisitive, creative, unconventional and easily bored.	⟷	**Preserver** Like operating in familiar territory; tend to be traditional, conventional and conforming.
C	Conscientious	**Focused** Focus their energies on accomplishing their goals; tend to be ambitious, hardworking, diligent and organised.	⟷	**Flexible** Are spontaneous and work to their moods; tend to be good at multiskilling; can be inefficient and disorganised.
E	Extroversion	**Extrovert** Like to be where the action is; tend to be sociable, assertive, gregarious and dominant.	⟷	**Introvert** Are happy to let others get stuck into where all the action is; tend to be quiet, reserved and private.
A	Agreeableness	**Adapter** Are accommodating when it comes to others' needs or wishes; tend to be kind, sympathetic and courteous.	⟷	**Challenger** Focus on their own priorities over others'; tend to be competitive, quarrelsome and sometimes callous.
N	Need for emotional stability (or Neuroticism)	**Reactive** Can feel crippled by stressful situations; tend to be anxious and emotional and often feel nervous and insecure.	⟷	**Resilient** Are able to stay quite calm in stressful situations; tend to be secure, relaxed, steady and stable.

Source: Adapted from Howard and Howard (2001).

Table 2.2 Measure yourself on the Big Five

The scales show descriptions associated with each of the Big Five factors. Read the words at both ends and place yourself where you think you actually are, not where you'd like to be. Then ask a friend or family member who knows you well to do the same thing. Are your impressions the same?		
Open to new experience, complex	|_|_|_|_|_|_|_|	Conventional, uncreative
Dependable, self-disciplined	|_|_|_|_|_|_|_|	Disorganised, careless
Extrovert, enthusiastic	|_|_|_|_|_|_|_|	Reserved, quiet
Sympathetic, warm	|_|_|_|_|_|_|_|	Critical, quarrelsome
Anxious, easily upset	|_|_|_|_|_|_|_|	Calm, emotionally stable

Source: Adapted from Gosling et al. (2003).

HOW DOES PERSONALITY INFLUENCE BEHAVIOUR AT WORK?

There are three questions you might consider before reading about how personality influences behaviour at work, particularly in relation to how organisations should act based on this information:

1   Are some personality traits better than others for effectiveness at work? If some traits are particularly important and you are a manager, you would most likely insist that your organisation uses personality tests to make sure you only hire people with these desirable traits.

2   Does effectiveness at work depend more on the situation? Perhaps some work environments suit some personalities better than others. Then it's a contingency argument and it's about fit. As a manager, you would be using personality tests to make sure job applicants have the right traits to fit with specific jobs.

3   Is it possible to have too much of a good thing? For example, if it's good to have a conscientious employee, is it better to have a very conscientious employee? Or are moderate amounts of desirable traits actually the most appropriate? As a manager, you would need a more detailed understanding of how personality tests are designed, how to interpret the scores and how to apply the results to the work context.

OPENNESS TO EXPERIENCE

People who are open (that is, those who are high on the openness to experience dimension, sometimes called Explorers) are creative, curious, complex and cultured (Howard and Howard, 2001; Saucier, 1994). Open employees tend to perform well in creative jobs that require them to come up with novel ideas and solutions. Since they have a built-in desire to learn and experience new things, they also tend to thrive in jobs that are dynamic and have rapidly changing job demands. Because they tend to get bored doing things in 'the same old way' they are quick to adapt and improve existing procedures that aren't working well.

They are less well suited to jobs that are repetitive, require precise rules to be followed and have little autonomy such as accounting, police work, sales and some service occupations.

CONSCIENTIOUSNESS

People who are conscientious are hard-working, organised, ambitious and persevering (McCrae and Costa, 1987; Saucier, 1994). Unlike openness, conscientiousness is thought to be important for all jobs and occupations. Can you imagine going into a job interview where they tell you that they are looking for someone who is lazy, disorganised and gives up easily? While people who are low on conscientiousness (sometimes called Flexible) are spontaneous, good at multitasking, and comfortable dealing with chaos (Howard and Howard, 2001), most research shows that conscientious employees are indeed productive employees (Barrick *et al.*, 2001; Judge *et al.*, 2008). Conscientious employees are motivated, committed and self-confident. They set higher goals for themselves than other employees and are more tenacious at attempting to reach their goals.

Conscientiousness has also been linked to a wide range of positive outcomes beyond job performance (Barrick *et al.*, 2001). For example, conscientious employees are more committed to their organisations and more satisfied with their jobs. Conscientious workers are more likely to employ citizenship behaviours and less likely to engage in counterproductive work behaviours. This is in part because of their high levels of job satisfaction. Feeling good about their job and the organisation promotes unprompted acts of citizenship and diminishes any feeling that they need to retaliate to negative treatment (Barrick *et al.*, 2001).

EXTROVERSION

Extroverts are sociable, talkative, assertive and dominant. Extroversion is considered to be important for some but not all jobs (Barrick *et al.*, 2001). You can undoubtedly imagine jobs that require long periods of working on one's own (for example, computer programmers, archivists, chemists, writers) that would be unsuited to people who are high on the extroversion–introversion continuum. Jobs like project managers, teachers, sales representatives and health care professionals are often recommended for people who are high on extroversion. It is perhaps surprising that extroverts don't always perform better in jobs that require a lot of social interaction, such as service representative jobs. This may be in part because extroverts tend to make their presence felt by dominating situations, and there are times when a back-seat is more appropriate (Stewart and Carson, 1995). Research has found that extroversion is easier than any of the other Big Five factors to guess correctly (Levesque and Kenny, 1993). Think of times when you were with a new group of people; it doesn't take very long to figure out who the extroverts and introverts are.

citizenship behaviours discretionary behaviour that is often not formally recognised or rewarded by organisations but benefits the organisation and/or its members

counterproductive work behaviours any intentional behaviour by an employee that is seen to be contrary to the organisation's interests

Extroverts are concerned with being influential and successful; they strive to increase their status and develop a strong reputation. Extroverts often emerge as leaders in group situations ▸ Chapter 8 ◂. They are energetic and outgoing and they fit with the stereotype of what followers expect leaders to look like. Extroverts also tend to be high in both job and life satisfaction (Judge *et al.*, 2002). Extroverts are typically high in positive affectivity across a wide range of situations which undoubtedly accounts for these findings (Thoresen *et al.*, 2003).

AGREEABLENESS

Agreeable people are kind, helpful, warm and cooperative. They focus more on getting along with others than they do on getting ahead in organisations. Once again, this set of traits is not right for all occupations. Agreeableness is very useful in jobs like nursing, teaching and service jobs in business, but may be less useful in jobs where being disagreeable is actually a requirement for being effective. For example, managers often have to make tough decisions that don't please their direct reports or other relevant stakeholders. Worrying too much about making everyone happy may lead to poor decisions or even complete indecision which would make no one happy.

Agreeableness has been found to be linked with several other positive and negative workplace outcomes. People who are high on agreeableness tend to have lower levels of career success when it's measured objectively by salary (Seibert and Kraimer, 2001). This is undoubtedly linked to their interest in getting along rather than getting ahead. Agreeable people are less likely to get involved in conflicts. However, if a conflict does arise, they are more likely to take a productive, integrative approach to resolve it, but are also more likely to feel distressed as a result of the conflict situation (Dijkstra *et al.*, 2004). They are less likely to engage in counterproductive work behaviours, especially behaviours directed towards others as opposed to the organisation (Judge *et al.*, 2008).

NEED FOR EMOTIONAL STABILITY

People who are high on the need for emotional stability (sometimes referred to as neurotic people) are nervous, insecure, moody and emotional. Like conscientiousness, this dimension relates to all jobs and occupations but, unlike conscientiousness, jobs benefit from employees who are low rather than high on this domain. Employees who are calm under pressure, steady and secure are much more attractive to employers than those who are anxious and insecure.

You'll recall that extroversion is associated with positive affectivity. Well, need for emotional stability is associated with negative affectivity which undoubtedly explains their lower levels of job, career and life satisfaction (Barrick *et al.*, 2001; Judge *et al.*, 2002). Some research has also found that need for emotional stability correlates negatively with

positive affectivity a dispositional tendency to experience pleasant moods such as enthusiasm and excitement

negative affectivity a dispositional tendency to experience negative moods such as nervousness, annoyance and hostility

objective career success although the results have not been consistent (Judge *et al.*, 2002). Stress is also an issue for people who are high on need for emotional stability. They perceive that they are exposed to greater amounts of stress, regardless of their actual workload; they feel more threatened by stressful situations; and they use less effective coping strategies when trying to deal with stressful events (Bolger and Zuckerman, 1995).

CONSIDER THIS...

You have recently been put into teams for a university assignment. You don't know your teammates and you are aware that personality will be a factor in how well you get along and how effectively the group will perform. Do you think you and your teammates should complete a personality instrument so that you can understand each other better from the start? Should you use scores on specific traits to decide who is best to lead the team? Are there any dimensions within the Big Five that might be too sensitive to assess?

© GETTY IMAGES/ISTOCKPHOTO/CATHERINE YEULET

CAN THERE BE TOO MUCH OF A GOOD THING?

At the start of this section, you were asked to consider a few questions, one of which focused on whether it's possible to have too much of a good thing.

As discussed in detail above, highly conscientious people are more motivated, organised and persistent and therefore are more likely to reach their goals and performance targets. However, research has questioned whether too much conscientiousness may actually be detrimental (Le *et al.*, 2011). Highly conscientious people may be compulsive perfectionists who are overly rigid and become focused on the minutiae rather than the big picture. Sticking too closely to plans and goals may make them unable or unwilling to change direction and/ or acquire new knowledge and skills, even when there are signs that these things are desirable. Similarly, very low and very high levels of neuroticism might also be more detrimental to performance. Feeling a certain amount of stress and anxiety might be useful for performance, but certainly very high levels can be crippling and lead to deterioration in performance. Le and his colleagues' research found what they expected. The relationship is not linear but rather curvilinear and more is better but only up to a point. After that point, high levels of conscientiousness and low levels of neuroticism were associated with lower levels of task performance and citizenship behaviour and higher levels of counterproductive work behaviours.

objective career success career success that can be assessed by a third party and is usually measured by hierarchical level reached, the salary attained and/or the number of promotions received

MEASURING INDIVIDUAL PERSONALITY CHARACTERISTICS

If you believe that personality is important for predicting behaviour in the workplace, then you may feel that it's important to assess it when making hiring and promotion decisions. The previous discussion will give you some indication of the traits that might be useful for different types of jobs and work environments. Even so, organisations must carry out detailed job analyses including person specifications for each job they're filling so that they know exactly what attributes are needed for success in each and every job. They must also then decide what selection method to use to determine whether a candidate has the right attributes. Interviews, psychometric testing, reference letters and assessment centres are potential options used by organisations in the selection process.

Personality is often 'assessed' during interviews, or by asking former employers about the person's personality during reference checking. A study carried out by Barrick *et al.* (2000) set out to determine how good interviewers are at assessing personality during their interviews. They found that interviewers were pretty good at assessing openness, agreeableness and extroversion, but they weren't as good at determining levels of conscientiousness or neuroticism. As you know from our discussion above, conscientiousness and neuroticism are extremely important personality traits for job performance; therefore better methods of assessment are needed. So, how do organisations actually go about measuring the personality traits that they want to assess in order to make their hiring decisions? It's much easier said than done.

First of all, how can you measure what you cannot see or touch? It's not like height and weight and other physical entities that simply require agreed measurement tools. At best we can make inferences about someone's personality based on what is observable. We know that some people are more sociable and talkative than others. The same can be said for intelligence. We know that some people are better at solving difficult problems. However, just because measuring personality is difficult and cannot be done directly doesn't mean it's a complete guessing game. Psychologists have developed a number of 'yard sticks' to assess personality called self-report personality inventories. These are often referred to as personality tests (even in this chapter) but that's technically not correct, as the term 'test' implies that there are right and wrong answers and that's not the case when measuring personality.

CONSIDER THIS…

When McCrae *et al.* (2005) administered the Big Five personality instrument to large numbers of university students in more than 50 countries, unsurprisingly they found country differences. On average, people in some countries are more agreeable/ extrovert/etc. than people in other countries. Do you think there is any danger that this type of research would reinforce national stereotypes? Why or why not? Do you think there is any value in carrying out similar research within organisations to find out what the dominant personality profiles are within organisational cultures? Why or why not?

Some self-report personality inventories are to be completed using pencil and paper methods while others are administered online. Some are developed by academics and have been critiqued through the blind peer review process, while others are available commercially where the quality can be variable. It's important that these instruments are of a very high standard, especially if they are going to be used for making selection decisions. In particular, it's important that they have both reliability and validity. There are several types of validity, but the most important in this context is predictive validity. If you were to look in academic journals, you'd find some measures of the Big Five include 240 items. These longer tools typically have very good psychometric properties (in other words, they're reliable and valid) but they can take up to half an hour to complete. Employers should be wary of self-report instruments that are much shorter; although job applicants might prefer them, they are less likely to have the necessary validity and reliability.

One criticism of using personality measures in employee selection is that applicants have a vested interest in engaging in impression management. In other words, they present a fake version of themselves in order to be more attractive to the employer. No doubt this happens in all aspects of the selection process. Can you imagine going to an interview and not putting your best foot forward? Even employers do this because they want to impress you as much as you want to impress them. However, when using psychometric tests, this can be a serious concern, especially if not everyone does it and those who do are not identifiable.

This topic has been debated extensively by academics because of the implications for employee selection. On the one hand, we want to use well validated measures to select the best employee and we know that interviews have poor predictive validity. On the other hand, if well validated psychometric tests and self-report instruments can be faked, then they are no better. A study by Hogan *et al.* (2007) provides strong evidence that faking isn't as much of a problem as once thought. In this highly sophisticated study, people were given a second chance to take personality assessments six months after their job application was rejected because their scores did not meet the required threshold, but the basic finding was that they did not do any better the second time around. Hogan and his colleagues argued that even though these applicants were motivated to improve their scores, they were unable to do so. In other words, any attempt at faking or managing impressions did not lead to better scores. Since well validated instruments were used, they argued that faking is not the concern that many think it is.

OTHER CLASSIFICATIONS OF PERSONALITY CHARACTERISTICS

MYERS-BRIGGS TYPE INDICATOR

Although most psychologists believe that the Five-Factor Model is the best system for examining personality, it is certainly not the only lens available. The Myers-Briggs Type Indicator (MBTI)

reliability the extent to which a measure is consistent or repeatable

validity the extent to which a measurement tool measures what it purports to measure

predictive validity the extent to which a measurement tool accurately predicts future job behaviour or performance

Personality Profiling and Sports

Recent reports indicate that more and more top-level teams, in a wide range of sports, are using personality assessments to help give them a competitive advantage over their opponents.

In 2013, the English Cricket Team used the Myers-Briggs Type Indicator (MBTI) (see below) 'to help 11 wildly different individuals to coalesce into a team' (Moody, 2013, p. 63), with apparent success: 'Reconciling divergent personalities into a well-oiled, cohesive team is no easy feat. England's behaviour on the field this month displays a maturity far removed from the discord and tensions of the recent past' (Rainey, 2013, p. 21). Kate Green, the England Cricket Board's lead on personal development stated that the more they understand their players, the more support they can give them in areas such as managing conflict and handling pressure both on and

IN THE NEWS

off the field. One of the coaches said that the MBTI helped him to overcome a problem he was having with one of his players. When he realised that they were completely opposite types in their personality profiles, he adjusted his coaching style and that helped them to overcome their problems.

AC Milan uses personality testing for a wide range of purposes including individual player assessment and development as well as understanding the team dynamic (Pepi, 2005). According to the head of European development at SHL (the business psychology consulting firm used by AC Milan), personality testing is even used for succession planning, including selecting the team captain. Furthermore, they have found that they can develop better recovery plans for injured players by considering their personalities and tailoring the plans to the players' needs.

In the United States, top level coaches in both men's and women's basketball also use personality assessments at the individual and team level. Jeff Bower, who has coached both professional (NBA) and US college teams, uses personality profiling with all his potential recruits. Bower said, 'We're not looking for any one quality in particular. We're looking for how individuals function best and what their natural instincts are. We think it's a tool that will help us blend personalities together and bring the right kind of person here' (Eisenberg, 2013). Similarly, a high-profile women's basketball coach, Pat Summit, uses personality profiling to help her manage her players more effectively. After players have completed the personality inventory, she analyses the results with them. Those who thrive under pressure in the most intense situations are managed very differently from perfectionists who are hard on themselves whenever they make mistakes.

It seems that some coaches do have concerns however. When US college basketball teams are vying for the best talent, they don't want to scare anyone off before they've signed on the dotted line. The recruitment process has been described as 'a courtship' where 'romancing' is more the norm than psychological testing (Eisenberg, 2013).

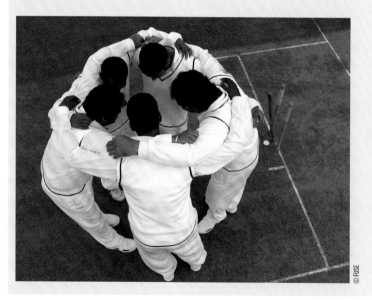

Questions

1 Several advantages of personality profiling in sport are discussed above. Can you think of any additional uses or benefits? Can you think of any potential drawbacks to using

it? If you were managing a top-level sports team, would you use it and for what purposes?

2 Can you think of any top athletes whose personality helps them to be successful? What specific traits do you think they have that are so beneficial? Can you think of any top athletes whose personality gets in the way of their success? What traits are holding them back? Do you think anything can be done to help them overcome or deal with these negative traits?

3 Do you think a coach or manager of a top-level sports team should prioritise skill-fit or personality-fit? A player with the best skills for a specific position might disrupt the team because of personality-fit. Can the manager justify putting in another player who isn't as talented but works better in the team? Would your answers be different for business organisations than for sports teams? Why or why not?

Sources

Eisenberg, J. (2013). Personality profiling is latest method coaches are using to evaluate potential recruits. Retrieved from http://sports.yahoo.com/blogs/the-dagger/personality-profiling-latest-method-coaches-using-evaluate-potential-143500770.html (last accessed on 17 August 2015).

Moody, O. (2013). England find Jung mind games give them the edge, *The Times*, 25 July, p. 63.

Pepi, S. (2005). Top Scorers. *People Management*, 13 January, pp. 38–40.

Rainey, S. (2013). Will Jung win us the Ashes?, *The Daily Telegraph*, 26 July, p. 21.

is arguably the most widely used personality instrument in the business world. This may be because the commercial providers are better at marketing it than other instruments, or it may be because its positive stance and simplicity make it attractive to people working in business. The different dimensions are shown as being opposites, but they're not described as being good or bad. Not having any negative definitions is a real advantage when introducing personality concepts into the workplace where trainers, managers and consultants are trying to improve morale and effectiveness and do not want to label people as having the 'wrong' personality.

The MBTI was originally designed to test Carl Jung's theory of personality type. Carl Jung, who once worked with Sigmund Freud (and then split from him), was the first to develop the terms extroversion and introversion. In his work he was drawn to understanding differences in the way people prefer to use their perception and judgement. He strongly believed in the notion of opposites. If you are not an introvert, then you must be an extrovert; there is no middle ground. A major difference between the MBTI (based on Jung's theory) and the theory underpinning the Big Five is the notion of opposite types. You'll recall from the discussion above that the Big Five dimensions are on a trait continuum. You may be very extroverted, a little bit extroverted, right in the middle of the continuum or somewhere towards the introvert end of it.

In the MBTI classification system, there are four dichotomies which lead to 16 different personality types, as shown in Table 2.3.

No doubt you can see a number of similarities between this classification scheme and the Big Five. Intuition is similar to Openness to experience; Feeling is similar to Agreeableness; and Judging is similar to Conscientiousness. The Extroversion link is obvious and Neuroticism doesn't have a parallel in the MBTI. The beauty of the MBTI is its simplicity. Someone's personality type can be captured by four letters. You might be an ENTP or an IFSJ. You can then read a short description of yourself that feels pretty accurate and fairly positive.

Table 2.3 Myers-Briggs Type Indicator dimensions

Extroversion (E) – being energised by people and things in the outer world	Introversion (I) – being energised by thoughts, feelings and impressions in the inner world
Sensing (S) – gathering information by focusing on facts and details that can be confirmed by experience	Intuition (N) – gathering information by focusing on possibilities and relationships among ideas
Thinking (T) – making decisions by using impersonal, objective and logical analysis	Feeling (F) – making decisions by using subjective analysis and focusing on others' needs
Judging (J) – approaching tasks by planning, being organised and reaching closure	Perceiving (P) – approaching tasks by being spontaneous, flexible and open

The MBTI does emphasise weak spots for each of the types to work on, but the tone and language is positive. This makes it appealing to managers in organisations who want a lens for understanding individual differences but don't want to unearth any 'bad types'. The MBTI is only available via commercial providers and must be administered, scored and interpreted by qualified practitioners. However, if you would like to complete an online version of Jungian Typology to see what your own type is, you can do so at: www.123test.com/jung-personality-test/ (last accessed on 17 August 2015).

Psychologists have starting coming out pretty strongly against the MBTI, arguing that it is not a good measure and it is not based on a good theory. For a succinct yet interesting critique, refer to Adam Grant's hard-hitting assessment in the Huffington Post: www.huffing tonpost.com/adam-grant/goodbye-to-mbti-the-fad-t_b_3947014.html (last accessed on 17 August 2015).

CORE SELF-EVALUATIONS (CSE)

Core self-evaluations (CSE) as a collective emerged around 2000, which makes it quite a new addition to the personality literature. CSE is a basic, bottom-line set of evaluations that individuals make about themselves in determining their own self-worth (Judge et al., 2003). While it includes self-esteem, it is broader than that. These four traits are closely linked to one and another and are well established in the psychology literature in their own right. See Table 2.4 for explanations of each of these concepts and some sample questions that you can use to assess yourself. As you can see, there is some overlap with the Big Five in that both include emotional stability (that is, neuroticism), but the emphasis of this personality lens is quite different to that of the Big Five.

Those who are higher in CSE tend to appraise situations more positively, have greater confidence in their ability to influence the world in a positive way, and generally feel pretty good about themselves. This self-belief and self-confidence mean they have higher levels of

CSE a broad trait indicator that includes four more specific traits: internal locus of control, emotional stability, self-esteem and generalised self-efficacy

Table 2.4 The meaning and self-assessment of CSE

CSE dimension	Meaning of CSE dimension	To what extent do you agree with the following sample statements? (1 = strongly disagree and 5 = strongly agree)
Internal locus of control	Beliefs about the causes of events in one's life – internal locus is when individuals see events as being the result of their own behaviour (rather than luck or external circumstances)	1 My life is determined by my own actions. 2 When I get what I want, it's usually because I worked hard for it.
Emotional stability	The tendency to have a positive belief/style and to focus on the positive aspects of oneself	1 Too often, when things go wrong, I get discouraged and feel like giving up. (R) 2 I often feel inferior to others. (R)
Self-esteem	The overall value that one places on oneself as a person	1 I feel that I have a number of good qualities. 2 I feel that I am a person of worth, at least on an equal basis with others.
Generalised self-efficacy	An evaluation of how well one can perform across a variety of situations	1 If something looks too complicated, I will not even bother to try it. (R) 2 When I make plans, I am certain I can make them work.

(R) These questions are 'reverse coded' items. They are negatively worded whereas the others are positively worded. You therefore need to reverse the scoring such that 5=strongly disagree and 1=strongly agree for these items.

Source: Based on information in Judge et al. (2003).

motivation. Think about it in relation to yourself. When you feel pretty good and you think you can do something, chances are that you stick at it until you succeed. This in turn leads to greater self-belief and you are on an upward spiral. When you are feeling down and/or have self-doubt, you are more likely to give up. This of course can lead to a downward spiral.

Research (by Kacmar *et al.* (2009), for example) has found that these four dimensions are collectively very good at predicting many important organisational outcomes. Those who have high levels of CSE not only perform better in their jobs, but they are also more satisfied in them and in life in general. They have more successful careers (for example, they earn more) and experience lower levels of stress and conflict. They are good at capitalising on opportunities and they cope well with setbacks. They are more effective at customer service and adjust better to foreign assignments. They persist more at job searching when unemployed and experience reduced levels of work–family conflict. In short, core self-evaluations are important for employers to consider when evaluating individual differences in the workplace. Researchers are enthusiastic about CSE as a way of looking at individual differences because it explains behaviour within (and outside of) organisations beyond what is explained by the Big Five.

DARK TRIAD OF PERSONALITY

After reading the section on CSE, you might be feeling pretty positive: 'If I feel good about myself, I'll perform better and then I'll feel even better about myself. I can create my own virtuous cycle!' Sorry to change your mood, but we're now going to take a look at the dark side of personality. There are three 'offensive' personalities that have also received a lot of attention in the literature: Machiavellianism, narcissism and psychopathy (Paulhus and Williams, 2002, p. 556).

They are described in more detail below, but in brief, *Machiavellianism* is the manipulative personality, *narcissism* is the superiority personality and *psychopathy* is the highly impulsive, thrill-seeking personality that also includes low levels of empathy. These three personality traits have a number of features in common, including self-promotion, emotional coldness, aggressiveness and deception. Not surprisingly, all three correlate significantly and negatively with the Big Five dimension of agreeableness (Wu and LeBreton, 2011). These are not characteristics you would want in your friends, bosses or co-workers.

If you think about how these personality traits might play out in the workplace, you'll get a good sense of the problems they can cause. Machiavellian types are scheming, planning and manipulative. They are playing a game in which everyone is under their control. They form strategic friendships that last only as long as they are useful. They thrive on conflict and make sure that they are a step or two ahead of everyone else ▸ **Chapter 9** ◂. Narcissists make everything relate to them. They take credit even when others do all the hard work and they promote themselves at every opportunity. They tend to be condescending to anyone who threatens them, treating them as inferior so that they can feel superior. They want to be admired by others and thought of as better than everyone else. For anyone working with a psychopath, the combination of lack of empathy and thrill-seeking is dangerous. Psychopaths will happily walk all over others, not caring about the consequences, and they do it just for the thrill of it all. Your misery seems to make them happy.

It's not surprising, in fact it's reassuring, that research has found negative workplace consequences for people with these dark personality traits (Judge *et al.*, 2006; Spain *et al.*, 2014). People who are high on these dark traits tend to receive lower performance appraisal ratings from their boss. Machiavellianism is also negatively associated with citizenship behaviour and positively linked to unethical decision-making in organisations. Leaders who are high in psychopathy engage in less corporate social responsibility and lower levels of support for their employees. They also respond less well to leadership training and development, in part because their overconfidence makes them less likely to take on board negative feedback. While narcissists claim to be very creative, the evidence suggests that they are no better at creative performance than others. All three of the dark triad traits have been linked with counterproductive work behaviours.

One area of particular concern for our purposes is that individuals with Machiavellian and/or narcissistic traits can make very good first impressions which might help convince employers to hire them. Narcissists tend to be talkative and good at self-promotion, both of which are advantageous at interviews. Machiavellian types seem to be more willing to engage in faking; they also seem to be better at it. However, researchers have argued that these initial good impressions wear off pretty quickly and others soon see them for what they are (Spain *et al.*, 2014).

BrewBite

Michael O'Halloran has recently been appointed HR manager of BrewBite, a new and promising micro brewery based in the UK. While completing his undergraduate degree in business, Michael did part-time bar work and was also actively involved in clubs and societies. He was Chairperson of the Gaming Society, which won numerous awards including Best Newcomers, and was also Public Relations Officer for the Ultimate Frisbee Club, which won Most Improved Club. After graduating, Michael worked as the Assistant Manager for a local bar and restaurant for 3 years then completed a Master's degree in HRM.

Michael is looking forward to the many challenges he knows he will face at this young and growing company. He is the first person they have ever hired to work in the area of HR and he wonders if he has the experience needed to be successful. He's recently learned that it is his capacity for innovation, which he demonstrated mostly through his leadership roles in the clubs and societies, that piqued BrewBite's interest in hiring him.

One of the first challenges Michael will face is devising a plan for a recruitment drive. BrewBite is expanding into new markets and needs to hire people for several positions from Sales Reps to Accountants. He has not been given a lot of guidance from the Senior Managers at BrewBite about how to do this, except from Jonathan Geary who is BrewBite's co-founder:

'We want people who are as passionate about our craft as we are, and that craft is making awesome beer and breaking down any walls of tradition in the process. The more walls we break – the better!'

BrewBite projects an image of a rebellious, non-conventional organisation with an almost rock star, tongue-in-cheek attitude. Jonathan Geary heads the influential Culture Management Team whose job it is to ensure that BrewBite stays true to its values and that its culture remains strong as the company grows.

Although Michael has experience in management and with the adult beverage industry, it has become clear to him that this organisational structure and culture are not what he has worked with in the past. Despite this, he is determined to do a good job and make a good impression. He recognises the importance of working with the Culture Management Team as he develops his recruitment plan. Not only are they a powerful and influential group, but they have a good point about not wanting to dilute BrewBite's values and culture as the company grows. When employees all share the same assumptions about 'how things are done around here', things run more smoothly. It's easy to see that someone who doesn't fit into the organisation's culture would struggle to be effective. They would probably also be quite unhappy and would therefore leave. These are things that Michael wants to avoid. However, he also recognises the importance of hiring people with the right knowledge, skills and abilities to do the job they are hired to do. He worries that the Culture Management Team might want him to emphasise organisational fit more than actual job competencies.

There is a second issue: BrewBite has received a lot of publicity lately and the organisation is highly attractive

© IMAGE SOURCE

(Continued)

BrewBite (*Continued*)

to potential job applicants. Michael worries about how they will manage the barrage of applications they anticipate receiving shortly after the online announcement of job listings is made. He's considering screening applicants using psychometric testing. Only those who are successful will be invited for interviews.

Questions

1 When hiring new employees, do you think Michael should give priority to the knowledge, skills and abilities deemed necessary for the specific positions he needs to fill or to the fit applicants have with BrewBite's culture? How might the external consultant ensure Michael that the methods of testing used tap into the experimental question "Are you right for BrewBite?"

2 One of the first few positions that Michael has to recruit for is Accountants. He has done some research on the personality traits of effective accountants and found that they tend to be detail-oriented, introverted, logical and structured. They also prefer stability over change. Do you think it's possible for Michael to find someone with these traits who will also fit into BrewBite's culture? Is it crucial that BrewBite's accountants fit the mould set in place by its CEO? How might Michael and the external consultancy counter-argue that sentiment?

3 Michael also needs to hire Sales Reps. Research on the Big Five has found that successful Sales Reps tend to be extroverted and conscientious. They are outgoing and ambitious, and they strive for status

and accomplishment. A potential candidate with an excellent sales track record makes it to interviews. Upon interviewing, the candidate appears shy and reserved, yet in the group role play, there is no question that he or she is a natural. Why might this be the case?

4 Work in a group and answer the following questions individually first, then share your answers with the group. What in your opinion is a personal attribute or individual quality that has the highest possibility of being overlooked by psychometric testing alone? How often does the situation or context come into play? How might we account for that?

Written by Dario Di Ruzzo, University of Limerick.

 SUMMARY

IN THE EBOOK, CLICK TO HEAR AN AUDIO SUMMARY

This chapter has shown that as individuals, we differ quite significantly in a number of ways. These differences influence the way we think, feel and behave at work and outside of work. They also influence how effective and happy we are in different contexts. Research shows that, while environmental factors are important, our genes also play a very important role in determining our personalities. It also shows that personality is pretty stable throughout our lives. The Big Five model is a useful tool for understanding these similarities and differences. It's also useful for understanding how and why different people are effective in different work situations. An important issue that came up throughout this chapter was around the area of fit. While having the right fit for our job, work colleagues and organisation is important, we must ask ourselves whether fit is more important than having the right knowledge, skills and abilities. This is something you should think about if you are planning to manage people in your future career. You also need to think about what you would do to ensure you are adequately trained in psychometric assessments if you think your organisation should be using these 'tests' in the selection process.

While the Big Five Model is extraordinarily useful for understanding individual differences and how these differences influence behaviour at work, it is not the only lens for assessing personality. We finished off the chapter by examining what might be described as 'the bad, the good and the ugly'. The 'bad' could be used to describe the Myers-Briggs Type Indicator. While it is extremely popular, and one might argue is unlikely to do much harm since there are 'no bad types', it has been severely criticised for its substantial limitations. It is much better to use the Big Five which has so much good science to back it up. The 'good' refers to core self-evaluations. Even a quick read of this section illustrates how important positive self-belief is to so many aspects of our lives. And finally…the 'ugly'. Personality isn't all about the bright side and there are a number of personality traits, beyond the Big Five and CSE that managers, employees and HR practitioners need to understand because of their potentially toxic influence in the workplace.

CHAPTER REVIEW QUESTIONS

1   In your own words, what is meant by the term personality? Is it important for HR practitioners and line managers to understand personality? Why or why not?

2   What is the nature–nurture debate and why is it important to our understanding of personality?

3   What are strong and weak situations? In which one is personality more likely to affect behaviour and why?

4   What are the five domains that make up the Big Five? List the traits that are associated with each of the five domains.

5   If you were hiring someone to work in a factory where the work was quite repetitive and there was little opportunity for people to talk to one another, what personality characteristics might you look for in job applicants and why?

6   Think about your friends. How similar are their personalities to yours? How do your similarities and differences influence your friendship? Has your friendship changed over time because of personality similarities and differences?

7   Your team at work is experiencing interpersonal conflict and you feel that it's because of personality differences. You think it would be useful to have a team-building training session using personality as a way of discussing how and why the team members approach things differently. Would you use the Big Five or the MBTI and why?

8   What characteristics are associated with the dark triad? How might you deal with a work colleague who displayed some of these characteristics?

MULTIPLE CHOICE QUESTIONS

In your ebook, click to take a multiple choice quiz to test your understanding of this chapter.

FURTHER READING

Bratton, J. (2015) *Introduction to Work and Organizational Behaviour*, 3rd edn. London: Palgrave.

Cohen, R.J. and Swerdlik, M.E. (2005) *Psychological Testing and Assessment: An introduction to tests and measurement*, 6th edn. New York: McGraw-Hill.

Colquitt, J.A., Lepine, J.A. and Wesson, M.J. (2011) *Organizational Behavior: Improving performance and commitment in the workplace*, 2nd edn. New York: McGraw-Hill Irwin.

Hogan, J., Barrett, P. and Hogan, R. (2007) Personality measurement, faking, and employment selection. *Journal of Applied Psychology*, 92(5), 1270–1285.

Judge, T.A., Klinger, R., Simon, L.S. and Yang, I.W.F. (2008) The contributions of personality to organizational behavior and psychology: Findings, criticisms, and future research directions. *Social and Personality Psychology Compass*, 2(5), 1982–2000.

WWW USEFUL WEBSITES

www.bbc.co.uk/science/humanbody/mind/index.shtml?personality

The BBC provides a great deal of information about personality including a number of personality assessments. One of the assessments you can access from this website is based on the Big Five, while others focus on careers and even on the relationship between personality and food preferences.

www.youtube.com/watch?v=z11DeKK13vM

This is a short video clip originally shown on ABC television in America. It discusses the Barnum Effect and shows how easily we can be fooled into believing horoscopes or mind readers. Barnum is the man credited with saying, 'There is a sucker born every minute.' Personality assessments that are not designed and validated by experts can also take advantage of Barnum-type statements, resulting in people mistakenly believing that the assessment they are given is a true reflection of their personality.

www.careersportal.ie/

Most universities offer their students access to online career advice and resources. Some of these websites, like the Irish one whose link is provided here, are hosted at the national level. These websites offer students access to a wide range of resources including personality assessments.

www.123test.com/personality-openness/

123test® is a Dutch-based, privately owned company that creates and publishes psychometric tests online. It provides a wide range of tests covering IQ, personality, and career assessment.

www.personal.psu.edu/~j5j/IPIP/

Professor John A. Johnson at Pennsylvania State University set up a website in which anyone can find out how they score on the Big Five. You can take the long or short version of the IPIP-NEO which is the International Personality Item Pool representation of the NEO PI-R™.

3 PERCEPTION

Jennifer Hennessy

LEARNING OUTCOMES

BY THE END OF THIS CHAPTER YOU SHOULD BE ABLE TO:

- Define perception.
- Discuss how the perceptual process works.
- Understand the concept of selective attention in an organisational context.
- Identify common perceptual distortions that can occur during a work activity.
- Explain how attribution theory assists us in explaining behaviour at work.

© ISTOCK.COM/NICOLA FERRARI

THIS CHAPTER DISCUSSES:

IN REALITY

Have you ever heard the old adage 'what you see is what you get'? We tend to think that our perceptions are relatively stable and unfaltering and that what we perceive closely matches the real world. However, in fact, our perception can often be manipulated to change what we experience. Many companies invest significant marketing and advertising resources to try and create a certain perception of their product. In a study conducted by researchers at Columbia University and MIT, participants in a pub were asked to evaluate regular beer and an 'MIT brew' to which a few drops of balsamic vinegar had been added (Lee *et al.*, 2006). The researchers discovered that disclosure of the additional ingredient of the balsamic vinegar significantly reduced people's preference for the MIT brew *only* when the disclosure took place prior to tasting. This suggests that participants' perceptions changed enough to influence how they experienced the subsequent tasting of the beer. What is also interesting is the fact that the addition of the balsamic vinegar can actually enhance the flavour of the beer, yet people's perception of the taste of vinegar produced a negative connection to its taste in the beer. This connection was strong enough to alter subjects' perception of what the beer would taste like!

This experiment demonstrates how our perception can be influenced to such a degree that it can change our subsequent experience of an event. Our perception of an event or experience is therefore subject to various influences and is not as objective as the old adage would lead us to believe.

INTRODUCTION

Appreciating how people perceive the world around them is a fundamental part of understanding why they behave in the way that they do at work. Perception is a significant psychological process and understanding the relationship between people's perceptions and their behaviours is very important in any organisational context. This chapter provides an overview of perception, the perceptual process and its relevance in a work environment. We begin by defining perception, noting its importance and how we all perceive things in our own unique way. How the perceptual process actually occurs is then examined and we explain how people move from detecting stimuli in the environment to actually taking action in response to them. For example, a manager who perceives that an employee is being bullied by another worker will take action to deal with the situation by carrying out an investigation. Within the perceptual process we as individuals often take shortcuts in making judgements about others and we will explore how this occurs in the workplace through perceptual distortions and attribution theory.

WHAT IS PERCEPTION?

Our five senses of hearing, sight, smell, touch and taste enable us to take in information from our environment, which we then filter and organise through complex processes in order to create meaning. Our **perception** relates to how we 'take in', process and interpret a stimulus. This is an important concept because how we perceive things can have significant outcomes. A good example of this is Milgram's (1974) well-known obedience experiment which illustrates the power of a person's perception of authority. Milgram set up an experiment to test how much pain ordinary people would inflict on an individual because they were ordered to by a figure of authority. He found that people (albeit reluctantly) administered perceived dangerous levels of electric shock to a research subject because they were told to by the scientist in charge of the experiment. The shocks were only an illusion and no harm was done to the subject but the research participants were unaware of this. This experiment shows the extreme lengths that adults could go to because of their perception of authority. The experiment was replicated in a French television documentary called *The Game of Death* in 2010 with similar results.

As illustrated above, how we perceive a situation does not necessarily represent a true or accurate picture of what is actually going on. However what we perceive is what we *think* is reality. A 'Public Perceptions' poll carried out by the market research agency Ipsos/MRBI for *The Irish Times* explored public perception of life in Ireland. One of the questions asked people to rate Ireland in terms of what it is like to live there on the basis of wealth, health, education, happiness and safety in comparison to other counties. The average rating given was 35th when in actual fact Ireland ranks 7th out of 187 participating countries under the United Nations Human Development Index. This demonstrates that people's perception of how highly Ireland ranked was quite different to how it actually ranked in reality.

It is important to understand that individuals perceive the world in their own unique way; as Oscar Wilde once noted 'we are all in the gutter, but some of us are looking at the stars'. Therefore, your perception of the world can be very different from that of other people. For example, if you look at the picture in Figure 3.1 what do you see? Some people will see an old woman, whereas others will see a young girl. How difficult is it for you to see both?

In a work context, a manager who sets challenging goals for an employee may perceive that these goals are motivational and provide a welcome challenge. The employee, however, may perceive the goals as unrealistic and unattainable and therefore become demotivated. It is necessary to recognise that people perceive things in different ways, and a failure to acknowledge these differences may potentially cause conflict in a work environment.

It is also worth noting that different approaches to the study of perception can be adopted. For example, research studies rooted in the positivist tradition may be more concerned with the measurement of perceptual differences and often use experiments to manipulate variables and test hypotheses. A researcher may be interested in, for example, investigating

perception the term perception comes from the Latin 'perceptio' and means 'comprehension' or literally 'a taking in'

Figure 3.1 Old lady or young woman illusion

what facial characteristics influence an interviewer's judgement when hiring someone for a job. More interpretive studies are interested in people's different interpretations of and the inferences they make about a situation based on their perception of that event. These types of studies will commonly use more qualitative methods to elicit rich data on the subject matter. For example, a researcher may be interested in exploring how individuals perceive their fit with the organisation in which they work.

Having learned a little about what perception actually is, we need to answer the question, 'how does perception actually take place?' A camera can be used as a very simple metaphor. It captures an image, processes that image and produces a picture. We as humans take information in, process it and produce an output. Let's now look at the actual process of perception in more detail. We will begin by looking at the factors which influence perception.

HOW PERCEPTION WORKS

Perception is an active process; we process everything that we see, smell, touch, hear and taste. Through our senses we take in information about the world around us. It is through the **process of perception** that we select stimuli from the environment, make sense of them, create meaning from them and react. It is important to be aware of each of the senses, although we predominantly focus on sight in this chapter.

FACTORS WHICH INFLUENCE PERCEPTION

As can be seen in Figure 3.2, there are a number of variables which influence perception. These include characteristics of the perceiver, the object or target being perceived and the context

process of perception the process of how we attend to, organise, interpret and react to stimuli

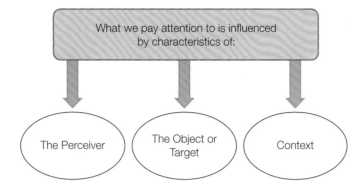

Figure 3.2 Variables which influence our attention

of the situation in which perception occurs. We will now explore these factors before turning our attention to the process of perception.

THE PERCEIVER

Our attention to and selection of stimuli is influenced by our perceptual set and this includes our personality, our goals and motives, prior learning and experiences, our emotions and our attitudes (Mullins, 2007). It is useful to look at some examples of how these factors influence how we attend to information.

Our personality traits may predispose us to attend to and react to stimuli in different ways ▸Chapter 2◂. For example, an extrovert may approach a Christmas night out organised by the company's social club with a very positive mind set and be happy to go along, whereas someone who is more introverted may feel a degree of apprehension about the night and find a reason not to go. Our motivational needs can also influence what we pay attention to. An employee who is interested in getting on in their career may be particularly tuned in to internal job vacancies that are sent to employees through the company's email. An employee who is reaching retirement age may pay far more attention to emails about how his pension is performing than an employee who is in the early stages of his career. These examples raise an important feature of motivation – the salience or importance of a motivational need may have an impact on the level of attention paid to a stimulus. In our examples career progression and planning for retirement are salient needs for each individual and, therefore, that individual pays more attention to the stimulus.

With regard to prior learning and experience, an employee working in an accounting role may quickly pick up an error made by a colleague on a spreadsheet because of his training, or an HR manager may perceive that a negotiation process with the company's union is going well because of her past experience of dealing with that type of situation. Our emotional

perceptual set a set of internal factors which influence what stimuli we select and pay attention to

and attitudinal state can also influence what we pay attention to in certain situations. An employee who is worried and nervous about the security of his job may pay little attention to a manager making a motivational speech about teamwork. An employee who has a negative attitude towards the organisation where he works may perceive that it is a poor place to work and may not be able to see the positive aspects of his work environment, such as a generous compensation and benefits package.

THE OBJECT OR TARGET

External factors also influence the way in which we perceive things. These factors relate to the nature of the stimulus itself and the stimulus may have a number of characteristics that can influence the level of attention that we pay to objects. These may appear individually or as a combination of elements, and include:

- *Size:* We tend to notice large objects; this is why a billboard advert will often catch our attention.
- *Intensity:* We notice stimuli which have a greater intensity; for example fire alarms have a high intensity noise in order to attract your attention.
- *Contrast:* People tend to be more aware of stimuli which are contrasting. The McDonald's 'M' sign is yellow to contrast with its environment and thus stands out.
- *Degree of motion:* People tend to pay more attention to objects that are moving. Adverts on a webpage are often moving up and down in order to attract your attention.
- *Level of repetition:* A stimulus that is repeated is noticed more. For example, in a busy train station an announcement which is repeatedly played over a messaging system is more likely to be noted by commuters.
- *Novelty:* Something which is different or new stands out more. An unknown visitor to the workplace will attract attention, as will a new notice board put on a wall at the entrance to the offices.
- *Familiarity:* We are more likely to notice something familiar to us in a situation where most objects are unfamiliar. For example, we can easily pick out a familiar face in a photograph where we don't know anybody else in the picture.

CONTEXT

The context or situation in which the stimulus is observed should also be considered as it can influence what we pay attention to. For example, employees who are called into a plant meeting when they know that the company has been performing poorly may have a different perception of what the meeting will be about from employees called to a plant meeting when they know that the meeting is being held in the context of the increasingly successful performance of the business. From a manager's perspective, being aware of context is particularly important. A manager might perceive that an employee has a very negative perception of his job. However, by exploring the context the manager may learn that this employee perceives that he is not being given any opportunities to advance in the role and is therefore simply feeling disheartened. Qualitative researchers who are interested in learning about perception will normally include a study of context in their investigation in order to gain a deeper understanding of the topic.

The perception questionnaire in the link below measures how much support you perceive that you receive from your instructor in your current learning environment.

www.selfdeterminationtheory.org/pas-learning-climate/ (last accessed on 18 August 2015)

Attention should be paid to the influence on perception of two other factors: culture and language. These dimensions will now be explored.

CULTURE

Our national culture can predispose us to react in different ways to certain stimuli. A study (Jack et al., 2012) demonstrated how people from different cultures perceive facial expressions in different ways. The research found that East Asians and Western Caucasians differed in the recognition of various facial expressions which included happiness, surprise, fear, disgust, anger and sadness. HSBC's advertisements illustrate variations in cultural perception. In one, it is noted how some American management consultants believe that it is better to have meetings standing up in order to save time which is perceived as precious, but in Japan company chairmen perceive that it is important to have time to contemplate what has been discussed so would prefer to sit down. Another notes how in America, if you hit a hole in one on the golf course, you are expected to buy your partners a drink, but in China you are expected to buy everyone expensive gifts! Finally, let's look at differences in perceptions with regard to the role of food. In the UK, for example, people are expected to finish the food on their plate, whereas if a person clears their dish in China the person's hosts may think the individual is questioning their generosity and will place more food on their plate. These examples reflect how people in different cultures may perceive their environment in different ways. Hofstede et al. (2010) have conducted research exploring cultural differences and developed a categorisation scheme to explore cultural dimensions ▸Chapter 12◂.

LANGUAGE

Language and how we use it has an important impact on the way in which we perceive the world. Our language enables us to recognise stimuli and to identify their role. For example, at one time petrol stations were places to purchase fuel for your car; now they are called service stations and you can buy anything from a sandwich to lottery tickets. As our needs changed in terms of what we expected a petrol/service station to be, the label used to describe what it does also changed. Our perception of the purpose of a petrol/service station is now different. Language can also influence whether we actually perceive a stimulus or not. Let's look at a simple example. Alaskans have many different word variations for snow, enabling them to perceive many different types of snow, whereas in the UK and Ireland there is just one word, so they don't tend to perceive these variations. Some researchers interested in discourse analysis study the way in which we construct words, sentences and phrases in order to understand the meaning of people's discourse. Now that we have a better understanding of the factors which influence perception, let us look at how perception actually works.

Lived Reality in the Health Service

OB IN THE NEWS

In 2014 reports in the Irish media reflected the different perceptions of patient care within the healthcare system. Members of the Irish Emergency Medicine Trainees' Association (IEMTA), who are employed on the health care front line, focused on potential dangers to patient safety, whereas the management group – the Health Service Executive (HSE) – concentrated on improvements in numbers of patients waiting to be admitted to hospital over the previous three years.

The IEMTA had sent a letter signed by its members to the Health Information Quality Authority (HIQA) and the HSE, stating that overcrowding in hospital emergency departments is essentially dangerous for patients and that recommendations from a 2012 HIQA report on overcrowding were being ignored by senior hospital management.

Members were concerned that waiting numbers remained very high. The letter stated that 'the overcrowding has to stop as the current situation is dangerous for patients and stressful for doctors'. The letter also noted that 'the appalling conditions that our patients endure in emergency departments should not go unchallenged. In any human rights issue such as this, there are inevitably bystanders and up-standers. We ask you to stand with us and stand up for our patients'.

In response, the HSE stated that hospitals had been experiencing pressures in recent weeks, mainly as a result of normal seasonal fluctuations in hospital activity. They noted how a similar pattern had occurred in services in Northern Ireland and England. The Head of the HSE accepted the association between overcrowding in emergency departments and the quality of care that can be given, yet he also noted that 'it is important to stress that we have nonetheless seen very significant improvements in the way hospitals nationally are dealing with emergency care'. He stated that there had been a 34 per cent reduction in the number of people waiting on trolleys in emergency departments over the past three years.

However, Chris Luke, a consultant in emergency medicine at Cork University Hospital, said in a radio interview that 'it infuriates me when people try to change the reality by debating the politics of perception', and he noted how the lived reality was different from the perception that things have improved. In his interview he highlighted how nurses and

© GETTY IMAGES/ISTOCKPHOTO/THINKSTOCK/DECISIVEIMAGES

doctors who have chosen to work in emergency medicine are coming into departments which are full of people, with patients on trolleys and packed waiting rooms. He stated how it was 'extremely difficult to work in our emergency departments' and that 'congestion compromises care'. He suggested that beds needed to be made available and that nurses and doctors working in emergency departments should be paid a premium which could help to deal with the high cost of emergency staff cover.

Questions

1 What is the main difference in the perception of patient care between the Irish Emergency Medicine Trainees' Association and the Health Service Executive, and can you give some reasons why these two parties might have different perceptions of the situation?

2 Can you think of a recent example in the media where a story influenced (either fairly or unfairly) public perception of the event?

Sources

www.independent.ie/irish-news/medics-lash-appalling-ae-situation-as-hse-says-trolley-list-down-29938297.html (accessed on 18 August 2015).

www.irishexaminer.com/ireland/doctors-claim-ae-report-ignored-256059.html (accessed on 18 August 2015).

THE PERCEPTUAL PROCESS

We will now move on to examine the process of perception (see Figure 3.3) and look at each of the elements in the perceptual process in turn. It is important to remember that the meaning we extract from what we have perceived is unique to us.

ATTENTION AND SELECTION

The first stage in the perceptual process is that of attention and selection. Because our senses are constantly bombarded with stimuli, we have to find a way to choose the information that

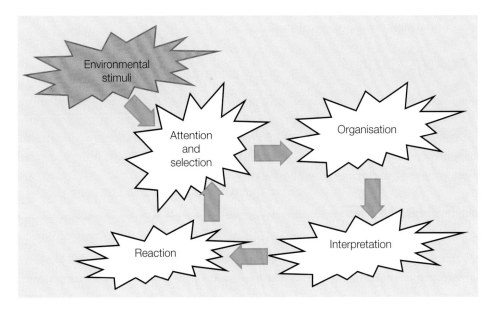

Figure 3.3 The perceptual process

we need to attend to and filter out the information that is irrelevant; otherwise our senses would be overloaded. This process is known as **selective attention**. For example, an employee who is immersed in a work project on his PC may still notice his manager coming into his office to talk to him, but may not be aware of two colleagues having a conversation outside his office door. There must also be certain levels of a stimulus present before our senses will register its presence. In the example above the employee's work colleagues may have been speaking too quietly for him to notice, but the noise of his office door opening was loud enough to cause him to pay attention to it. People's sensory thresholds vary with regard to the amount of sensation that needs to be present before they pay attention to it, and with the level of sensation that they are comfortable with. People also vary as to the impact that sensory deprivation has upon them.

Sensory deprivation is sometimes used as a technique by military forces to interrogate prisoners, yet Brian Keegan, who was kidnapped by Islamic Jihad in Beirut, writes of his experiences in his book *An Evil Cradling*, 'You are in the dark, there are no windows, you can't see. But, tiny and oppressive as it is, you find in your mind ways to push the walls back'. This quote illustrates his ability to survive in captivity, even under extreme conditions of sensory deprivation.

CONSIDER THIS...

Close your eyes. Imagine that you are working as a machine operator on the factory floor of a large manufacturing company. Imagine the pictures and sounds that you could potentially see and hear. What do you think you would particularly note? These images and sounds are reflective of your selective attention in action.

We now know that we select certain stimuli to attend to, and that what we decide to pay attention to is influenced by various internal, external and contextual factors. Let's now look at the other stages in the perceptual process.

ORGANISATION

The next stage of the perceptual process is organisation. The Gestalt School of Psychology, which was established in the early 20th century, proposed a number of principles which help us to organise and give meaning to the information that we have attended to and selected. Many of these principles can be applied in a work context. These include the figure-to-ground effect, grouping and closure and will be discussed below.

FIGURE-TO-GROUND EFFECT

This first principle suggests that figures are usually seen against a background. For example, as you type on your keyboard the black letters stand out from the white background. However, sometimes this is not as straightforward as it seems. In Figure 3.4 do you see a vase or do you

selective attention process through which we attend to certain stimuli and select out others

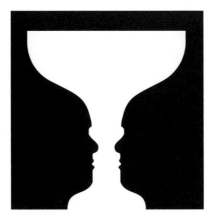

Figure 3.4 Rubin's (1915) vase illusion

see two faces? Most people attend to one part of the picture at a time, either the figure (the faces) or the background (the vase), but not both at the same time.

Mullins (2007) notes how this principle can have application in an organisational context. Employees need to be able to decide which elements of their job are salient and which are less important. Individuals who get stressed in their work may find it difficult to determine which parts should take priority.

GROUPING

In trying to make sense of what we perceive, we tend to group stimuli together rather than viewing them as separate entities. This is based on the Gestalt principle that the whole is greater than the sum of its parts. Wertheimer (1958) developed a number of laws to illustrate the principles underpinning these processes, the most common of which are described in Table 3.1.

INTERPRETATION

The third stage of the perceptual process is interpretation. During this phase of the process we interpret the information that we have attended to and organised in order to create meaning.

Table 3.1 Examples of grouping principles

Proximity: when we see things close together we tend to think of them as a group.	When we see a group of people sitting together in an office we assume that they are part of the same department.
Law of Continuity: we perceive items that appear to have a continuous form as making a pattern.	In a manufacturing plant, we may perceive that a row of machines on the factory floor produce the same element, when in fact they all produce different parts.
Similarity: we tend to group together elements that have similar characteristics.	A manager might think that payroll should be part of the finance function because payroll works with figures. However, the person working in payroll might feel that he would be better placed in the HR department because he deals a lot with people.
Law of Closure: we tend to close off or finish any objects that we perceive as being incomplete.	The IBM logo comprises a number of lines which do not actually connect but in our mind we join up the lines to create the logo.

We use information that we have already processed and stored to make sense of the new information that we receive. This process is very subjective. We use pre-existing schemas and scripts to help us interpret information. A **schema** is a unique mental representation of the world around us and is based on information from our memories. We also hold schemas about ourselves which are known as self-schemas; for example we may view ourselves as intelligent, caring or funny (or even all three). **Cognitive scripts** are predetermined steps in our mind that we follow to help us know how to behave in a certain situation. In a theatre actors use scripts to tell them what they are expected to do next. An employee who is about to do a performance review with his manager has a pre-existing schema as to what the review will involve and how he should act out this situation. The schemas and scripts that we create in our minds are unique to each of us, and our prior experiences influence how we construct them. Returning to our example, an employee who previously had a very negative experience of a performance review may have developed a very different cognitive script for performance reviews as compared to an employee whose past experience of the review process was positive. It should be noted that our pre-existing schemas and scripts also influence the information

CONSIDER THIS...

© PHOTODISC/GETTY IMAGES

Mercer is a global HR consulting company which has teamed up with intercultural training and learning specialists RW3 LLC to create a new product for Mercer's clients. Cultural Training Passport is an online learning tool that prepares employees for international assignments. As part of the training programme employees can build up a cultural profile of the country in which they will be based that enables them to understand how business and society may operate there and how this differs from what they are used to. The e-learning tool can help international assignees to be aware of cultural differences in how people perceive things and also how their perception can influence their actions. Part of the tool explores Hofstede's cultural dimensions ▸ **Chapter 12** ◂ and employees can develop a profile of their own cultural preferences. A sample of the Cultural Training Passport can be found on Mercer's website (www.imercer.com, last accessed on 18 August 2015). Consider how having an understanding of cultural differences could be useful to you once you begin your career.

---

schema is a unique mental representation of the world around us and is based on information from our memories

cognitive scripts are predetermined steps in our mind that tell us how to behave in a certain situation

that we attend to in the first stage of the perceptual process. Schemas and scripts help us to structure and make sense of our world, but we must also be aware that they can increase our tendency to make perceptual errors such as stereotyping because we make assumptions based on pre-existing thought patterns.

REACTION

The final stage in the process of perception occurs when our interpretation of a stimulus elicits a reaction. Our response may manifest itself as an internal reaction, such as feeling a particular emotion or as an external behaviour or as a combination of both. For example, in an organisational context an employee who perceives that she is likely to receive a promotion may worry about the extra responsibility that she will be asked to take on, or she might go and talk to another employee who has previously carried out the role to learn more, or she could do both. The perceptions and reactions of an individual in a given situation will of course be influenced by their personality, past experiences, social context and so on. It is important that leaders in an organisational context understand that people's perceptions influence behaviour and that they manage the organisational activities which can influence perception and can help shape behaviour. Many of these activities are carried out by the organisation's HR function.

A number of HR departments attempt to gauge the perceptions of their employees through the use of surveys. Some organisations develop their own surveys and others use external consultants to design data collection instruments. The Great Place to Work Institute administers a Trust Index Assessment to assess employees' perceptions of trust in their organisation. Once the organisation gains an understanding of how their employees perceive the organisation they can take actions to ensure that their employees perceive it in a positive light and that the employees' actions reflect this positive perspective.

We have covered how the process of perception takes place, how we pay attention to a stimulus, organise and interpret the information we have received and react to it in some way. Yet this process is often flawed and we will now explore some of the ways in which our perception can be obscured.

PERCEPTUAL DISTORTIONS

As we have mentioned previously, how people perceive events is not a perfect representation of reality. **Perceptual distortions** occur when people misinterpret the information they have received. Perceptual distortions are common and vary in the types that occur. They happen when people take mental shortcuts in order to speed up the perceptual process. It is important that we are aware of these shortcuts and work on trying to reduce the resultant perceptual errors. Common perceptual errors include:

perceptual distortions the errors that people make in their perception of others and events

Contrast effect: The contrast effect occurs where people tend to compare individuals against each other, as opposed to assessing them independently on their own merits. An interesting study by Palmer and Loveland (2008) found that a greater contrast effect occurred after a group discussion on performance evaluation. The Bia interview example in the 'Building Your Skills' feature later in the chapter also looks at this phenomenon in an organisational context.

Horns/halo effect: This is where we tend to focus on either one positive or negative aspect of an individual and use that characteristic to evaluate the person as a whole. In the work environment an example of the halo effect could be an employee who has a perfect time and attendance record and so may be perceived as being a good overall performer, despite the lack of any positive evidence about their performance. An example of the horns effect might be an employee who had received a verbal warning being regarded as generally difficult and troublesome, despite being a very good performer with just one aberration. To avoid the horns or halo effect when evaluating employees, a manager needs to try and evaluate each employee across a range of criteria and must also try to examine each criterion independently of each other. In a study by Turnipseed (2002) individuals who were perceived as being 'more ethical' were also perceived as being more productive than those who were considered to be 'less ethical', demonstrating the existence of the halo effect.

SPOTLIGHT ON SKILLS

The concept of perception is very important for managers within an organisation. It influences them in their selection of employees through the interview process, and they have to be careful not to let perceptual errors taint their judgment. Later when successful candidates become employees of the organisation the manager has to try and ensure that these employees have a positive perception of the organisation.

1 Have you seen other interviewers making any perceptual errors when carrying out interviews in the organisation?

2 As a manager how do you try to ensure that employees in your company have a positive perception of the organisation?

To help you answer these questions, in your ebook click the play button to watch the video of Gavin Connell from University of Limerick talking about perception.

Stereotyping: We tend to assign a set of characteristics to a group of people or to an individual. More often than not, however, these perceptions are inaccurate and are not reflective of the true characteristics of others. For example, we may perceive that salespeople are always outgoing and that librarians are all mild mannered. Sometimes we can actually discriminate against people because of the stereotypes we assign to them. Within an organisational context a manager might perceive that all younger workers are lacking life experience, or he might think that older employees aren't willing to learn new skills. Roberson and Kulik (2007) refer to the concept of 'stereotype threat', which is where individuals who belong to certain groups feel that they are judged negatively based on a stereotype. Stereotype threat has been found under certain conditions to have negative impacts on people's performance. In other words, people who feel that they are judged negatively by being labelled with a stereotype may feel under more pressure to perform particularly well. This pressure can potentially have the opposite effect and may cause them to underperform. Steele and Aronson (1995) first demonstrated that stereotype threat can undermine intellectual performance. They carried out an experiment on entry tests in US colleges and found that stereotype threat could reduce the performance of Black college students. The same studies also showed that if stereotype threat was reduced through subtle changes in instructions (such as stating that the test was a simple problem-solving exercise as opposed to a measure of ability) the test results improved. Employment equality legislation highlights some of the most common stereotypes that people use to label others and helps to protect these groups against discrimination, including gender, age, disability, ethnic origin, religion, sexual orientation.

Prejudice: This is where people hold a negative or positive impression of members of a group which has no foundation. For example, the Nazis held extremist views of the Jewish people in terms of their behaviour and preferences which were not based on facts but on hatred. Not all negative prejudice is as obvious or extreme as this, but it can still be very damaging. Prejudices can be subtle, such as people in a disadvantaged area finding it difficult to even gain an interview in a local company. Research conducted in the US by Harrison and Thomas (2009) found that there was a skin-tone preference with regard to job selection. They found that among Black candidates, lighter skinned job applicants received significantly higher selection ratings than their darker skinned counterparts. They describe this prejudice as 'colourism'. Stereotyping, which we described above, is a feature of prejudice.

Projection: This perceptual distortion is where we perceive that others are feeling or thinking in a similar way to ourselves. We project what we are thinking onto another person and we assume that we are both 'on the same wavelength'. In a work context a manager who is very goal oriented and production driven may perceive that his employees are also like this when in fact they may have other priorities, such as wanting to finish work on time rather than when the work is done. A good manager recognises that people may have different perspectives on certain matters and that it is important to pay attention to alternative viewpoints.

stereotyping the tendency to assign a set of characteristics
to a group of people or to an individual

Participating in cross-functional work teams can help organisational members to recognise diverse perspectives and put them to good use.

Similarity to me bias: We tend to show a preference for those who are most similar to ourselves. For example, in a performance review meeting a manager may rate employees with a similar work style to his own higher than those who have a different work style, even though they are equally good workers. He may also show preference for applicants who have a similar educational background and work experience record to him. A manager must try to put his or her personal preferences aside when evaluating staff.

Self-fulfilling prophecy: This is based on a premise by Merton (1948) that because we make a prophecy it is more likely to happen. From a perception perspective this means that when an individual has stated something, she will do all that she can to make it come true so that she can validate what it is that she has said will happen. For example, in a work environment, an employee who feels that an organisation is going to close may become demotivated and put very little effort into their work. In turn productivity levels go down which affects profitability and the company is ultimately forced to shut down. In this way the employee has unwittingly contributed to a self-fulfilling prophecy. Individuals need to take responsibility for their actions and to be aware of the potential outcomes.

PERCEPTUAL DEFENCE AND CONFIRMATION BIAS

As individuals we don't like to be wrong or faced with information that challenges our existing view of things. **Perceptual defence** is where an individual discounts any information that might threaten his or her existing perception of a stimulus. An example of this might be the manager who perceives a particular employee to be very diligent; in a situation where the employee forgot to do something, the manager would downplay this oversight in order to preserve her opinion about that person. **Confirmation bias** is where we actively see out information to support our initial hypothesis, even when all the evidence suggests that this hypothesis is incorrect. This phenomenon can be useful in explaining why people persevere with a course of action and seek out information to support them in their endeavours, even when all of the indicators suggest that their chosen path is not the right one. It can be useful in such a situation to play the role of devil's advocate and to challenge ourselves on the decisions we make. An example might be useful as an illustration of confirmation bias.

---

perceptual defence where an individual discounts information in order to defend his or her existing perception

confirmation bias where we actively seek out information to prove we are right even when the evidence suggests we are incorrect

BUILDING YOUR SKILLS

Being Aware of the Dangers of Confirmation Bias

A company needs a specific HR software program to make the HR function operate more efficiently. A manager in the organisation is given responsibility for the project and after much deliberation chooses a company she feels offers the best value to the organisation. The program is piloted tested by the organisation and several major issues are reported back to the software design company. Even though some of the issues are sorted out, employees who have tested the updated software still report that the program is not user-friendly, is incompatible with other existing HR software, and has several major operational flaws because of coding errors. Only one employee reports no problems with the software. Based on the opinion of this employee the manager decides to go ahead and adopt the software anyway, despite the problems with the software that have been identified by the other employees. The behaviour of the manager in this scenario can be explained by confirmation bias. If you were in the manager's position would you have gone ahead with the implementation of the new HR software? Explain your rationale. What potential issues do you see arising from the manager's decision?

Within a work environment perceptual errors such as those highlighted above can lead to workers being discriminated against. Managers must be particularly cognisant of the dangers of perceptual errors with regard to the recruitment and selection process and when conducting performance appraisals.

ATTRIBUTION THEORY

Another potential perceptual error is connected to attribution theory. Attribution theory explores how people form explanations for why they and other people behave in the way that they do. Individuals like to be able to make sense of their world and the term 'attribution' is used to describe the processes that individuals engage in to explain behaviours. One of the original researchers in this area was Heider (1958) who suggested that behaviour in a particular situation is primarily attributed to either personal attitudes (internal forces) or situational factors (external forces).

Kelley (1973) developed a theory of causal attribution to explain how people make attributions about the behaviour of others. He suggested that there are three variables which influence people's explanations for the behaviour of others. These variables are consensus,

BUILDING YOUR SKILLS

Perceptual Errors

Bia is a small food company in start-up phase. The general manager has been with the company for nine months and came from a finance role in a multinational organisation. Along with her other duties she has responsibility for HR. The production manager has been with the organisation for six months and has recently been promoted from a quality role. Neither manager has had any formal training in interviewing job candidates. They have just finished interviewing five external candidates for a potential team leader role in the production department. They are discussing how the interviews went.

General Manager:	Before we look at how the interviewees performed against our selection criteria, how do you think that they got on?
Production Manager:	I thought that first interviewee was particularly good, we actually play golf together and I would see us as having a lot in common.
General Manager:	Yes, maybe. What about that young candidate, I'd be worried she doesn't have the life experience to be able to cope with the role.
Production Manager:	I don't know, I thought she performed well in the interview. I also thought that guy from the pharmaceutical company might be good. He has an engineering background and must be good with figures.
General Manager:	Yes. Do you remember the candidate who was ten minutes late? I don't think he did particularly well in the interview, and if he was late for the interview…
Production Manager:	I agree with you. I thought the second candidate we interviewed was excellent; I thought she was very goal oriented and seemed to have a very similar mind set to us. Finally then, the last candidate – remember he spoke about how he didn't get on too well in his last performance appraisal. I wonder, has he a poor work ethic?
General Manager:	Perhaps. Ok, maybe we should try and evaluate their performance using our selection criteria now that we have an overview.

1 Identify the different types of perceptual errors made by the interviewers.

2 If you were the interviewer how could you have avoided making similar perceptual errors?

consistency and distinctiveness, and they can be linked together in different compositions. Let's look at what these terms mean:

1 *Consensus* refers to whether the person's behaviour is similar to that of other people in similar situations.
2 *Consistency* refers to how often the person behaved in a particular way in the past.
3 *Distinctiveness* refers to how often the individual behaves in the same way across different situations.

These variables can be organised in a number of different ways and this can lead people to attribute behaviours to internal or external factors. It is particularly useful in a work context to be able to understand how individuals attribute certain explanations to other people's behaviours.

Let's look at how attribution theory can help to assist us in explaining people's behaviour at work. We will explore two different scenarios using the same example of an employee who has received a poor result in a performance evaluation from his supervisor.

In scenario one, the employee's supervisor has noted that the employee usually performs poorly in the performance evaluation (high consistency), other workers doing the same job and working in the same area have not performed poorly (low consensus), and the employee's performance is poor despite having been placed into different work situations across the factory (low distinctiveness). The manager may then attribute the poor result to a lack of effort and a poor attitude to work (internal factors).

In scenario two, the employee's supervisor has noted that the employee usually performs well in the performance evaluation (high consistency), other workers doing the same job and working in the same area have also performed poorly (high consensus), and the employee's poor performance is very unusual as the individual usually works well in any work environment (low distinctiveness). The manager may then attribute the poor result to a lack of training or persistent problems with the machines that the individual is operating (external factors).

As you can see, depending on the pattern of the variables, behaviour in a given situation can be mainly attributed to internal or to external factors.

FUNDAMENTAL ATTRIBUTION ERROR

This is something which sounds serious yet has quite a simple explanation. The **fundamental attribution error** is another example of a perceptual error and is where individuals tend to

> Scenario One:
>
> Low Consensus, High Consistency, Low Distinctiveness = Internal Factors
>
> Scenario Two:
>
> High Consensus, High Consistency, Low Distinctiveness = External Factors

Figure 3.5 Patterns of attribution elements

fundamental attribution error where individuals attribute external causes to their own behaviour, and internal causes to the behaviour of others

attribute external factors to the causes of their own behaviour, and internal factors to the causes of the behaviour of others. For example, if we perform poorly in an evaluation we are more likely to attribute our performance to a poor evaluator or to a difficult work environment (external factors), whereas we are more likely to attribute others' poor performance to a lack of a positive work ethic or work apathy (internal factors). We do this in order to maintain our existing perspective and to support our self-beliefs. We don't like to have to make adjustments to how we think about things, and we will do what we can to preserve our viewpoint. Having an awareness of our tendency to preserve our self-belief can help us to determine whether our viewpoint on a particular matter is relatively accurate or is potentially skewed.

Bridgewater

ACTIVE CASE STUDY

Bridgewater is a manufacturing plant located in Germany. The company is aware that the key to their survival is their ability to provide a low-cost, high-quality product to their customers. Their strategy is twofold; firstly to contain cost through constant innovation and secondly to respond to their customer needs faster than any of their competitors. The company's 700+ employees are seen as a key contributing factor to their business success. A number of organisational and functional initiatives reflect the company's commitment to its employees.

One initiative which seems to have had a particular impact on company culture and employees' perception of the organisation is the continuous improvement process. The company has implemented a process of continuous improvement since 2007, using various tools such as value stream mapping, total productive maintenance, 5S, visual management systems and demand smoothing to increase efficiencies. The company management team has tried to promote a continuous improvement culture in the organisation whereby the

employees themselves are the drivers of improvement initiatives. Bi-monthly meetings are held with the directors in which they provide information on company performance, new initiatives and any relevant operational and strategic issues that employees need to be aware of. Employees are encouraged to ask questions and make suggestions at these meetings. Some employees are seconded onto continuous improvement projects to examine ways in which work processes can be improved, but even employees who are not working on specific projects consider it is important to look for ways of making improvements to the way in which they carry out their work. One employee, for example, spoke about developing a board which helped to make the checking of the guide wires more efficient.

Supervisors in the plant are rotated through continuous improvement roles and there is a focus on internal promotion. Approximately 60 per cent of the supervisors and team leaders in the plant have been promoted from within the organisation. Employees go through a performance appraisal and are evaluated on both their performance and their behaviour. The company has a

© GETTY

set of ten standards of behaviour to which all employees are expected to adhere. Employees are recognised for high performance or suggestions which lead to cost savings or an improvement in work processes. Sometimes this takes the form of a luncheon voucher, but more often a simple thank you card is regarded as sufficient recognition. The HR director states that when people start with the organisation they come with their 'hands and the head', and if you look after them the 'heart will follow'. Initiatives should, as do those outlined above, drive a continuous improvement culture. Employees have a good attitude towards their work environment and also have a positive perception of the organisation. One team leader noted how 'you are in tune with what's going on in the organisation, and they are in tune with what you are doing as well'. A member of staff working in a support function observed when she joined the organisation how 'you do feel a part of something when you come in, which was lovely'.

Questions

1 Why do you think that the continuous improvement initiative has created positive employee perceptions of the organisation?

2 What other type of initiatives might the company introduce to create a positive view of the company?

3 Can you think of examples which might change employees' positive perceptions of the work environment?

4 Plan out a specific event for your university/college that could be held for all staff and students in order to encourage a positive perception of the organisation.

 SUMMARY

 IN THE EBOOK, CLICK TO HEAR AN AUDIO SUMMARY

In this chapter we have explained what perception is and how the process of perception works. We explored the concept of attention and how people select and attend to some environmental stimuli and not others, how they organise and interpret that material and finally how they react to what they have taken in and processed. We also discussed and identified some of the perceptual errors that people commonly make during the process of perception in a work context. Attribution theory which explains the processes that we as humans engage in to explain behaviours was also described and the fundamental attribution bias, which is also a perceptual error, was studied. Perception is an important psychological phenomenon and having knowledge of how it works can help us to better understand how people behave in certain ways within a work context.

CHAPTER REVIEW QUESTIONS

1 Explain the concept of perception.

2 Why is an understanding of perception important to the study of organisational behaviour?

3 There are a number of stages in the process of perception. Can you explain each of the four main phases?

4 What we pay attention to is influenced by a set of internal elements known as our perceptual set. Can you describe the factors that make up our perceptual set?

5   What are schemas and scripts, and how are they connected to perception?

6   What are the most common perceptual errors that people make?

7   Can you give some examples of perceptual errors that might occur in a work context?

8   Based on attribution theory, what is the fundamental attribution error?

☑ MULTIPLE CHOICE QUESTIONS

In your ebook, click to take a multiple choice quiz to test your understanding of this chapter.

📖 FURTHER READING

Ariely, D. (2010) *Predictably Irrational, Revised and Expanded Edition: The Hidden Forces That Shape Our Decisions*, US: Harper Perennial.

Buchanan, D. and Huczynski, A. (2013) *Organisational Behaviour*, 8th edn, UK: Pearson Education Limited.

Goldstein, E. (2013) *Sensation and Perception*, US: Cengage Learning.

Mullins, L.J. (2013) *Management and Organisational Behaviour*, 10th edn, NY: FT Publishing International.

WWW USEFUL WEBSITES

www.greatplacetowork.ie/

Check this website out and explore their Employee Trust Survey which examines employees' perceptions of satisfaction with their work environment.

http://video.ted.com/talk/podcast/2009G/None/BeauLotto_2009G-light.mp4

An interesting presentation on perceptual illusions which teaches us that we shouldn't always believe what we see!

http://dragon.uml.edu/psych/illusion.html

A website which demonstrates a range of optical illusions.

www.pearnkandola.com

This website offers lots of information on perceptual errors. Check out the research section in particular.

4 WORK-RELATED ATTITUDES AND VALUES

Ultan Sherman

LEARNING OUTCOMES

BY THE END OF THIS CHAPTER YOU SHOULD BE ABLE TO:

- Explain what is meant by the term 'attitude'.
- Understand the process of attitude formation.
- Explain how attitudes and behaviour are connected.
- Discuss what is meant by the term 'job satisfaction' and why it is an important

concept in the organisational behaviour literature.

- Distinguish between important work-related attitudes and the implications they have for the organisation.

© WWW.IMAGESOURCE.COM

THIS CHAPTER DISCUSSES:

IN REALITY

Many believe that people's attitude to work has been profoundly affected by the economic turbulence since 2008. Indeed, the global recession had a dramatic impact on the work environment. Hundreds of thousands of people lost their jobs as organisations restructured to remain competitive and previous research has shown that difficult economic times do influence how an individual views their job (Kinnunen *et al.*, 1999). However, De Hauw and De Vos (2010) found that certain types of employees did not change their attitudes towards their job because of the recession. They found that 20- to 30-year-olds had high expectations of their employer in relation to career development, job content and financial rewards. This finding supported results in similar studies carried out before the economic recession (Wey Smola and Sutton, 2002). The suggestion here is that these expectations have been embedded in a generation which remains resistant to changes in the economic climate. This study raises interesting questions about the factors that influence attitude formation and attitude change.

INTRODUCTION

This chapter explores the relationship between our attitudes and the work environment. Often employees are referred to as having a 'good' or 'bad' attitude. Indeed, important decisions to be made about an employee can often be based on their attitude in relation to work, for example, recruitment and selection, and promotion. 'Attitude' is among the most widely researched concepts within the broad field of organisational behaviour. It is central to our understanding of why people act the way they do in the workplace. But what do we mean when we say a good or bad attitude? Can we observe someone's attitude in the workplace? There are a number of important issues that must be examined before we can answer these questions. This chapter assesses the key issues within the literature on work-related attitudes, starting with the various theoretical approaches to analysing attitudes, then looking at the formation of attitudes in terms of the main factors that shape the creation process. It then looks at how attitudes influence behaviour and how attitudes can be changed. The chapter also discusses the prominent work-related attitudes that are of most significance to employers. Finally, the importance of 'work values' in explaining organisational behaviour is analysed.

EXPLAINING THE TERM 'ATTITUDE'

The eminent social psychologist Gordon Allport wrote:

> The concept of attitudes is probably the most distinctive and indispensable concept in…social psychology. (1935, p. 798)

This statement is still true today because our attitudes are akin to our view of the world. The term 'attitude' has entered our everyday vernacular. We have different attitudes to our families, friends, work, music and so on which direct how we behave in relation to each one of them. Some of you might *believe* that Beyoncé is the greatest pop star in the world. As a result you may have bought all her albums and attended some of her concerts. Others might *feel* she is overrated and change the station when they hear her music on the radio. So, what is an attitude? Examining the italicised words suggests that attitudes are beliefs or feelings. Like many concepts within the organisational behaviour field, competing theories have been extended to define the term 'attitude', although Allport is arguably the father of attitude research and most subsequent work is congruent with his definition. We define **attitudes** as evaluative judgements relating to people, events or objects.

There is much debate as to what constitutes an attitude. Some theorists prefer a one-component attitude model, specifically the *affective* component (for example, Thurstone, 1931). Other theorists propose a two-component attitude model, incorporating a *cognitive* element into the one-component model (for example, Petty and Cacioppo, 1986). They argue that exploring the cognitive underpinnings of attitudes can tell us something different about how they function in a way that the affective component cannot. A third approach is the three-component model incorporating a *behavioural* component. Therefore, there are potentially three different components of an attitude:

a *Cognitive component:* the values and beliefs that the individual holds about a particular person or thing. For example, a first year student at the National University of Singapore may have particular values and beliefs about her new university. One belief may be that she is now studying at one of the world's most prestigious academic institutions. This is likely to be a source of pride for the student – the underlying value supporting the belief.

b *Affective component:* the feelings and emotions arising from an evaluation of the two elements in the cognitive component. The Singapore student would typically develop feelings about the university related to the inherent beliefs and values she holds about it. For example, she might have a great sense of accomplishment for having been accepted into the university. However, she might also feel greater pressure in terms of her academic performance given the high standards expected of students at the National University of Singapore. The affective component of attitude structure tends to be learned from our environment (see below).

c *Behavioural component:* the behavioural outcome of the process which stems from the affective component of the model. Again, using the Singapore student as an example, she may make an extra effort at her studies given the expectation of success for National University of Singapore students. Of course, the cognitive and affective components can change over time, which in turn results in a change in behaviour. She could, perhaps, lose interest in her course, resulting in a change in behaviour (for example, she might change her course or drop out of the university).

attitudes evaluative judgements relating to people, events or objects

These three components have a profound influence in our everyday life. They essentially make up the ABCs of attitudes. Reich and Adcock (1976) argue that if attitudes refer to phenomena that are not directly observable but only inferred, then the behavioural component of an attitude by itself cannot fully illustrate the attitude. Broadly speaking, the cognitive, affective and behavioural components need to be assessed together to fully understand the dynamics of the attitude itself.

CONSIDER THIS...

From what you now know about the components of attitudes, what are your own feelings about your university or college? How have these feelings shaped your behaviour? Do they influence how you speak to others about your course and lecturers?

ATTITUDE FORMATION

Our attitudes are a manifestation of cognitive, affective and behavioural processes. However, it is important to examine how these attitudes are created in the first place. Many philosophers believe that we are born with a mental 'tabula rasa' (Latin for 'blank state'), effectively without any mental content. Our knowledge and perception come from experience as we develop. The argument here is that our attitudes are also formed as we develop, with new experiences shaping how we view the world. This developmental process is complex with a number of competing theories often cited to explain it. We will examine the main theories put forward in the literature to explain how our attitudes are created.

a   *Dispositional characteristics:* It is generally accepted that underlying personality predispositions influence attitude formation. Our personality is relatively stable but can change over time with the onset of new experiences. A number of studies have shown how different personality traits affect behaviour (for example, 'extroversion' and public speaking; 'conscientiousness' and adhering to rules; 'emotional stability' and staying calm under pressure) ▸ **Chapter 2** ◂. In the work environment, behavioural manifestations of inherent personality characteristics can be easily observed. For example, air stewards are expected to be knowledgeable of the rules and regulations concerning air travel and to adhere to them at all times. They are also expected to be stoic when interacting with the passengers. For this reason, when airlines are recruiting for these positions, conscientiousness and emotional stability are two personality dimensions that they seek in candidates. Their attitude towards established procedure must be unwavering, even in challenging situations.

b   *Direct experience:* Many of the attitudes people hold are the result of direct experience with 'attitude objects'. Attitude objects are the 'things' in our environment with which we directly interact (for example, school, friends, social media). People tend to have positive or negative experiences with attitude objects, which can go some way to influencing their attitudes. After a number of unsuccessful interviews a jobseeker may view future interviews in a pessimistic light. A famous example from psychology is the Little Albert case. Albert was an infant participating in an experiment investigating associations between different stimuli. In the experiment, Albert played with a pet rat and displayed no visible signs of fear or panic. Later, loud, frightening noises were repeatedly made whenever Albert played with the rat and he began to cry. Eventually, just seeing the rat (no longer paired with the loud noises) aroused feelings of panic and fear in the infant. Accordingly, due to his unpleasant encounter Albert formed a very negative attitude towards the rat. In a broader sense, this experiment investigated classical conditioning, an important concept in learning and behaviour. Classical conditioning emphasises the role of direct experience in shaping an attitude and associated behaviour.

c   *Social learning:* While direct experience certainly plays a significant role in the construction of attitudes, another approach views attitude formation solely as a social learning process. The actions of other people in our social environment shape our attitudes too. For an infant, parents are arguably the most important source of information in attitude formation. Often, we follow a similar career path to our parents'. However, Connell (1972) found that, although a positive correlation existed between the specific attitudes of parents and their children towards a given issue, it was also a rather weak relationship. Beyond a family context, wider socio-cultural factors influence how we view the world. Bandura (1986) developed a social learning theory that people learn by observing the behaviour of other people in their social environment. He also likened attitude formation to a process of modelling whereby one person models their behaviour on a referent other.

His famous 'Bobo' Doll experiment neatly captured this modelling process. Children watched adults attacking an inflatable doll, and receiving encouragement and positive feedback for their actions. Later, when the children were alone in the room with Bobo, many attacked him in a similar way to the adults. To most children, adults are seen to be significant models on which to base behaviour.

While parents have a powerful influence on the child, adults are also shaped by the behaviour of others in their social environment. In a work context, new recruits model their behaviour on what Morrison (1993) refers to as 'organisational insiders'. Many new recruits are assigned a mentor upon organisational entry in the hope that they will acquire important information, understand the culture of the organisation, and learn the 'right' attitude from their more experienced counterpart. Indeed, co-workers pass on social cues to the new entrant throughout the socialisation process, resulting in a broad 'homogenisation' of the workforce. For example, if a new employee notices that his first 'staff night out' is very well attended by the employees, then this will be perceived as a cue to guide future behaviour. It is likely that the new recruit will continue to attend future staff events in light of this newly acquired information. Many organisational factors play a role in attitude formation such as leadership style, organisational culture ▸Chapter 12◂ and work design.

---

classical conditioning through repeated association, a formerly neutral stimulus can elicit a reaction that was previously elicited only by another stimulus

socialisation the process by which a person is immersed into a social environment

So, the source of our attitudes originates from our interaction with our social environment, through direct experience and vicariously through observation and modelling. We can now say that our attitudes are shaped by and shape our interaction with the world.

CONSIDER THIS...

Beginning university can be an exciting time for students. It often can be a very confronting time as they try to adjust to things like the new surroundings and their coursework. Reflecting on this early experience, what effect did other students have on you? Did you model your behaviour on them? In what way? Did it make it easier to adjust to life as a student?

CONNECTING ATTITUDES AND BEHAVIOUR

Attitudes and behaviour are closely linked, but it is a complex relationship. Simply holding an attitude towards an object does not predict behaviour in relation to that object. For example, an employee may feel that team-building exercises are a waste of time. However, this does not mean that she will refuse to participate in any such activity. There are other factors at play.

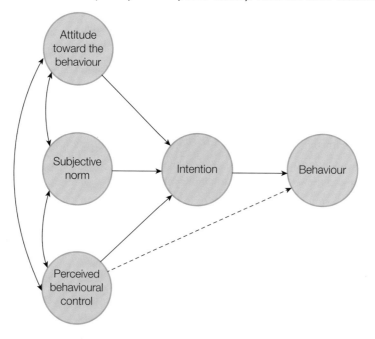

Figure 4.1 Theory of planned behaviour

Source: Adapted from Ajzen (1991).

Ajzen (1991) has developed an important model capturing this association. His theory of planned behaviour posits that attitude toward the behaviour, subjective social and environmental norms (discussed above) and perception of behavioural control (the extent to which the person believes they are in control of the situation) lead to the formation of a behavioural intention. Behavioural intention then predicts behaviour.

Ajzen's model highlights that holding an attitude towards a specific object does not directly predict that a person will behave in a corresponding way to that object. Social norms and behavioural control beliefs mediate the relationship between attitudes and behaviour. Let's say an employee is thinking about applying for a position within the same organisation. She may view this post as an exciting opportunity (attitude toward the behaviour). If she believes she has a good chance of being successful (perceived behavioural control) and if the organisation is one that encourages internal promotion (subjective norms) then it is likely that she will intend to apply for the position.

Indeed, people are often very inconsistent in their espoused attitudes and beliefs and how they subsequently behave. For example, people often value their health, yet they smoke. How many of you believe using your mobile phone while driving is reckless, but still do it? Festinger (1957) developed the concept of cognitive dissonance to explain the often complicated relationship between the different components of attitude structure. Cognitive dissonance is an unpleasant cognitive state that motivates an individual to resolve perceived conflict among beliefs, attitudes and behaviours. The dissonance is an uncomfortable or stressful feeling that one often experiences with perceived inconsistency between cognitions and behaviour. For example, a director of an environmental charity who regularly takes first-class flights around the world may experience dissonance as a result of the conflict between his travel patterns and the values of the organisation he leads. However, if an attitude is not terribly important to the individual, then the incongruent behaviour creates relatively little dissonance.

Of course, different contexts will lead to different levels of dissonance. This unpleasant feeling can be resolved by changing one element of the structure to restore consonance, for example, changing your view of the object, in the case of cigarettes, (cognitive), giving up smoking (behavioural), rationalising that smoking light cigarettes is less harmful (belief). In the early 2000s, many schools in Britain found themselves under the spotlight for the nutritional content of the food provided to their students. Both parenting groups and the media questioned how a school could, on the one hand, espouse the principles of science yet, on the other, neglect to educate their students on the values of healthy dietary habits. As a result of this negative press, many of these schools removed vending machines containing sugary snacks and ensured canteens served more nutritious food to the students. Cognitive dissonance is an important concept in organisational behaviour as it furthers our understanding of the link between attitudes and behaviour.

cognitive dissonance an unpleasant cognitive state that motivates an individual to resolve perceived conflict among beliefs, attitudes and behaviours

BUILDING YOUR **SKILLS**

Conflict Management

Imagine you are the human resource director in a small medical supplies company with 205 employees. You are a smoker and like some other employees at the firm you regularly use the designated smoking areas. One day you receive an email from an employee with a petition containing the signatures of more than 150 non-smoking employees asking for smoking to be prohibited from all areas of the organisation. How do you resolve this issue?

ATTITUDE CHANGE

Earlier in the chapter we examined the environmental forces that influence the creation of attitudes. Similarly there are myriad factors that are responsible for bringing about attitude change. From a management perspective, social norms help shape the new recruit to align with the culture of the organisation. When employees join an organisation they bring with them a belief system that has been constructed and developed over time with experience. This belief system dictates how they view the new work environment. Studies have shown that employees adjust their attitude and behaviour in accordance with the information that they have received. Thus, new employees' attitude and behaviour are likely to change towards those of experienced insiders as they become accepted as an integral part of the company (Thomas and Anderson, 1998).

There are many other organisational forces that can bring about attitude change, such as punitive procedures, rewards and so on, but it is important to directly examine how the change itself occurs given the central role cognition plays in attitude formation. Certainly, the process of attitude change is a matter of great interest to managers and those in positions of authority. Hovland *et al.* (1953) were among the first researchers to explore the factors that contributed to attitude change. For Hovland and his colleagues the key issue was understanding the principles of persuasion. Persuasion is a form of learning, so the underlying theoretical mechanism of their study was learning theory. Any factor that influenced the learning of a message was considered central to understanding attitude change. They divided these factors into three separate categories: the communicator; the audience; and the communication. A credible source of communication was predicted to produce persuasion because it was believed to be more rewarding to agree with someone who is more likely to be perceived as correct (reported in Forgas, 2008). However, the researchers found that less credible sources were often more persuasive in certain circumstances, undermining their proposition. The audience were assumed to impact the persuasion process through their attention levels. The study found that the persuasiveness of the message was associated with how well the audience attended to it. Finally, the message itself was examined in terms of its content, for example the strength of the inherent argument, and this too had an effect on the level of persuasiveness. While the scientific merit of Hovland's study has been questioned, it is an important milestone in attitude change research.

In attempting to examine the factors that influence persuasion the Hovland study calls attention to the reasons explaining why and how people change their attitudes. Arguably, the most dominant theory to explain the attitude change process is Cognitive Response Theory. Often the thoughts generated trigger an attitude change. An individual interprets the message using pre-existing thoughts they hold about the subject. An attitude is then changed (or not changed) depending on the degree of incentive to generate their attitude in the first place (Greenwald, 1968). For example, during a presidential election campaign a voter with a slight preference for one candidate may change her mind upon hearing a rallying speech by the opponent. On the other hand, a staunch supporter of one candidate is unlikely to change her mind under any circumstances. Cognitive response theory highlights the importance of initial thoughts to a message in triggering an attitude change.

Other factors influencing the persuasion process have been examined in the literature. For example, Popovich and Wanous (1982) highlight how the medium through which the message is delivered is an important factor influencing persuasion, particularly at the beginning of employment. Indeed, *how* important information is communicated to employees influences their response. If an organisation is forced to make a number of staff redundant the medium through which the message is communicated takes on greater significance. Informing staff members that they are to be sacked through a text message or via Twitter is likely to evoke a negative reaction. (Think about the fact that more and more football managers appear to learn of their dismissal through unofficial sources before they hear from the club itself, and the impact this must have not only on the manager but on the remaining staff too.)

One agent for attitude change is 'forced contact' which has been shown to decrease racial prejudice (Deutsch and Collins, 1951). The contention here is that forced interaction will 'normalise' relations between different groups of people. Relating this to an organisational example, a teacher may 'relocate' an errant student to an area in the class where she will interact with more diligent students with the intention that this 'forced contact' will bring about a change in that student's attitude and subsequent behaviour. All of these studies highlight both the multiple causes accounting for attitude change and the cognitive activity intrinsic to the change process.

PREJUDICE, STEREOTYPES AND DISCRIMINATION

Earlier in the chapter we explained how certain social factors influence how attitudes are formed. A significant concept in this area is that of in-groups and out-groups. Attitudes towards members of both groups are one of the most widely researched topics in the field.

Cognitive Response Theory a thought created in response to persuasive communication

in-groups and out-groups in-groups are social groups to which an individual believes he or she belongs. In contrast, out-groups are social groups to which the individual believes he or she does not belong

Winning the Lottery

In June 2006, high-school janitor Tyrone Curry (56) won $3.4 million in the Washington state lottery. To celebrate his victory he went bowling with his friends that evening at the local alley. The following morning his alarm sounded at 4am and he headed into work, just as he did every morning. Today, Tyrone still works at the same high school. When asked why he kept up his job he replied, 'You need to be doing stuff. That's my philosophy'. For Tyrone, it seems that his job at the high school means more than simply a way to pay the bills. Tyrone viewed 'work' in a different way.

OB IN THE NEWS

If you were in Tyrone's position, would you continue to work? Trying to predict how a person would answer this question is difficult. There is a wide range of factors that could influence their response. For example, age is likely to be a relevant factor in the decision. A person close to retirement may be more likely to quit their job than someone in their thirties. The occupation itself is likely to be an important variable affecting the decision. If someone is working in a job perceived to be particularly unpleasant then it is reasonable to assume that they would not continue to work, or that they'd certainly change their job. However, in November 2014, George Kinghorn (60) won £1 million pounds in the EuroMillions lottery. However, when asked whether he would give up his grueling offshore oil rig job, he insisted that he would carry on working. In George's case, winning the lotto did not change his perception of his job. Both of these examples clearly demonstrate that there is more to work than simply money.

Arvey *et al.* (2004) examined the post-award work behaviour of lotto winners. They found that the size of the jackpot as well as level of 'work centrality' determined their decision to continue working. Work centrality is an important concept in work-related attitudes and it refers to the general importance of work in an individual's life compared with other activities such as leisure, spending time with friends, or family (Kanungo, 1982). When someone attaches a significant degree of importance to their employment they are likely to behave in a certain way in and around their job. Indeed, understanding a person's level of work centrality allows us to better predict their behaviour in the work environment. Work centrality is just one of many work-related attitudes assessed in the organisational behaviour field.

Questions

1   How big would a jackpot have to be to convince you to never work again? How would you fill your time? Do people need 'to be doing stuff'?

2   Besides the financial reasons, what does an individual gain from working? Are these factors important?

Sources

www.dailymail.co.uk/news/article-2012235/Lottery-winner-works-school-janitor-Tyrone-Curry-won-3-4m.html (last accessed on 19 August 2015).

www.pressandjournal.co.uk/fp/news/north-east/415759/north-east-couple-scoop-1million-on-euromillions/ (last accessed on 19 August 2015).

© ISTOCK.COM/TFONIMAGES

Broadly speaking, we have a preference for people similar to ourselves (that is, members of the in-group) over those considered dissimilar (that is, members of the out-group). Accordingly, intergroup attitudes are particularly prone to irrational, affective distortions (Allport, 1954). There is an affective element pervasive in intergroup relations and interaction with the in-group and out-group can evoke positive and negative emotions respectively. Affect (or emotion) is thus likely to influence intergroup judgements, both through the information processing strategies used and the way further information is selected and used (Forgas *et al.*, 2007). When an individual encounters an out-group, their level of anxiety is heightened, which reduces their capacity to process information effectively and accurately. For this reason, the individual resorts to stereotyping ▸ **Chapter 3** ◂. The tendency to see all out-group members in stereotypical ways can be observed in a variety of contexts (for example, 'salespeople are exploitative and aggressive'; 'Irish people have a drink problem' and so on). However, this chapter solely addresses stereotypes about people in a work context.

Stereotyping is a mental shortcut that helps individuals to make sense of another person or a group of people. It allows us to 'fill in the blanks' on an individual about whom we know very little. Often, this can lead to benefits. In the work environment stereotyping allows us to categorise employees into groups. For example, those entering an organisation from college or university often join as part of a graduate programme. The underlying notion is that every graduate (and the organisation itself) will be best served by the various processes of this programme (that is, induction, training, mentoring). Such a programme supposes that each graduate requires a comprehensive introduction to the work environment given their assumed lack of work experience. It is argued that this socialisation process can have a positive effect on reducing turnover among new entrants (for example, Feldman, 1981). However, stereotyping can also lead to problems for an organisation. It is likely that one may overlook the array of differences and level of individuality of people being stereotyped. For example, an organisation may not select a female candidate for a position on the assumption that she plans on having children in the near future, thus creating a future short-term vacancy. This, of course, limits the applicant pool for the organisation and may result in the best candidates being overlooked.

Stereotyping often has an enduring quality. Even in the face of contradictory information, people can go to great lengths to sustain the original stereotype. They seek out information that supports and protects the established view and ignore information that may refute it. Thus, **confirmation bias** is closely linked with stereotyping. For example, when a line manager is rating an employee's performance as part of the performance management process he may focus on incidents where the employee performed poorly and ignore instances of high performance, in line with his existing negative view of the employee.

When an individual holds a stereotyped view of certain types of people they are often accused of being prejudiced. The concept of **prejudice** falls neatly within the attitude domain. It can be considered to be an example of an extreme attitude. Prejudice can be defined as a negative attitude towards members of a specific group and can either be explicit or implicit. Prejudicial attitudes can be consciously or unconsciously held. Prejudice can either be explicit and conscious (for example, critical remarks about a person based on their race) or implicit

---

confirmation bias a tendency to seek out information that is in line with expectations and existing knowledge

prejudice a negative attitude towards members of a specific group and can be either explicit or implicit and unconscious (for example, believing it is important to show female employees the crèche facilities on site during induction but not the male employees). In line with the ABC structure of an attitude, to be prejudiced against someone implies that we feel, behave and think about that person in a negative way (Reich and Adcock, 1976).

SPOTLIGHT ON SKILLS

You are the HR manager in a small call centre. The work is repetitive and monotonous. Labour turnover is high. In fact less than 50 per cent of your staff have more than one year's service with the firm. Starting salary for operators is €22,000 per annum.

What can you do to ensure operators hold positive attitudes towards their work?

How important is job design in shaping an individual's work-related attitudes?

To help you answer these questions, in your ebook click the play button to watch the video of Melissa Challinor at Which? talking about attitudes.

As we saw above, prejudice tends to endure even in the face of conflicting evidence. For example, a successful encounter with a builder may not dispel the view that all builders are lazy and unscrupulous. The prejudiced person is capable of rationalising the incident in such a way (for example, 'this was a one-off') so that the stereotype prevails. In a famous study of anti-Semitism among female university students in the US, Frenkel-Brunswik and Sanford (1945) found that those women who held deep-rooted prejudice against Jews displayed repressed hatred and suspicion of parental figures. In effect, the students were projecting onto the Jews their entrenched attitudes that would normally be directed at their parents. This is a good example of how innate factors, stemming in this case from the students' relationship with their parents, can shape how we see the world. Glick and Fiske (2001) propose that prejudice is determined by two social factors:

- The extent to which the target group has a cooperative or competitive relationship with society. A group is categorised as cooperative if its members are perceived to be undemanding (for example, self-sufficient elderly people), contributing (for example, homemakers) or as needing help through no fault of their own (for example, disabled);
- The social status of the target group within mainstream society. Examples of relatively low-status groups are homeless people and working-class people. Examples of relatively high-status groups are rich people and highly educated people.

Table 4.1 Three forms of prejudice

Group's relative social status	Group's relationship with mainstream society	
	Cooperative	Competitive
High	No prejudice	Envious prejudice
Low	Paternalistic prejudice	Contemptuous prejudice

Source: Adapted from Glick, P. (2002). In Understanding Genocide by L. S. Newman and R. Erber: Table 5.1 (p.132). © by Oxford University Press, Inc. By permission of Oxford University Press.

How the target group is the recipient of prejudice is dependent on how it is categorised across these factors. For example, contemptuous prejudice occurs when the target group has a competitive relationship with mainstream society and is perceived to have lower social status. Envious prejudice occurs when the target group has a competitive relationship with mainstream society and is perceived to have higher social status. Finally, paternalistic prejudice occurs when the target group has a cooperative relationship with mainstream society and has low social status (Franzoi, 2009) (see Table 4.1).

While stereotyping is a belief and prejudice is an attitude, discrimination is an act. Believing all female employees are too emotional in the workplace is a stereotype. Resenting them for this perceived characteristic is an attitude. Actively overlooking them for a position because of their group membership is discrimination. As we have discussed, behaviour does not always follow attitude and discrimination is not an inevitable consequence of prejudice. An employer may be prejudiced against men but she may not act upon her negative attitude for fear of the consequences. Nevertheless, discrimination is a significant issue in the work environment. Many countries have established legislation that protects employee rights in terms of workplace discrimination. Sex, age, ethnicity, religion and sexuality are all grounds against which an individual can be discriminated. As the workplace becomes increasingly diverse the threat of discrimination becomes more apparent. In response to this, organisations invest significant amounts of time and money in ensuring all work practices are free of discrimination. Important decisions involving, for example, recruitment and selection, promotion, and so on, should not be made on grounds that may be perceived to be discriminatory.

Of particular relevance to a work context is the issue of positive discrimination. The argument here is that, in order for minority groups to receive the same opportunities as the majority group, some form of discrimination must occur. A famous example is the 'Rooney Rule' in American football (named after the former US state ambassador to Ireland who went on to be chairman of the Pittsburgh Steelers football team). National Football League (NFL) teams are required to interview minority candidates for high-ranking coaching and operation positions in the team. In almost 80 years before the Rooney Rule was established in 2003 only six Black head coaches had been appointed. In the decade since, twelve had been hired. Had this rule not existed it is unlikely that these dozen coaches would have been given such an opportunity.

discrimination a negative action towards members of a specific group

positive discrimination the preferential treatment of members of a minority group over a majority group

WORK-RELATED ATTITUDES

Many different work-related attitudes have been examined by researchers. For the purposes of this chapter we will only explore those that have received the most attention in the literature. First, job satisfaction is a type of work attitude. It is one of the most widely researched measures in organisational behaviour literature due to the much hypothesised view that it has a direct effect on important workplace outcomes. Job satisfaction according to Locke (1976) is a pleasurable or positive emotional state resulting from the appraisal of one's job or job experiences. When employees have a high level of job satisfaction they tend to view their job in a positive light. When dissatisfied with their job they tend to hold a negative attitude towards it. There are an unquantifiable number of factors that cause job satisfaction and researchers agree that it is difficult to develop a comprehensive model of its antecedents. We next explain three perspectives on job satisfaction, with each approach offering a unique insight into the origins of this attitude (Baker, 2004):

- *Task characteristics approach:* This perspective proposes that certain task characteristics are related to employee attitudes. Five key dimensions have been identified that influence levels of job satisfaction: autonomy, job feedback from the job, job variety, task identity and task significance. Consequently, this argument contends that if an employee is in a job where these criteria are being fulfilled there is an increased likelihood of reported job satisfaction.
- *Social information processing approach:* This situational approach has been proposed as an alternative to the task characteristics approach (Salancik and Pfeffer, 1978). As has been discussed, job attitudes are shaped by social cues processed from the work environment. A number of studies have found that certain socio-organisational factors impact upon job satisfaction: for example, leadership (Lok and Crawford, 2004), organisational culture (Egan *et al.*, 2004) and teamwork ▸**Chapter 7**◂ (Griffin *et al.*, 2001).
- *Dispositional approach:* This perspective indicates that the individual possesses dispositional characteristics that impact upon levels of job satisfaction. Studies show support for intrinsic motivation (for example, Schonfeld, 2000), positive/negative affectivity (such as happiness/anxiety, for example Simmons *et al.*, 2001) and self-efficacy (for example, Judge and Bono, 2001).

Therefore, we can view job satisfaction as a function of three factors: the characteristics of an employee's job, the information sourced from referent others in the organisation or a person's dispositional characteristics.

MEASURING JOB SATISFACTION

Since attitudes are not directly observable, they can only be measured indirectly. This presents a number of methodological difficulties for researchers. The most obvious approach is to simply ask people, and the majority of research has adopted this line of enquiry.

job satisfaction a positive emotional state which exists as
a consequence of appraising one's job and job experience

Typically, attitude questionnaires ask respondents to indicate whether they agree or disagree with a series of 'belief' statements about an attitude object. Questionnaires, or 'instruments' as they are known, are designed using 'factor analysis' (a scientific method to reduce a large set of variables into a smaller set). The technique ensures the instrument has the correct number of statements that best capture the variability of the attitude being measured. Each statement is referred to as an 'item'. The number of items in an instrument varies markedly depending very much on the type of attitude being measured. For example, a job satisfaction questionnaire might ask candidates to what extent they are happy about their current career opportunities in the organisation, or their current level of salary. Regardless of the number of items used, the final statements included in an instrument need to be carefully selected. Each item should represent a different and independent perspective of the attitude being measured. Building on the work of Thurstone (1928), Likert (1932) developed an effective technique to measure attitudes. Figure 4.2 shows an example of a Likert Scale in which a number of attitude statements are presented to respondents. They are then asked to determine the extent of their agreement or disagreement with these statements using a 5-point scale, with the two poles typically labelled 'strongly agree' and 'strongly disagree'. Other techniques have been used to measure attitudes, such as *Guttman's Scalogram Method* and *Osgood's Semantic Differential*, but the Likert Scale has been the dominant methodological approach used in modern questionnaires.

There are of course a number of problems to be considered when measuring attitudes. Participants' responses can be affected by a wide variety of biases which render the outcome of the instrument invalid. For example, in an effort to portray a socially acceptable view of the world the participant may not answer truthfully. This is known as social desirability. Alternatively, the score of a respondent holding a prejudiced view against a certain group of people (for example, women) would run counter to a prevailing norm (for example, equality). Often attitude measurement suffers from definitional and operational difficulties, which goes some way to explaining why the field of attitude measurement frequently contains conflicting results. Satisfaction can be measured in a number of different ways, for example surveys, interviews

---

Respondents specify their agreement ranging from strongly agree (5) to strongly disagree (1) to the following six items:

1. The most important things that happen in life involve work.
2. Work is something people should get involved in most of the time.
3. Work should be only a small part of one's life (reverse scored).
4. Work should be considered central to life.
5. In my view, an individual's personal life goals should be work-oriented.
6. Life is worth living only when people get absorbed in work.

The higher the score, the higher the level of work centrality.

Figure 4.2 Work centrality scale

Source: Based on Arvey et al. (2004).

and critical incident technique. Each method for measuring job satisfaction has its own limitations and it is recommended that a mixed-methods approach be used to more accurately measure the concept (for example, combining interview and questionnaire approaches).

JOB SATISFACTION AND PERFORMANCE

The big question in research on job satisfaction concerns its consequences. Does job satisfaction predict job performance? The 'human relations' movement in the middle of the 20th century called attention to the positive outcomes of job satisfaction, such as higher levels of performance and productivity. Empirical support for this notion is, however, somewhat weak. For example, Vroom (1964) found a correlation of 0.13 between overall job performance and overall job satisfaction, which represents a very tenuous relationship between the two. A similarly weak relationship has been found in a number of subsequent studies (for example, Riketta, 2008; Podsakoff and Williams, 1986). Judge *et al.* (2001) outline six possible ways in which job satisfaction and job performance are linked (see Figure 4.3).

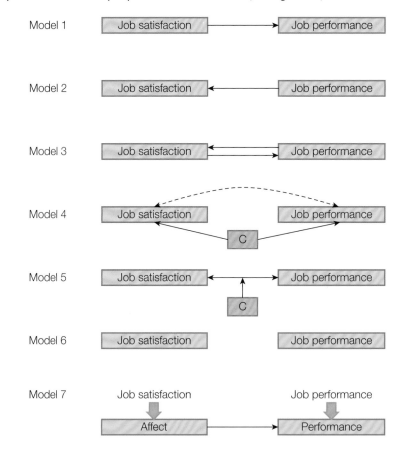

Figure 4.3 The relationship between job satisfaction and job performance

Source: Judge et al. (2001).

The oft-cited expression that 'happy workers are productive workers' is a good example of people's assumptions about the association between attitudes and behaviour. As we can see in Figure 4.3, the relationship is a lot more complex than simply cause and effect. Judge *et al.*'s (2001) research is seen as a landmark study in this area. Their findings suggest a modest relationship between satisfaction and performance. However, the multi-faceted nature of job satisfaction and job performance presents methodological difficulties for researchers investigating the causal link between the concepts. Universal measures of both concepts lack scientific value. It is a much more valid approach to investigate the relationship between specific components of satisfaction and specific components of performance. More attention needs to be paid to the moderator variables or third variables, such as rewards, as outlined in Model 4 and Model 5 in Figure 4.3. For example, do satisfied employees with a salary of €75,000 perform better than satisfied employees with a lower salary level? Answering questions like this will further our understanding of the relationship between job satisfaction and job performance.

ATTITUDES TOWARDS THE ORGANISATION

The concept of organisational commitment has received considerable attention from researchers since the 1980s. Most employers seek commitment from their employees as a means of ensuring goals and targets are met and of achieving overall strategic roles. However, a sense of organisational commitment can be difficult to engender in the workforce. There are many variables that influence it. For example, job security may not be seen as a credible notion. The upheaval caused by the financial crisis of 2008 saw millions of people around the world lose their jobs. How can an organisation gain commitment from the employees if their jobs may not exist in six months' time? For this reason, employees now seek security from their profession and no longer from the organisation. The idea here is that the employee will remain committed to the organisation as long as the employer increases their level of employability, for example through up-skilling and providing educational opportunities. If the employee is then made redundant he or she knows that they are likely to find new opportunities elsewhere because of this higher level of employability. This 'new deal' has characterised the employment relationship since the 1990s (Guest, 2004). It is important to understand the context in which the employment relationship plays out. As explained earlier, socio-economic factors can also shape an employee's commitment to the firm.

Similarly to job satisfaction, commitment does not guarantee a higher level of work performance. Also, it is generally accepted to be a multi-faceted construct. For example, Allen and Meyer (1990) have distinguished between different types of commitment:

organisational commitment an individual's comparative strength of identification and involvement with an organisation

   a *Affective commitment*: An individual's emotional investment with their organisation.
   b *Continuance commitment*: An individual's perception of the risks involved in leaving the
      organisation. Two factors are likely to influence the perception process: the personal
      sacrifice in leaving and the alternative sources of employment available.
   c *Normative commitment*: An individual's perceived moral obligation to remain with the
      organisation.

Let's say an employee has been offered a position in another company. She may perceive this
role as more attractive in terms of salary and benefits (continuance commitment) but because
of her emotional ties to the organisation (affective commitment) and the fact that she is overseeing a major project for the firm (normative commitment) she decides to stay and commit to
the firm. It is clear that this model is founded on the tri-dimensional model of attitudes, that is,
affective, behavioural and cognitive. While the validity of the model has been criticised by some
researchers (Solinger *et al.*, 2008) it has served as a very useful guide for investigating commitment. It is also important to consider what exactly constitutes the organisation. Who represents
the organisation? Indeed, Rousseau (1995) has highlighted how individuals will feel numerous
commitments at work, such as to their line manager, their colleagues and their subordinates.
Organisations consist of many different groups of people, each with their own goals and ambitions, and the relationship the individual has with these groups shapes that sense of commitment. This is one of many reasons why organisational commitment is a contentious issue.

Wasti and Can (2008) found that commitment to the organisation predicted outcomes
such as increased turnover, whereas commitment to the supervisor predicted extra-role
behaviours such as staying at work late. This type of behaviour, in which the employee often
willingly goes above and beyond the agreed terms of the employment relationship, has been
termed **organisational citizenship behaviour (OCB)**. It refers to individual behaviour that is
discretionary, not explicitly recognised by the formal reward system and promotes the effective functioning of the organisation (Organ, 1997).

Like job satisfaction, a wide range of factors have been identified that influence an
individual's sense of commitment. Again, dispositional characteristics such as motivation,
personality variables and job characteristics such as autonomy and other related variables
have been identified. There is a causal connection between all these factors and organisational
commitment. However, this interrelationship is extremely complex and more work is needed
in building a theoretical framework to explain commitment. Similarly to job satisfaction,
commitment is generally measured using Likert scaling such as the Organisational Commitment Questionnaire (OCQ) developed by Mowday *et al.* (1979) (see Figure 4.4). Again, the
important issue within the literature on organisational commitment is the relationship with
job performance. Does the committed employee perform better than the less committed
employee? Again, it is difficult to answer this question because organisational commitment

organisational citizenship behaviour voluntary behaviour from the employee that is likely to have positive
consequences for the organisation

is a multi-faceted construct. Broadly speaking there is modest support linking both variables (for example, Harrison *et al.*, 2006), but there is more robust evidence supporting the idea that organisational commitment is a predictor of an employee's intention to leave a job (for example, Solinger *et al.*, 2008).

Job satisfaction and organisational commitment are important concepts in understanding how attitudes manifest in the work environment. As has been explained, a conclusive model capturing the interrelationship between these variables and job performance has yet to be developed. However, given that they do indirectly impact upon how an employee behaves in the work environment there is a considerable need for employers to understand their causal factors.

Organisational Commitment Questionnaire (OCQ)

Instructions

Listed below are a series of statements that represent possible feelings that individuals might have about the company or organisation for which they work. With respect to your own feelings about the particular organisation for which you are now working please indicate the extent to which you agree or disagree with each statement, ranging from strongly agree (5) to strongly disagree (1) (R = Reversed Score)

1 I am willing to put in a great deal of effort beyond that normally expected in order to help this organisation be successful.

2 I talk up this organisation to my friends as a great organisation to work for.

3 I feel very little loyalty to this organisation. (R)

4 I would accept almost any type of job assignment in order to keep working for this organisation.

5 I find that my values and the organisation's values are very similar.

6 I am proud to tell others that I am part of this organisation.

7 I could just as well be working for a different organisation as long as the type of work was similar. (R)

8 This organisation really inspires the very best in me in the way of job performance.

9 It would take very little change in my present circumstances to cause me to leave this organisation. (R)

10 I am extremely glad that I chose this organisation to work for over others I was considering at the time I joined.

11 There's not too much to be gained by sticking with this organisation indefinitely. (R)

12 Often I find it difficult to agree with this organisation's policies on important matters relating to its employees. (R)

13 I really care about the fate of this organisation.

14 For me this is the best of all possible organisations for which to work.

15 Deciding to work for this organisation was a definite mistake on my part. (R)

Figure 4.4 Organisational commitment questionnaire

Source: Mowday et al. (1979).

WORK-RELATED ATTITUDES AND BEHAVIOUR

How work-related attitudes manifest in the organisation will be of particular interest to those in managerial positions. Indeed, understanding the attitudes held by employees can allow managers to better predict how workers are likely to behave. In recent years, there has been a great deal of interest in employee engagement. Organisations seek to have employees engaged in the workplace because engagement is associated with a number of desirable behaviours, such as intention to stay with the firm and organisational citizenship behaviours, for example (Saks, 2008). Research suggests that engaged employees are more alert, more efficient in their jobs and achieve a higher level of task performance (see Rich *et al.*, 2010). Disengaged employees on the other hand are lethargic, inefficient and rate worse on task performance. Let's say two employees working for the same organisation have similar jobs and salaries. The reason that one employee is outperforming the other could be attributed to his level of engagement. Of course, there may be other viable explanations for his work performance but increasingly organisations are trying to understand the antecedents of engagement. Again, there are myriad factors that shape engagement, such as job rewards, relationship with supervisor and job content. Job satisfaction and organisational commitment are also associated with level of engagement (see Harter *et al.*, 2002 and Saks, 2008) emphasising the centrality of these two concepts in the organisational behaviour field.

Another widely studied concept in this area is job involvement. Once again, job involvement has been linked with organisational outcomes such as performance and attendance and is shaped by many factors, including leadership and personality. (See Brown, 1996, for a comprehensive review of job involvement.) It may seem that many of the terms examined in this section are relatively similar from a definitional perspective but it is important to recognise that each concept is distinct from the other. Each tells us something different about an employee's relationship with his or her work. (See Hallberg and Schaufeli, 2006, for an in-depth discussion of this issue.)

The behaviours explored so far in this chapter can all be broadly described as pro-social. Within the context of the organisation, these behaviours are beneficial because they result in positive outcomes for the organisation. Of course, not every behaviour will be pro-social. Employees often hold attitudes towards the firm that result in behaviours at odds with the goals of the organisation. In the literature, these behaviours are often referred to as deviant. Many of these behaviours may seem inconsequential if they only happen very occasionally. While not encouraged by the employer, the consequences to the organisation of one employee calling in sick to take a three-day

---

employee engagement the degree to which an individual is attentive and absorbed in the performance of their roles

job involvement the extent to which an employee psychologically identifies with their job

pro-social pro-social behaviours are those that benefit another party

deviant deviant behaviours are those that are counterproductive to an organisation

weekend are relatively minor. However, if many employees (or the same employee) repeatedly fake illness then this can cause great disruption to the organisation. Call centres typically experience higher levels of 'voluntary absenteeism'. Many researchers point to the repetitive, monotonous nature of the work as a primary reason to explain this behaviour. Again, this explanation highlights the shaping role of organisational factors on employee behaviour. Sometimes employees view their job in a negative way and have high turnover intentions. Assembly line workers often have high turnover intentions (see Bakker *et al.*, 2003) which, again, may be explained by the repetitive nature of the work.

On the other hand, not every counterproductive behaviour can be traced back to a negative attitude. Since the early 2000s, both employers and researchers have directed their attention to the concept of presenteeism. Being ill is a legitimate reason not to turn up to work. However, many of you will remember times when you have gone to work or attended an important lecture despite feeling under the weather. While this behaviour can be seen as admirable or even necessary for one-off occasions (for example, a sales pitch to important new clients or a mid-term exam), attending work while ill for a prolonged period creates a number of difficulties for the organisation. For instance, an employee suffering from depression is likely to make poorer decisions, be less productive and experience relationship difficulties in their personal life. Of course, these problems do not disappear when in the work environment. If this worker decides to attend work and not take time off, the consequences of these difficulties for the organisation can be considerable, such as decreased productivity and interpersonal conflict. As this is an under-developed area within organisational behaviour research we have limited insight into the causes of presenteeism. There is evidence to suggest that the economic climate plays an important role. It seems likely that a temporary employee fearing for her job would be more likely to attend work in spite of illness when compared to a permanent member of staff. (For a detailed study of the causes and consequences of presenteeism see Johns, 2010.)

We have already explored the relationship between attitudes and behaviours, and it is clear that important workplace behaviours can to some extent be attributed to work-related attitudes. The consequences of these behaviours for organisations can be significant and managers need to understand their root causes. A recurring theme in this chapter is the shaping role of organisational factors on the various attitudes and behaviours discussed. This suggests that the organisation can go some way towards influencing employee behaviours. Decisions concerning pay, work design, autonomy and other work-related factors will have considerable bearing on how employees interact with the organisation.

turnover intentions an employee's self-reported intentions to leave their job

presenteeism refers to attending work while suffering with illness

BUILDING YOUR SKILLS

Managing Relationships

© GETTY IMAGES/ THINKSTOCK IMAGES/ MEDIOIMAGES/PHOTODISC

You have just hired an employee on a six-month fixed-term contract. While this is currently a very important role within the organisation it is unlikely that the contract will be extended. The employee is aware of this. Can you expect the employee to be committed to the organisation during the six months? If so, how do you bring about this commitment?

WORK VALUES

Values are different from attitudes. For example, most of us would prefer to work for an organisation that is socially responsible. However, some of us would *only* work for an organisation that is committed to corporate social responsibility (CSR). For these people, ethical behaviour is fundamental to their career choice. Therefore, we can say that social responsibility is a value they hold regarding their job. Simply, values are the degree of importance underpinning our attitudes. However, like attitudes, a person's value system is shaped by social factors such as the values of their parents, teachers and friends, and the cultural influences to which they are exposed. The resulting values often endure throughout their lifetime. Therefore, when a person enters the work environment for the first time they bring with them relatively stable expectations.

According to James and James (1989) these work values serve as a filter through which individuals interpret their work environment. They help people to make sense of their environment. Individuals' work values determine the meaning that work, their career and the organisation have for them. **Work values** are defined by Super and Sverko (1995) as the general and relatively stable goals that people try to reach through work. They are expressions of more general human values in the context of the work setting. The central idea put forward in the domain of work values is that they lead individuals to seek jobs or organisations that are characterised by certain attributes (Rentsch and McEwen, 2002). For example, work–life balance has emerged since the 1990s as a value that many employees particularly seek. The option of, for example, beginning work at a later time or working three-day weeks are all flexible work arrangements that were largely unheard of before the 1980s. That these options

values refer to the degree of importance an individual ascribes to a particular belief they hold about an object

work values the general and relatively stable goals that people try to reach through work

are available to employees reflects the changing societal needs and values that have emerged since (Guest, 2004). Employees with young families appreciate flexible work practices and they seek employment opportunities in organisations where such arrangements are valued and practised.

Of course, people's values can also change over time for a variety of reasons such as the life-stage they are at and the different experiences they encounter through their lives in terms of work–life balance: a 19-year-old employee with no children will typically have a very different value system from a middle-aged employee with four children. Indeed, employees often search for an organisation whose cultural values are congruent with their own value system. De Vos *et al.* (2005) found that new employees in an organisation constantly seek information that directly relates to the fulfilment of their values. For example, an employee who values personal development in their job will explicitly seek out information from the employer regarding issues like training opportunities and development plans.

Work values play an important role in helping an employee to identify a suitable organisation and also in how the employee behaves after organisational entry. However, as we have discussed already, the organisation can deliberately shape the employee through socialisation tactics as a means of ensuring greater alignment between values. While an individual's values often remain stable over their lifetime, the effect of socialisation can influence how employees view their work. Like attitudes, our experience at work is shaped by and shapes our values.

Pulsate

Pulsate is a well-established English franchise that has its headquarters in London, from where it directs the operations of its 16 sites across Europe. It is one of the leading 'home entertainment' brands in the UK, specialising in high-definition televisions and smart devices. It employs more than 350 people across four countries. Last week, Pulsate bought Phonic – a large independent trader in home entertainment based in Dublin with more than 50 employees. Within five months they expect the transition from Phonic to be completed and for the Dublin office to be operational as Pulsate's 17th site. To speed up this process, a number of senior managers from their London and Scottish sites are to be temporarily transferred to Phonic to oversee day-to-day operations during the changeover.

Phonic has been well served by its loyal staff for over 25 years, many of whom have been with the company from its very first day. Five years ago Phonic had a sterling reputation in its field. However, recently the company has 'fallen behind' the technological advancements that are considered an integral part of 21st-century home entertainment. While Phonic pride themselves on their customer service, the actual goods and services on offer are both limited and dated. As a result they have seen some of their customers move to more 'modern' service providers. However, they still have a large pool of customers which Pulsate believe can be significantly grown with the introduction of more desirable goods and the provision of a better service. Pulsate's stores are designed to minimise the number of shop assistants on the floor by using an in-house catalogue ordering system. Customers shop in Pulsate because the service provided is efficient and the average length of time spent by a customer in a Pulsate store is 9 minutes. The majority of Pulsate's staff, therefore, work in

(Continued)

Pulsate (*Continued*)

the warehouse next to the shop floor, obtaining the customer's product.

Pulsate were surprised to learn of Phonic's persistence in selling outdated goods and customer service. For Pulsate, it is essential that every employee is proficient with both modern technology (for example, Tablets, H.D. televisions) and the functioning of the catalogue system. However, they also see the value in 'face to face' interaction with customers and will continue to offer this service, albeit to a lesser degree. The company wants to minimise redundancies and believes a role can found for each of the 51

employees at Phonic, but will not prevent anyone from leaving. They feel this acquisition will cement their position as a European leader in home entertainment.

Understandably, Phonic's employees have been a little apprehensive about the takeover. Firstly, they have heard whispers of large-scale redundancies with many consultants losing their jobs to the new catalogue service. They fear being replaced by younger, technologically savvy employees – the perceived profile of a typical Pulsate employee. They believe that a failure to upskill in the necessary areas will result in their exit

from the company. Some of the employee representatives have voiced their concern over the uncertainty that surrounds the takeover, and they are still awaiting the director's response. Ultimately, they believe abandoning existing services will jeopardise the long-term relationship with established customers.

You are the Director of Phonic and you will assume a similar position within Pulsate in the coming weeks. You are concerned about how the employees have responded to news of the takeover.

Questions

1 How would you describe Phonic employees' attitude to the takeover? How is this likely to affect their behaviour over the coming months?

2 Is it possible to change the employees' attitude to be more positive about the takeover? If so, how can this be achieved?

3 Guest (2004) argues that technology has changed the relationship between the employee and the organisation. Has technology changed employees' attitudes towards their job? Explain your answer.

© PHOTOALTO

IN THE EBOOK,
CLICK TO HEAR
AN AUDIO SUMMARY

SUMMARY

It is clear that the concept of attitudes can help us understand behaviour within an organisation. In assessing attitudes, it is important to understand their tri-dimensional structure. Certainly, the cognitive, affective and behavioural components of attitudes need to be explored together to fully understand the dynamics of the attitude construct itself. However, there are many variables mediating the relationship between attitude and behaviour. It is reasonable to argue that it is a complex relationship. Similarly, there are multiple antecedents of attitudes. Broadly speaking, our attitudes are shaped by personal or dispositional characteristics, direct experience and social learning. Indeed, prejudice, discrimination and stereotyping are often learned from our parents or our friends. In a work context, the organisation passes information to the employee in a strategic way as a means of ensuring greater conformity. Over time, our work-related attitudes can change. While our attitudes are relatively stable and enduring, our interactions with the work environment and information received from this environment can influence how we view the world. Often we learn to view our jobs differently.

Arguably, the most widely researched topic in the literature on attitudes is job satisfaction. Again, there are myriad factors that impact our level of job satisfaction, which accounts for the difficulties associated in measuring it. The same can be said for organisational commitment. While a definitive model capturing the full complexity of the relationship between work-related attitudes and job performance has yet to be developed, it is important for the organisation to better understand the factors that affect issues such as job satisfaction, given that they indirectly influence behaviour in the workplace. Both pro-social and deviant behaviours can often be traced back to an attitude held by an employee but it is important to highlight that the relationship between attitudes and behaviours is complex. Finally, work-related values can also help to explain behaviour in the organisation. Certain attitudes will have an inherent level of importance which dictates our social interactions. Indeed, work-related values serve as a filter through which our employment is understood.

Overall, much of our behaviour can be explained by attitude theory. Of course, this is just one lens through which organisational behaviour can be understood. Given that attitudes influence both how we view and how we behave in the world, it is critical for the employer to understand the attitudes held by their employees towards the organisation.

CHAPTER REVIEW QUESTIONS

1 What is the difference between a 'good' attitude and a 'bad' attitude?
2 What are the key factors that influence a person's attitude? In what way can an organisation influence the attitude formation process?
3 Explain the association between attitudes and behaviour. Can the organisation predict an employee's behaviour in the workplace?
4 Why is job satisfaction such a complex issue for organisations? Is there any merit in measuring it?
5 What is positive discrimination? What are your thoughts on the criticism that it restricts the capacity of the recruitment process to find the best candidate?
6 Is it easy to change an attitude? Can a person learn to be prejudiced? Can a person unlearn their prejudice?
7 Can you explain what is meant by the 'ABCs' of attitude formation?
8 How are values different from attitudes? How do they influence behaviour in organisations?

MULTIPLE CHOICE QUESTIONS

In your ebook, click to take a multiple choice quiz to test your understanding of this chapter.

FURTHER READING

Albarracin, D., Johnson, B.T. and Zanna, M.P. (Eds.). (2014). *The Handbook of Attitudes*. Psychology Press.

Burnes, B., Patterson, F., Robertson, I.T., Silvester, J., Cooper, C.L. and Arnold, J. (2004). *Work Psychology: Understanding Human Behaviour in the Workplace*. Financial Times Prentice Hall.

Currivan, D.B. (2000). The causal order of job satisfaction and organizational commitment in models of employee turnover. *Human Resource Management Review*, 9(4), 495–524.

Kowske, B.J., Rasch, R. and Wiley, J. (2010). Millennials'(lack of) attitude problem: An empirical examination of generational effects on work attitudes. *Journal of Business and Psychology*, 25(2), 265–279.

Sutton, R. and Douglas, K. (2013). *Social Psychology*. Basingstoke. Palgrave.

USEFUL WEBSITES

www.cipd.co.uk

This is a useful website for students. The CIPD is the governing body of human resources in Britain and Ireland. Here you will find real-life examples of how organisations manage attitudes in the workplace.

http://www.bps.org.uk/networks-and-communities/member-microsite/division-occupational-psychology

This is the Division of Occupational Psychology within the British Psychological Society. Here you will find information on how psychologists work with organisations to better understand workplace attitudes and behaviour.

www.pearnkandola.com

Pearn Kandola is a firm of psychologists who work closely with employees and organisations on issues relating to attitude and behaviour. They have regular blogs and examples of how real-life organisational problems are tackled.

5 MOTIVATION IN THE WORKPLACE

Colette Darcy

LEARNING OUTCOMES

BY THE END OF CHAPTER YOU SHOULD BE ABLE TO:

- Explain why motivation is important in the workplace.

- Distinguish between need theories of motivation and process theories of motivation.

- Understand the difference between extrinsic and intrinsic sources of motivation.

- Describe the link between job design and motivation.

- Explore the application of reinforcement theory as a means of motivation.

- Understand the impact of situational factors on workplace motivation.

© ROYALTY-FREE/CORBIS

THIS CHAPTER DISCUSSES:

IN REALITY

We have all heard the phrase 'money is the greatest motivator', yet we can all think of times when money has not been the driving force behind us doing something. In his book *Drive* (2011), Daniel Pink describes what he says is 'the surprising truth' about what motivates us. Pink tells us that true motivation can be condensed into three elements: autonomy – the desire to direct our own lives, mastery – the desire to continually improve at something that matters to us, and purpose – the desire to do things in service of something larger than ourselves. These are important issues for consideration by those who are responsible for managing people in organisations. However, executives still think that bonuses are the dominant incentive for most people, and this is reflected in the pay-for-performance approach adopted in many organisations.

INTRODUCTION

Motivation is a set of forces that makes people behave in certain ways (Steers *et al.*, 2002). It is an important concept in the workplace as the challenge for managers is to maximise the likelihood of staff working as hard as possible. This key issue is highlighted in a large scale study of American work attitudes in which over 50 per cent of workers admitted that they only did the minimum to avoid being fired. Over 80 per cent said they could work 'much harder' (Spitzer, 1995). On any given day an employee may choose to work as hard as possible, or work just hard enough to avoid a reprimand. While it is often relatively easy to motivate someone in the short term, to achieve an immediate goal for example, it is often much more difficult and complex to motivate someone for longer periods of time. Motivation and the ability to motivate individuals and groups of workers has, therefore, been the focus of much research. If an organisation, or managers within an organisation, can master the skills which allow them to motivate their staff then they are likely to witness higher performance from individuals (Locke and Latham, 1990), greater team cohesiveness (Evans and Dion, 1991), lower absenteeism (Mowday *et al.*, 1982), greater job satisfaction (Judge *et al.*, 2001) and a strong positive organisational culture (Milne, 2007). You can see, therefore, why organisations are so keen to understand what drives their employees and, equally, why anyone with people responsibility within an organisation should have a fundamental understanding of what motivates and drives individual performance. This chapter begins by looking at the drivers of individual performance and how these impact upon motivation. Several theories of motivation are relevant when it comes to work settings, with three main groups of theories identifiable: content theories, process theories and situational factors that influence motivation. These theories relate to individual sources of motivation, and the chapter finishes with a look at the special case of team motivation.

motivation a set of forces that make people behave in certain ways

WHAT DRIVES INDIVIDUAL PERFORMANCE?

Individual performance is generally determined by three things: motivation – the desire to do the job; ability – the capability to do the job; and the work environment – the resources needed to do the job (Griffin, 2014) (see Figure 5.1).

Without all three drivers in place simultaneously the chances of the individual performing a job to the optimal level is drastically reduced. Consider an individual who might be highly motivated to become a doctor. Since a very early age, all he has ever wanted to do was to become a doctor. Yet when it came to completing the final school examinations he was unable to achieve the points required to gain access to an undergraduate medicine course. He was highly motivated but *lacked the ability* to achieve the desired outcome. Take another example. Within a college there is a lecturer who is a world-recognised expert in entrepreneurship. This lecturer has published her research in the very top academic journals and has written numerous books. However, the lecturer does her best to avoid having to teach and when she does, her students report that it is a disastrous experience. The lecturer clearly has the ability, yet *lacks the motivation* to teach. Her interests lie elsewhere in terms of getting her work published and she finds teaching an unnecessary distraction.

Equally, we could have a highly motivated and capable employee who wants to launch a new product onto the market. The product he has developed has clear selling points and initial studies have confirmed that customers would be willing to buy it. Yet the senior management team is reluctant to invest in a national marketing campaign to launch the product. In this case the individual is highly motivated and has clear ability but due to the work environment and specifically a *lack of organisational support* for the marketing campaign, he is unlikely to be successful in launching the new product.

From a management perspective, therefore, it not sufficient to simply recruit capable individuals – that is just the first step. We must ensure that when we recruit these capable individuals we convince them to invest their ability and skills in their work to achieve the organisational goals, and make sure that we will provide them with the necessary resources

Figure 5.1 What drives individual performance?

to do that. This chapter is therefore concerned with not only what motivation is, but *how* managers can leverage theories of motivation to convince their employees to use their skills to best effect in the workplace.

Human capital theory recognises individuals as cognitive and emotional beings who possess free will (Wright *et al.*, 2001). It is the employee who decides what behaviours they will engage in. The employee owns their knowledge, skills and abilities, not the organisation they work for. Therefore, it is the individual who makes a conscious decision whether or not to invest their knowledge, skills and abilities for the strategic benefit of the firm. If an employee lacks ability it could be argued that a development plan could be put in place to tackle this deficit. If resources are lacking, again a manager could intervene to correct the problem by making these available. However, if motivation is lacking, the problem for the manager becomes more complex. The idea of **discretionary effort** (MacDuffie, 1995) is really at the heart of the challenge of motivating employees. How do we get our employees to maximise their discretionary effort? What factors positively influence this discretionary effort and what factors have a negative impact?

WHAT IS MOTIVATION?

Motivation can be thought of as the set of forces that energise, direct and sustain behaviour (Hitt *et al.*, 2012). Much of the literature focuses on the initial galvanisation of employees in order to motivate them to take on a particular task and to focus this energy in order to complete it. In one way this is the easy piece of the jigsaw. It is the ability to sustain the initial burst of motivation that is difficult for managers.

These forces can come from the person, the so-called *'push' of internal forces*, or they can come from the environment that surrounds the person, the so-called *'pull' of external forces*. We are going to concentrate on the push, or internal forces, first. As the name suggests, these forces are internal to the individual, so in essence they are the forces within an individual which cause them to act in a certain way.

Psychologists typically categorise motivation theories as they relate to individuals into two types:

1 *Content theories* which focus on what needs a person is trying to satisfy and on what features of the work environment seem to satisfy those.

2 *Process theories* which focus on the way different variables or factors combine to influence the amount of effort people are willing to make in order to gain some outcome.

discretionary effort the level of effort people could give if they wanted to, but above and beyond the minimum required

'push' of internal forces motivational forces which come from the person

'pull' of external forces motivational forces which come from the environment that surrounds the person

content theories focus on the needs that motivate people. The internal drive that motivates specific behaviours in an attempt to fulfil the needs

process theories focus on how people decide what actions to choose in order to meet their needs and how they decide whether these actions were successful

CONTENT THEORIES

Content theories of motivation focus on the personal needs that workers attempt to satisfy while also taking account of the features in the work environment that satisfy their needs. In this way managers can design work to meet these needs and hence elicit appropriate and successful work behaviours. There are three main content theories: Maslow's need hierarchy, Herzberg's two-factor theory and McClelland's acquired needs theory.

MASLOW'S NEED HIERARCHY

Maslow's hierarchy of needs proposes that people are motivated to satisfy five need levels, starting with the most basic (physiological needs such as hunger) and, once those are satisfied, moving to the next level (safety needs), then the third (need for a sense of belonging) and fourth levels (need for self-esteem), and finally to the need for self-actualisation (see Figure 5.2). The theory was not developed specifically with the work environment in mind but we will consider how each of the five levels might relate to a work setting.

According to Maslow's theory the single motivator is an unsatisfied need and only when the individual's more basic needs have been met will they be able to concentrate on satisfying higher-order needs. Interestingly, the theory would argue that, should a lower-order need come under threat despite an individual having previously satisfied this need and moved on to

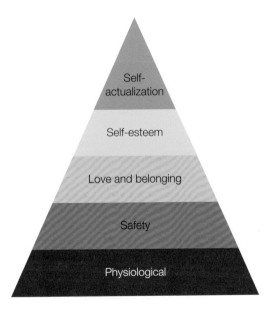

Figure 5.2 Maslow's hierarchy of needs theory

Source: Maslow (1943).

self-actualisation refers to a person's desire to reach their full potential, to grow and develop to achieve your absolute potential and to use your abilities to the greatest extent

higher-order needs, that person would be likely to revert to focusing on the need under threat and decrease their efforts to satisfy higher-order needs until such time as the threat had passed.

Think about someone working in a senior banking role where they have high levels of responsibility and status attached to their job. In such a role an individual will probably have met all their needs up to and including self-esteem. However, should there be an announcement that compulsory redundancies are required within the management level of the bank, it is likely that this individual will revert to focusing on lower-order needs such as safety, that is, his job security. His ability to concentrate on higher-order needs such as self-actualisation will be temporarily displaced until such time as his safety needs have been satisfied and reassurance provided that he is not going to be one of the compulsory redundancies.

IMPLICATIONS OF MASLOW'S HIERARCHY OF NEEDS FOR MANAGERS

The key to understanding a person's motivation from a needs hierarchy perspective is to identify the individual's most basic need that is not yet being met. Once a need has been satisfied it ceases to be a motivator unless its fulfilment is threatened again.

While Maslow's work persists in terms of popularity, it has its critics. As with most theoretical developments in the area of motivation, this one has its roots firmly in the US and as such it is reasonable to question whether a similar set of needs or indeed the order of these needs are equally applicable to individuals in different countries with different cultural emphases. The answer is 'probably not' (Gambrel and Cianci, 2003). There is no evidence to suggest that the order of the needs is the same from person to person, or that everyone has these specific needs (Sackett, 1998). As individuals, it is likely that we have distinct needs and drivers which are unique to us and that this model is too simplistic to capture this complexity (Wahba and Bridwell, 1976). Equally, the model presupposes that once a need is met an individual moves to a higher one in a linear, orderly fashion, going from one to the next on the list (Rouse, 2004). Yet, it would seem probable that individuals might be concerned with more than one need at any one time – think of the example of the banking executive. He may be concerned with job security while also focusing on belongingness. Indeed how realistic is it that individuals move in a linear way through each need to reach the highest need of self-actualisation? Could an individual not jump from one to another, bypassing some along the way? Equally, at what point is each individual satisfied that the need has been met?

HERZBERG'S THEORY ON WHY MOTIVATION MUST COME FROM WITHIN

Around the same time that Maslow was working on his hierarchy of needs theory, Frederick Herzberg, was also tackling the issue of motivation. According to Herzberg (1966), at work individuals are not content with satisfying the lower-order needs set forth by Maslow, but rather they look for the satisfaction of higher-level psychological needs such as a sense of achievement, recognition, advancement and the nature of the work itself. Herzberg was particularly intrigued by the commonly held view among managers that the best way to motivate employees was through a 'KITA' approach. What is 'KITA'? 'Kick in the ass.' At that time, and even in some organisations today, there was a strong belief that you could motivate someone by metaphorically or literally giving them a kick up the bum to get them to do what is was that you needed. The problem with this approach, however, is that every time you want someone to do something you need to apply a KITA. Also, Herzberg made the point that when a manager applies the KITA, it is the manager who is motivated and not the employee. The employee moves (a kick in the backside will do that all right!) but he was not himself motivated to move. Herzberg argued that motivation can only really come from within and therefore that one must want to do it – no outside stimulation should be required. Movement, Herzberg argued, needs to be distinguished from motivation.

Movement is a function of fear of punishment or failure to get **extrinsic rewards**. On the other hand, motivation is a function of growth from getting **intrinsic rewards** out of interesting and challenging work. Movement requires constant monitoring and reinforcement with a focus on short-term results. To get a result, management must constantly add to the extrinsic rewards on offer. It is a constant drive upwards in terms of extrinsic rewards. Let's look at an example of this in operation. Last year I was rewarded with a bonus of €5,000 for exceptional performance. This year, despite working as hard, I received a bonus of €3,000. Even though I received a bonus in both years the fact that I *only* received €3,000 this year means that I *lost* €2,000. The result of this is that I feel like I have been short-changed and I am demotivated rather than positively motivated. The only way to maintain 'motivation' in this situation is to continue to increase my bonus, or, at a minimum, maintain it until eventually I am no longer motivated by it and accept it as a given.

CONSIDER THIS…

Think of what needs might fall into each level of Maslow's needs hierarchy. To start you off, an example of a physiological need in a work-based setting might be an adequate basic salary. (See possible answers on http://www.palgrave.com/carbery-ob.)

Maslow's need level	Work based example
Physiological	Adequate basic salary
Safety	
Love and belonging	
Self-esteem	
Self-actualisation	

HERZBERG'S TWO-FACTOR THEORY OF MOTIVATION

Having established in theory that motivation must come from within, Herzberg set out to consider the notion that the presence of one set of job characteristics or incentives leads to worker *satisfaction* at work, while another and separate set of job characteristics leads

extrinsic rewards rewards that are tangible or physically given to an individual for accomplishing a task

intrinsic rewards outcomes that give an individual personal satisfaction such as that derived from a job well done

to *dissatisfaction* at work. What is most interesting is that Herzberg was convinced that satisfaction and dissatisfaction were not opposites at either end of a continuum, but rather completely separate phenomena. Herzberg's real breakthrough was to argue that managers need to focus on both the motivators and the factors that create dissatisfaction in order to ensure that satisfaction is increased while dissatisfaction is minimised.

Herzberg interviewed 200 accountants and engineers in an attempt to understand the factors associated with satisfaction and dissatisfaction. He asked participants to recall occasions when they had been satisfied and motivated, and occasions when they had been dissatisfied and unmotivated. His two-factor theory of motivation was the result by which he attempted to distinguish between factors that increase job satisfaction (**motivators**) and those that can prevent dissatisfaction but cannot increase satisfaction (**hygiene factors**).

Unsafe working conditions will cause people to be dissatisfied, but an improvement in working conditions such that they are deemed safe will not lead to a high level of motivation. Hygiene factors are therefore the minimum required to allow employees to avoid feelings of dissatisfaction. Motivators, however, must be in place before employees will be highly motivated to excel at their work. Motivators influence the level of satisfaction gained from individual experiences, and so are the intrinsic factors that are directly related to *doing* a job. They focus on achievement, recognition, responsibility, the work itself and elements of personal growth directly received by performing the work. Hygiene factors are extrinsic to performing the job. They are associated with conditions *surrounding* it such as pay, company policies and interpersonal relationships. When hygiene factors are poor, work is dissatisfying.

So, the factors involved in producing job satisfaction and motivation are separate and distinct from the factors that lead to job dissatisfaction – this is the key to understanding Herzberg's two-factor theory of motivation. Unlike movement, true motivation has longer-lasting effects. Because the reward is intrinsic, focused on personal growth and satisfaction, employees don't need to be rewarded incrementally.

IMPLICATIONS OF HERZBERG'S TWO-FACTOR THEORY OF MOTIVATION FOR MANAGERS AND JOB DESIGN

What does this all mean for managers attempting to motivate their workers? The model proposes a very simple message: to motivate employees, focus on improving how the job is structured and what the individual is asked to do. Providing hygiene factors will remove employee dissatisfaction but will not motivate workers to high achievement levels. On the other hand, recognition, challenge and opportunities for personal growth are powerful motivators and will promote high satisfaction and performance.

However, as with all theories, this one is not without its critics. It has been claimed that the model is overly simplistic; for example, is it always possible to distinguish hygiene factors from motivational ones? Supervision would be classed as a hygiene factor in Herzberg's theory,

motivators influence job satisfaction based on fulfilling higher-level needs such as achievement, recognition, responsibility

hygiene factors focus on lower-order needs and involve the presence or absence of job dissatisfiers, such as working conditions and pay

BUILDING YOUR SKILLS

Pay as a Motivator

There is increasing understanding among managers of the importance of employee recognition given the difficulties associated with using pay as a motivator. In economically difficult times how do you motivate employees if you have no financial rewards to offer? Or if you do offer employees financial rewards, do you simply keep paying more and more to continue to motivate them? Is there a limit to the amount of money available to motivate staff? If there is a limit to how much you can offer them, what happens when you reach the maximum? How do you motivate those employees who previously were in receipt of financial-only rewards?

© IMAGESOURCE

but we know that the type of supervision an individual receives can potentially increase their motivation to perform at a higher level as well as reduce their dissatisfaction (Locke and Latham, 1990). In this case, the division of factors into those that impact on *doing* the job and those concerned with the conditions *surrounding* the job, while appealing, falls down.

One of the main contributions of Herzberg's two-factor theory was the increased emphasis it placed on how jobs are designed; for example, how different tasks and skills should be combined into jobs so as to maximise the motivation of the individual to perform them. Designing jobs in such a way as to give employees greater feelings of responsibility, accomplishment and achievement can affect their individual motivation.

JOB CHARACTERISTICS MODEL

The work of Herzberg became fashionable again in the 1970s, despite the criticisms levelled against it, because of its implications for job design, and in particular the idea of job enrichment. The ability to revise jobs to give employees a greater feeling of responsibility, accomplishment and achievement which can in turn impact on their motivation is a powerful message which appeals to organisations. This approach is more likely to come from internal sources and thus have a longer-lasting effect.

job enrichment increasing the complexity of a job to provide a greater sense of responsibility, accomplishment and achievement

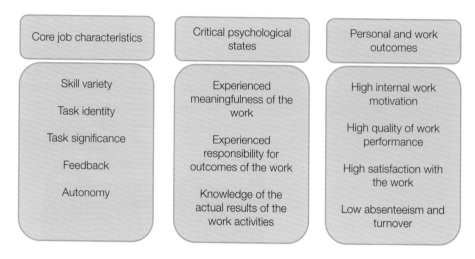

Figure 5.3 Job characteristics model

Source: Adapted from Hackman and Oldham (1975).

The **job characteristics model** developed by Hackman and Oldham (1976) emphasises three components of jobs with high potential for increased motivation (see Figure 5.3):

- Core job characteristics – the level of skill variety, task identity, task significance, feedback and autonomy.
- Critical psychological states – the level of experienced meaningfulness of the work, the experienced responsibility for outcomes of the work, and knowledge of the actual results of the work activities.
- Expected outcomes – high outcomes would result in internal work motivation, growth satisfaction, work effectiveness and general job satisfaction.

Not all employees will seek out more responsibility or more challenging work, but many do, particularly over time. Who wants to go to work day after day, week after week and undertake the same tasks, using the same skills while having little, if any, say in how, when, where or why things are done the way they are? Who would not rather work in an organisation where every day you get to do different things, where you are faced with different problems or challenges and have to use different problem-solving skills to get results? More and more organisations, therefore, have paid attention to the motivational content of their employees' jobs and are thinking about structuring roles in such a way as to maximise their motivational content for the person charged with undertaking them. The job characteristics model states that the more the five core job characteristics can be designed into a role, the higher will be the employee's motivation and performance, quality of work and overall job satisfaction.

The following questions are useful in identifying the five core characteristics for each job:

1 *Skill variety:* How many different activities and skills does the job require?
2 *Task identity:* Do you complete an entire piece of work or just a part of it?
3 *Task significance:* Do others see what you do as important? Does what you do have an impact? Does it make a difference to others?

4   *Autonomy:* Can you plan and schedule your work in your own way?

5   *Feedback:* How much information do you receive about your performance?

Skill variety, task identity and task significance tend to influence the employee's psychological state of experienced meaningfulness of work. This essentially means that improving these factors can ensure that the work itself is satisfying and provides opportunity for intrinsic rewards for the employee. If work can be designed in such a way as to provide workers with situations in which they are required to use different skills, to achieve an identifiable piece of work which has a visible outcome and has a meaningful impact on the lives of other people within the organisation then it is likely to be highly motivational.

Autonomy influences workers' experience of responsibility. This speaks to the degree to which an individual has freedom and discretion to decide the individual scheduling of the work and to determine the approach or procedures used to carry it out. The greater the level of autonomy an individual has, the more likely it is to be motivational. Finally, feedback provides the worker with knowledge of actual results. The employee thus knows how he or she is doing and can change work performance to increase the likelihood of achieving desired outcomes.

MANAGERIAL IMPLICATIONS OF THE JOB CHARACTERISTICS MODEL

The job characteristics model highlights a number of important considerations for managers. In creating or redesigning roles, the more managers can include elements of the core job characteristics into the role, in terms of skill variety, task identity and significance with feedback and high levels of the autonomy, the more likely those roles are to motivate the individual tasked with completing them. Having input regarding *how* and *when* you do certain parts of your job are important motivating factors for individuals, as is the opportunity to see how your job fits into the broader fulfilment of the goals of the team or organisation. A sense of 'my job matters' and 'I understand how it contributes' is a very powerful motivator for most employees. For managers looking at implementing the insights from this model, a good rule of thumb is to try to make the roles of those who report to them more like their own!

BUILDING YOUR SKILLS

Applying the Job Characteristics Model

Choose a job you are familiar with – it could be a job you currently have or have done in the past or one that someone you know has. Don't just pick a job at random because you really need to have background knowledge of the responsibilities, drawbacks, challenges, plusses and minuses of the job in order to do this exercise. Now look at the core job characteristics and see how you might, as a manager, increase the motivational potential of the role in question by adding greater depth or complexity to the role under each of the five headings.

ACQUIRED NEEDS THEORY

David McClelland (1985) adopted a similar but slightly different approach to factors which influence individuals' motivation. He argued that certain types of needs are acquired during a person's lifetime. Individuals have very different life experiences and the learned or acquired needs which come from these become 'enduring predispositions' that are almost like personality traits and can be activated by certain cues in the environment. The three key needs he identified are:

- *Need for achievement* – the drive to accomplish something difficult, surpass others, and master complex tasks.
- *Need for affiliation* – the desire to form close personal relationships and avoid conflict.
- *Need for power* – the desire to influence or control others and have authority over them.

Individuals with a high need for achievement tend to prefer work which has a moderate level of task difficulty, have a preference for personal responsibility for their actions, like taking moderate risks, and desire specific and concrete feedback on their performance. The need for achievement has received the most widespread attention from researchers and it appears to be present in all cultures, although the percentage of those with a high need for achievement varies from country to country (Erez and Earley, 1993). Individuals with a high need for affiliation seek to resolve conflicts, make decisions, and interact with others in the organisation in a positive and collaborative manner. They seek to enhance their relationships with others and develop a common understanding. These individuals are concerned with being liked and respected by their supervisors, peers and subordinates in the workplace.

Finally, the desire for power is a tremendous source of motivation ▶ **Chapter 9** ◀. Not only does power determine an individual's standing within an organisation, but it is also a reflection of the individual's importance to that organisation. McClelland argued that some individuals actively seek to gain and use power. Having power to influence decisions or other people can itself be a source of great personal satisfaction. A high need for power has been associated with aggressive reactions as well as with managerial success (McClelland, 1971). McClelland suggested that a high need for power, if unrestrained, can lead to actions indicative of a desire to dominate others and to triumph, particularly at someone else's expense.

To recap, content theories of motivation are those theories which focus on what needs a person is trying to satisfy and what features of the work environment appear to satisfy those needs. So, content theories focus on both the particular needs of the individual, which are internal to them and act as a source of motivation, and the external forces, which need to be in place to satisfy the individual's needs. We move on now to look at process theories of motivation.

PROCESS THEORIES

Process theories of motivation focus on the way different variables combine to influence the amount of effort people are willing to put into something. Where content theories of motivation focus on *which* variable affects motivation, process theories focus on *how* the variable affects it. Three process theories will be discussed in this section, namely equity theory, expectancy theory and goal setting theory.

EQUITY THEORY

Equity theory was developed in the early 1960s by Stacy Adams and emphasises the social aspect of motivation. This focus on the social dimension of motivation is a recognition that individuals do not work in a vacuum; they work with people in various social networks. The theory proposes that individuals are motivated to change their effort levels in response to comparisons between their own situation and that of others. So in essence the theory assumes that individuals are fully aware of the kind of effort and skill they put into their jobs and the level of outcomes, for example, salary and promotions, they expect to receive in return. The theory also assumes that individuals are likely to compare the amount of effort they put into their job to the level of outcomes they receive; in other words, they evaluate whether the amount of effort they expend is worth the outcome they receive as a result. In addition, the individual will also look around to see what effort others expend and what outcomes *they* receive as a result. By comparing these situations an individual determines whether he or she feels fairly treated.

So, what does this look like in reality? Suppose that you have a job working in a supermarket. Part of your role is to restock the shelves and you agree to do this for €8 per hour. You feel that €8 an hour is a reasonable rate of pay for this task. It is not the best paid job in the world, so you take a view that you are not prepared to go above and beyond what is required. You will do what you can, within the time you are there. Honestly, you could probably do more but you feel that for the level of pay that is on offer you are not prepared to exert yourself more than necessary, and you see this as a reasonable trade-off. You begin your first week of work and something surprising happens. You talk to your co-workers and they tell you that they are being paid €11 an hour, which is €3 hour per hour more than you. You feel that they work no harder than you and that they expend no more effort than you. You stack as many shelves as they do, in the same way and in the same time period. Why should they get €3 more? You think this situation is grossly unfair and so you reassess your situation, about which you are pretty angry. It *feels* unfair. Why should you get paid less than the others for the same work? The options available to you are straightforward: you can quit your job, you can approach your boss and ask to be paid the same as your work colleagues, or you might decide that a pay rise is unlikely and that you need the job even though it isn't fair that you get paid less for doing the same work as others. In this case, you could decide to decrease your level of effort to reflect the amount of pay you received.

Alternatively, you could take a slightly different approach and try to rationalise why you are paid less than the others. You might decide not to compare yourself to this group at all but instead to your university friends (referent group) who all earn the same as you, making you feel that perhaps this is a fair rate for the work. You could also re-evaluate the individuals you

equity theory a process-based motivational theory that focuses on how individuals compare their circumstances to those of others and attempts to explain how such comparisons may motivate certain kinds of behaviour

work with in terms of their experience or skill set and decide that they bring something to the role which merits them getting paid more than you. They may have worked there for longer, or have an additional responsibility attached to their role. In this way you can re-evaluate your sense of unfairness about the situation. All these scenarios are summarised in Table 5.1.

But what happens if, rather than perceiving yourself to be disadvantaged, you perceive yourself as having an advantage? What happens if you are the one being paid €11 when someone else is being paid €8? In this case the theory suggests that you would increase your inputs or decrease your outputs to realign the balance between effort and return. That is to say, you would work harder to justify your extra pay or seek a reduction in your pay to regain balance. In reality, however, common sense suggests that most people would be happy to be paid more, to just take the cash and run!

The difficulty with equity theory is that it doesn't help us to predict which method people will use in which specific setting or situation. It doesn't indicate who will quit, who will reduce their efforts or who will change their comparison group. What the theory does do, however, is emphasise that it is the individual's *perception* of equity when compared to others' circumstances which is so powerful and has such a magnified impact upon motivation. The important lesson from equity theory for managers is the ability to recognise that not all employees will be motivated in the same way or react in the same way. It is their perception of fairness, whether based in reality or not, which will ultimately influence how they react.

EXPECTANCY THEORY

Expectancy theory focuses on individuals' thought processes as they choose between alternative actions in the workplace (Vroom, 1964). In deciding how much effort to put into a task, individuals first perform an internal assessment, or calculation inside their head. The first thing they consider is the effort to performance ratio – the probability that a certain amount of effort on their part will lead to a certain level of performance. For example, if I do 100 stomach crunches a day I would have a reasonable expectation that after a year my stomach would be flat and toned. The second thing people consider is the probability that a particular level of performance will lead to particular outcomes. So, if I have a flat stomach my chances of getting a new boyfriend are greatly increased! From a work perspective, the answer to these internal questions in relation to effort and outcome will result in an employee being motivated to perform a certain task at a certain level or to be demotivated to undertake such a task.

The third point they consider is the valence of a particular outcome – the anticipated value that a person attaches to it. In our example this would be that I would like to have a new boyfriend as I haven't had one in more than three years (high valence) or I already have

expectancy theory a process-based theory of motivation that focuses on the thought processes people use when choosing between alternative courses of action and their anticipated consequences

valence the extent to which an individual values a particular outcome

Table 5.1 Basics of equity theory explained using the example of a job in a supermarket

If	the ratio of my outcomes to my inputs	is	equal to the ratio of the others' outcomes to inputs	then	I am satisfied	and I am motivated to	do nothing
If	the €8 an hour I am paid for the work	is	perceived by me to be equal to the pay and effort of my colleagues	then	I am happy with my pay and the work I am asked to do	and I am motivated to	do nothing
HOWEVER							
If	the ratio of my outcomes to my inputs	is	less than the ratio of the others' outcomes to inputs	then	I am dissatisfied (inequity)	and I am motivated to	increase my own outcomes by either: • decreasing my own inputs, or • re-evaluating the others' inputs, or • changing the referent, or • leaving the situation
If	the €8 an hour I am paid for the work	is	perceived by me to be less pay for the same effort of my colleagues doing the same work	then	I am really annoyed. I am seriously unhappy that I get paid less	and I am motivated to	either: • quit my job, or • put in less effort, or • re-evaluate why I am paid less by considering my colleagues may have other responsibilities, or • rationalise it by looking at my university friends who are all paid €8 an hour

a boyfriend who I deeply love and respect (low valence). If the valence of rewards offered is high, there is potential for increased motivation. Equally, if the anticipated value of the reward is low or the offered rewards are not relevant to the individual, motivation is likely to be weak. Let's take another example. I believe that studying hard will lead to higher grades in my final year exams. In turn, by achieving higher grades in my final year exams I believe that I will be more likely to get my dream job. I am therefore more likely to study hard because I believe that this effort will lead in the first place to higher grades, which in turn is likely to result in the job that I have always wanted. However, if I genuinely believe that no matter how hard I study I am unlikely to improve my grades, I am unlikely to invest that effort despite really wanting that dream job. Equally, if I believe that, despite working really hard and studying all day and night, my high grades are unlikely to get me a foot in the door of my dream job, it is unlikely that I will be motivated to go that extra mile. Therefore, the three variables are multiplicative rather than additive. Low values in any one of the variables lead to low motivation, as we can see from the example. If any variable is zero, there is zero motivation to make any effort. So, if I don't believe that extra study will result in a higher grade, if I don't believe that higher grades will lead to a job or I don't value that job in the first place then I will not be motivated to make any extra effort. This relationship can be expressed as an equation:

$$\text{Effort} = (E \rightarrow P) \times (P \rightarrow O) \times V$$

where:

E→P is the expectancy that a particular level of effort will lead to a particular level of performance

P→O is the probability that a particular level of performance will lead to particular outcomes

V is the anticipated value a person attaches to an outcome

IMPLICATIONS FOR MANAGERS ARISING FROM EXPECTANCY THEORY

Expectancy theory has been widely embraced by both academic researchers and managers in organisations. One of the reasons for its popularity with managers is that it suggests explicit ways to improve workers' performance. If managers can improve workers' confidence in their performance ability by increasing training to improve skills or by mentoring or providing feedback, then it is likely that employees will be more motivated because they will believe that their increased ability to perform will result in some sort of reward. Managers should be consistent in their application of rewards and positive feedback to facilitate this. They should also think carefully about what rewards and outcomes are really valued by their employees. There is little point in offering an employee reward that is of little perceived value to them personally. A good example of this is offering employees very generous retirement benefits when younger employees would probably place more value on the cash equivalent or additional days of annual leave. Organisations have a habit of assuming they know what employees value, yet they rarely do a sense-checking exercise to see if this is really true. Managers need to know their employees and understand what it is that they value in order to make whatever rewards and outcomes they offer have high valence to them.

GOAL-SETTING THEORY

The third process theory is goal-setting theory which emphasises the importance of conscious goals and intentions in directing human behaviour (Locke, 1968). The idea is that if managers can influence employees' goals and intentions then they can directly influence performance. What is critical to the success of this approach is an understanding of the importance of the *level* at which the goals are set and the *commitment* of individuals to the goals. We know that the more challenging (higher or harder) goals result in more effort than easier goals, but only if the individual accepts and commits to the goal achievement (Nicholson, 2003). General or vague goals are less effective. Equally, goals that are perceived as too easy will not result in any additional effort so it is unlikely that they will be seen as motivational. Specific and clear goals are more likely to result in higher levels of effort (Britt, 2003).

SMART goal-setting requires that goals should be Specific, Measurable, Achievable, Realistic and Time-bound. Crucially, it is important that goals are not set so high as to make them unachievable, but also when setting goals managers must work hard to get employee buy-in and commitment to their achievement; otherwise they quickly become pointless. There is little point to setting a goal which is unachievable, and in doing so you are likely to demotivate employees. The 'Goldilocks' principle needs to be applied to the setting of goals – not too high, not too low but just challenging enough to stretch individuals while ensuring that, when the goals are achieved, they are appropriately recognised.

IMPLICATIONS FOR MANAGERS ARISING FROM GOAL-SETTING THEORY

For managers it can be difficult to correctly assess whether or not a goal is set too high for an individual. In the workplace it is often the case that individuals are tasked with more than one goal and so the balancing act becomes more complex as more goals are added to the mix. Most organisations use goal setting as part of their performance management system. Without clear performance goals and feedback, most people are not committed to work and are not inclined to give their best effort (Locke and Latham, 2002). Participation in the goal-setting process is likely to lead to greater employee acceptance of the goal and therefore higher motivation to achieve it, but again this is challenging for managers to balance. What happens when you have 15 people reporting to you directly and each has 6 goals? How much time do you spend working through the goal-setting phase, let alone the measurement of their success? It can very quickly become a time-consuming process and particularly where the goals have to be documented, as in a performance management system, for example.

goal-setting theory emphasises the importance of conscious goals and intentions in directing human behaviour

SMART goal-setting goals which are specific, measurable, achievable, realistic and time-bound

Finally, feedback on the achievement of goals is a very important aspect of the critical success of goal-setting theory. The more feedback an individual receives about how they are doing in terms of achieving the goals set the better. There is little motivational value in waiting until 12 months after the goal was set, only to inform a person that they have failed to achieve it. Regular feedback in terms of how the individual is doing against the target is more likely to result in increased effort and/or continued high performance. It is just as important to recognise high performance among staff as it is to tackle poor performance.

To recap what we have just learned in the first two sections of this chapter, content theories are those which focus on what needs a person is trying to satisfy and on what features of the work environment seem to satisfy them. On the other hand, process theories are those which focus on the way different variables combine to influence the amount of effort people are willing to make in order to gain some outcome. Although these two sets of theories offer us insights into what, how and when people are likely to be motivated we must also consider what happens to an individual following the action they have taken, that is to say, what the consequences of the behaviour were. The consequences can be positive (in terms of reward for desired behaviour) or negative (in terms of punishment for undesirable behaviour). Consideration of the consequences and the use of reinforcement theory will provide managers with another set of tools to use in motivating their employees to engage in behaviours which help the organisation as a whole to achieve its goals.

The Influence of Organisational Culture on Motivation at Netflix

Netflix has been a real success story in the US and is rapidly expanding across the globe. This success has attracted a lot of attention from rivals in industry, academics and practitioners alike. The facts that during 2013 alone the stock price for Netflix more than tripled and that the company's US subscriber base was up to nearly 29 million are likely to explain some of this interest. So what is it about Netflix and its approach which is so compelling? Firstly, the company set out to 'craft a culture of excellence.' This is evident in everything they do, but particularly in relation to their

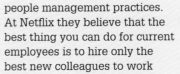 OB IN THE NEWS

people management practices. At Netflix they believe that the best thing you can do for current employees is to hire only the best new colleagues to work alongside them. This sentiment is captured beautifully in the statement that 'adequate performance gets a generous severance package!' Netflix managers do not tolerate people who only perform to a passable standard and, when they recruit an individual who turns out not to be a true high performer, they let him or her go, albeit with a generous payment.

Netflix also does not conduct any formal reviews. The organisation believes that performance should be discussed on an ongoing basis, year round. They strongly advocate that managers be as honest as possible with their subordinates about how they are doing and where an employee is not up to standard, that they let them go. They do not believe in performance improvement plans for low performers on the basis that it just prolongs the inevitable. If someone isn't a good fit for the organisational culture ▶Chapter 12◀ then they should let them go. This approach is very different from that of other organisations which have formal review systems in place and a lengthy process to deal with underperformance issues, including providing employees with time to improve or address shortcomings. The approach advocated by Netflix appears harsh, yet the logic is hard to argue with, particularly if the underperforming employee receives a generous severance package on leaving.

Furthermore, Netflix don't pay bonuses because they believe they are unnecessary if you hire the right person in the first instance. A bonus is unlikely to motivate the 'right' person to work harder or smarter; if they are committed to the company and believe in its values then they will work to their absolute best all the time and a bonus isn't going to make them more motivated. Compared to other high-tech companies, the reality is that the financial reward or pay that

they do offer their employees is likely to be as good, if not higher, than competitors, which allows them to recruit the best people in the first place. But a decision not to pay bonuses is a brave one, given the fact that they are the norm in other organisations. Yet Netflix has a reputation for this strong culture and those who go to work there appear to embrace it.

This strong organisational culture is built around a clear understanding of how the company operates and what drives the business. This, they believe, is the key to motivating employees. Even when you have recruited well you need to clearly communicate how the company makes money and what behaviours will drive its success. In doing this you demonstrate to employees the direct link between the impact of their actions and the success of the organisation. Netflix also acknowledges that not all employees are the same and that within any

© ISTOCK/NIOLOX

company there are subcultures that need to be managed differently. The employees who work in the company call centre are very different from those who work at company headquarters. Awareness of the different subcultures and what makes each tick is the key to good leadership.

Questions

1 Do you think this non-traditional approach to the management of people is likely to be effective in all organisations? Do you think you would find it motivating if you were an employee of Netflix? Explain your answer.

2 Paying bonuses is typical in most high-tech companies, particularly in the US. Why do you think Netflix has been so successful in attracting and retaining talented staff despite this fact?

3 What dangers, if any, can you see with having such a strong dominant organisational culture?

4 Reading through the Netflix case, what theories of motivation do you recognise as being deployed by the organisation?

REINFORCEMENTS AND CONSEQUENCES

Managers have the ability to use reinforcements and consequences as motivational tools for their employees. If an individual receives a reward for a particular behaviour, then he or she is more likely to repeat that behaviour. If on the other hand, an individual receives a rebuke/punishment for a particular behaviour he or she is less likely to engage in that activity again. The consequences of exhibiting certain behaviour can be positive or negative, and both can be used to equal effect by managers in a deliberate way to drive desired behaviour among their employees.

POSITIVE REINFORCEMENT

Positive reinforcements are desirable consequences that follow a behaviour and are likely to increase the chances of that behaviour being repeated in the future. We often use positive reinforcement with children – good behaviour can result in a treat being offered. The hope is that the child will remember the treat and the link to their good behaviour and will be more likely to repeat the behaviour in future. Good behaviour in the form of achieving specific goals or reaching challenging targets in a work setting may result in a financial reward in the form of a bonus. The organisation gives the bonus to signal to the individuals that this kind of behaviour is desirable and valued. Basically the organisation is saying, if you do more of this kind of work we will reward you with more of this kind of reward.

Positive reinforcements, however, can result in unintended consequences. Imagine a call centre where the supervisor informs staff that they will receive a bonus if they answer 200 calls in any two-hour period. Without any link to the quality of the call in terms of customer satisfaction, it is likely that the employee will answer those 200 calls but not deal with them fully, or in a manner which would be expected by the organisation. In this way managers need to be careful of the behaviours that their positive reinforcement promotes and ensure that there are no unintended consequences.

NEGATIVE REINFORCEMENT AND PUNISHMENTS

Negative reinforcement occurs when an undesirable consequence decreases the likelihood of an individual engaging in an undesirable behaviour again. Once the individual stops engaging in the undesirable behaviour, the undesirable consequence also stops or is removed.

Punishments are exactly that – unwanted consequences following an undesirable behaviour that are intended to decrease the likelihood of that behaviour being repeated. The effectiveness of punishments as a way to motivate desired behaviour is questionable. For one thing. an individual has to have already engaged in undesirable behaviour before the punishment can be dealt – it comes after the fact and so can have limited impact. It can also be difficult to predict the impact of these kinds of punishments on employees, and in some cases it may even demotivate employees further. Within an organisational context, an example of punishment might be the use of the disciplinary policy if an individual is persistently late in attending their place of work. The policy may state that the individual is given a verbal warning in the first instance, followed by a formal warning if the behaviour continues, leading ultimately to dismissal if there is no attempt to amend or explain why the lateness continues.

positive reinforcements desirable consequences that follow a behaviour and are likely to increase the chances of that behaviour being repeated in the future

negative reinforcement an undesirable consequence that decreases the likelihood of an individual engaging in an undesirable behaviour again

punishments unwanted consequences following an undesirable behaviour that are intended to decrease the likelihood of that behaviour being repeated

EXTINCTION

Extinction is simply the absence of positive consequences in an effort to decrease undesirable behaviour. If you don't want a behaviour to be repeated, then don't praise the behaviour or acknowledge it in any way. Managers often use this approach at the same time as praising the behaviours they want to be repeated. An example of this would be where an individual demonstrates overly aggressive behaviour in arguing a point at a team meeting. Rather than respond to the aggression, the manager simply moves the meeting on to the next point on the agenda. In doing so, the manager hopes that the individual is given a clear message that overly aggressive behaviour at meetings is something which the team are not willing to engage with. There is a danger, however, that managers can lose focus and simply forget to reinforce a desired behaviour, which can also result in the extinction of that behaviour.

CONSIDER THIS...

A mother is concerned about letting her teenage son borrow the family car. In particular, she is concerned that he may be tempted to drive above the legal speed limit. To overcome her concern that her son might engage in undesirable behaviour (speeding) when she isn't around she has the car fitted with an alarm which sounds when the car is driven at an excessive speed. Once her son reduces his speed below the legal limit the alarm will stop. While very simplistic, it is very effective. No matter how hard the son tries to drown out the noise of the alarm with the radio it is extremely annoying.

© BANANASTOCK

WHAT ROLE DO SITUATIONAL FACTORS PLAY IN INFLUENCING MOTIVATION?

There is more to motivation than simply looking at individual behaviour. What role, if any, does the situational context have on motivating behaviour? People do not work in a vacuum. According to Gallup's 2013 State of the American Workplace report, only 30 per cent of employees in the US actively apply their talent and energy to move their organisations forward. Fifty per cent are just putting their time in, while 20 per cent act out their discontent in ways which are directly negative for the organisation – negatively influencing

extinction the absence of positive consequences in an effort to decrease undesirable behaviour

their co-workers, taking sick days while not actually sick, providing poor customer service or at the most extreme sabotaging the organisation by ignoring problems. It is clear that, while there are individual factors which influence motivation (push factors which are internal to an individual), there are also pull factors which operate externally to an individual and have the potential to influence motivation. This section will take a closer look at three of those factors, namely the influence of co-workers, supervisors and the organisation's culture.

INFLUENCE OF CO-WORKERS

One of the biggest situational factors which impact upon individual motivation is the influence of the immediate work group. The ability of groups to strongly influence the motivation of individual members cannot be underestimated. This influence can be either positive or negative but is equally powerful in either direction. The ability of groups to influence individual behaviour is prefaced on there being a strong group identity, an in-group, with established norms which have been developed over time, whose members seek the approval of the rest of the group ▶ **Chapter 4** ◀. Where such a strong in-group identity exists, the group's influence will almost certainly impact on the level of effort or motivation a person exhibits.

Consider this example. John began working as a porter in a children's hospital. His job required him to collect patients from wards and departments and bring them to other areas of the hospital for various appointments and procedures. One of the most important aspects of the role was ensuring that patients were brought down to the surgical units on time so as not to delay the surgical list. John was enthusiastic and keen to make a good impression when he began his new job. He went about his work as quickly and efficiently as possible and believed he was doing a good job. He managed to get through all his allocated tasks quickly and without fuss. Over lunch one day, however, a number of John's new colleagues told him he needed to slow down because his fast-paced work was making them look bad. To John the message was clear: if you want to be 'one of us' you need to toe the line. John strongly wanted to get the approval of his work colleagues and did not want to be excluded, so he subsequently altered his behaviour to bring it into line with their expectations. He worked more slowly and as a result maintained his position as one of the in-group but at the expense of the organisation he worked for.

INFLUENCE OF SUPERVISORS

In the same way that co-workers and the desire to be a part of an in-group can drive motivational levels either positively or negatively, so too can the influence of supervisors ▶ **Chapter 8** ◀. Supervisors, as we know from an earlier section, have within their power the ability to reward or punish employees. They equally have the ability to set expectations around what is and is not acceptable behaviour. However as with rewards, the ability of supervisors to motivate performance varies from individual to individual. The same supervisor can be a source of increased motivation for some employees, while having the opposite effect on others. The potential impact of the supervisor on subordinates is heavily dependent on the one-to-one interpersonal relationship they have developed over time.

Consider this example. When managing a football team the coach needs to pay attention to what motivates each individual player. There are always players who require gentle handling, a quiet word in their ear and encouragement to drive on their performance. There are others who respond better to the side-line calls and shouted demands for better performance. The key to getting the very best out of each player from a coaching perspective is to know each individual and what motivates him or her. It is a mistake to think that talented employees are so skilled and motivated that they don't need supervisor attention. The reality is that superstar performers need as much, if not more, of their manager's attention. High performers want their manager to track their performance, to recognise their efforts and give them rewards for those efforts. They crave feedback on a job well done and want to be seen to be doing a good job. Often high performers are looking to develop and move to the next level in terms of challenge. The role of a supportive, motivational manager is to recognise this need in their star performers and to ensure these opportunities for development are available to them to maintain this level of high performance.

SPOTLIGHT ON SKILLS

Given what you know about motivation how would you approach the challenge of motivating a group of colleagues at work to get involved in training for four months for a charity 10k fun run?

1 What factors would you emphasise to motivate them? What measures would you put in place to monitor and track their performance?

2 What action would you take if someone was not motivated over the stretch of the four months?

3 Why do you think that people are motivated initially towards a goal or objective, but then find it hard to maintain this over the long term?

To help you answer these questions, in your ebook click the play button to watch the video of Clare Hodder, a freelance rights consultant, talking about motivation.

INFLUENCE OF ORGANISATIONAL CULTURE

O'Reilly (1989) talks about culture as a form of social control. By this, he argues that individuals who work together and share a common set of expectations will try to live up to the expectations of their colleagues if they agree with them. This idea is often more effective than formal control systems. Culture is frequently defined simply as 'how we do things around here' ▸Chapter 12◂. The beliefs that such a culture nurtures result in norms that powerfully shape the behaviour of individuals and groups. Norms are expectations about what are appropriate and inappropriate attitudes and behaviour. Where a strong culture exists within an organisation these acceptable norms are very evident and send strong messages to employees.

MONEY AS A MOTIVATOR – A SPECIAL CASE

Organisations use money to attract, motivate and retain employees. It is used to reward good performance, to motivate work yet to be done and withheld from those who have not performed as expected in their work. Yet we know that a reward that effectively motivates one individual doesn't necessarily work for another, and we also know that there are other problems associated with offering financial rewards to employees to motivate them. Yet despite this, most organisations persist in using financial rewards as their primary motivational tool. So let's take a closer look at the arguments against using monetary rewards to motivate employees.

Money or financial incentives are often criticised as motivators. They tend to have a short-term focus and are, by their very nature, temporary. Once you receive the reward you are no longer motivated by it. In this way there is a danger that they become the focus and that the employee loses interest in the actual work. For example, imagine you are a sales representative in a mobile phone shop and you have been told that if you achieve your target of selling 500 phones in the coming year you will receive a 20 per cent bonus. You achieve your target after only six months. Where is the motivation or incentive for the remaining six months of the year? What is the likely impact? Would you work as hard as you had been for the previous six months or do you think you might take your foot off the pedal?

In some organisations the setting of specific targets like this can negatively impact upon performance because employees are only interested in achieving the target set and are not incentivised to go beyond it. Worse still, by setting targets like this you may even be incentivising individuals to delay their performance so as to increase their chances of achieving their target the following year. This doesn't just apply in a sales environment, but across organisations. The achievement of a target or goal can mean that better ways of working and serving clients' needs may go undiscovered because there is no incentive to improve the process if the target can be achieved.

Financial rewards assume that people are motivated by lower-level needs. While money is important, and we all need a certain amount of it, it would appear that it is no substitute for higher-level needs. When met, these higher-level needs have a much more long-lasting effect. When an individual is focused on the achievement of a particular extrinsic goal it often comes at the expense of intrinsic rewards. If we take the example of our sales representative in the mobile phone shop, what if, rather than a 20 per cent bonus for achieving a target of selling 500 phones in any given year, the staff were told that those sales representatives who consistently performed above expectation would be in line for promotion to store manager? What do you think would be the likely impact of this incentive over pure financial incentives for the sales representatives? Do you think they would be more or less motivated? Do you think they would be likely to focus on long- or short-term goals? Do you think they would be more or less likely to engage in mis-selling products to customers knowing they were not what the customer needed? Why do you think this might be?

We move now to look at the issue of motivating people in groups or teams, rather than individually.

TEAM MOTIVATION

While individual motivation is obviously very important, most of us work in teams at least some of the time and it is therefore important to consider three additional motivational issues that arise specifically in relation to teams. Team motivation arises when there is agreed collective effort on the part of a group of people aimed at achieving a common goal. In order for a team to be motivated two key features are required. Individual members of the team must believe that other members of the team have the variety of skills and knowledge necessary to achieve the team's goals. In addition, however, the team must be able to bring these together in order to effectively perform the task that has been set ▶ Chapter 7 ◀.

Let's take an example. Imagine you have been tasked with a group-based assignment as part of one your modules. The lecturer has assigned students to each team – you didn't get to choose your team members. The first thing you do when the details of the assessment are announced is to check who is on your team. You check firstly to see if the people on your team are the brighter students from your class, if they are known to be good at presentations, report writing or analysing cases. If they are, you begin to feel confident that you can achieve a high grade for the assignment. However, if you doubt that any one member of the team, or worse, more than one, is unable to perform at the level required, then your motivation suffers dramatically. Enhancing team motivation therefore requires that team members must be encouraged to have confidence in each other's ability and if that confidence is damaged, it must be repaired quickly and effectively (Clark, 2003).

Your attention then turns to how well the group will work together to get the job done. At the first team meeting it becomes clear that, despite the fact that you have a strong team of individuals, there are very different opinions about how to get the task completed. Although there is a wide range of skills and knowledge within the team, the group is unable to agree on how best to proceed, or what the main focus of the assignment will be. This is the second factor impacting on team motivation. Collaboration is an essential requirement for team success. Teams must be able to find a way to work together for the common good of achieving the overall goal set for them. Uncooperative, highly independent but talented team members can wreck team motivation by refusing to work effectively with other team members (Clark, 2003).

This brings us to another problem that is often encountered among teams, and not just in a college assignment setting: social loafing. Social loafing refers to a team member who

team motivation arises when there is agreed collective effort on the part of a group of people aimed at achieving a common goal

social loafing refers to a team member who benefits from team membership but does not actively participate in, or contribute to, the team's work

benefits from team membership but does not actively participate in, or contribute to, the team's work. How many times have you been working in a team where one member has not been pulling their weight? Some people believe that because they are part of a team they need not work as hard as if they had to complete the task on their own. They are happy to let others do most of the work and while they are prepared to contribute, their contribution is often less than if they had to complete the task on their own. There can be many reasons for social loafing. Sometimes an individual is not technically as competent as other team members and therefore takes a back seat, sometimes they find it difficult to speak up and have their views heard, and sometimes the individual is quite happy to hide behind the efforts of others.

So how do you tackle social loafing? Clark and Estes (2002) found there was a very simple answer. When you assess the individual contribution of each member of the team, social loafing disappears. Therefore in a business context, in order for teams to be motivated, each team member must understand what their contribution is and how this contribution will be measured by the organisation.

A Tale of Two Sports

Soccer

In 2013 Welsh forward Gareth Bale completed a world record £85 million (€100 million) transfer from Tottenham to Real Madrid. His earnings were reported to be £300,000 a week for the six-year contract. That meant that Bale's new contract would see him earn in one week what many of those who watch him from the stands in the Estadio Bernabeu would earn in ten years. This prompts a number of questions but first among them has to be, 'Does any football player deserve to be paid so much?'

It has been argued that footballers' wages are dictated by the market. It is simple supply and demand and where a footballer is believed to be

so talented as to make the difference between winning and losing for his club, then the market price of that player is likely to increase significantly, particularly when more than one club is interested in securing his talents. Football clubs are no different from any other business. They expect to see a return on their investment and they believe their club will be more successful and their brand more lucrative as a result of paying such a high price for a player. If Real Madrid increase their level of success at competitions both nationally and internationally, through winning La Liga and then the Champions League, for example, they are more likely to attract bigger corporate sponsors and increase their sales and

advertising revenues, not to mention the in-flow of cash from merchandising. Football is now big business.

To be fair you could argue that a footballer's career is a relatively short one and so they have a very limited timeframe in which to make all the money they will need for the rest of their days. The average career span of a footballer is just eight years, with the longest careers spanning between sixteen and twenty years. This does not take into account the fact that many never make it to the top tier of football or that those that do may suffer a career-ending injury. Many footballers have no alternative career path should football not work out. While the junior academy system set up in most major clubs supports players in gaining an education, this tends to be relatively limited. There are few job advertisements seeking nearly-good-enough ex-football players. It is by no means an easy route to becoming a millionaire.

The payment of such extravagant wages to footballers appears to have spiralled out of all proportion, yet it remains to be seen whether paying such high salaries to some players results in better team performances on the pitch. Given that team motivation rises when a group of people agree on a collective effort aimed at achieving a common purpose, it is difficult to see how such payments can assist in this goal.

Source: www.bbc.com/news/uk-23931053 (accessed 19 August 2015).

Rugby

European soccer compares starkly with the experience of the New Zealand rugby team. Between 2004 and 2011, the All

© DIGITAL VISION

Blacks took their winning record from an extraordinary 75% to an almost unbelievable 86%. This incredible winning record has been attributed to a new values-led approach instilled in the team which focuses on a purpose-driven high performance culture. The key to success is the development of the characters of the players off the pitch so that they perform better on it.

The management team looked to put a strategy in place to develop rituals around key behaviours which they believed would drive superior performance. Two rituals stand out in terms of team motivation. The first is 'sweeping out the sheds'. This principle speaks to the value of humility and requires that all players take it in turn to sweep out the dressing room after each training session and/or match. Senior and junior team members are required to take their turn, no one is deemed above it and no one is excused. This simple but effective ritual is based on the principle that success can only be achieved by keeping the players' feet firmly on the ground.

The second ritual is entitled 'follow the spearhead'; grounded in Maori tradition it essentially speaks to the fact that no one player is bigger than the team. The management team deliberately select character over talent, believing that character will deliver better long-term results than short-term individual-driven talent. This has led to the colourful expression 'no d**kheads'

but it means that the All Blacks strive to be a true team, a collective rather than exemplars of individual shows of talent. There is no 'me' in the team, only 'we'.

Another element to the strategy is the idea of 'leaving the jersey in a better place'. This concept of legacy is central to the team's success. Players recognise that their jersey was handed down to them by the great players of the past and that they wear it temporarily before passing it on to the next generation. They are challenged with 'leaving the jersey in a better place'. The All Blacks seek to 'add to the legacy' in everything they do, knowing that higher purpose leads to higher performance.

Questions

1 Which of the approaches do you think is likely to yield better performances from the teams involved? Explain your answer.

2 What is the impact of paying one 'star' player significantly more than their team-mates likely to have on team motivation?

3 Is there any merit in paying all starting members of a team the same rate of pay? Discuss the pros and cons of both approaches.

4 In your groups discuss the likely reactions of Gareth Bale's team-mates to his arrival and the impact on their individual performances.

Source: www.hrzone.com/feature/people/better-people-equals-better-business-lessons-all-blacks/141131 (accessed 21 November 2014).

 SUMMARY

 IN THE EBOOK,
CLICK TO HEAR
AN AUDIO SUMMARY

We can see that motivation in the workplace, while offering enormous potential benefits to both the organisation and the individual, is a highly complex phenomenon. Motivation influences people's decisions to actively choose to undertake a task and to persist at that task over time until it is complete. If managers understand the theories of motivation they offer the potential of a highly motivated and engaged workforce who are likely to drive higher performance. For the individual, being highly motivated is likely to lead to greater job satisfaction, greater sense of achievement and a more fulfilling career. The difficulty, however, is that all individuals are unique and what motivates one may not motivate another. The ability of managers to understand the sources of motivation, both in terms of the internal individual factors which drive motivation and the external situational factors which motivate, are key in organisational life.

CHAPTER REVIEW QUESTIONS

1 Why is an understanding of motivation so important to the success of any organisation?
2 What are 'push' and 'pull' motivational forces? Provide some examples.
3 How can managers affect motivation by changing the content of a job?
4 What are some of the characteristics of an individual with a high need for achievement?
5 According to equity theory, what would happen if some one felt they were being paid less for the same effort as colleagues doing the same work? What options would be open to the individual to address the imbalance?
6 According to expectancy theory, how can managers influence employees' level of motivation?
7 What role do situational factors play in influencing motivation?
8 How is team motivation different from individual motivation?

MULTIPLE CHOICE QUESTIONS

In your ebook, click to take a multiple choice quiz to test your understanding of this chapter.

FURTHER READING

Britt, T.W. (2003). Black Hawk Down at Work. *Harvard Business Review*, 81(1), 16–17.

Clark, R.E. (2003). Fostering the Work Motivation of Individuals and Teams. *Performance Improvement*, 42(3), 21–29.

Kalleberg, A.L. (2008). The Mismatched Worker: When People Don't Fit Their Jobs. *Academy Of Management Perspectives*, 22(1), 24–40.

Kehoe, M. (2013). *Make that Grade: Organisational Behaviour*, 2nd edn, Dublin, Gill & Macmillan Ltd.

McCord, P. (2014). How Netflix Reinvented HR (cover story). *Harvard Business Review*, 92(1/2), 70–76.

Nicholson, N. (2003). How to Motivate Your Problem People. *Harvard Business Review*, 81(1), 56–58.

🌐 USEFUL WEBSITES

http://hbr.org/magazine

The *Harvard Business Review Magazine* website is useful for short, up to date and easy to read management insights into all areas.

www.ted.com/talks/dan_pink_on_motivation

This TED talk on motivation contains some very interesting ideas.

www.motivate.com.au/

This website covers all aspects of motivation from workplace motivation to student motivation.

www.mindtools.com/pages/article/newLDR_57.htm

This links to a short quiz where you can score yourself on how self-motivated you are.

6 EMOTIONS AND THE WORKPLACE

Deirdre O'Shea

LEARNING OUTCOMES

BY THE END OF THIS CHAPTER, YOU SHOULD BE ABLE TO:

- Understand what emotions are and distinguish between affect, mood and emotions.
- Explain the functions of emotions – why do we experience them?
- Explain the various ways in which emotions have an impact in the workplace.
- Identify the impact that 'emotion work' has on employees.
- Learn ways in which employees can effectively manage their emotions in the workplace.

© GETTY IMAGES/ISTOCKPHOTO/XIXINXING

THIS CHAPTER DISCUSSES:

IN REALITY

Research in organisations often assumes that emotions are best left at home; that we make better decisions when we don't engage our emotions, and that emotions are 'bad' in the workplace. However, a world or even a workplace without emotions could be quite different from that which is posited in the rational decision-making models and in economics research that assumes a *homo economicus* (an 'economic human' who is entirely rational and makes decisions based on judgements about how to maximise utility).

Professor of Neuroscience at the University of Southern California, Antonio Damasio, proposed that when we are required to make decisions in complex situations, we cannot rely only on our logic because we are often missing key information. In fact, we can never possess all the information we need to make a completely logical decision. Without the emotional signals that help us to 'mark' each choice as good or bad, we find it almost impossible to decide what to do (Dunn, 2012). Damasio had the opportunity to study a man called Elliot who was completely undisturbed by emotions as a result of a brain tumour. Instead of being a master decision maker, Elliot was unable to perform the most simple of actions. For example, Elliot would endlessly contemplate the pros and cons of writing with a black or blue pen. Even deciding on a restaurant for lunch was a mammoth task. He would evaluate the restaurants' seating arrangements, pricing, menu, and sometimes would even drive to the restaurants to see how busy each one was. Without being able to rely on his 'gut feeling', that is without the ability to consult his emotions, Elliot had to evaluate all the objective evidence in order to decide which restaurant was the best one (see Van Der Lowe, 2012 for a more detailed summary). The effect of this 'paralysis by analysis' was detrimental to Elliot's life; he lost his job, went bankrupt, and his wife divorced him (Van Der Lowe, 2012).

In the workplace, there are famous examples of when decisions made using our 'gut' or because it 'felt right' have had incredible outcomes. For example, Stanislav Petrov has been credited with averting the onset of nuclear war on the basis of a decision that 'felt right'. A lieutenant colonel in the Soviet Defence Forces, he was in charge of the Oko nuclear warning system command centre. On 26 September 1983, the system detected a missile launch from the United States. Instead of initiating a chain of responses to launch a retaliatory attack (which was protocol, and thus the 'rational' response to the threat), he correctly judged that this was a false alarm. When he was asked afterwards by a reporter how he made this decision, he said 'I had a funny feeling in my gut. I didn't want to make a mistake. I made a decision, and that was it.' (See Dunn, 2012, for a more detailed summary).

INTRODUCTION

The study of emotions is central to understanding organisational behaviour, and is becoming an increasingly important topic that both researchers and practitioners need to consider. Indeed, the increased interest in the role of emotions in organisational behaviour has been termed the 'affective revolution' (Barsade *et al.*, 2003). Whether in the workplace or outside of it, emotions determine how we feel, shape our behaviour and influence how we interact with others. At times, emotions can help us in the situations we encounter every day, but at other times, our emotions can get the better of us and become more of a hindrance. In this chapter, we focus first on defining emotions and then consider the role that emotions play in our behaviour. We discuss the relevance of emotions to the workplace, consider specific work environments with expectations of emotional displays, examine how employees can manage their emotions in such situations, and discuss whether it is possible for managers to influence the emotions of their employees.

WHAT ARE EMOTIONS?

Ask anyone how they feel, and you will get an array of adjectives by way of response. Most of these responses will probably be vague (for example, 'I feel good', 'I feel bad'), but if probed, just about everyone will be able to give you a more detailed description of what they are experiencing (for example, 'I feel happy', 'I feel excited', 'I'm upset'). We call these experiences our 'emotions'.

So, we, as human beings, are pretty good at recognising our own emotions, and we can often recognise those same emotions in other people as well. We may ask ourselves at times, where do these emotions come from? The answer to this is more complex than one might expect, and lies in our interpretation of the interaction between our brain and bodily responses to our environment. Most experts agree that emotions have a particular infrastructure that includes dedicated neural systems . In addition, emotions appear to influence cognition (thinking) and behaviour, and help us to respond to situations in our environment (Izard, 2009).

ARE FEELINGS, EMOTIONS AND MOODS THE SAME?

Frequently, we use the terms 'feelings', 'emotions' and 'moods' interchangeably. However, for psychologists, there is a distinction between these. Feelings, emotions and moods all stem from affect, a more general term describing all emotional experiences. Affect is an umbrella term that encompasses a broad range of feelings, including 'feeling states', which are in-the-moment, short-term emotional experiences, and 'feeling traits', which are more stable tendencies to feel and act in certain ways (Barsade and Gibson, 2007). Having affective responses to things or people in our environment is fundamental to our behavioural functioning (Baumeister *et al.*, 2007a).

Emotions and moods are specific types of affective response. The main difference between these two terms is the length of time that the affective response is experienced for. Emotions are brief and directed at specific events or people. Similar to feeling states, they are conscious (that is, we know we are experiencing them), they are accompanied by bodily arousal (for example, the physical feeling of tenseness or excitement) and they make themselves observable through expression and behaviour (Tice, 2009). Consider, for instance, a sports fan attending

---

affect automatic and mainly non-conscious responses to stimuli

emotions a conscious affective state accompanied by bodily arousal

a rugby match. When his team scores, he will experience a range of positive emotions, such as joy, delight and excitement. These emotions are also likely to be accompanied by a shout or a roar, and possibly by physical actions such as jumping and raising a fist in the air. These physiological reactions to emotions come from our peripheral nervous system.

Emotions can change rapidly as well. Consider the same rugby fan for a moment: if his team ultimately loses the match, at the end of the game his joy and delight will have disappeared and been replaced by disappointment. He may also experience other negative emotions such as fear (for example, fear that his team will not now get to the finals) and anger (for example, he felt the referee was unfair to one of the best players on the team). These mixed negative feelings are representative of another characteristic of emotions: they are a collection of cognitive evaluations and labelling processes. For example, both disappointment and anger are negative emotions, which include an evaluation of the person or event that is their source; in this case they are labelled as disappointment because the team lost, and anger because the referee was unfair.

In contrast to the rapidly changing emotions that we experience, mood refers to an affective response that lasts much longer (Tice, 2009). Moods may last for several minutes, for hours and sometimes even for days. The other key characteristic of moods is that they are objectless, meaning that there is not a clear event or object that elicited them (Niedenthal *et al.*, 2006). If you pause for a moment, you can probably think of someone you would describe as 'moody'. Typically, this person's moods will swing between being in 'good humour' and 'bad humour' without any apparent cause, and they will be likely to express or take their 'bad humour' out on others, again without any apparent cause. The teenage years are a stereotypical period in our life when we may be subject to moods. Normally, as a teenager becomes an adult these moods lessen and more likely than not disappear. However, some researchers suggest that each of us have a tendency to experience different levels of positive and negative affect, outside of any environmental or age factors, and this is what we term trait affectivity

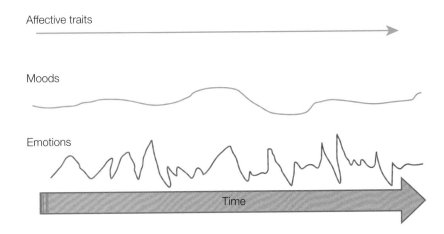

Figure 6.1 Distinctions between affect, moods and emotions

mood a long-term objectiveless affective response   trait affectivity people's tendency to experience pleasant or unpleasant emotional states

IS THERE SUCH A THING AS AN EMOTIONAL TRAIT?

Whether they last only for moments or for days and weeks, both emotions and moods do change, and so we refer to them as affective *states*. However, some would suggest that affect can also be a *trait*, which is a more stable, unchanging attribute of a person. Positive and negative affectivity describe differences between people in terms of their tendency to experience pleasant and unpleasant emotional states. High levels of trait positive affectivity are evidenced by frequent feelings of cheerfulness, enthusiasm and energy, and are character-ised by joviality, self-assurance and attentiveness (Watson and Naragon, 2009). In contrast, trait negative affectivity is associated with experiencing discomfort at all times and across all situations, even those that are not inherently stressful. It is also associated with a tendency to focus on the negative side of oneself and others (Watson and Clark, 1984). Here's an example that we are all familiar with. If an individual high on positive affectivity sees a glass that is filled with liquid comprising half its volume, this person is likely to describe the glass as 'half full'. In contrast, an individual high in negative affectivity will describe the glass as 'half empty'.

Positive affectivity has a number of benefits in the workplace because of its association with perceiving as challenges those situations that people with negative affectivity would perceive as threats, and because it broadens attention, thinking and behavioural reper-toires. What this means is that we will consider a wider range of possibilities or options when we experience positive affect, and we will engage in a wider range of behaviours. As a result of this, positive affectivity is also potentially better for creative problem solving and potentially associated with more resilient people. On the other hand, individuals who experience high negative affectivity may be less ready to embrace the norm of change that applies in many organisations and to be generally less flexible. Employees who experience more positive moods are more likely to receive higher ratings of their job performance (Staw *et al.*, 1994), to help customers and engage in prosocial behaviours (George, 1991), such as helping a colleague in need, and are less likely to be absent from work (George, 1989). That is not to say that negative emotions do not have a role to play in the workplace, and later in the chapter we will consider some of the benefits of negative emotional states.

TRAIT AFFECTIVITY – TEST YOURSELF

Are you a person who sees the glass as half full or half empty? Complete the questionnaire below to find out!

Consider the items below and rate the extent to which you tend to experience each emotion *in general*. Do not think too much about your answer to each item. Instead go with your immediate reaction and be honest.

	Very slightly or not at all	A little	Moderately	Quite a bit	Very much
1. Enthusiastic					
2. Scared					
3. Interested					
4. Afraid					
5. Determined					
6. Upset					
7. Excited					
8. Distressed					
9. Inspired					
10. Jittery					
11. Alert					
12. Nervous					
13. Active					
14. Ashamed					
15. Strong					
16. Guilty					
17. Irritable					
18. Proud					
19. Hostile					
20. Attentive					

(*Continued*)

SCORING AND INTERPRETATION:

Positive affect:

Add together the following items and then divide by 10
[1, 3, 5, 7, 9, 11, 13, 15, 18, 20]/10
Interpretation: Your score on positive affectivity will range between 1 and 5. Low scores indicate that you typically do not experience much positive affect, moderate scores (for example, 3) indicate that you sometimes experience positive affect, and high scores indicate that you experience positive affect very frequently.

Negative affect:

Add together the following items and then divide by 10
[2, 4, 6, 8, 10, 12, 14, 16, 17, 19]/10
Interpretation: Your score on negative affectivity will range between 1 and 5. Low scores indicate that you typically do not experience much negative affect, moderate scores (for example, 3) indicate that you sometimes experience negative affect, and high scores indicate that you experience negative affect very frequently.

ABOUT THIS SCALE:

The Positive and Negative Affect Scale (PANAS) was developed by Watson, Clark and Tellegen (1988), and is one of the most widely utilised measures of trait affectivity. It has been adapted here with permission from the American Psychological Association. Copyright © 1988 by APA.

WHERE DO EMOTIONS AND MOOD COME FROM?

In order to understand the role that emotions, mood and affect play in the workplace, it is beneficial to consider why we have emotions in the first place and where they come from. To do this we must take a short trip into the fields of biology and psychology. Psychological explanations suggest that states such as mood and emotions, as well as traits such as positive and negative affectivity, derive from a common concept called core affect (Russell, 2003; Russell and Barrett, 1999). Core affect refers to momentary, elementary feelings of pleasure or displeasure and of activation or deactivation (Russell and Barrett, 1999). These result in feeling good or bad, energised or tired, which in turn influences our thoughts and behaviour (Russell, 2003). Russell and Barrett (1999) propose that core affect stems from primitive, universal, patterned alterations in ongoing neurological states and autonomic activity (that is, the autonomic nervous system which regulates involuntary vital functions), which are part of all emotion-related concepts.

core affect momentary, elementary feelings of pleasure or
displeasure and of activation or deactivation

One of the central propositions of this model of core affect is that an individual has the experience of a momentary, elementary feeling of pleasure or displeasure, and then attributes this to a cause. It is only when a person decides on the cause of his or her affective experience that they express an emotion, such as anger, fear or sadness, and this guides his or her attention and behaviour (Russell, 2003; Russell and Barrett, 1999). A second central proposition of core affect is its two-dimensional structure (see Figure 6.2). We are familiar with labelling our emotions as either positive or negative, and this is what we call the *valence* of an emotion. However, we less frequently think about how active an emotion is, yet the *level of activation* is the second important component of core affect. It refers to the extent to which an emotion energises us or prompts us to take action. For example, our rugby fan was experiencing highly active emotions, whether they were positive (for example, excited) or negative (for example, upset). However, we can also experience less active emotions, such as when we feel calm and relaxed (positive) or depressed and fatigued (negative). Core affect forms a circle around these bipolar dimensions (Niedenthal *et al.*, 2006), and so this model is often referred to as the circumplex model of core affect (see Figure 6.2). The activation of an emotion is an important consideration later in the chapter when we look at how our emotions influence our behaviour in the world of work.

Core affect may also be an important affective influence on our work motivation ▸**Chapter 5**◂. Seo, Barrett and Bartunek (2004) suggest that core affect is responsible for influencing both the processes and outcomes of work motivation, such as direction, intensity and persistence, as well as goal level, goal commitment, expectancy judgements and progress judgements.

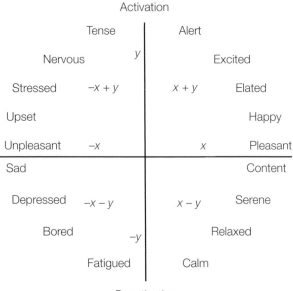

Note: The letters *x* and *y* represent semantic components
of core affect: *x* = pleasantness; *y* = activation

Figure 6.2 The two-dimensional structure of core affect

Source: Feldman Barrett and Russell (1998).

WHAT FUNCTION DO EMOTIONS SERVE?

To understand the role that emotions play in the workplace, we must also consider the functions that emotions serve for us. Although we primarily associate affect with the way we feel, it also serves a purpose for us as human beings. One of the most basic functions of emotions is that they help us in making sense of our environment and what happens in it. This sense-making in turn allows us to adapt to our surroundings. Think for a moment about walking through a city at night. Have you ever 'had a feeling' that a certain street was not safe? In this type of situation, our emotions can help us to adapt our behaviour to keep us safe (perhaps we turn around and take a different street that 'feels safer' in order to get to our destination). Thus, emotions serve an adaptive function.

Emotions are also a source of information; indeed, some would suggest that this is their main purpose (Schwarz and Clore, 2003). The affect-as-information model (Clore *et al.*, 2001; Schwarz, 2001) suggests that people may directly use affect in order to decide on an appropriate response to social situations. Put simply, this theory suggests that 'we know how we judge something by how we feel towards it' (Suri and Gross, 2012; p. 13). Emotions play a role in readying our behavioural responses, tuning our decision-making, enhancing our memory for important events and facilitating our interpersonal interactions (Gross and Thompson, 2007). In doing so, emotions allow us to adapt to different contexts and to profit from current experiences for the future (Baumeister *et al.*, 2007b; Tice, 2009).

Some researchers argue that the adaptive function of emotions is evolutionary, that is, emotions have been shaped by encounters with a small number of problems posed repeatedly by our environment (Niedenthal *et al.*, 2006). A typical example of this is the 'flight or fight' response by which, in response to a threatening stimulus (for example, a bear in a forest), we make a decision to run away (flight) or to stay and fight. This is largely based on our emotional response to the threatening stimulus. It is claimed that emotions provide us with cues as to whether we should approach or avoid situations and people, and that this originates in our evolutionary hardwiring. One of the critical aspects of emotions that provide such cues is affective valence (discussed above) and the feelings of pleasure or pain (Frijda, 2008) which are involved in our appraisal processes (Lazarus, 1991a). We experience pleasure as something to approach and pain as something to avoid. For example, imagine yourself walking across a road at a pedestrian crossing. You have waited for the green man to appear and so perceive yourself to be safe to cross the road. However, as you approach the middle of the road, you see a truck hurtling towards you at breakneck speed. In this situation, you experience fear, and this active negative emotion results in an increased intake of sensory information. The focus of your attention also narrows; you no longer notice any sounds or sights other than the approaching truck. This allows you to very quickly and efficiently process the information that will help you to take the appropriate action to avoid pain. It allows you to evaluate the probable outcomes of the situation very quickly, and to decide whether to keep moving forward or to run back to the footpath you have just left. Either way, in this situation, you try to avoid the experience of pain, and your emotions facilitate you in making quick decisions and taking effective action.

Such emotional reactions can also benefit us in the workplace, and can provide us with information on whether the actions we are taking are effective or not, and whether we are making appropriate progress towards our goals. Thus, when we experience positive emotions, we perceive that what we are doing is fine, and we keep doing it. Alternatively, we may exhibit a tendency to 'coast' and to keep our effort level constant and make no attempts to increase it (Carver and Scheier, 2008). In contrast, when we experience negative emotions, we perceive that our actions or decisions are poor or insufficient, and thus we may change these or increase our effort (Carver, 2001).

In addition to using the valence of an emotion to direct our behaviours, specific emotions can be useful for different activities. For example, joy can be useful in motivating readiness for novel exploits and expanding competencies (Fredrickson and Cohn, 2008), which are beneficial for creativity and training. In addition, experiencing joy can help us to recover from stress. For example, research has shown that individuals exposed to joyous radio clips showed substantially greater cardiovascular recovery from stressful events than those who were not exposed to such clips (Suri and Gross, 2012). Negative emotions such as feeling guilt or shame are beneficial in managing our social interactions (Hoffman, 2008). For example, we may use anticipated guilt or shame to evaluate whether a particular action would be immoral, unethical or dishonest, and the anticipated guilt or shame prevents us from engaging in this behaviour. We must keep in mind, however, that individuals may differ in how they experience feelings (such as their intensity) and also in what they do about such feelings, or in the extent to which they pay attention to the information they convey and whether they integrate it into their judgements, decisions and behaviours (Seo and Barrett, 2007). Thus, individuals can experience intense feelings during decision-making, and can simultaneously regulate the possible bias-inducing effects of those feelings on their decisions. For example, during a disciplinary meeting, a manager may experience high levels of anger towards an employee who has done something wrong. However, if she recognises that this has the potential to influence her action (that is, to dole out undue punishment), she may regulate her feelings to ensure that the consequences are in line with the wrongdoing and that her decision is not unfair.

BUILDING YOUR SKILLS

Learning to Reappraise

Reappraisal can be a powerful tool to help us use our emotions more effectively. Research has even shown that reappraising one's bodily reactions to stress can significantly reduce its negative effects (Jamieson *et al.*, 2013). Kelly McGonigal talks about how to do just this in an interesting TedTalk:

www.ted.com/talks/kelly_mcgonigal_how_to_make_stress_your_friend.html (last accessed on 20 August 2015)

Watch this talk, and make a list of how you can build your skills in reappraising stress. What impact do you think this would have in the workplace?

EMOTIONS IN THE WORKPLACE

The role of emotions in the workplace is an area of research that was rediscovered in the mid-1980s and 1990s and continues to grow in popularity for both researchers and practitioners (Brief and Weiss, 2002; Fisher and Ashkanasy, 2000). Emotions have been shown to play a role in performance, decision-making, creativity, group dynamics and individual behaviours such as turnover intentions, helping behaviour, negotiation and leadership (Barsade and Gibson, 2007). For example, Lyubomirsky, King and Diener (2005) demonstrated that an individual's tendency to experience positive emotions and moods is associated with increases in a number of performance indicators, such as more positive emotions from one's supervisors, higher income, enhanced negotiating ability and the performance of discretionary acts for the benefit of the organisation. However, affect is not always adaptive (that is, it is not always used in a constructive way) and its influence on thoughts and behaviours in organisations is highly dependent on context (Forgas and George, 2001).

The study of emotions in the workplace is often confused with related areas investigating broader states such as stress and satisfaction ▸ **Chapter 5** ◂, but there are distinct advantages to understanding more specific feeling states (Briner, 1999). Considering stress and satisfaction alone is limited, because they are non-specific and only examine why people feel good or bad at work in a general way. For example, two employees may report on an employee satisfaction survey that they are satisfied in their jobs, but may be experiencing very different specific emotions; one feeling content and calm, while the other feels excited and enthusiastic. From the circumplex model of core affect, we know that the first is experiencing passive positive emotions, while the second is experiencing active positive emotions. Active emotions are associated with being more engaged in proactive behaviour and with creativity and innovation (Fredrickson, 1998; Parker *et al.*, 2010). Passive positive emotions do not show the same relationships. Thus, it is important to distinguish between specific emotional states.

When considering the role of emotions in the workplace, it is also important to distinguish between the *expression* and the *experience* of emotions. In considering the function of emotions, we predominantly focus on how they are *experienced*. However, the *expression* of emotions tends to be the focus when considering topics such as emotional labour. Both of these areas are discussed below.

WHY ARE EMOTIONS BENEFICIAL IN THE WORKPLACE?

Managers often ask questions such as 'are happy workers also more productive workers?' The answer is not quite as straightforward as it seems. In short, sometimes they are and sometimes they are not. Returning to our circumplex model, positive emotions will only lead to higher effort (which in turn is likely to lead to higher productivity) when these emotions are in the active quadrant of the circumplex. Less active or more passive emotions do not have the motivating potential to drive an employee to action. This raises an interesting question about whether managers really want satisfied workers. Satisfaction is a passive emotion, so when an

CONSIDER THIS...

Ashton-Jones and Ashkanasy (2008) showed how specific discrete emotions have different effects on our behaviour and actions. Consider the impact of the following emotions in these work-related contexts:

1 If moral emotions (for example, guilt, shame) have the effect of making us less likely to engage in unethical behaviour and acting on immoral decisions, why do people still engage in unethical and immoral acts?

2 If an employee has an angry exchange with his manager, how might this impact his trust of that manager? Are there other factors that this depends on?

3 What is the effect of fear versus anger during organisational change ▶ **Chapter 13**◀?

employee is very satisfied with their job, they have no reason to change or to try anything differently. Researchers have suggested that managers want *engaged* workers, rather than satisfied workers (Bakker and Oerlemans, 2011). Work engagement is associated with active positive emotions and so provides this motivational drive to strive for higher effort and performance.

Emotions can also help us to learn. By providing feedback, emotions may stimulate retrospective appraisal of actions, and in this way, conscious emotional states can promote learning and alter guidelines for future behaviour (Baumeister *et al.*, 2007b). Furthermore, emotions amplify the nature of consequences and outcomes in terms of reward and punishment (Tice, 2009). Finally, emotions stimulate counterfactual thinking, which can enhance the prospects of improving behaviour by considering alternatives to events that have already occurred (Tice, 2009). Hence, emotions can lead to adaptive improvements in behaviour by improving learning. For example, Keith and Frese (2005) demonstrated that emotion control contributed to more effective learning when individuals were encouraged to make errors during training.

EMOTIONS AND GOAL PROCESSES

Emotions may benefit us in the workplace by helping us to achieve our aims because they serve two functions in goal-directed behaviour. Firstly, they provide feedback about the extent to which we are achieving our goals: their informational function. Secondly, they can direct and energise us to take action, to make plans or to monitor our progress towards goals:

counterfactual thinking a human tendency to create possible alternatives to events that have already occurred, for example, asking 'What if…?' or lamenting 'If only I had…'

their motivational function (Bagozzi *et al.*, 2003). This function has many overlaps with the affect-as-information theory.

The motivational function of emotions is linked to the role they play in readying us to take action. Emotions have been defined as states of action readiness that allow us to maintain or modify our relationship with work or ourselves (Frijda, 2008). These emotional 'action tendencies' lead people to engage in specific forms of behaviour directed towards the reversal or maintenance of an emotional state they are experiencing (Frijda, 1986). Specific emotions result in different action tendencies. Ashton-Jones and Ashkanasy (2008) summarise these relationships as follows:

- Anger
  - Triggered by an event or object in the environment that is perceived to be a demeaning offence against oneself or one's own (Lazarus, 1991b).
  - Anger provokes an action tendency to preserve or enhance self-esteem against threat or assault.
- Sadness
  - Triggered by a real or perceived absence, loss or threat of loss (Ekman, 1984). This is not characterised by heightened action readiness, but rather associated with resignation and disengagement accompanied by the appraisal tendency for helplessness in the face of loss.
- Disgust
  - Involves a strong innate impulse to avoid or get rid of something offensive.
  - Associated with intensified action readiness and a strong desire to remove or to avoid a stimulus that is a threat in terms of physical or social integrity (Lazarus, 1991b).
- Fear and anxiety
  - Common action tendency for fear and anxiety is to avoid or escape, which is accompanied by physiological arousal.
  - The distinction between these two emotions is that fear relates to a knowable object, while anxiety is a result of ambiguity, for example, when the future is uncertain and poses a threat.
- Joy/happiness
  - These emotions arise from the attainment of a goal (Ekman, 1984).
  - Joy is a more intense form of happiness, frequently associated with the unexpected attainment of a personal goal. It is also associated with heightened states of physiological arousal which motivate action.

From this summary, we can see that specific emotions can prepare us to take different forms of action. Thus, it is important when considering the role of emotions in organisational behaviour to look at the effects of specific emotions on behaviour (Gooty *et al.*, 2009).

Some interesting research from social psychology has shown that certain individuals can actually modify their emotional states when they want to engage in a specific action or behaviour. Tamir and Ford (2009) demonstrated that people may be motivated to experience unpleasant emotions when these emotions are useful for goal attainment. They showed that individuals increased their level of fear when they were preparing to engage in an avoidance goal (for example, an employee who does not want to change their core work tasks even though their manager has told them this is necessary). It is not only fear that can be utilised in this manner. More recently, Tamir and Ford (2012) demonstrated that individuals try to increase anger when preparing to negotiate with a person who they are expecting to have to confront, as opposed to collaborate with ▶ **Chapter 9** ◀. Interestingly, the experience of anger also led to better outcomes for those individuals. The ones with higher levels of anger were more successful at getting others to concede to their demands. These are interesting findings because they show that sometimes people prefer to feel bad if doing so can lead to benefits for them.

SPOTLIGHT ON SKILLS

Goette and Huffman (2007) conducted a study on how bicycle couriers used emotions for choices about work effort. The results of the study showed that windfall gains (that is, earning more than they expected) in the morning had an impact on work effort in the afternoon. The researchers suggested that messengers attach emotional significance to a daily earnings goal. A messenger with a windfall gain works harder than other messengers in the first part of the day, but less hard later.

Affective reactions occur because we do not want to fall short of a reference point or goal, and our emotions act as a psychological incentive to exert effort as long as we are below our goal. However, there is a tendency for us to experience stronger emotions as we become closer to achieving our goal, and this is called the goal gradient effect.

1 Bicycle messengers were a good choice of subjects for examining how emotions can motivate effort because they have substantial discretion over how hard they work and when they work during the day (Goette and Huffman, 2007). Could a manager use this knowledge to motivate workers who have less discretion?

2 Would this apply to employees who were not on piece-rate (that is, getting paid for each delivery made)? Would it be ethical to induce negative emotions in one's staff?

To help you answer these questions, in your ebook click the play button to watch the video of Fiona Fennell at Cregg Group providing her perspective on these issues.

EMOTIONS AND DECISION-MAKING

The motivational function of emotions is also seen in the context of how we use emotions to help us make decisions. Frequently, emotions are considered to have a negative influence on decision-making. This was the assumption in early economic theories of decision-making and rational decision-making models, which considered people to be entirely logical when it came to this activity. They saw them as *Homo economicus* (Van Der Lowe, 2012), the perfect decision maker who bases all decisions on completely rational criteria. For example, if you were to base your food choices on a perfectly rational decision-making model, you would always choose the most nutritious food which was also the best value. You would never choose to eat chocolate or ice cream, both of which have low nutritional value, just because you like them. Clearly, most people do not behave in this manner in the real world.

One of the best examples of how emotions affect decision-making in the workplace involves economic and investment activities. For example, we may use emotions to guide decisions by anticipating how we will feel when the consequences of the decisions play out (Baumeister *et al.*, 2007b). Potential investors often imagine how overjoyed they will feel if their investment pays off, and use this to justify making a risky investment. Similarly, they may anticipate feeling regret if they did not purchase a stock and it rose in value. These types of emotions are referred to as anticipated emotions. Imagine how happy you will feel when you do well in your organisational behaviour exam and all your hard work has paid off!

Bagozzi, Baumgartner and Pieters (1998) developed a model of goal-directed emotions to explain the process through which anticipated emotions help our decision-making and goal pursuits. Appraisals of the consequences of achieving or not achieving goals elicit anticipatory emotions which influence our volitions (intentions, plans and the decision to expend energy) in pursuing goals. After this, goal-directed behaviours arise as a response to volitions and lead to goal attainment. According to this model, it is the intensity of anticipatory emotions that gives them their motivational potential. For example, using a stock investment simulation, Seo and Barrett (2007) found that individuals who experienced more intense feelings achieved a higher decision-making performance. In addition, those who were better able to identify and distinguish their current feelings achieved higher decision-making performance through their enhanced ability to control the possible biases induced by those feelings. Thus, anticipated emotions play an important and beneficial role in making decisions (Baumeister *et al.*, 2007b).

Hence, emotions have an important function in influencing our behaviour. Behaviours may come about as a consequence of an emotion, or because behaviour may be directed towards achieving or avoiding certain anticipated emotions.

anticipated emotions the emotions experienced when one imagines how one will feel in the future once certain desirable or undesirable future events have occurred

Emotional Marketing

Emotions have long been used in marketing and advertising campaigns to influence consumers to purchase products or to remain loyal to a particular brand. For example, emotional marketing expert, Graeme Newell, shows how emotional reactions to heroes and villains are frequently used in marketing. For example, he demonstrates how Nike uses this approach in their marketing. However, rather than using external heroes and villains, they make it personal by putting the hero and the villain inside our own heads – we need to get over our own internal 'demon on our shoulder' or our own laziness, while the hero is our best self who gets out of bed on a cold winter morning to train.

Newell shows that companies often use this type of emotional marketing to influence consumers' brand loyalty and purchasing behaviour. Emotional contagion explains why shop assistants are frequently asked to engage in emotional labour: if the person attending to you in a shop displays positive emotions, you are more likely

OB IN THE NEWS

to experience positive emotions also, and feel more positively towards the products you are looking at. It has also been shown that emotional contagion does not require direct contact between people. Kramer, Guillory and Hancock (2014) demonstrated in a large-scale experiment using Facebook's News Feed algorithm that emotional states can be transferred to others, without their awareness. They showed that emotional contagion can occur without direct interaction between people – exposure to a friend expressing an emotion is sufficient – and in the complete absence of non-verbal cues.

However, this study, which was undertaken in conjunction with Facebook, has been heavily criticised because it did not seek prior informed consent from Facebook users, which is considered an ethical issue from a research perspective. The research has also sparked media criticism regarding its motives and the potential for social media to influence users' emotions, both positively and negatively. For example, the *Guardian* reported a Facebook spokesperson as saying that the research was carried out 'to improve our services and to make the content that people see on Facebook as relevant and engaging as possible'.

The ethics of participant consent are an ongoing issue for debate. Regardless of this, however, it seems that many people simply do not like the idea of having their emotions manipulated without their consent or awareness. This presents an interesting point of reflection for

us, given the extent to which marketing campaigns influence our emotions.

For more information on the Nike branding strategy using emotions, see: http://602communications. com/2013/02/nike-brand-strategy-emotional-branding-using-the-story-of-heroism/

For more information on the Facebook emotions experiment, see Kramer *et al.* (2014).

Questions

1 Think about some of the products you own; do you have an emotional connection to a particular brand(s)? How does this influence your purchasing behaviour?

2 Is your purchasing behaviour based on your mood (for example, do you ever engage in impulse buying)? Have you ever noticed companies or employees attempting to influence you to engage in impulse buying using emotional language?

3 Has reading this article influenced your attitude towards using social media?

4 Facebook were criticised for conducting their emotion experiment without informed consent from their users. This is considered unethical when conducting research. When utilised for business reasons, is it ethical to influence either employees' or consumers' emotions?

Sources

http://www.theguardian.com/technology/2014/jun/29/facebook-users-emotions-news-feeds (last accessed 5th November 2015).

www.bbc.com/news/technology-28051930 (last accessed 5th November 2015).

© ROYALTY-FREE/CORBIS

EMOTIONAL LABOUR

Workplaces are inherently social environments, and as such the emotions that individuals display play a central role in the interactions that occur there (Briner, 1999). Emotional expressions are the means by which emotions are communicated; for example, if a customer looks angry, it may change the way a customer service representative approaches him or her. At a minimum, most of us would expect to be nice to our co-workers, and have them be nice to us. In the main, this suggests keeping the expression of negative emotions to a minimum. However, in some workplaces, there are greater expectations for the level of emotional expression. For example, we tend to expect positive emotional displays from flight attendants, supermarket cashiers and hairdressers. We expect nurses and teachers to be caring. On the other hand, we probably expect high negative emotional displays from debt collectors or criminal interrogators. Any work that requires or expects certain emotional displays is referred to as emotional labour. Importantly, emotional labour is sold for a wage and therefore has an exchange value (Hochschild, 1983). Although the jobs mentioned above are classic emotional labour jobs (that is, the expectations of emotional display are relatively explicit), there are many other types of jobs where the management and display of emotions are more implicit. Hence, one of the criticisms of research on emotional labour is that the distinction between those jobs that require emotional labour and those that do not is unclear (Briner, 1999). Indeed, it could be argued that every job requires some kind of emotional labour to some degree.

There are two types of 'rules' in emotional labour which determine employees' expression of emotions. *Feeling* rules specify the range, intensity, duration and object of the emotions that employees should experience. In contrast, *display* rules specify which particular emotions can be expressed. Displays of emotions may or may not match people's experienced feelings (Ashforth and Humphrey, 1993). For example, we expect a sales assistant to continue to display positive emotions and remain polite when interacting with a rude customer. This is an example of a display rule. In contrast, we expect nurses and doctors to not only display, but also feel, empathy for their patients. This is an example of a feeling rule. These 'rules' dictate the emotions that employees are both expected to feel and expected to express.

Similarly, Hochschild (1983) suggested that there were two main ways to control emotional expressions: surface acting and deep acting. Surface acting refers to displaying emotions that are not felt, where the focus is on the display of the emotion rather than the inner experience. Thus, surface acting involves the overt behavioural display of emotion including our facial expressions. Because it involves the facial or behavioural display of emotion, it often leads to an inauthentic display – in other words, it appears fake to an observer. For example, consider a time when you entered a fast food restaurant and were immediately greeted with a 'Hi, how are you doing today?' Did you ever respond, and receive a surprised look from your

---

emotional labour any job that requires the management of feeling to create a publicly observable facial and bodily display, including tone of voice

surface acting displaying an emotion that is not felt

server? This is an example of surface acting. The second way to control emotional expression is **deep acting**. This refers to a situation in which someone attempts to experience the emotions that are going to be displayed by using thoughts, images, or memories that evoke the emotion. For example, this is a technique that actors often use when they need to cry. Because an individual engaged in deep acting tries to both change the experience and expression of the emotion, it is more likely to produce an authentic display. However, it also requires greater effort, and is more difficult to achieve.

CONSIDER THIS...

Emotional labour results from an implicit assumption that customers expect a certain type of experience when they interact with shop assistants in making purchases in stores, or when they interact with restaurant staff when they go out for a meal. Do you think emotional displays enhance the performance of employees? As you think about the answer to this question, consider some of the factors that

might be important. For example, if you get the impression that a shop assistant is only telling you that an outfit looks good on you in order to get you to buy it so that their commission is increased, how do you feel? The other side of this story is how it feels to be the employee who is expected to display these various emotions. What do you think is more difficult: to display an emotion that you do not feel, or to force yourself to feel a certain emotion before you display it? Are there costs to surface acting and deep acting for employees in service industries like the ones above?

MANAGING EMOTIONS IN THE WORKPLACE

Emotional labour is an example of a work context in which employees are expected to manage their emotions in order to present a particular display. However, deep acting and surface acting do not inform us about the strategies that they use to either display or experience an emotion. Theory and research on emotion regulation provide us with deeper insights into the strategies individuals use to manage the emotions they experience in the workplace.

Emotion regulation refers to the set of processes whereby people manage their emotional states, including specific emotions such as anger or sadness, moods such as depression and euphoria, general stress responses and rapid affective reactions that may or may not be

deep acting efforts to change the actual experience of an emotion in order to display this emotion in the workplace

emotion regulation the processes by which people manage their emotional states

consciously experienced (Koole, 2009b). Emotion regulation processes are used to influence the emotions individuals experience and whether they eventually express these emotions (Gross, 1999), and they may increase, maintain or decrease positive and negative emotions (Koole, 2009a).

Basic components of emotion regulation include recognition and understanding of one's own emotions, managing these emotions by inducing, modulating or preventing them, and using emotions for action and goal attainment (Pekrun, 2006), as discussed above. Before people can regulate their emotions, they must be aware of their current emotional state and the possible consequences an emotion has, both for themselves and for others (Niedenthal *et al.*, 2006). Emotion knowledge includes knowledge about the causes of emotions, their associated bodily sensations and expressive behaviour, and about possible means of modifying them. Such knowledge facilitates emotion regulation because it provides information about the appropriateness of the emotional experience, and about the possible actions that can be taken to deal with discrepant emotions.

Emotion regulation has links to the concept of emotional intelligence (Salovey *et al.*, 1993) as referring to three interrelated skills or abilities: accurate appraisal of mood and expression of emotion by oneself and others, adaptive regulation of emotion in self and others, and utilising emotions (for example, in problem-solving) (Briner, 1999). The concept was popularised by Goleman in *Emotional Intelligence: Why it can matter more than IQ* (1995) and also applied to the workplace by Goleman (1998) and others (Briner, 1999). Goleman's Emotional Competence Inventory assesses 20 competencies, subsumed under four clusters: self-awareness, social awareness, self-management and social skills (Conte, 2005). Although this approach to emotional intelligence is very popular in organisations, particularly in management development programmes, it has a number of weaknesses. Among these is Goleman's failure to clearly identify whether this concept is, in fact, an intelligence. Indeed, if it is considered an intelligence, then it would not be amenable to development because intelligence is a relatively fixed entity. The approach has attracted considerable criticism, with research evidence suggesting that the Emotional Competence Inventory is actually more closely related to personality and should not receive serious attention (Conte, 2005).

To address the issues pertaining to the definitions and measurement of emotional intelligence, Petrides (2011) provides a clear distinction between ability emotional intelligence and trait emotional intelligence. As an ability, emotional intelligence can be described as the capacity to monitor one's own and others' feelings and emotions, and to use this information to guide one's thinking and actions (Salovey and Mayer, 1990). Ability emotional intelligence is a cognitive–emotional capability that concerns emotion-related cognitive abilities that should be measured via maximum-performance tests, while trait emotional intelligence concerns emotion-related self-perceptions, which is similar to a type of trait emotional self-efficacy (Petrides, 2011). Trait emotional intelligence is thus more accurately classified as personality, while ability emotional intelligence is theoretically within the domain of cognitive ability. However, in reality, it is very difficult to measure emotional intelligence as an ability because of the subjectivity of emotional experience (Petrides, 2011; Robinson and Barrett, 2010).

Research has examined the extent to which trait emotional intelligence differs across cultures. Gökçen *et al.* (2014) investigated cultural differences in emotional intelligence between Hong Kong and the UK, demonstrating that there was pronounced cross-cultural variation in global trait emotional intelligence scores. British participants scored consistently higher than their Chinese counterparts. The researchers explain this by way of the cultural accommodation effect. Chinese participants completing the questionnaire in English scored higher on global trait emotional intelligence and on sociability than Chinese participants completing the questionnaire in their own language. The researcher suggests that this illustrates the influential role of language in bilinguals' responses to questions concerning cultural norms and values.

Research has demonstrated that individuals high on trait emotional intelligence are faster at identifying and recognising emotional expressions in others, and are more sensitive to mood induction (Petrides and Furnham, 2003). In other words, they are more likely to be influenced by emotional displays in their environment or exhibited by others. Similarly, there is research to support a relationship between trait emotional intelligence and psychological and physical health (Martins *et al.*, 2010; Schutte *et al.*, 2007). However, the role of emotional intelligence in the workplace has been exaggerated by popular literature, its applicability varying as a function of the context and task (Petrides, 2011; Petrides and Furnham, 2003; Zeidner *et al.*, 2004). As such, it may be of more benefit for managers and employees to understand how to manage their own and others' emotions, and for this we must turn to emotion regulation strategies.

Emotion regulation, as discussed above, refers to one's attempts to influence the emotions one experiences, when one has them, and how these emotions are experienced and expressed (Gross, 1998). As such, emotion regulation can be considered as a set of competencies which are amenable to development and, for this reason, emotion regulation strategies may have practical benefit in the workplace.

STRATEGIES FOR MANAGING EMOTIONS

As individuals, we can learn ways of managing our emotions. Two of the most common ways of doing this are to reappraise or to suppress our emotions. The strategy we use to manage our emotions can also have an impact on our well-being.

Reappraisal is a form of cognitive change, and begins with the idea that no situation in and of itself generates an emotion. It is the individual's appraisal of the situation that does so. Hence, this strategy involves changing a situation's meaning in a way that alters its emotional impact (Gross and Thompson, 2007). Reappraisal is an antecedent-focused strategy because one intervenes before an emotion has been fully generated and, hence, can efficiently alter the entire subsequent emotional experience. Gross and John (2003) suggest that it should successfully reduce both the extent to which we experience negative emotions and how we act upon these emotions. Beal *et al.* (2006) argue that deep acting in emotional labour is a form of regulation that is typically achieved through cognitive reappraisal of the events surrounding the emotional experience.

BUILDING YOUR

Enhancing Positive Emotions

Savouring our emotions is a way of regulating them, specifically focusing on how to enhance our positive emotions and happiness. We can learn strategies that help us with this. Try some for yourself (Quoidbach *et al.*, 2010):

1 Behavioural display
   ● Smile as much as you can!

2 Be present
   ● Direct your attention to a pleasant experience in the present. Focus on the positive emotions that this creates.

3 Capitalize
   ● Share positive things that have happened with others.

4 Positive mental time travel
   ● Try to remember a positive event that occurred to you in the past as vividly and in as much detail as you can.
   ● Think about a positive event that will occur in the future and imagine the positive emotions that you will experience.

Research has shown that engaging in strategies such as these on a regular daily basis, even for short periods of time, can increase our positive emotions and well-being (Lambert *et al.*, 2013; Quoidbach *et al.*, 2010).

Suppression, in contrast, involves inhibiting the expression of emotion (Gross, 1999). It is a response-focused strategy, and modifies the behavioural aspect of emotion response tendencies (Gross and John, 2003). Butler and Gross (2009) demonstrated that suppression leads to increases in physiological responding and decreases in cognitive functioning. It requires individuals to exert effort to manage emotional expressions as they arise, and this effort may consume cognitive resources that could otherwise be used for optimal performance (Gross and John, 2003). Comparing the effectiveness of these two strategies, Gross (1998) found that reappraisal is more effective than suppression. Reappraisers cope with stress by using reinterpretation, have a well-developed ability for negative mood repair, and show a capacity for negative mood regulation. Furthermore, they tend to experience and express greater positive emotion (Gross and John, 2003). In contrast, suppressors cope with adversity by 'battening down the hatches', so they feel inauthentic and do not vent their true feelings. They tend to evaluate their emotions in negative terms, and the lack of clarity they experience around their emotions is associated with a lower ability to repair their mood, lower estimates of their own ability to regulate negative mood and increased rumination.

Doctors on Duty

Employees in the medical profession are faced with many emotions that need to be dealt with on a daily basis. They need to deal with distraught and upset patients and their relatives, as well as their own feelings when faced with often life-threatening decisions on the operating table, for example. In addition, doctors are part of a profession that is highly competitive and they must consistently perform at a very high standard in order to progress their careers and remain employed. There is a paradox in the medical profession whereby doctors are 'required to reproduce medicine as an abstract system – an objective, trustworthy, reliable, effective, competent and fair mode of healing – and yet individual practitioners are also required to be caring, emotionally intelligent, intuitive and sensitive' (Nettleton *et al.*, 2008; p. 18).

Traditionally, doctors were seen in an unemotional way

as the diagnostician, while nurses and other health care professionals were associated with more caring post-diagnosis roles, and thus, with emotional labour. The conventional stereotype that doctors are fairly emotionless is still true today (Ofri, 2013). However, emotions affect the thought processes and actions of doctors in the same way as they affect all of us. They are part and parcel of the human experience and we cannot expect anyone, or any profession, to just 'turn them off'. Rather than trying to ignore emotions, it may be better to understand their effects. In doing so, we can better manage their impact. This is true for doctors also, whose cognitive errors may be influenced by their unrecognised emotions. For example, Ofri (2013) explains that, because individuals who experience positive emotions are more likely to succumb to attribution bias, doctors who fall prey to this bias are more

likely to attribute a disease to who the patient is, rather than their situation. They may attribute a disease to the fact that the patient is a drug user, rather than to their exposure to bacteria. However, negative emotions are associated with anchoring bias, and this is a key factor in diagnostic error which may cause doctors to stick with an initial impression and avoid considering conflicting data.

In her book *What doctors feel*, Danielle Ofri discusses the range of emotional reactions experienced by doctors to both the physical maladies experienced by their patients and to less-than-desirable personality characteristics which can present a challenge to showing empathy with some patients. Just as we may squirm when we watch medical procedures on TV, doctors may experience similar reactions when first presented with patients who present with repulsive conditions.

The globalisation of work presents further challenges for the medical profession. As highly qualified professionals, many choose to study and work abroad, which leads to a highly multi-cultural profession. This can present challenges for both doctors and patients from different cultures. For example, research has demonstrated that there are differences in the integration of positive and negative emotions between independent cultures (for example, US) and interdependent cultures (for example, China) and in social norms for emotional displays. It has also been demonstrated

© GETTY IMAGES/MONKEY BUSINESS IMAGES LTD/THINKSTOCK IMAGES

that collectivist cultures (for example, Japan, China, Brazil and India) tend to use suppression as an emotion regulation strategy more frequently than individualist cultures (for example, US, Australia, UK and Canada). Such cultural differences may present challenges for doctors when treating patients from other cultures to their own, who may expect different emotional displays.

In addition to this, doctors are pressurised by the social norms of the profession to work long hours, and to work while sick. This can lead to medical errors that can cause patient harm, especially if they become infected from the doctor, and can result in emotions such as fear and guilt in doctors.

Questions

1 Do you think that medicine should be an 'emotional' profession? Do you prefer it when your doctor shows emotions or does not show emotions when you visit them?

2 What might be the implications for doctors of *not* showing their emotions?

3 What do you think would be the consequences of:

a Doctors suppressing their emotions?

b Doctors showing, or at least acknowledging, their emotions?

4 If you were the HR manager in a hospital, what would your thoughts and recommendations be on this subject?

5 Get into groups and develop a 'training plan' for how to help doctors deal with their emotions as they do their work. What might be some of the contextual factors that need to be taken into account – for example, what events might be very emotional in a doctor's work? Does the training plan need to consider dealing with both negative and positive emotions?

Sources:

Cromie, W.J. (2006). Doctor fatigue hurting patients: Interns feel guilt, lose empathy. *Harvard University Gazette*, 10 December. Available at: www.news.harvard.edu/gazette/2006/12.14/99-fatigue.html (last accessed 5th November 2015).

Nettleton, S., Burrow, R. and Watt, I. (2008). How do you feel doctor? An analysis of the emotional aspects of routine professional medical work. *Social Theory and Health, 6*, 18–36.

Ofri, D. (2013). *What doctors feel: How emotions affect the practice of medicine*. Boston: Beacon Press.

Ofri, D. (2013). 'Why doctors don't take sick days. *The New York Times Sunday Review*, 15 November. Available at: www.nytimes.com/2013/11/16/opinion/sunday/why-doctors-dont-take-sick-days.html?ref=contributors&_r=1& (last accessed 5th November 2015).

 SUMMARY

 IN THE EBOOK, CLICK TO HEAR AN AUDIO SUMMARY

Emotions are an important component of our working lives. They influence the decisions that we make and how we reach our goals, and they provide us with an important source of information. In this chapter, we considered how we experience emotions and attribute them to a cause (core affect). We examined the distinction between emotions, moods and affective traits. Then we identified the ways in which emotions can serve a purpose in helping us to achieve our goals and take action. We also explained how workplaces can influence our emotions, and the importance of emotion regulation skills in workplaces characterised by high levels of emotional labour. Workplaces themselves also influence our emotions: those that are characterised by high levels of emotional labour require us to manage our emotions in particular ways. The effectiveness of our emotion regulation and the effort that it requires may impact on our performance and well-being at work. Despite this, experiencing emotions in our working life is a much better alternative to not experiencing them at all.

CHAPTER REVIEW QUESTIONS

1   What is the distinction between mood and emotion?

2   What functions do emotions serve for us as human beings?

3   In what ways can emotions be beneficial for achieving our goals?

4   In what ways can emotions help or hurt when we make decisions?

5   Describe the ways in which emotional labour could be considered an affective event.

6   Are the concepts of deep acting and surface acting similar or different from reappraisal and suppression? In what ways?

7   Explain what is meant by the concept of emotional labour. Have you any experience of this type of work?

8   Do you believe in the concept of emotional intelligence? Why or why not?

MULTIPLE CHOICE QUESTIONS

In your ebook, click to take a multiple choice quiz to test your understanding of this chapter.

FURTHER READING

Barsade, S.G. and Gibson, D.E. (2007). Why does affect matter in organizations? *Academy of Management Perspectives*, 21(1), 36–59.

Briner, R. (1999). The neglect and importance of emotions at work. *European Journal of Work and Organizational Psychology*, 8(3), 323–346.

Gooty, J., Gavin, M. and Ashkanasy, N. M. (2009). Emotions research in OB: The challenges that lie ahead. *Journal of Organizational Behavior*, 30(6), 833–838.

Jamieson, J.P., Mendes, W.B. and Nock, M.K. (2013). Improving acute stress responses: The power of reappraisal. *Current Directions in Psychological Science*, 22(1), 51–56.

Niedenthal, P. M., Krauth-Gruber, S. and Ric, F. (2006). *The Psychology of Emotion: Interpersonal, Experiential and Cognitive Approaches*. New York: Psychology Press.

Totterdell, P. and Niven, K. (2012). *Should I strap a battery to my head? (And other questions about emotion)*. Self-published.

USEFUL WEBSITES

www.obweb.org/index.php?option=com_content&view=category&id=54&Itemid=82
This is the website of the Academy of Management: Scholars of Organizational Behaviour. Listen to the interview with Neal Ashkanasy on studying emotions in the workplace. Neal is one of the world's leading scholars on emotions. In the podcast he provides a very interesting overview of his work, and answers some key questions on why emotions are important to consider in the workplace.

www.obweb.org/index.php?option=com_content&view=category&id=42&Itemid=66

It will also be useful to listen to the podcast interview with Amir Erez, entitled 'Charismatic Leadership and Emotions'. He looks at why emotions are important to consider in leaders, and how effectively managing others' emotions is an important function for charismatic leaders.

www.eiconsortium.org/index.html

This website provides further information on emotional intelligence and why it is important in organisational settings.

www.emotionsnet.org

This is a network and website dedicated to the study of emotions.

www.mindtools.com/pages/article/newCDV_41.htm

This webpage provides an overview of why it is important to manage one's emotions at work.

www.ted.com/speakers/antonio_damasio

In this TedTalk, Antonio Damasio discusses his research and, particularly, that considering case studies of individuals with impaired emotional functioning.

http://knowledge.wharton.upenn.edu/article/managing-emotions-in-the-workplace-do-positive-and-negative-attitudes-drive-performance/

In this podcast, research on how to manage emotions by Sigal Barsade is reviewed and discussed.

SECTION ONE CASE STUDY

Francois joined Dax in August 2010 as a regional sales manager. He has a degree in Management from Toulouse Business School and worked in the medical sales industry for ten years before joining Dax, which specialises in the manufacture and sale of computer components. It is a medium sized company employing 250 people, with its headquarters in Munich in Germany. The manufacturing is undertaken in Japan. Dax's engineering teams develop a wide range of products and the manufacturing facilities allow time to market in the shortest of lead times. The company also has a sophisticated warehousing and distribution system which ensures the availability of components as customers need them. The sales team is split into six regions with a sales manager and six to eight sales people per team.

In his previous role in the medical device industry Francois excelled in terms of sales performance. However, in that role he was selling mainly to large public sector-based organisations and his role involved finalising sales after product marketing engineers had provided product demonstrations on site to the customers. Working in a large organisation meant that Francois had access to significant support from finance and administration teams, by and large leaving him to focus on processing sales. While Francois has experience in the sales area he is lacking in product knowledge of the IT industry and in managerial experience more generally. This is a fact that the sales team are aware of. Prior to Francois' appointment to the position there had been an expectation among the sales team that one of the existing staff would be appointed to the role. Three members of the sales team applied for the position and were interviewed; however they were unsuccessful. This has had a significant impact on morale among the sales team and one member – Serban – has begun to talk about leaving. Serban joined Dax in 2000 as a graduate straight from her marketing degree. She believed that she had the required knowledge and experience to get the position. What's more, she believes that Dax should have valued her loyalty to the organisation over the years, particularly because she has been headhunted by competitors in the past and remained with Dax instead of leaving. She is telling everyone how unhappy she is at being overlooked for promotion. She is a bubbly character and is not afraid to voice her opinion when others may remain silent. The other two who applied (Konrad and Jack) did not believe they had the required experience but wanted to show that they were interested in promotion within the firm. Both had joined the sales team in the last year and are performing well.

When Francois starts his new job he spends the majority of the first two months getting to know the product range and the existing customer base. He gets up to speed quickly and the sales team are impressed with how quickly he understands both the product range and manufacturing processes. He keeps the same sales targets that were set by his predecessor because these are set until the end of the year; however he has quietly expressed his opinion that 'the bar has been set too low' in terms of targets and that changes are afoot for next year. He works long hours and travels across Europe and Japan frequently, meaning he is out of the office a lot. Privately, Francois has questioned why the organisation does not have technical staff travelling to sites, as was his experience in his previous organisation. Francois believes that if other members of the organisation were travelling to customer sites then that would free up the sales team to concentrate on identifying new opportunities and expanding growth. Due to his frequent travel the team see little of Francois in the office. When the sales team do see him he comes across as quiet and conscientious, if somewhat withdrawn. The sales team expect that he will be more accessible once he has settled into the role. The rest of the team regularly socialise as a group, and their previous manager encouraged group activities such as dinner and golfing sessions, always taking part herself in these. As yet, Francois has demonstrated no interest in getting to know his colleagues outside of working hours.

Time passes, and it is January . New sales targets have been set but these have only been communicated via email to the sales team. Some of the team have been surprised at what they perceive to be 'unachievable targets', Serban chief among these. Levels of motivation are low at the start of the year among the sales team and Francois' manager (the sales director) is beginning to worry whether they have chosen the wrong person for the role and that they should have appointed Serban instead. Serban is still complaining about how she should have been promoted into the role and takes every opportunity during team meetings to dismiss Francois' ideas. The working relationship between Francois and Serban is strained. She, however, always meets her sales targets and in doing so has demonstrated to the rest of team that these are not unrealistic expectations. Therefore Francois has no issue with her work.

The sales director arranges a meeting with Francois to discuss the 'issues' within his sales team. Francois is surprised to discover that the meeting will be about his management of the sales team because the sales targets for last year were met by everyone. He is even more surprised to learn that the issues the team have raised with the sales director include a lack of communication, unfair treatment and autocratic leadership style.

QUESTIONS:

1   Identify the key issues in this case from an organisational behaviour perspective.
2   What theories of motivation could help inform the sales director for her conversation with Francois?
3   Why is Francois surprised that the meeting is taking place? What theories of personality inform your answer?
4   In what ways does the concept of perception impact on the issues in this case?
5   How could Francois manage Serban's emotions?
6   Describe how Francois' attitude to his new role is impacting on the sales team's performance?

7 GROUPS AND TEAMS IN THE WORKPLACE

Christine Cross and Caroline Murphy

LEARNING OUTCOMES

- Discuss the role of groups in organisational life, and identify the different types of groups.
- Recognise and evaluate key aspects of group composition and formation, including stages of group development, norms, and roles.
- Consider some key group decision-making dynamics such as cohesiveness, conformity, groupthink and social loafing.

- Outline the key differences between groups and teams in the workplace.
- Identify the characteristics of an effective workplace team.
- Demonstrate an understanding of different types of teams in an organisational setting.

© GETTY IMAGES/ISTOCKPHOTO/THINKSTOCK/BEN BLANKENBURG

THIS CHAPTER DISCUSSES:

IN REALITY

It is a commonly held belief that the most effective groups consist of like-minded individuals who share similar backgrounds and interests, because the common experiences among their members will promote greater group cohesion, facilitate group understanding and communication, and ensure that everyone has the same end goal in sight. It is partly because of this belief that in a recent survey of 500 hiring managers, 74 per cent reported that their most recent hire had a personality similar to theirs. However, research has shown that groups with more diverse members are more innovative and creative and facilitate better, more productive intra-team processes. This is particularly evident when the team includes female members. Studies from MIT, Carnegie Mellon and Union College have found that the teams which were best at collaborating and demonstrating effective problem-solving in an efficient timeframe were the teams with the highest numbers of women (see Engel *et al.*, 2014). These studies showed that the more women on the team, the better it performed. This was attributed to women being found to have higher levels of emotional intelligence ▸ **Chapter 6** ◂. Women consistently scored higher on tests which involved looking at images of people's faces in which only their eye regions were visible and identifying what complex emotion they were feeling, from shame to curiosity. Even in a virtual setting, tests revealed that when teams were not physically together and could not see their fellow team members' faces, women performed better than men at gauging team members' emotions. So what does this mean for teamwork and for virtual teams? In essence, it may mean that in the absence of female team members, the opinions of individuals in the team are less likely to be fully explored and conflict may arise from the failure of others to notice early cues of, for example, disagreement or distress. Managers should bear this in mind when forming teams in their own companies. Even in the event that a female team member's technical knowledge is replicated elsewhere in the group, her emotional intelligence may prove invaluable.

INTRODUCTION

Feeling part of a group or team can be motivating, energising and rewarding, and collaborating is a great way of sharing resources and getting things done. Groups and teams have the potential to deliver more together through the experience of interaction than individuals working alone (Katzenbach and Smith, 2005). However, we also know that none of this is guaranteed. It is not easy to join a group, navigate group dynamics or hold on to our individuality once we are a part of a group. Indeed, in order to 'fit in' we sometimes find ourselves behaving differently in a group setting than we might do alone (Ross and Nisbett, 1991). This means that groups do not always benefit from interaction as much as they might do. Groups can lose their way and are prone to decision-making traps; for example everyone might agree to a certain course of action because they do not want to appear to contradict the majority. Also, the need for coordination means progress can be slow, and working within a group or a team is by nature more complex than going it alone.

In this chapter we consider groups and teams and their popularity in organisations and workplaces. We explore the impact of group dynamics such as group development, roles and patterns of group behaviour, and we consider cohesiveness, conformity and group decision-making. We also look at the difficulties that arise in groups and the mixed feelings we sometimes have about them. Finally, we examine the differences between groups and teams, the characteristics of effective teams, and the implications for their support and management in the organisation.

WHAT ARE GROUPS?

Groups are a pervasive feature of organisations and working life (Delarue *et al.*, 2008). This is no surprise, because both collaboration and competition are deeply rooted behaviours within the natural and social world. We are in effect 'social animals' (Aronson, 2007) and often need to be able to interact with others in order to function individually. Sometimes it is about shared interests, or pooling resources and getting things done. Sometimes it is rooted in identification, such as the need to belong, to interact with those who share our outlooks and to feel solidarity with them. It can also be about attraction. A group is perhaps best understood by what it is *not*. For instance, a group is not just a collection of people occupying the same space or sharing a demographic factor such as being over 60 years of age. It is only when something connects people and causes them to develop that they take on the internal identity of a group. For example, people waiting on a platform for a train would not be classified as a group because they are not working towards achieving a common objective. Schein's definition of a group assists us with this classification process: 'any number of people who interact with each other and perceive themselves to be a group' (1980, p. 145). Table 7.1 lists some possible groups. Identify which ones can be accurately categorised as groups based on our definitions.

Table 7.1 To be a group or not to be!
Identify which of the following fall into our categorisation of a group.

	Yes/No
People with red hair	
The government	
Students waiting for a lecture to begin	
People in a queue for lunch	
A rugby team	
Rugby fans at a match	

Check the companion website at www.palgrave.com/ carbery-ob to see if you answered correctly.

groups two or more people who interact together to achieve a common objective and who are interdependent

Groups serve a major purpose in that they support *collective action*, which is getting things done through shared effort and knowledge or making larger tasks manageable by breaking them down into specialist roles and responsibilities. The potential for synergy within groups is what makes them so important for organisations, which increasingly rely on this enhanced group performance to achieve an advantage over their competitors (Purcell *et al.*, 2003). The galvanising energy of a group is interdependence. If a group does not have a sense of interdependence it will have to work much harder to stay together because it has little real incentive to collaborate beyond a superficial level. This is an important point. Organisations sometimes try to harness the identification benefits of groups by assigning workers into *nominal* or *pseudo teams* rather than fostering real task interdependence. This can arise from how work is organised or space is shared (pooled interdependence), from connected processes or work flows (sequential interdependence) or from shared needs for information, skills and relating (reciprocal interdependence), known as relational interdependence. Think of groups you are involved in at university. Are they groups assigned by the lecturer or are they groups of your own choice? How has the method of selection impacted on them in terms of interdependence?

A core insight from psychology, anthropology and sociology is the motivating effect of the feeling of belonging. Indeed, many view belonging as a basic human need ▸**Chapter 5**◂. Interestingly, social psychologists have found that when we become part of and belong to a group, we consciously or unconsciously tend to be influenced by the beliefs, expectations and actions of the other people in the group. This is the dynamic of group conformity, where group members may feel pressurised to agree with the opinions and ideas of other group members. Put more simply: we sometimes come to think, feel or behave differently in a group than we might do if we are working alone. We will explore this further when we examine group formation later in the chapter.

Social identity theory (Tajfel, 1974) tells us that we divide the world into 'us' (known as our in-groups) and 'them' (known as out-groups) in a process of social categorisation. We exhibit in-group bias by favouring members of our own group over members of other groups. Indeed, Tajfel (1974) states that the in-group will discriminate against the out-group to enhance their perception of themselves ▸**Chapter 3**◂. Others who we believe share our particular qualities are in our in-group, and those who do not are in our out-group. This distinction is one that is used a lot in the sports arena. Rivalry between certain terms is seen as a way to drive group performance. The creation of a 'them' and 'us' approach, where a strong identification is made with your own team – the in-group – over the other team – the out-group – is commonplace in team sports such as football, cricket and basketball. For example, in football,

---

synergy occurs when the effect of combining efforts leads to more creative or effective outcomes than would have been achieved had each individual operated alone

task interdependence the degree of mutual reliance and reciprocity within the group

relational interdependence the degree of mutuality or give and take

group conformity the tendency of group members to consciously or unconsciously align their beliefs and behaviours with the apparent beliefs and behaviours of the group

in-group bias the process whereby members of a group favour members of their own group over members of other groups

Alex Ferguson, former manager of Manchester United, regularly used the 'us-against-them' approach, fostering a siege mentality to motivate his group of players.

We've seen so far that working together can be energising and rewarding, but it can also be complicated and time-consuming, and does not always lead to positive outcomes. Struggles to communicate, to agree and to coordinate mean that groups are not always efficient or effective, and at times they may not feel comfortable places to be. We will deal with these issues later in the chapter; now we will move on to a discussion of different types of groups.

TYPES OF GROUP

In a work context groups can be transient, only coming together for a specific amount of time, or ongoing. You might currently be a member of a group project for some of your modules, of the organising committee for an end of year ball, or perhaps at work you are part of a new group working on product development or a member of the engineering department. Group membership can be relatively static or highly changeable. Groups can be self-selecting or organisationally defined, and range from nominated structures such as committees and boards, to organisational principles such as departments, occupational groupings and staff categories. They can also arise through shared interests, such as trade union membership, sports and social groups. As a result, groups are normally categorised as formal or informal. Formal groups are to be found in every organisation. They are deliberately formed in order to allow the organisation to achieve its objectives. Membership of these groups is usually determined by those in authority in the organisation and they also set out the rules of operation. Formal groups can also be classified as command or task groups. Command groups are permanent formal groups that are formed as a result of organisational structures. From the example above, the new product development group and the engineering department fall into this category. Task groups are temporary groups designed to deal with specific issues and are dismantled once the task is complete. An example would be the group at a book publisher consisting of marketing managers, editors, IT systems executives and project managers brought together to launch the company's new website.

Informal groups emerge in the organisation from the informal interaction of people at work. Their membership and rules of engagement are internally rather than externally defined. Group membership often crosses the boundaries of the formal groups. The people we normally have lunch with or see socially after work are members of our informal group. These groups can often be a source of concern for management because they have no control over group membership. As the Hawthorne Studies (Roethlisberger and Dickson, 1939) famously revealed, informal groups can be powerful and have a significant effect on what gets done

formal groups are officially established, usually as a result of the organisation's structure, with a specific purpose

command groups permanent formal groups that are formed as a result of organisational structures

task groups temporary groups designed to deal with specific issues and are dismantled once the task is complete

informal groups are those which develop naturally in the workplace in response to a need for belonging in the workplace ▸**Chapter 1**◂. This 'below the surface' dynamic is often forgotten about in the formal structures of organisations, but is one of the reasons why the study of groups is interesting and insightful. Have you ever worked anywhere where the informal group was able to impact either negatively or positively on the organisation?

CONSIDER THIS...

Take a moment to draw a circle and divide it into pie-shaped pieces reflecting the group affiliations that are part of your life and identity, sized by how important they are to you.

What do they mean to you? How do they affect you? Are they formal or informal? How would you feel if you were no longer part of each of the groups?

GROUP DEVELOPMENT

Regardless of the type of group, groups take time to come together and become cohesive. Research by Tuckman (1965) indicates that groups pass through clearly defined stages of development (see Figure 7.1). In the first stage, *forming*, individuals are getting to know each other and finding out about each other's attitudes and backgrounds. There is often a nervousness associated with this stage because individuals are assessing one another and trying to make a good impression. As a collection of individuals meet, they are confronted with the advantages of becoming a group, and equally, the challenges. Questions for each member at this time are: Will this be OK? What will I gain and what will I lose? Will I fit in? Will everyone work to get the job done? There is a high level of uncertainty and – for most of us – uncertainty is uncomfortable. In general, members will take a low-stakes approach, rather than offering immediate commitment. The more confident or experienced in the group may push forward to suggest how the group might work and offer route maps, but everyone knows that this early stage is critical and full of judgements. If you have ever watched the TV programme *Big*

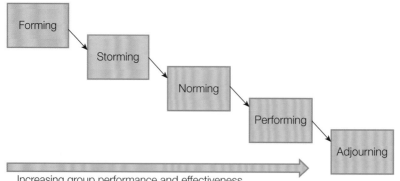

Increasing group performance and effectiveness

Figure 7.1 Stages of group development

Brother you will have seen how people are reticent to reveal much of themselves when they initially meet the others in the Big Brother house.

The second stage, *storming*, is where the group members are getting to know each other better. People begin to settle into the group and this is the stage when the most conflict arises between group members. It may be that more than one person wants to be identified as the leader of the group, or that differences in personal goals are revealed. This stage is critical to group development as a group can end up 'stuck' here for a considerable amount of time. Group roles – the pattern of behaviour expected of each group member – are identified in this stage. Benne and Sheats (1948) have identified three broad types of roles people play in small groups: task roles, building and maintenance roles, and self-centered roles. *Task roles* focus on completing the group objective, for example, taking the minutes of a meeting. *Building or maintenance roles* focus on building interpersonal relationships, for example, someone who offers encouragement by providing positive feedback. *Self-centered roles* focus on preventing the group from achieving its goal, for example, the person who does not pull their weight. This issue is known as social loafing (Karau and Williams, 1993) and people who engage in social loafing often think others in the group do not notice their lack of contribution. We have all been part of a group in which one person does not contribute an equal amount and yet expects to benefit from membership in the same way as those who have contributed. It happens when individuals feel other people will 'pick up the slack' and thus they do not have to do their share of the work (Latane *et al.*, 1979). It is an aspect of group work that is of particular concern where individual contributions are not measured.

Once the group members have developed ways of working together the group decides who will do which tasks and how they will be done. The third stage, *norming*, identifies the norms within the group. All groups have norms that govern their behaviour. They have a strong effect on group behaviour and can be difficult to change (Feldman, 1984). For example, everyone will arrive punctually at meetings and there will be time after the meetings for some social chat, but not during the meetings. Street gangs and prison gangs have been a useful source of information on the study of group norms because their norms are often very obvious to outsiders, for example gang tattoos and clothing (Hughes and Short, 2005; Vigil, 2010; Skarbek, 2012). Norming is a comforting process of converging so that there is less need to question and more agreement, and goals and roles are relatively clear to each member. This phase travels the interesting tightrope between cohesion and conformity, which we discuss in more detail shortly.

The final stage, *performing*, relates to the effective performance of the group. Here the group has developed effective productive methods of working and is meeting its goals. Not all groups make it to this stage, however. In Figure 7.1 we see a further stage called *adjourning*,

group roles the pattern of behaviour expected of each group member

social loafing where a group member exerts less effort in the group than if they were working alone

norms the unwritten and unspoken rules and expectations of behaviour that apply to the group's members

which is a late addition to the original model. This is the stage where the group disbands, either because it has achieved the group task or because the members have left the group. For a high-performing team this stage can bring feelings of sadness because they will no longer be working together as a group. This stage was added to the group development process some 10 years after the original model was developed (Tuckman and Jensen, 1977).

While this group development process may look linear, it is often the case that groups move from one stage to the next and back again, before moving forward once more. The 'punctuated equilibrium' view, for example, observes that a group may move back and forth through these stages as new things happen (such as the arrival of a new member, or a significant change in group context or task). In the Big Brother house the group may find it difficult to move out of the storming stage, depending on the motives of the group members. They may move from the storming to the norming stage and back to the storming stage on a cyclical basis until some 'difficult' members of the group are voted out of the house.

GROUP PROPERTIES

There are many variables which affect overall group performance, such as roles, size, cohesiveness and conformity. Group dynamics such as these have been the subject of a significant amount of research which has resulted in a number of theories (Lewin, 1948; 1951). In this section we deal with some of the key properties and processes that impact on the performance of groups.

GROUP ROLES

We have briefly looked at the way in which people take on roles in a group. If we consider the example of the Big Brother house, people will take responsibility for cooking, or cleaning the house, or for being the 'mother' of the group, or the 'entertainer' of the group. The roles people take on have an important impact on the group's development and its effectiveness. In life we have many roles, such as sister/brother, friend, waitress/waiter, student and girlfriend/boyfriend, many of which may conflict with each other. For example, if your work as a waitress/waiter interferes with your work as a student, but you need to earn money to pay for tuition fees, you are experiencing *role conflict*. This happens when two or more *role expectations* (the way other people believe you should act in a given context) are contradictory. One of the most interesting studies on roles was conducted by Philip Zimbardo and his colleagues from Stanford University in the US. Seemingly normal and well-adjusted students were recruited to participate in this landmark 1971 study about the psychology of imprisonment. The results showed that students took their role-playing as prisoners and guards to extremes, with the 'guards' turning power-hungry, violent and occasionally sadistic, resulting in the shutting down of the experiment after only 6 days. You can see this experiment on the big screen in a movie based on the study, *The Stanford Prison Experiment* (2015).

Personality Profiling and Effective Team Performance

As research highlights, the dynamics of interpersonal relationships in teams depend more on individuals' personalities than on hard skills or expertise. You can put world-class talent together on a team, and it may still fail to perform as a cohesive unit. In fact, leading researchers believe that the only way to create a team that's worth more than the sum of its individual contributors is to select members on the basis of personality, soft skills and values.

Personality profiling can be a very useful tool in helping us better understand how to relate to team members. While we know that personality type doesn't explain everything about us, that people with the same personality type often behave differently and that no personality type is inherently better than another, certain personality types work better together and some

OB IN THE NEWS

are more suited to certain roles on the team.

Most leaders understand the benefits of collaboration – they've seen plenty of evidence that it increases firms' competitiveness. By building teams that can collaborate across boundaries of geography, ethnicity and loyalty, they'll be better equipped to deliver what their organisations need, even in this age of matrix reporting and globally dispersed workforces.

To that end, a number of organisations are using personality profiling to build their teams. For example, Edmunds, a sort of TripAdvisor for cars, uses personality tests to identify the most promising candidates for its executive team, and Buffer, a social media firm, uses them to create virtual teams and pilot novel organisational structures that eschew managers and formal roles. Personality profiles aren't just a tool for new recruits, either. They would be ideal for existing team members as well. They can help members understand the current team dynamics, and learn strategies for improving communication, respect and trust. This could greatly help to turn around underperforming teams, or teams that are negatively affected by interpersonal conflict.

Interestingly, a recent article posted on Yahoo! Sports identifies personality profiling as a technique that is being successfully used by a growing number of sports coaches and recruiters at the college level to evaluate the strengths and weaknesses of

© ROYALTY-FREE/CORBIS

potential team members. With increasing frequency, college coaches have been asking prospective recruits to take a personality test before making them an offer. This is a practice that has been in use at the professional level for years. NFL and NBA teams grade potential draft prospects on their speed, strength or proficiency in certain drills; they also use clinical interviews, aptitude tests and personality surveys as evaluation tools. The goal is to determine which potential draftees will thrive under pressure, respond when challenged and fit in the locker room culture. Personality profiling is a natural fit as an evaluation tool during the recruiting process, it can also help coaches to figure out what motivational techniques to use to bring out the best in their current teams too.

Questions

1 Do you believe personality profiling can make a positive contribution to team member selection?

2 In what way do you think personality profiling can help an already established team?

Sources:

https://hbr.org/2015/03/personality-tests-can-help-balance-a-team (last accessed on 20 August 2015).

http://sports.yahoo.com/blogs/ncaab-the-dagger/personality-profiling-latest-method-coaches-using-evaluate-potential-143500770.html (last accessed on 20 August 2015).

www.discinsights.com/blog/education/trend-watch-coaches-use-personality-profiling-as-a-recruitment-tool (last accessed on 20 August 2015).

GROUP SIZE

The size of the group has a direct impact on group performance and productivity. The larger the group the more difficult it is to have clear lines of communication and to coordinate tasks. The old saying 'too many cooks spoil the broth' is borne out of this type of situation. Conversely, where the number of group members is small and the task is complex, there may not be enough resources to complete the task. In a small group of three people, issues like social loafing are more easily visible and communication within the group is more intimate. For example, research from Seijts and Latham (2001) highlights that individual performance in seven-person groups was significantly lower than individual performance in three-person groups. However, research evidence varies in relation to the optimal size of a group, with some indicating that seven is the optimal number (Blenko *et al.*, 2009). In general, the appropriate group size is dependent on both the task and the context in which the group operates.

GROUP COHESIVENESS

Group cohesiveness can be thought of as the glue that binds the group together and represents a form of solidarity between group members (Beal *et al.*, 2003). In a cohesive group, members place a value on being part of the group and interpersonal relationships are strong. Group cohesiveness is identified as a key factor in successful sports teams (Carron *et al.*, 2002). The main factors that influence group cohesiveness are:

- Group size;
- Members' similarity;
- Entry difficulty;
- Group success;
- External competition and threats.

As it is easier for smaller groups to coordinate their activities, they are often more cohesive than larger groups. The more group members are similar to each other on various characteristics the easier it is to reach cohesiveness. As discussed earlier, we know from social identity theory (Tajfel, 1974) that people feel closer to those they perceive as similar to themselves ▶Chapter 3◀. In addition, coming from a similar background makes it more likely that members share similar views. In a survey of 500 hiring managers, 74 per cent reported that their most recent hire had a personality similar to theirs. This is not necessarily a good thing, however. The study interviewed professionals from elite investment banks, consultancies and law firms about how they recruited, interviewed and evaluated candidates, and concluded that among the most important factors driving their hiring recommendations were shared leisure interests. As explained by one attorney, 'The best way I could describe it is like if you were going on a date. You kind of know when there's

group cohesiveness the force that binds a group together

a match' (see http://stamfordglobal.com/insights/20150305/they-are-watching-you-work, last accessed on 4 September 2015).

Entry difficulty to the group also creates a sense of exclusivity. The more elite the group is perceived to be, the more prestigious it is to be a member in that group. Consequently, members are more motivated to belong and stay in the group. This is particularly true where the group is successful. Group rivalry, in the form of external threats, is often used to encourage competition and stimulate performance levels, particularly in sales.

Group diversity has been found to be an important factor impacting group performance. Diversity among employees can create better performance when it comes to creative tasks such as product development, and managers have tried to increase diversity to achieve the benefits of innovation and fresh ideas (Northcraft *et al.*, 1995). Strong group cohesiveness sounds like an ideal situation, and in many cases it is. However, strongly cohesive groups can also cause problems. They can become defensive of their group membership and output, and make it difficult for new members to join the group. They can resist change and become overly protective of their decisions. This can lead to issues of group conformity and groupthink, both of which are discussed below.

GROUP CONFORMITY

A seminal study by Asch (1951) highlights the pressure group members feel to conform to group norms. In his classic experiment he showed a group of volunteers a line and asked them to say aloud which of three other lines matched it in length (see Figure 7.2). However, only one of the subjects was a real volunteer. The others were planted by Asch and were told to give an incorrect answer to the question. In almost one-third of cases the volunteer went along with the wrong answer, even though it was very obviously incorrect. This study demonstrated how difficult it is to go against the opinions of others, even when you know their opinion is wrong. There is strong social pressure to conform when among our peers. Can you think of a time when you have found yourself in a situation like this? How did you feel and what did you do?

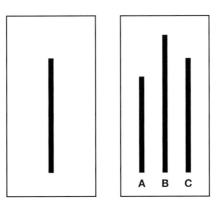

Figure 7.2 The Asch experiment

GROUPTHINK

Groupthink is similar to the concept of conformity, and as a term was created by social psychologist, Irving Janis. It occurs when a group makes faulty decisions because group pressures lead to a deterioration of 'mental efficiency, reality testing, and moral judgment' (Janis, 1972, p. 9). Janis noted that high levels of group cohesiveness can lead to groupthink and identifies eight symptoms of this phenomenon:

- Illusion of invulnerability – this creates excessive optimism that encourages extreme risk-taking.
- Belief in inherent morality – members believe in the rightness of their cause and therefore ignore the ethical or moral consequences of their decisions.
- Collective rationalisation – members have a collective mind set and discount warnings.
- Stereotyped views of out-groups – negative views of the 'enemy' make effective responses to conflict seem unnecessary.
- Direct pressure on dissenters – members are under pressure not to express disagreements with any of the group's views.
- Self-censorship – doubts and deviations from the perceived group consensus are not expressed.
- Illusion of unanimity – the majority view is assumed to be unanimous.
- Self-appointed 'mindguards' – members protect the group and the leader from information that is problematic or contradictory to the group's cohesiveness, view and/or decisions.

One of the key ways to avoid groupthink occurring is for the group to encourage its members to voice their opinions and to actively critically evaluate the group's decisions. Another technique is to appoint someone to the role of devil's advocate. Much of the analysis of the 2008 global financial crisis points to the possibility of groupthink having played a role in the collapse of some financial institutions.

CONSIDER THIS...

Can a minority influence a majority? What strategies are available to you to influence a group? *12 Angry Men* is an absorbing film about the dynamics of a jury faced with working out whether a young man is guilty of murder. Through the lens of the film we see one individual challenge the almost unanimous view of the group that the young man did commit the crime. You can watch clips of the film on YouTube to consider the way he did this.

groupthink when maintaining group conformity is more important than critically evaluating alternative viewpoints, even if it means actively discouraging dissenting opinions

GROUPS AND TEAMS

So far we have discussed groups in detail, including what they are, their different types, their purpose and how they develop. But what is the difference between a group and a team? Before you read further, think about your answer to this question. For some this distinction is very clear, but it is true that the terms are often used interchangeably in popular discourse. In an organisational behaviour context a team is defined as a group of people working together with a defined purpose in order to achieve a common goal. While individuals who have some relationship with one another or who share similar traits may be part of a group, a team essentially means that all members are involved in the same activity. Unsurprisingly then, organisations develop teams to achieve goals that are considered too complex, lengthy or challenging to be completed by individuals working alone. Hence, one of the fundamental differences between workplace groups and teams is that, while individuals who are part of a group will often share knowledge and expertise with each other, this is primarily to help others in the group achieve their own individual aims rather than to complete an overarching task together, which is the aim of a team. Table 7.2 outlines some of the core differences between groups and teams.

Table 7.2 Differences between groups and teams

Characteristic	Groups	Teams
Purpose	Knowledge and information sharing between group members. The aims of groups are generally broad and reflect the main aims of the organisation.	The achievement of a common goal by all individuals in the team. Team aims can be specialised and clearly defined for each member as part of the organisation's objectives.
Leadership	Since groups are not established with a shared specific goal to achieve, a single leader is generally appointed in a role much like a chairperson, to speak on behalf of the group rather than coordinate tasks.	An official team leader is appointed whose role may be shared or rotated among members.
Skills and task orientation	Group members can possess a diverse range of skills and no coordination of task completion among the members is required.	Members possess a range of skills which complement each other, and the allocation and achievement of tasks within the team is tightly coordinated.
Accountability	Accountable for individual performance only.	Both individually and mutually responsible for team performance.
Size	Unlimited.	Limited, but a team should have enough members to ensure the achievement of its goals. The CIPD (2002) suggests that 6–8 is optimum.
Synergy	Neutral.	Positive, with team performance greater than the sum of individual efforts.

team a group of people working together with a defined purpose in order to achieve a common goal

A vast array of management research now exists which clearly shows that in general teams outperform individual efforts. From an organisational perspective, teams have been found to improve levels of overall productivity, strengthen the competitive advantage of the organisation over its rivals, lead to advances in innovation and creativity, improve quality and to improve job satisfaction, motivation and commitment to the organisation among employees (Parker, 1990). As such, teams (of many different forms) are now a standard feature of most modern organisational structures. The way in which individuals and groups are structured and coordinated in terms of the task they perform within the organisation, and the way in which the structural aspects are configured are key elements in the success of an organisation ▸Chapter 11◂.

An understanding of team processes and structure is therefore an essential part of a manager's role.

> The leaders who work most effectively, it seems to me, never say 'I'. They don't think 'I'. They think 'we'; they think 'team'. They understand their job to be to make the team function. They accept responsibility and don't sidestep it, but 'we' gets the credit. (Drucker, 2011, p. 14)

As this quote from management guru, Peter Drucker, quite clearly shows, to be a successful manager in a modern organisation requires the ability to manage a team effectively.

TYPES OF TEAMS IN ORGANISATIONS

Teams can serve a variety of functions in organisations. However, depending on the task to be achieved or the working environment in which it is to be completed, different types of teams with varying structures can be developed. In today's globalised and competitive business environment traditional corporate structures aren't always best-placed to deliver fast efficient results to businesses and therefore must be reviewed. This often results in the creation of various types of teams in the organisation. In this section we will discuss five types of teams commonly found in organisations: cross-functional, self-managed, problem-solving, virtual and management.

CROSS-FUNCTIONAL TEAMS

A cross-functional team draws on members who are responsible for varying tasks in the organisation and brings them together to achieve a specific purpose. The bringing together of a cross-functional mix of members ensures that a range of diverse skills and talents are present in the team. For example, a cross-functional team in a manufacturing setting will have members from product development, production management, engineering, sales and marketing when designing a new product. Taking part in one of these cross-functional teams is often referred to as *boundary spanning*. Large organisations, particularly those in the automobile sector, have been

cross-functional teams have members from a range of functional departments within the organisation working towards a common goal

utilising cross-functional teams for decades. Toyota, for example, uses this type of team design in complex projects and in product development. While the great benefit of cross-functional teams is the varying insights and perspectives brought to them by so many different backgrounds, there are some drawbacks. The development of a cross-functional team can take time; also, with so many differing perspectives, achieving agreement and consensus decision-making can be difficult. Sobek *et al.* (1998) found that in the case of Toyota a dilution of knowledge within each functional level was a problem because individuals were spending too much time away from their core roles on other projects. This is an important difference between a cross-functional team and the creation of an entirely new division; the premise of a cross-functional team is that members will maintain substantial contact and links to their own departmental area. For example, an engineer working on a new product design may be part of a cross-functional team drawing on designers, engineers and marketers but ultimately she is still part of the engineering department.

SPOTLIGHT ON SKILLS

Teams are accepted as a feature of working life, whether we enjoy this aspect of work or not. How would you help a team in your organisation to be effective? Would you utilise training such as team roles analysis? Why or why not? If you would, how would you use it? Would you use team building? If you would, what would you do and how would you measure or perceive its effects?

To help you answer these questions, in your ebook click the play button to watch the video of Doug Howlett, a former rugby player who has played for the All Blacks (New Zealand) and Munster.

SELF-MANAGED WORK TEAMS (SMWT)

Self-managed work teams (SMWTs) can also be referred to as *self-directed teams*. SMWTs often perform tasks traditionally completed by managers (Orsburn *et al.*, 1990). The development and origin of SMWTs arose largely from the socio-technical systems approach and the quality of work life movement, hence such teams strongly feature elements associated

self-managed work teams (SMWTs) consist of a small number of employees who have been given autonomy to plan and manage their team's day-to-day activities with relatively little supervision

with job enrichment ▸ **Chapter 5** ◂ (Polley and Ribbens, 1998). During the 1990s SMWTs were commonly found to exist in product environments where TQM (total quality management) and JIT (just in time) manufacturing processes were also present (Proença, 2010). The role of the SMWT in such settings was to enhance the quality of goods produced and to reduce costs while simultaneously leading to improvements in the levels of job satisfaction and motivation among employees. For example, the introduction of a SMWT in a work setting where an assembly-line style of production existed could serve to improve job satisfaction by giving members of the team more control over their work and reducing monotony in the process. However, while there are many advantages to such teams, a number of problems can also arise. Research has shown that SMWTs can be prone to conflict between members regarding individual levels of productivity (Proença, 2010). It has also shown that employees on self-managing work teams can display higher rates of absenteeism and turnover, despite also supporting the view that employees in autonomous work groups report more favourable work attitudes than their counterparts in traditionally designed jobs. Cordery *et al.* (1991) argued that these are complex behaviours and, as previously suggested by Nicholson and Johns (1985), are caused by diverse reasons often beyond the organisational sphere. Examples of self-managed work teams can be found in a variety of industries. For example, Federal Express has utilised the concept with positive results. Also cited as an example of an organisation embracing the self-managed team idea is the food chain, Taco Bell. Organisations may even be able to reduce the number of management positions in some areas by encouraging teams at various sites to increase their levels of independence and accountability.

PROBLEM-SOLVING TEAMS

Typically, **problem-solving teams** are formed to find solutions to problems regarding quality, costs and efficiency that are identified as needing to be addressed in the organisation. Similar to cross-functional teams, a problem-solving team that has been created to solve a strategic-level issue is likely to draw individuals from different sectors of the organisation so as to facilitate a wider array of perspectives on the problem and identify an appropriate solution. At an operational level, a problem-solving team will generally consist of a small number of employees (fewer than twelve) who will discuss how processes and methods can be improved. Problem-solving teams do not always have the autonomy or resources to implement the recommendations they decide upon. The motor manufacturer Ford has championed the use of problem-solving teams. It operates a process known as 8D (eight disciplines of problem-solving) which involves the identification of the problem, its symptoms, the creation of a team and the design of permanent corrective and preventative actions.

problem-solving team one which is formed specifically to find a solution to an existing problem

VIRTUAL TEAMS

This type of team may never need to meet face to face in a traditional sense to achieve their aims. The presence and use of virtual teams has increased vastly since the 2000s as technological advances have made it possible for more organisations to adopt such work practices. The virtual team has a great number of advantages for both organisations and employees themselves. Cascio (2000) highlights some of these benefits as savings in time and expenses, since access to experts in a variety of locations through electronic collaboration reduces the need for travel within and between organisations. In addition, Cascio points out that virtual teams allow organisations to draw on a wider pool of talent when selecting team members because they are no longer restricted by geographical location. For employees, working as part of a virtual team can be beneficial in terms of gaining expertise through collaboration with a diverse group and from a work–life perspective cut down on travel and potentially facilitate a remote working or working-from-home option. However, in spite of the many advantages virtual working creates, drawbacks also exist with regard to communications style. In a virtual team many of the non-verbal signals and cues between members are neglected ▶**Chapter 10**◀. Furthermore, Mann (2013) shows that it can be challenging for managers to develop and foster a sense of trust between team members in a virtual setting. Virtual teams are now using a wide variety of settings within and beyond the technology sector. Take, for example, the university or college in which you are studying. It is very likely that the researchers and lecturers you meet on a daily basis work in virtual teams on international research projects. For many virtual teams the challenge is operating without a clear management structure and this is an issue which the team members may have to negotiate for themselves in some instances.

MANAGEMENT TEAMS

A management team is one which consists of individuals with managerial roles in different areas of the organisation who coordinate the work of their respective teams. It is therefore usually one which is ongoing and does not end or disband with the completion of a specific task or project. One of the fundamental roles of a top management team is to effectively coordinate the efforts of interdependent work teams at lower levels in the organisation. These managers also serve a coaching role and provide guidance for those in the teams they coordinate. Top management teams often experience problems in working effectively as a team due to the characteristics of high-powered individuals within the team who may find it difficult to share resources or adapt to being part of a team rather than a leader (Hart, 1996).

---

virtual team: one in which the team members are dispersed geographically and where the team communicates and collaborates together through the use of a variety of electronic systems

management team one which consists of individuals with managerial roles in different areas of the organisation who coordinate the work of their respective teams

CONSIDER THIS...

Understanding team roles

www.youtube.com/watch?v=E95Vw5fbQhU

Watch this YouTube clip in which Meredith Belbin (the founder of Belbin's team roles) discusses possible answers to questions such as: What role should we play in a team? What is the ideal size of team? Do we need all nine team roles present in a team at all times?

TEAM ROLES

A team role refers to a pattern of behaviour or set of characteristics that is displayed in the way one team member interacts with another when serving to progress the performance of the team towards its aims. As discussed earlier, for any team to perform effectively a sense of cooperation among its members has to exist. We pointed out that one of the key differences between groups and teams lies in the sense of purpose they have; in other words, teams have a clearly defined sense of purpose while the aims of a group are broad and less clearly defined. In order for teams to work cooperatively to achieve their goals, members must fulfil different roles. According to Belbin (1993b), for a team to cooperate successfully members need to perform a variety of functions and roles which complement each other rather than overlap, in which case conflict is likely to occur or possible aspects of the task could be overlooked. In the 1970s, management psychologist Meredith Belbin conducted research studies which sought to identify certain patterns of behaviour which could in turn be used to predict the success of teams in a variety of different projects. Belbin used the basic psychological personality types ▶ Chapter 2 ◀ to divide participants across simulated teams. She identified nine team roles which are described in Table 7.3.

Belbin's investigation showed that the difference between successful and unsuccessful teams was less dependent on factors related to intelligence and experience but primarily related to behaviour within the team. Factors included the way team members made decisions and cooperated with each other, and how each individual applied their abilities to reach the team goal (Batenburg et al., 2013). The Belbin model continues to be extremely popular and is used by many FTSE 100 companies in team development. However, there has been some criticism of the model, particularly regarding the validity of the psychometric measures and instruments used to determine each of the role types (Broucek and Randell, 1996). In examining the Belbin Team Role Self-Perception Inventory (BTRSPI), Furnham, Steel and Pendleton found the predictive or construct validity to be unimpressive. Belbin (1993a) responded to this criticism of the tool's validity by pointing out that Furnham and colleagues had not adopted the recommended method of use for the BTRSPI, insisting that the tool was designed to intimate to individuals what their team roles might be.

team role refers to a pattern of behaviour or set of characteristics that is displayed in the way one team member interacts with another when serving to progress the performance of the team towards its aims

Table 7.3 Belbin's nine team roles typology

Role Type	Description
Plant (PL)	The title derives from the fact that one such individual is 'planted' in each team . The Plant tends to display creative qualities and is skilled at problem-solving in unusual ways.
Monitor Evaluator (ME)	The Monitor Evaluator role describes a team member who is logical and impartial in their judgments. This individual is capable of assessing a team's available options in a calm, unemotional manner.
Coordinator (CO)	This role fulfils the requirement of focusing on the team's objectives and delegating tasks based on each person's expertise.
Resource Investigator (RI)	The Resource Investigator role describes a team member who is an extrovert, skilled at making contacts and ensuring that the team has identified clearly its challenges with respect to competitors and its future opportunities.
Implementer (IMP)	Implementers create practical plans and strategies of work to ensure that tasks are completed efficiently.
Completer Finishers (CF)	Completer Finishers display their talents most effectively at the end of task when quality and attention to detail are required for completion of a project.
Teamworker (TW)	Teamworkers help the team to work together by being versatile, identifying tasks and completing them for the team.
Shaper (SH)	Shapers are viewed as challenging individuals who are skilled at sustaining the momentum of the team and helping others to focus on the task at hand.
Specialist (SP)	Specialists present with the in-depth knowledge of a key area that is essential to team success.

Source: Based on information in the Belbin Team Role Report from www.belbin.com/rte.asp?id=8.

BUILDING YOUR

Team Building

You have provisionally been appointed team leader to a group of ten telesales operatives in a fundraising charity organisation. Your appointment is conditional on your achievement of excellent results in your final exams and winning a social enterprise business plan competition that has had a lot of media attention. However, you have no experience in management or telesales. How would you approach the first day and your first meeting with the team? What steps would you take to support, motivate and manage your team?

(Continued)

Team Building (*Continued*)

Guidance

The *Harvard Business Review Guide to Leading Teams* (https://hbr.org/product/hbr-guide-to-leading-teams-ebook-tools/10022E-KND-ENG, last accessed on 27 November 2015) by Mary L. Shapiro provides advice for managers in leading teams. The guide advocates six important facets in managing teams effectively. Firstly, choosing the right team members for tasks and cultivating their skills accordingly; secondly, setting clear goals for the group; thirdly, fostering a sense of camaraderie and cooperation among the team; fourthly, holding individuals accountable for their actions and setting expectations for individual and team behaviour; finally, maintaining team focus and motivation until tasks are accomplished. Shapiro also highlights the importance of the initial stages of meeting a new team. She states that a priority must be 'to get to know your team members and to encourage them to get to better know one another', and to 'resist the urge to immediately start talking about the work and the task outcome'. Team activities and icebreaker techniques are often suggested as really useful ways to foster this approach. Visit http://humanresources.about.com/od/icebreakers/a/my-10-best-ice-breakers.htm (last accessed on 21 August 2015) for icebreaker and team activity ideas.

HIGH-PERFORMING WORK TEAMS

Throughout this chapter we have emphasised that groups and teams possess a kind of synergy that is greater than the sum of individual efforts. However, it is important to bear in mind that this is only the case when they function successfully and achieve results which reflect those efforts. Naturally, in business just as in sport, no team can be successful and win one hundred per cent of the time. When a team's failure can be put down to strong external competition, lessons can be taken for future performance. However, when a team is unsuccessful because of internal factors such as a lack of cooperation between members, insufficient resources from management or the presence of groupthink, then an organisation must look at how team structures can be improved.

Although high-performing work teams will have many attributes, Nelson (2010) has identified seven key characteristics which capture most of these elements. These include purpose, empowerment, relationships and communication, flexibility, optimal productivity, recognition and appreciation, and morale (see Table 7.4).

While Table 7.4 outlines the value of each of the characteristics of high-performing teams from an organisational perspective it is also important to focus on what this means for individual and team behaviour in the workplace. Take for example an individual working in a health care setting. An understanding of the sense of purpose of the organisation and of each individual within it is vital, thereby ensuring quality health care not just in terms of medical interventions but in all other functions from administration to cleaning and maintenance. Furthermore, if we look at empowerment and flexibility, we see the importance of individuals

Table 7.4 Characteristics of high-performing work teams

Characteristic	Value
Purpose	All members are aware of the team's mission and why it is important. They have a precise understanding of the aim that needs to be achieved and they develop mutually agreed upon goals that relate to that aim. Clear action strategies are created and each member understands his or her role.
Empowerment	Mutual respect within the team enables members to share responsibilities, support each other and take the initiative, providing personal as well as collective power. Sets of rules and processes exist to enable members to do their jobs more easily.
Relationships and communication	An atmosphere of trust and acceptance is created through open communication, and differences of opinion are valued. Methods for managing conflict are established. Members provide honest and constructive feedback to each other.
Flexibility	Members are flexible and perform different functions as needed. Members recognise that change is inevitable and are willing to adapt to changing conditions.
Optimal productivity	High-performing teams display a commitment to high standards. Effective decision-making and problem-solving methods result in optimal task accomplishment.
Recognition and appreciation	Both individual and team accomplishments are regularly acknowledged by the leader, the other team members and the organisation as a whole.
Morale	Members share a sense of pride in being part of the team and a strong sense of team spirit exists.

Source: Based on information in Nelson (2010).

being able and having the authority to take on alternative roles and work within a team in order to deal with issues such as absenteeism or employee turnover on a day-to-day basis. Previously in this chapter we discussed how groupthink can be detrimental to decision-making. The collapse of Swissair in 2002 is often cited as an example of groupthink in an organisation. The airline was nicknamed 'the Flying Bank' because of its strong financial status. On its collapse, it was found that the board of managing directors of the airline was insufficient in size and indeed lacked expertise in a broad range of areas (see Hermann and Rammal (2010) for a wider discussion of corporate groupthink).   Strong communication channels and good working relationships between team members are essential in avoiding situations of groupthink or poor decision-making by putting people on the team in a position to voice opposition to ideas. From a management perspective, providing recognition for work and fostering a sense of pride in team achievements is hugely important to task achievement. This is true even in a voluntary setting. Take for example the success of the 2012 London Olympics, much of which was attributed to the successful management of thousands of volunteers.

As with leadership, a key determinant of the success or failure of team structures is the context. Does the context support and empower team operation? Teams are often presented as a kind of universal solution to organisational problems, but of course, this is unrealistic.

Teams, no more than anything else, can only thrive if they are well matched to their environment. Teams are now a much more integral part of the organisational landscape than they were in the past. However, this is not always comfortable or effective. With justification, a lot of effort goes into team-building activity in organisations – giving teams the chance to bond, the structural and cultural support to thrive, and the knowledge to understand potential group difficulties and how to overcome them.

Quality Teamwork?

SemTech Inc. is a world leader in the manufacture of semi-conductor technologies for use in both large and small electronic-based consumables. The organisation was established as a medium-sized manufacturing company in Portland, Oregon in 1972 but has since grown into a publicly traded multinational corporation employing 8,000 people across 16 countries worldwide. The organisation is widely recognised as a leader in the market, both in terms of quality of items produced and the excellent service it provides to its corporate customers. In 2010 the company was valued at over US$3bn. While the main manufacturing sites for the organisation have traditionally

been US and Europe-based, in 2010 SemTech purchased a large-scale manufacturing facility in Guangzhou, China. This action was in line with the organisation's strategic plan to increase sales in the Asian market where it was struggling to compete on price with other manufacturers. By 2012, the facility was operational with a workforce of almost 700 people. Unlike the European and US plants, production workers in the new facility have very little autonomy in their roles. The facility has so far had excellent production statistics, and this has contributed to rising sales in the Asian market.

SemTech operates a state of the art quality system in all its operations, utilising quality management processes such as 5S, Lean technology and Six Sigma practices. These systems are designed to improve production efficiency and quality. While each manufacturing operation has its own internal quality and reliability teams, the main quality function is based at company headquarters in Portland. The quality office is made of three main teams: the Internal Quality Processes (IQP) team, the Product Reliability and Test (PRT) team, and the Defective Product and Customer Returns (DPCR) team. The quality function in Portland employs approximately 50 people mainly from engineering, science and technology backgrounds. The quality function is led by the Quality Director, Jon Traynor, who has been employed by SemTech since 1999. Jon and the three other team managers travel to each of the manufacturing sites on an annual basis, but beyond that they keep in touch with local-level quality teams via teleconferencing, email and online virtual meetings.

Since the end of the second quarter in 2013 the Defective Product and Customer Returns (DPCR) teams had noted an unacceptably high level of customer returns based on

© ISTOCK.COM/CGFFEEYU

products from the Guangzhou site. This led to some internal conflicts in the Portland office between the DPCR team and the IQP and PRT teams. The leader of the DPCR team, Peter Harris, made it clear that he feels it is unfair that his team should have to deal with so many returns which clearly wouldn't have occurred if the other teams had been liaising effectively with the local-level quality team in Guangzhou. The other team leaders responded similarly by informing Jon Traynor, the Quality Director, that the quality teams in Guangzhou were extremely 'difficult to deal with'. For example, the IQP team noted that they routinely failed to supply documentation of quality processes on time. In addition, the PRT team reported that the Guangzhou team regularly delayed or cancelled vital system shutdowns which were required as part of the reliability check process, choosing instead to use the time to increase production levels in the factory. Jon was aware that there were some issues to iron out with the new facility, such as the level of information sharing. However, until then he had not acted upon anything. Because the top management team had been so impressed with the impact of the new facility on sales he felt it unwise to bring up problems prematurely and planned instead to go and visit the site in the coming months.

In the first quarter of 2014, just before Jon's planned visit to Guangzhou, an unexpected crisis occurred. One of the micro imaging engineers in the DPCR team discovered that the part which was being returned was in fact not produced by SemTech at all. The part, which had the company trademark, was in fact counterfeit. An investigation by the quality team as a whole revealed that this counterfeit part had been installed in at least 100,000 units and perhaps many more. To have produced such a part the company making the counterfeit must have had a high level of knowledge of the processes and material used by SemTech, not to mention the potential customers for such goods. The team immediately pointed to a lack of tight quality controls at the Guangzhou plant and a failure of the quality team there to keep certain patents and plans confidential.

The presence of counterfeit goods in the market alone has the potential to cost SemTech millions in lost sales, not to mention the costs associated with customer returns of products containing actual SemTech parts produced in China. The top management team pointed the finger firmly at Jon and his team and told him to 'sort this mess out'.

Jon decided to form a crisis problem-solving taskforce of eight people from within his own team in Portland who would spend the eight weeks (or as long as it took) to sort out the problems in Guangzhou. Of course, first he had to try and solve the problem of the bad feelings between the three teams in Portland, not to mention the fact that none of them would want to be part of his new taskforce.

Questions

1 A range of teams are present in this case. While each of the sub-teams appears to be a cohesive unit, problems clearly exist between a number of them. Identify what these problems are and what their root cause might be.

2 We have seen that a virtual team situation exists between the Portland and Guangzhou plant that doesn't presently function well, and in addition defective products have caused division among the main quality team in Portland.

   a Outline how Jon Traynor could develop a more cohesive virtual team between the two sites.

   b Recommend some ways by which Jon could fix the divisions in his own team.

3 The problem-solving task force will not only need to identify problems but also implement changes at the Guangzhou plant. Get into groups and identify a variety of team roles that will be required to ensure a successful intervention over the eight-week period.

 ## SUMMARY

 IN THE EBOOK, CLICK TO HEAR AN AUDIO SUMMARY

The reality of today's world is that every one of us will be part of a group or a team at some point during our working lives. While a distinction is made between groups and teams in this chapter, this difference is not always as obvious. For most organisations the aim of group work is to achieve the results of a high-performing team. In this chapter we have identified that synergy and interdependence can create high levels of performance. However, as we have seen, group work is fraught with difficulties, such as social loafing and groupthink. In order to help us achieve the ideals of teamwork, a number of characteristics and team roles have been identified. The point to remember is that teams, generally, need a lot of support and investment for their potential effectiveness to be optimised.

CHAPTER REVIEW QUESTIONS

1   What is the difference between a group and a team?
2   What are the stages of group development? Discuss and reflect on the characteristics of each stage.
3   What are the challenges and advantages of working in a group, from your own experience?
4   What is group conformity? Discuss and assess the dynamics of conformity using the Asch studies as a reference point.
5   Using Table 7.2, outline three ways in which groups may differ from teams in an organisational setting.
6   List three features of high-performing work teams and outline how these features might differ in an underperforming team.
7   Critically evaluate the advantages for organisations of using virtual teams over traditional teams based in a central location.
8   Identify two drawbacks of:
    (a) self-managed teams;
    (b) cross-functional teams.

MULTIPLE CHOICE QUESTIONS

In your ebook, click to take a multiple choice quiz to test your understanding of this chapter.

FURTHER READING

Bond, M. (2014) *The Power of Others: Peer Pressure, Groupthink and How the People Around Us Shape Everything We Do*, London: Oneworld Publications.

Cain, S. (2012) The Rise of the New Groupthink, *The New York Times*. January 12.
http://www.nytimes.com/2012/01/15/opinion/sunday/the-rise-of-the-new-groupthink.
html?pagewanted=all&_r=0

Sennet, R. (2012) *Together: The Rituals, Pleasures and Politics of Cooperation*, Boston: Yale University Press.

Wheelan, S.A. (2010) *Creating Effective Teams: A Guide for Members and Leaders*, Thousand Oaks, California: Sage.

USEFUL WEBSITES

www.tavinstitute.org/

The Tavistock Institute of Human Relations applies social science insights to contemporary issues and problems. It promotes a learning culture, and helps groups, organisations and individuals to think and reflect. Their website is an interesting source of research, historical background and case studies, looking at organisations and groups through the lens of socio-technical systems.

www.belbin.com/

Belbin Associates is a company founded by Meredith Belbin and others to promote knowledge about Belbin's team roles. While this is a commercial site, it is a useful resource for locating information about the history, sample reports, research and contemporary insights relating to the team roles inventory.

www.ted.com/talks/susan_cain_the_power_of_introverts?language=en

In this highly acclaimed TED Talk, Susan Cain talks about the power of introverts, making a simple but very timely argument about the challenges of being an introvert and navigating a world where being social and outgoing is prized. This is the basis of Cain's subsequent *New York Times* article 'The New Groupthink' and is an interesting perspective on the composition of effective groups. There are further useful resources and counterpoints on her website www.quietrev.com/.

8 LEADERSHIP

Ronan Carbery

LEARNING OBJECTIVES

BY THE END OF THIS CHAPTER YOU SHOULD BE ABLE TO:

- Define leadership and understand the differences between leaders and managers.
- Distinguish between trait, behavioural and contingency leadership theories.
- Explain leader-member exchange theory.
- Recognise the contribution of charismatic leadership theories and articulate what we mean by transformational leadership.

- Explain the issues that need to be considered when deciding whether a leader can be developed.
- Understand why organisations invest in leadership development and recognise different approaches to developing leaders.

© ISTOCK.COM/STUDIOTHREEDOTS

THIS CHAPTER DISCUSSES:

IN REALITY

Some are born great,
some achieve greatness,
and some have greatness thrust upon 'em
Shakespeare, *Twelfth Night* (1602)

This quote touches upon whether people are born leaders or whether it is something that can be developed. We often assume that those who make good leaders possess some attributes that allow them to excel in this role, attributes that the rest of us simply do not have. But are leadership qualities innate or acquired? This is a question that has been debated for decades. Researchers are fascinated by the links between personality and leadership in order to better understand what differentiates leaders from everyone else. Trait theories of leadership identify the specific personality characteristics that distinguish leaders from non-leaders. They are based on the premise that leaders are 'born, not made'. But while early research focused on the relationship between personality and leadership, it reported little supporting evidence. Nevertheless, research interest in this area continues, with Judge and Bono (2000) reporting that 12% of all leadership research published between 1990 and 2004 included the keywords 'personality' and 'leadership'. Interestingly, a 2013 study looking at brain functions in 103 US Army officers found that neural networks in the frontal and prefrontal lobes of those who were deemed to be 'leaders' were different from those who were not (Hannah *et al.*, 2013). These areas of the brain are associated with self-regulation, decision-making and memory.

What are the implications of this? It could potentially revolutionise how organisations assess and develop leaders, with brain scans being used to identify those with the 'leadership gene' early and train them accordingly.

INTRODUCTION

There exists a school of thought which suggests that leadership is in the genes – you are either a born leader or you are not. Others take the view that it is life experience that makes the leader. It is possible that *both* views are correct in that innate factors as well as knowledge and skills that have been acquired over time are considered to be important in explaining the behaviour of leaders. Cognitive abilities and personality traits are partly inherent, suggesting that natural characteristics may enhance or limit the ability to be a leader. Another view is that a leader's basic characteristics are fixed. However it is also possible that different environments may explain whether certain leadership traits are manifested.

Leaders are important because they help organisations to develop an organisational culture ▸Chapter 12◂ and manage organisational change ▸Chapter 13◂. Leaders develop a vision for the future along with strategies for producing the changes needed to achieve that vision. They articulate this vision to employees in order to get their commitment to its achievement and to motivate them to keep them moving in the right direction by appealing to basic but often untapped human needs, values and emotions. Successful leaders who have done this include Jack Welch (General Motors), Steve Jobs (Apple), Hillary Clinton (former US Secretary of State) and Alex Ferguson (Manchester United).

This chapter examines the concept of leadership and considers the importance of effective leadership in organisations. We look at the different theoretical approaches to leadership, including the trait, behavioural, contingency and process approaches, and consider different approaches to leadership development.

WHAT IS LEADERSHIP?

Leadership has been of interest to researchers for decades. According to Bass (1990), 'The study of leadership rivals in age the emergence of civilization, which shaped its leaders as much as it was shaped by them. From its infancy, the study of history has been the study of leaders – what they did and why they did it' (p. 3). The study of leadership has been characterised by not only a significant amount of research, but by shifting interpretations of what it means to be a leader and what leadership actually involves. Over 50 years ago, Bennis (1959) suggested: 'Of all the hazy and confounding areas in social psychology, leadership theory undoubtedly contends for top nomination. And, ironically, probably more has been written and less is known about leadership than about any other topic in the behavioral sciences' (p. 259). In more recent times, thankfully, a more cohesive overview of the nature of leadership has emerged.

Defining leadership in a concise manner isn't an easy task, with Fiedler (1971) highlighting that 'there are almost as many definitions of leadership as there are leadership theories – and there are almost as many theories of leadership as there are psychologists working in the field' (p. 1). Broadly, however, leadership can be characterised as the nature of the influencing process that takes place between a leader and followers, and how this influencing process is affected by the leader's dispositional characteristics, their behaviours, followers' perceptions and the context in which the influencing process takes place.

It is important to differentiate leadership from power and management, because these concepts are often confused with leadership. Power ▶Chapter 9◀ refers to the means leaders have to potentially influence others; for example, referent power (that is, followers' identification with, or respect for the leader), expertise, or the ability to reward or punish performance. In terms of a comparison between leadership and management, leadership is more purpose-driven, resulting in change based on values, ideals and emotional exchanges, whereas management takes a more objectives-driven approach, resulting in stability based on bureaucratic means and the fulfilment of contractual obligations.

There is considerable debate as to how a leader is different from a manager. Cunningham (1986), for example, identifies three different viewpoints on the relationship between

leadership the ability to lead, guide and inspire a group of followers

leadership and management. The first position assumes that leadership is one competency among a range required for effective management. A second position advocated by Bennis and Nanus (2003) suggests that the two concepts are separate but related, whereas the third position sees them as partially overlapping. Academics have identified a need to conceptually distinguish leadership from management, often at the expense of the latter. Management as an activity and concept is frequently viewed as a 'second class citizen', something which is very transactional in nature.

Kotter (1988) has argued that leaders and managers have distinct roles and functions. He considers management to be concerned with planning and organising, whereas leadership is concerned with creating, coping with change and helping organisations to adapt in turbulent times. Other contributions have similarly emphasised that these concepts are different. Boydell *et al.* (2004) consider management to be about implementation, order, efficiency and effectiveness whereas leadership is concerned with future directions in time of uncertainty. They argue that management may be sufficient in an organisation in times of stability, but it is insufficient when organisational conditions are characterised by complexity, unpredictability and rapid change. Research suggests that how well a leader influences his or her followers is related to their self-confidence. However, in order to be an effective leader, it is also important to have the capacity to motivate. Judge and Bono (2000), for example, found that warmth, trustworthiness and altruism are the strongest and most important predictors of leadership. Other studies have found that effective leaders are less critical and aggressive than non-leaders. Leaders are often characterised as having the ability to 'move people' or the ability to inspire others with a vision of the future to which they can aspire. To express this vision with enthusiasm, leaders are expected to be optimistic and energetic.

The ability to provide effective leadership is one of the most important skills that a manager can possess. It is being increasingly recognised that all managers, including first-line supervisors, need at some level to be leaders and to understand the concept of leadership, albeit the higher the organisational level, the more complex leadership becomes and the more it is concerned with broader and long-term aims. In some organisations people may be senior professionals, such as doctors or scientists, but not defined as managers (at least in terms of the formal organisational hierarchy). It would be naive, however, not to think of them as leaders or potential leaders.

Leadership theories can be divided into a number of categories, of which three are covered here: trait, behavioural and situational or contingency theories.

CONSIDER THIS...

A curious statistic emerged during the French Presidential election campaign in 2012. The two main candidates were François Hollande, a socialist, and the incumbent President, Nicolas Sarkozy of the UMP, France's major right-wing political party. Prior to voting, polls suggested that a majority of French voters wanted Hollande as their next President. However, opinion polls also suggested that the French rated Sarkozy more

(Continued)

(Continued)

highly than Hollande for traits associated with leadership. Sarkozy scored better for having 'the authority of a head of state' (53% to 23%), for being 'capable of taking difficult decisions' (49% to 23%), and for being 'capable for taking the right decisions faced with the current economic and financial crisis' (41% to 27%).

On 6 May 2012, François Hollande was elected President of the French Republic with 51.7% of the vote. French political analysts suggested that the result was not out of enthusiasm for Hollande, but borne out of disappointment with Sarkozy's perceived behaviour and attitudes during his five years as President.

This presents an interesting conundrum for politicians. Is being perceived to be a 'leader' sufficient to gain support from voters, or do people prefer to vote for someone who is deemed to be a 'safe pair of hands'? Which do you think would have the biggest influence on your voting decision?

TRAIT THEORIES OF LEADERSHIP

Initial attempts at developing theories of leadership focused on individual traits that people possessed (Gibb, 1947) ▸ **Chapter 2** ◂. Research on leadership prior to the 1950s was based on the psychological focus of people having inherited characteristics or traits. Attention was directed at discovering these traits, often by studying successful leaders but with the underlying assumption that if other people could also be found with these traits, then they, too, could become great leaders.

Later research followed a similar path. Stogdill (1974) identified the traits and skills shown in Table 8.1 as being critical to leaders. For their part, McCall and Lombardo (1983) recognised four primary traits by which leaders could either succeed or fail:

- *Emotional stability and composure:* The ability to be calm, confident and predictable, particularly when under stress, is crucial for leadership success.
- *Admitting error:* Owning up to mistakes, rather than putting energy into covering up, is an important determinant of leadership ability.
- *Good interpersonal skills:* Being able to communicate and persuade others without resorting to negative or coercive tactics is necessary for effective leadership.
- *Intellectual breadth:* Successful leaders are able to understand a wide range of areas, rather than having a narrow area of expertise.

These traits are broadly similar to Richard Branson's (2014) three most important leadership principles: listening (interpersonal skills), learning (intellectual breadth) and laughter (composure).

There have been many different studies of leadership traits, and they agree only in the general honourable qualities needed to be a leader. One of the major criticisms of trait theory is its simplistic approach; that it fails to take account of other factors that will influence the development of a successful leader such as situational and environmental factors. For a long

Table 8.1 Leader traits and skills

Traits	Skills
• Adaptable to situations • Alert to social environment • Ambitious and achievement-oriented • Assertive • Cooperative • Decisive • Dependable • Dominant (desire to influence others) • Energetic (high activity level) • Persistent • Self-confident • Tolerant of stress • Willing to assume responsibility	• Clever (intelligent) • Conceptually skilled • Creative • Diplomatic and tactful • Fluent in speaking • Knowledgeable about group tasks • Organised (administrative ability) • Persuasive • Socially skilled

Source: Bass & Bass (2008).

period, inherited traits were sidelined as learned and situational factors were considered to be far more realistic reasons for why certain people acquire leadership positions. A significant issue regarding trait theories is that few traits seem to correlate strongly with leadership efficacy. Trait leadership theory usually only focuses on how efficacy is perceived by followers rather than on a leader's actual effectiveness (Judge *et al.*, 2009) e.g. in terms of the financial performance of the organisation they lead.

Interestingly, more recent research by De Neve *et al.* (2013) may take us full circle back to the inheritability argument, in that it suggests the possibility that a 'leadership gene' exists. They have identified a specific DNA sequence associated with the tendency for an individual to occupy a leadership position and estimate that one-quarter of the difference between how effective and ineffective leaders behave can be explained by genes.

BUILDING YOUR SKILLS

Leadership Skills

Rosenberg *et al.* (2012) highlight that leadership skills, management skills, interpersonal skills, critical thinking skills and a strong work ethic are among the most essential prerequisites for graduate employment. Leadership skills and information technology skills have also been identified as the strongest predictors of career advancement (Heimler *et al.*, 2012).

© IMAGESOURCE

At job interviews after graduation you are likely to be asked how you exhibited leadership skills in your educational environment. Identify those you have developed over the course of your studies to date.

BEHAVIOURAL THEORIES OF LEADERSHIP

From the late 1950s, there was a move away from the belief that leaders are born towards a desire to determine the types of behaviours that specific leaders displayed. Behavioural theories of leadership are based on the premise that certain behaviours differentiate effective leaders from non-leaders. Seminal behavioural theories of leadership were proposed by studies in Ohio State University (Stogdill and Coons, 1957) and the University of Michigan (Likert, 1961). We will look next at both of these studies and also the concept of participative leadership.

OHIO STATE STUDIES

In an attempt to measure leadership styles, researchers at Ohio State University developed an instrument known as the *Leader Behavior Description Questionnaire (LBDQ)*. Respondents to the questionnaire perceived their leader's behaviour toward them on two distinct dimensions or leadership types, which they eventually called initiating structure and consideration. An example of the type of question on the survey asks respondents to think about how often the leader: acts as the spokesperson of the group, waits patiently for the results of a decision, and lets group members know what is expected of them. The questionnaire is freely available at http://fisher.osu.edu/research/lbdq/ (last accessed on 22 August 2015). The initiating structure leadership style focuses on the extent to which a leader defines and structures their role, and the roles of their followers, in achieving organisational goals and objectives. The consideration leadership style is essentially the same as an employee-centred leadership style; it focuses on meeting people's needs and developing relationships.

Because a leader can be high or low on initiating structure and/or consideration, four types of leadership style were developed: low structure and high consideration; high structure and high consideration; low structure and low consideration; and high structure and low consideration. The results of the research demonstrated that leaders who were rated high in both initiating structure and consideration were more likely to achieve greater performance among their followers.

UNIVERSITY OF MICHIGAN STUDIES

The University of Michigan Leadership Model identifies two leadership styles: production-centred style and employee-centred style. The production-centred style refers to the extent to which the leader takes charge of technical aspects of the role to get the job done. Employee-centred style looks at the extent to which the leader focuses, similarly to the consideration style mentioned above, on meeting the needs of employees while developing relationships. Unsurprisingly, employee-oriented leaders consistently achieved higher levels of both productivity and job satisfaction. It should be noted, however, that the technical aspects of the role cannot be ignored. Truly successful leaders who adopted an employee-oriented approach reported that production was one of their primary responsibilities.

THE MANAGERIAL GRID

Recognising that leaders need to be concerned for their people while also having concern for the work to be done, Blake and Mouton (1962) built on the Ohio State and Michigan studies and developed the Managerial Grid (see Figure 8.1). The grid is similar to both the Ohio State studies and Michigan studies in that its two axes – Concern for People and Concern for Production – link to Ohio's initiating structure and consideration, and to Michigan's production-centred and employee-centred styles.

The grid identifies five key styles:

1 *Impoverished management*: Minimum effort to get the work done. A basically lazy approach that avoids as much work as possible.
2 *Authority-compliance*: Strong focus on task, but with little concern for people. Focus on efficiency, including the elimination of people wherever possible.
3 *Country Club management*: Care and concern for the people, with a comfortable and friendly environment and collegial style. But a low focus on task may give questionable results.
4 *Middle of the road management*: A weak balance of focus on both people and the work. Doing enough to get things done, but not pushing the boundaries of what may be possible.
5 *Team management*: Firing on all cylinders: people are committed to the task and the leader is committed to people.

Many other task–people models and variants have appeared since this grid was proposed in 1962. The dimensions they present are a useful starting point for understanding aspects of leadership, but as other models point out, there is more to leadership and management than this.

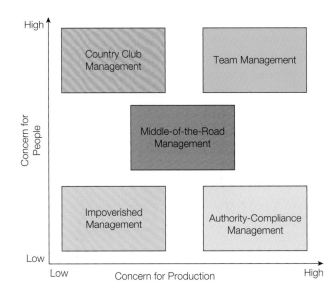

Figure 8.1 The managerial grid

Source: Adapted from Blake and Mouton (1964).

Not participative				Highly participative
Autocratic decision by leader	Leader proposes decision, listens to feedback, then decides	Team proposes decision, leader has final decision	Joint decision with team as equals	Full delegation of decision to team

Figure 8.2 Continuum of leadership participation

PARTICIPATIVE LEADERSHIP

A participative leader, rather than taking autocratic decisions, seeks to involve other people in the process, possibly including subordinates, peers, superiors and other stakeholders. Often, however, the extent to which leaders give or deny control to their subordinates is subject to their whims, and as such, most participative activity takes place within the immediate team. The question of how much influence others are given may vary depending on the leader's preferences and beliefs, and a whole spectrum of participation is possible, as demonstrated in Figure 8.2. Involvement in decision-making improves the understanding of the issues involved by those who must carry out the decisions. People are more committed to actions when they have been involved in the relevant decision-making and are less competitive and more collaborative when they are working on joint goals. When people make decisions together, the social commitment to one another is greater and thus increases their commitment to the decision. Several people deciding together make better decisions than one person alone.

There are many varieties on this spectrum, including stages where the leader sells the idea to the team. Another variant is for the leader to describe the 'what' of objectives or goals and let the team or individuals decide the 'how' of the process by which the objectives or goals will be achieved. The level of participation may also depend on the type of decision being made. Decisions on how to implement goals may be highly participative, whilst decisions during subordinate performance evaluations are more likely to be taken by the manager. There are many potential benefits of participative leadership, as indicated in the assumptions above.

This approach is also known as consultation, empowerment, joint decision-making, democratic leadership, management by objectives (MBO) and power-sharing. Participative leadership can, however, be ineffective when leaders ask for opinions and then ignore them. This is likely to lead to cynicism and feelings of betrayal.

CONTINGENCY THEORY

In this approach the leader's ability to lead is contingent upon various situational factors, including the leader's preferred style, the capabilities and behaviours of followers and also various other situational factors. This theory is also often referred to as situational theory. Contingency theories

contingency theories a belief that there is no best way to
lead

sit within the behavioural approach and argue that there is no one best way of leading and that a leadership style that is effective in some situations may not be successful in others.

One outcome of this is that leaders who are very effective at a certain place and time may become unsuccessful either when transplanted to another situation or when the factors around them change. This helps to explain how some leaders who seem to have the 'Midas touch' suddenly appear to go 'off the boil' and make very unsuccessful decisions. Contingency theory is similar to situational theory in that there is an assumption of no simple one right way to do things. The main difference is that situational theory tends to focus more on the behaviours that the leader should adopt given situational factors such as how followers behave, whereas contingency theory takes a broader view that includes contingent factors about leader capability and other variables within the situation. Two of the main contingency theories are Fiedler's contingency model and House's path-goal theory.

FIEDLER'S CONTINGENCY MODEL

Fiedler (1971) started from the premise that anyone appointed to a leadership position should have a certain standard of technical knowledge; therefore he wanted to determine what aspects of leadership behaviour influence how well groups work together. Fiedler's situational contingency theory suggests that group effectiveness depends on an appropriate match between a leader's style and the demands of the situation. Fiedler considers situational control (the extent to which the leader can control what their group is going to do) to be a significant factor in determining the effectiveness of leadership behaviour. Fiedler's contingency model is a dynamic model in which the personal characteristics and motivation of the leader interact with the current situation that the group faces.

Fiedler and Chemers (1974) then identified the Least Preferred Co-worker (LPC) scoring for leaders by asking them first to think of a person with whom they worked who they would least like to work with again, and then to score that person on a range of scales between positive factors (friendly, helpful, cheerful and so on) and negative factors (unfriendly, unhelpful, gloomy and so on). A high LPC leader generally scores the other person as positive and a low LPC leader scores him or her as negative. High LPC leaders tend to have close and positive relationships and act in a supportive way, even prioritising the relationship before the task. Low LPC leaders put the task first and will turn to relationships only when they are satisfied with how the work is going.

Three factors are then identified about the leader, member and the task, as follows:

- *Leader–member relations*: the extent to which the leader has the support and loyalty of followers and relations with them are friendly and cooperative.
- *Task structure*: the extent to which tasks are standardised, documented and controlled.
- *Leader's position-power*: the extent to which the leader has authority to assess follower performance and give reward or punishment.

The best LPC approach depends on a combination of these three (see Table 8.2). The scale includes factors such as Friendly/Unfriendly, Relaxed/Tense, and Cheerful/Gloomy. Generally, a high LPC approach is best when leader–member relations are poor, except when the task is unstructured and the leader is weak, in which a low LPC style is better.

Table 8.2 LPC approaches

#	Leader–member relations	Task structure	Leader's position-power	Most effective leader
1	Good	Structured	Strong	Low LPC
2	Good	Structured	Weak	Low LPC
3	Good	Unstructured	Strong	Low LPC
4	Good	Unstructured	Weak	High LPC
5	Poor	Structured	Strong	High LPC
6	Poor	Structured	Weak	High LPC
7	Poor	Unstructured	Strong	High LPC
8	Poor	Unstructured	Weak	Low LPC

Source: Fiedler, Fred E.; Chemers, Martin M., Leadership & Effective Management, 1st Ed., © 1974. Reprinted by permission of Pearson Education Inc., New York.

This approach seeks to identify the underlying beliefs about people, in particular whether the leader sees other people as positive (high LPC) or negative (low LPC). This is another approach that uses the focus on task versus people as a major categorisation of the leader's style.

PATH-GOAL THEORY OF LEADERSHIP

The path-goal theory of leadership (House, 1971) was developed to describe the way that leaders encourage and support their followers in achieving their goals by making their path clear and easy. In particular, leaders:

- Clarify the path so subordinates know which way to go.
- Remove roadblocks that are stopping them going there.
- Increase the rewards along the route.

Leaders can take a strong or limited approach in each of these. In clarifying the path, they may be directive or give vague hints. In removing roadblocks, they may scour the path or help the follower move the bigger blocks. In increasing rewards, they may give occasional encouragement or pave the way with gold. This variation in approach will depend on the situation, including the follower's capability and motivation, as well as the difficulty of the job and other contextual factors.

House and Mitchell (1974) describe four distinct styles of leadership behaviour within their path-goal theory:

1 *Supportive leadership*: Leaders consider the needs of the follower, show concern for their welfare and create a friendly working environment. This includes increasing the follower's self-esteem and making the job more interesting. This approach is believed to work best when the work is stressful, boring or hazardous.

2 *Directive leadership:* Leaders tell followers what needs to be done and give appropriate guidance along the way. This includes giving them schedules of specific work to be done at specific times. Rewards may also be increased as needed and role ambiguity decreased by telling employees what they should be doing. This may be used when the task is unstructured and complex, and the follower is inexperienced. Directive leadership increases the follower's sense of security and control and therefore is appropriate to the situation.

3 *Participative leadership:* Leaders consult with followers and take their ideas into account when making decisions and taking particular actions. This approach is best when the followers are expert and their advice is both needed and expected.

4 *Achievement-oriented leadership:* Leaders set challenging goals, both in work and in self-improvement (and often together). High standards are demonstrated and expected. The leader shows faith in the capabilities of the follower to succeed. This approach is best when the task is complex. Leaders who show the way and help followers along a path are effectively 'leading'. This approach assumes that there is one right way of achieving a goal and that the leader can see it and the follower cannot. This casts the leader as the knowing person and the follower as the dependant. It also assumes that the follower is completely rational and that the appropriate methods can be deterministically selected depending on the situation.

Holacracy and Zappos

'Zappos Says Goodbye To Bosses,' read the headline in the Washington Post. 'Zappos is going holacratic: no job titles, no managers, no hierarchy,' wrote Aimee Groth in Quartz, an online news outlet. Zappos.com is an online shoe and clothing

 **IN THE NEWS**

shop based in Las Vegas. It is known for its unconventional corporate culture. A quarterly meeting in 2013 opened with a *Lion King* performance put on by employees at the Smith Center in downtown Las Vegas and closed with an after party at the museum next door. Employees who don't want to stay with the organisation can be paid up to $2000 if they quit [see *In*

Reality feature in Chapter 12 for more information]. Focusing on company culture and customer service is how CEO Tony Hsieh built Zappos into a billion-dollar online retailer.

Zappos has embraced a new management trend known as 'holacracy'. This essentially means abandoning the traditional hierarchy and abolishing managers' usual roles and job titles. Instead, employees form themselves into self-governing and interlinking circles based around core tasks.

Popularised by Robertson (2007), holacracy was conceived around the idea of role, which represents a breakdown of the organisation's work. Roles work together in 'circles' that self-

organise. Circles can spawn sub-circles, and connect with other circles with 'links' – roles that form conduits between circles. People 'energise' roles, and one person can energise multiple roles. Circles are supposed to have regular governance meetings in which people talk about roles, accountabilities, authority and policies. Holacracy is essentially a set of inward-looking hierarchical mechanisms that connect the circles. Each circle is required to be run democratically and openly, with comprehensively detailed procedures on how things like meetings are to be managed and how decisions are to be made.

Alexis Gonzales-Black, one of the individuals tasked with

(Continued)

(Continued)

overseeing the transition to the new structure in Zappos, says: 'One of the core principles is people taking personal accountability for their work. It's not leaderless. There are certainly people who hold a bigger scope of purpose for the organization than others. What it does do is distribute leadership into each role. Everybody is expected to lead and be an entrepreneur in their own roles, and holacracy empowers them to do so.'

Holacracy tries to address many things employees don't like about their companies, including:

1 The organisation chart on the wall has nothing to do with how people do their jobs.

2 The title an employee holds probably doesn't reflect what they actually do, unless they own the company.

3 Manager knows nothing about what an employee

does much of the time, and yet makes decisions that determine their success.

4 Traditional management creates a culture of distrust.

A similar, non-directive approach has existed at WL Gore, the engineering firm (and makers of Gore-Tex), since the 1990s. In WL Gore no one tells anyone else what to do. 'Want to know if you're a leader?' a WL Gore employee asked the management guru Gary Hamel, 'Call a meeting and see if anyone shows up.' The concept has a number of high-profile adoptees – Twitter co-founder Evan Williams uses it at his company, Medium, and productivity specialist David Allen uses it to run his firm, but Zappos is by far the largest company to adopt the idea.

Google's leadership has also displayed some unconventional characteristics. In the early years of rapid growth employees were encouraged to spend up to one-fifth of their time working on

new ideas that interested them. When Eric Schmidt, executive chairman of the company, first started attending meetings there he said he could not tell the difference between graduate interns and the most senior staff: you led with ideas and argument, not rank. Google has become more conventional as it has grown, but analysts suggest that the origins of its success lie in the rejection of many elements of old-school leadership.

Questions

1 What types of leadership skills are required to operate a holacratic system?

2 What industries might be more likely to adopt a holacratic system?

3 Does holacracy mean that leaders are no longer required?

Sources:

Groth, A. (2013) Zappos is going holacratic: no job titles, no managers, no hierarchy, *Quartz*, http://qz.com/161210/zappos-is-going-holacratic-no-job-titles-no-managers-no-hierarchy/

Holocracy.org

http://holacracy.org/how-it-works

http://holacracy.org/blog/evan-williams-on-building-a-mindful-company

McGregor, J. (2014) Zappos says goodbye to bosses, *The Washington Post*, 3 January, www.washingtonpost.com/blogs/on-leadership/wp/2014/01/03/zappos-gets-rid-of-all-managers

Robertson, B. (2007) Evolving organization, *Integral Leadership Review*, 7 (3).

© ISTOCK.COM/ZHUDIFENG

SITUATIONAL LEADERSHIP THEORY

Another popular leadership model that has its roots in the Ohio State leadership studies is the Hersey and Blanchard (1969, 1982) theory of situational leadership. This suggests that leaders should match their leadership style to the readiness level of the person, or group of people, being led. In their leadership model they describe development level in terms of the follower's competency (ability) and commitment (willingness). Ability is the knowledge, experience and skill an individual or group brings to a particular task or activity. Willingness is the extent to which an individual or group has the confidence, commitment and motivation to accomplish a specific task. Situational leadership is about the extent to which followers are able and willing to accomplish a specific task, and the style that the leader adopts to achieve this. It is not a personal characteristic of the individual, but simply how ready they are to perform a particular task. According to this theory, there are no good and bad styles, only those that are appropriate for the given situation of the task and people who are being led. One of the key characteristics of effective leadership is to assess the leadership situation correctly, select and apply the appropriate style, and continuously review the choice.

Hersey and Blanchard (1969, 1982) proposed four leadership styles (S1 to S4) that match the readiness level of the people the leader is attempting to influence. The four styles suggest that leaders should put greater or less focus on the task in question and/or the relationship between the leader and the follower, depending on the readiness level of the follower. Leadership style in the situational model is based on the amount of task and relationship behaviour the leader engages in. The difference is based on structure initiation versus consideration. Task behaviour is the extent to which the leader details the duties and responsibilities of an individual or group. It includes giving directions and setting goals. Relationship behaviour is the extent to which the leader engages in two-way or collaborative communication. It includes such activities as providing encouragement, listening and coaching.

The main point of situational leadership theory is that as an individuals' readiness increases, the leader should concentrate more on relationship behaviour and less on task behaviour. When a group member becomes more ready, less task or relationship behaviour is required of the leader.

Four degrees of readiness have been identified by Hersey and Blanchard (1969, 1982) and these can be used to identify the appropriate leadership style that should be used by the leader.

a) *Low readiness*. Where followers are unable, unwilling, or insecure.

b) *Moderate readiness*. Where followers are unable but willing or confident.

c) *Moderate-to-high readiness*. Where followers are able but unwilling or insecure.

d) *High readiness*. Where followers are able, willing, or confident, and are self-sufficient and competent.

By mapping the amount of task and relationship behaviour the leader engages in with the readiness of the follower, we get four distinct leadership styles (S1-S4).

STYLE 1: TELLING

Follower: Low readiness
Leader: High task focus, low relationship focus

When the follower cannot do the job and is not motivated, then the leader takes a highly directive role, telling him or her what to do and without a great deal of concern for the relationship. The leader may also provide a working structure, both for the job and in terms of how the person is controlled.

This is taking a particularly managerial stance, using whatever legitimate coercive power the leader has to make the person do the job that they do not want to do. The relationship is less important here, first because the person may be replaced if they do not perform as required, and second because the lower standing of the person is assumed to lead to an attitude that does not respond well to a relationship-based approach.

STYLE 2: SELLING

Follower: Moderate readiness
Leader: High task focus, high relationship focus

When the follower wants to do the job but lacks the skills or knowledge, the leader turns on the charm, acting in a friendlier manner as they persuade and help the follower to complete the task.

STYLE 3: PARTICIPATING

Follower: Moderate-to-high readiness
Leader: Low task focus, high relationship focus

When the follower can do the job, but is refusing to do it, the leader need not worry about showing them what to do, and instead is concerned with finding out why the person is refusing and then persuading them to cooperate.

STYLE 4: DELEGATING

Follower: High readiness
Leader: Low task focus, low relationship focus

When the follower can do the job and is motivated to do it, then the leader can basically leave them to it, trusting them to get on with the job.

One thing to note is that the situational leadership model is based on assumptions that can be challenged; for example, the assumption that at the 'telling' level, the relationship is of lower importance.

LEADER-MEMBER EXCHANGE THEORY

Another relatively recent leadership theory concerns relational theories. Leader-member exchange theory, also called LMX or vertical dyad linkage theory, is the classic social exchange leader–follower approach that investigates the quality of the relationship experienced between leader and follower (Graen and Uhl-Bien, 1995). LMX focuses on followers and describes how group leaders maintain their position through a series of unspoken exchange agreements with their members. In particular, leaders often have a special relationship with an inner circle of trusted assistants and advisors, to whom they give high levels of responsibility, decision influence and access to resources. This in-group essentially pay for their position. They work harder, are more committed to task objectives and share more administrative duties. They are also expected to be fully committed and loyal to their leader. Individuals not in this group, on the other hand, are given low levels of choice or influence. This can put constraints upon the leader. They have to nurture the relationship with their inner circle, balancing giving them power with ensuring they do not have enough to strike out on their own. These relationships, if they are going to happen, start very soon after a person joins the group and follow three stages: role-taking, role-making and routinisation.

1. ROLE-TAKING

The member joins the team and the leader assesses their abilities and talents. Based on this, the leader may offer them opportunities to demonstrate their capabilities. Another key factor in this stage is the discovery by both parties of how the other likes to be respected, and gender, racial and cultural differences may be significant here.

2. ROLE-MAKING

In the second phase, the leader and member take part in an unstructured and informal negotiation whereby a role is created for the member and the often-tacit promise of benefit and power in return for dedication and loyalty is offered.

Trust-building is very important in this stage, and any betrayal felt, especially by the leader, can result in the member being relegated to the out-group. This negotiation includes relationship factors as well as purely work-related ones, and a member who is similar to the leader in various ways is more likely to succeed. This perhaps explains why mixed-gender relationships tend to be less successful than same-gender ones. The same effect also applies to cultural and racial differences.

3. ROUTINISATION

In this phase, a pattern of ongoing social exchange between the leader and the member becomes established. Successful members are thus similar to or compatible with the leader in many ways (which perhaps explains why many senior teams are all white, male, middle-class and middle-aged). They work hard at building and sustaining trust and respect. To help this,

BUILDING YOUR SKILLS

Group Leadership

Consider a group project that you are currently working on or will be working on in the near future. How do you think the LMX approach could benefit you? For example, when joining a team, LMX suggests it is important to join the inner circle. How else can you use LMX theory?

---

they are empathetic, patient, reasonable and sensitive, and are good at seeing the viewpoint of other people, especially that of the leader. Aggression, sarcasm and an egocentric view confer the keys to the out-group wash-room. The overall quality of the LMX relationship varies with several factors. Curiously, it is better when the challenge of the job is extremely high *or* extremely low. The size of the group, financial resource availability and the overall workload are also important.

The principle works upwards as well. The leader also gains power by being a member of their manager's inner circle, which they can then share downwards. People at the bottom of an organisation with unusual power may get it from an unbroken chain of circles up to the hierarchy.

DISTRIBUTED LEADERSHIP

Moving on from the relationship between leaders and groups, distributed leadership is a relatively new approach to leadership which has encouraged a shift in focus from the attributes and behaviours of individual 'leaders' to a more systemic perspective, in which collaborative working is undertaken between individuals who trust and respect each other's contribution. Distributed leadership occurs as a result of an open culture within and across an institution, where actions are openly challenged, critiqued and developed by engaging in reflection.

Spillane and Diamond (2007) outline that distributed leadership roles are played by multiple individuals, whether in formal or informal positions. Distributed leadership is neither a top-down nor a bottom-up approach but recognises that leadership roles are played by different people at different times. Under distributed leadership, everyone is responsible and accountable for leadership within his or her area. Good ideas come from throughout an organisation, and many people cooperate in creating change. A central goal of the distributed leadership approach is for individuals to succeed in a climate of

distributed leadership the idea that leadership of an organisation should not rest with a single individual, but should be shared or 'distributed' among those with the relevant skills shared purpose, teamwork and respect. This approach has become popular in educational institutions.

Bolden *et al*. (2008) found that a distributed leadership approach may be most powerful as a rhetorical device, and can be used by those in positions of real power to disguise power differentials, offering the illusion of consultation and participation while disguising the methods by which decisions are reached and resources distributed.

CHARISMATIC LEADERSHIP THEORIES

More recent developments in leadership theory have supplemented the contingency approach with those which emphasise the leader's charisma and the theory of transformational leadership. The focus of these theories reflects the need to understand leadership within the context of a business environment characterised by crisis and change. This approach emphasises the personal characteristics of the leader and their ability to attract and influence others, suggesting that charisma is a quality that some leaders can effectively capitalise on to galvanise others into action. These new leadership theories seemed better able to account for the leader's ability to cope with radical change and manage the turnaround of failing businesses. A growing body of work also gave them substantial empirical support compared to the mixed findings of research into older theories. Transformational leadership is of particular importance.

SPOTLIGHT ON SKILLS

When it comes to selecting individuals for leadership development, organisations often start with the most basic of questions: How 'developable' is the individual? Given the investment in resources required to develop a leader, this represents the most fundamental question. It can be answered using a systematic leader assessment process that focuses on three key criteria:

- *Self-confidence:* It is well established that developable leaders possess strong self-confidence. They project confidence in their interactions with others. However, they are not arrogant. Arrogance is considered a significant derailing factor.
- *Competence:* Competence is considered an essential prerequisite for consistent, strong performance. Competence typically focuses on assessing baseline skills and behaviours that can be further developed. These competencies include drive for results, rapid and disciplined decision-making, strategic thinking and tolerance of ambiguity.

- *Emotional intelligence:* Emotional intelligence consists of both self and social awareness components and includes interpersonal skills, conflict management, influencing and relationship management components.

Careful attention to these characteristics when selecting leaders for development will significantly enhance the chance of future leadership success. With this in mind, how can organisations identify and assess these criteria? What can individuals do to ensure that organisations know that they possess these criteria?

To help you answer these questions, in your ebook click the play button to watch the video of Joanna Moriarty from Green Park Interim and Executive Search discussing her experience recruiting senior leaders for charities and social enterprises.

TRANSFORMATIONAL LEADERSHIP

We know that people will follow a person who inspires them. A person with vision and passion can achieve great things and it may be easier to get things done by injecting enthusiasm and energy into followers. One example of a transformational leader is Martin Luther King, an American pastor, activist, humanitarian and leader in the African-American Civil Rights movement of the 1950s and 1960s. King was an inspiring orator who motivated followers to have the level of courage required to practise non-violent protest in the service of justice. He also had the capacity keep a network of activists, both black and white, organised, while he worked to gain wider support through challenging Americans outside the movement to live up to the fundamental American principle that all citizens are created equal with rights to 'life, liberty, and the pursuit of happiness.' As a Christian minister, he also called upon members of his faith to remember that all races are God's children and the injunction to love your neighbour was not limited to people who look like you. As a realist as well as a visionary, he worked behind the scenes with another leader, President Lyndon Baines Johnson, to get civil rights legislation passed.

Transformational leadership starts with the development of a vision, a view of the future that will excite and convert potential followers. This vision may be developed by the leader or the senior team or it may emerge from a broad series of discussions. The important factor is that the leader is fully committed to it. The next step is to constantly sell the vision. This takes energy and commitment, because few people will immediately buy into a radical vision and some will join the show much more slowly than others. A transformational leader thus takes every opportunity and will use whatever works to convince others to climb on board the bandwagon. In order to create followers, the transformational leader has to be very careful in creating trust, and their personal integrity is a critical part of the package that they are selling. In effect, they are selling themselves as well as the

transformational leadership a leadership style that can inspire positive changes in those who follow vision. In parallel with their selling activity, the leader is seeking the way forward. Some transformational leaders know the way, and simply want others to follow them. Others do not have a ready strategy, but will gladly lead the exploration of possible routes to achieve a specific vision.

The transformational approach is often contrasted with the transactional leadership approach. Transactional leadership styles are more concerned with maintaining the status quo. Transactional leadership can be described as 'keeping a steady ship'. Transactional leaders use disciplinary power and an array of incentives to motivate employees to perform at their best. The term 'transactional' refers to the fact that this type of leader essentially motivates subordinates by exchanging rewards for performance (Bass, 1985).

BASS' TRANSFORMATIONAL LEADERSHIP THEORY

Bass (1990) defined transformational leadership in terms of how the leader affects followers, people who should trust, admire and respect the transformational leader. Awareness of task importance motivates people and a focus on the team or organisation produces better work. Bass identified three ways in which leaders transform followers:

- Increasing their awareness of task importance and value
- Getting them to focus first on team or organisational goals, rather than their own interests
- Giving personal attention to each follower

Charisma is seen as necessary but not sufficient; for example, in the way that charismatic movie stars may not make good leaders. Transformational leaders are able to evoke strong emotions and to cause identification of the followers with the leader. This may be through stirring appeals, but it may also occur through quieter methods such as coaching and mentoring.

BURNS' TRANSFORMATIONAL LEADERSHIP THEORY

Burns (1978) defined transformational leadership as the process whereby leaders and followers engage in a mutual process of raising one another to higher levels of morality and motivation. Association with a higher moral position is motivating and will result in people following a leader who promotes this. Burns believed that transformational leaders raise the bar by appealing to the higher ideals and values of followers. In doing so, they may model the values themselves and use charismatic methods to attract people to the values and to themselves.

Burns' view is that transformational leadership is more effective than transactional leadership, where the appeal is to more selfish concerns. An appeal to social values thus encourages people to collaborate, rather than working as individuals potentially in competition with one another. He also sees transformational leadership as an ongoing process rather than the discrete exchanges of the transactional approach. Using social and spiritual values as

transactional leadership a leadership style that focuses on managing and supervising employees

a motivational tool can be very powerful and also gives people an uplifting sense of being connected to a higher purpose, playing to the need for a sense of meaning and identity. Ideals are positioned quite high up in Maslow's hierarchy ▶ Chapter 5 ◀, which does imply that lower concerns such as health and security must be reasonably satisfied before people will pay serious attention to others.

GENDER AND LEADERSHIP

Women perform 66% of the world's work, produce 50% of the food, and own approximately 40% of all private businesses in the formal economy. In 2014 alone, women controlled approximately US$28 trillion in consumer spending. However, women are significantly under-represented when it comes to leadership positions in organisations.

Among Fortune 500 companies, women hold only 3% of CEO positions and 15% of board seats. In the UK, female membership of FTSE-100 company boards reached 17% in 2013, but women comprise only 6% of executive directors. While it makes sense to address this disparity from an equality and moral perspective, it also makes business sense. UK organisations with more women on their boards were found to outperform their competitors, with a 42% higher return in sales, 66% higher return on invested capital and 53% higher return on equity (Davies, 2011). So why do women struggle to obtain leadership positions? According to Eagly (2013), there are a number of reasons. Leadership stereotypes tend to be more 'masculine' (for example, highlighting traits such as assertiveness) than 'feminine' (for example, prioritising more communal, supportive traits).

Women experience a strong gender bias when being evaluated for promotions on both their level of performance as well as their potential impact. Research shows that women have to work harder than men to be perceived as equally competent (Lyness and Heilman, 2006). In addition, unfortunate assumptions are sometimes made about women's ambitions and abilities. Research by DDI (Development Dimensions International, 2009) shows that women do not progress because of a perceived lack of ambition and lesser company commitment due to family responsibility. However, women and men rarely differ in their ambitions (Catalyst, 2004). Furthermore, women struggle with so-called 'second generation gender biases', which are 'powerful yet often invisible barriers to women's advancement that arise from cultural beliefs about gender, as well as workplace structures, practices, and patterns of interactions that inadvertently favour men' (Ely et al., 2011, p. 4). It should be no surprise that men get selected for leadership positions more frequently than women ▶ Chapter 3 ◀ – people making selection decisions are likely to be strongly influenced by leadership stereotypes.

In order to succeed in leadership roles, many women leaders may need to live up to masculine (be tough) and feminine (be nice) stereotypes – a difficult challenge. In addition, the perceived demands placed on leaders at senior levels may be seen as a deterrent to women. As a result, women either 'fall off the track' to the top, have to take time out to have children, or forgo having children in order to have top-level leadership careers. There are often deep-seated prejudices from those in power, usually men, which prevent women from attaining leadership positions.

For example, Cuddy *et al.* (2004) carried out an experiment in which Princeton undergraduate students were presented with identical descriptions of two hypothetical job candidates, Kate and Dan, both consultants, depicted alternately as childless or as having a new baby. Dan was seen as equally competent in either scenario, whereas Kate as a mother was considered less competent than her hypothetical childless version, and the undergraduates were less willing to hire, train, or promote her. Similarly, Correll *et al.* (2007) found that study participants offered mothers a lower wage than they offered childless women, and saw them as less competent and committed. By contrast, parenthood made men seem more competent and committed!

Finally, some women's progress toward leadership positions is stalled by their own lack of belief in their abilities and their lack of persistence in driving towards these positions. Sheryl Sandberg, Chief Operating Officer of Facebook, has had a particularly strong impact on the gender and leadership debate through her book *Lean In: Women, Work, and the Will to Lead* (2013), in which she invites men in senior positions to engage more seriously in questions around gender, suggesting that their involvement is what will cause a change at the top.

DEVELOPING LEADERS

Having considered various perspectives on leadership theories and leadership styles, we now need to consider the extent to which leaders can be developed and the types of activities that are used to achieve this. Leadership development is an important organisational activity that is critical to organisational success. Despite this, historically when budgets were tightened during periods of economic downturn, investment in leadership development was one of the first activities to have its funding reduced. However, organisations increasingly understand the implications of failing to develop individuals who have responsibility for formulating an organisation's strategy, growing and developing its talent and managing the day-to-day operational issues. Indeed, of the $130bn spent worldwide on corporate training in 2014, 35% (over $45bn) was spent on leadership development (Deloitte, 2014).

Rather than taking the viewpoint that the only way leadership can be developed is through experience, it can be argued that development interventions combined with experience are necessary to create effective leaders. Leadership development interventions provide potential leaders with frameworks within which to examine particular leadership situations and give them the opportunity to use multiple perspectives in addition to their existing skills. The overarching goal of leadership development in organisations is the improvement of individuals' capacity to be effective in such roles. For leadership development to be effective, it must be closely aligned with the organisational context, including its strategy and culture, and also the specific needs of individual leaders. Leadership development competencies are frequently used to ensure that their leadership development practices are effectively aligned in this way.

Bearing in mind the complexities of the global business context, organisations need to determine whether leaders have the capabilities needed to contribute to fostering competitive

leadership development activities and practices that enhance the ability of leaders to work as part of a team to develop relationships with organisational stakeholders

advantage. Increasingly, organisations use competency models to help them identify the knowledge, skills and personal characteristics needed to achieve successful organisational performance (Noe, 2010). Competency models are considered an effective way of ensuring that leadership development practices make a contribution to the bottom line (Kapp and O'Driscoll, 2010).

Numerous definitions of the term competencies exist. The Society for Human Resource Management defined competencies as 'the knowledge, skills and abilities required to perform a specific task or function' (2010, p. 18). Competencies are a core integrating element of leadership development across the organisation. Swiercz and Lydon (2002) classified leadership competencies into functional competencies and self-competencies. However, Quinn *et al.* (2003) identified them in terms of the roles leaders were expected to perform. GlaxoSmith-Kline, for example, have 6 core values and 21 leadership competencies. They emphasise thinking strategically, being a change champion, leading courageously, managing execution and fostering enthusiasm and teamwork. Competencies are used to develop a consistent, reliable and standardised leadership development process.

CONSIDER THIS...

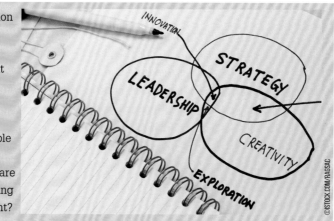

Why would an organisation choose to spend €15,000 to send one person to attend an open enrolment executive education program at a business school when they could conceivably train 25 people in-house with the same amount of money? What are the arguments for investing in leadership development?

Organisations have a large number of choices when it comes to selecting the optimal methods for developing leadership competencies. These include job assignments, formal coaching and mentoring, action learning, peer networks, job shadowing and technology-enabled practices. The Centre for Creative Leadership proposes a 70:20:10 development mix, in which lessons learned by successful and effective leaders are divided roughly into:

- 70% from tough jobs (on-the-job development);
- 20% from people (coaching, mentoring and networking);
- 10% from courses and reading (formal learning).

competencies are the practical application of knowledge, skills, attitudes, motivation, values, beliefs, cognitive style and personality that enables an individual to work effectively and autonomously in a clearly defined context

It is beyond the scope of this chapter to detail all of the practices that can be used by organisations. Some of the most relevant are:

- *360-degree feedback:* This is a very popular development practice. It involves the systematic measurement of the perceptions of an individual's leadership performance from an entire circle of relevant viewpoints, including self, subordinates, peers, supervisors and even external stakeholders such as customers and suppliers (McCarthy and Garavan, 2006). A comprehensive assessment from various role perspectives can provide an accurate picture of the impact of a leader's behaviour on others. The gap between self-ratings and others' ratings can be used to estimate individual self-awareness, which has been shown to be positively related to managerial performance. A weakness of 360-degree feedback is that the resulting ratings can lead to confusion if there is major disparity across rating sources.

- *Coaching:* Coaching is useful in helping leaders make sense of assessment data, put together actionable development plans and implement the plan, while also providing support and a follow-up assessment of behavioural change (Ellinger and Kim, 2014). An important factor to consider with coaching is the training and experience of the particular coach. Coaching is a very tailored and personalised intervention, and has lots of applications in a leadership development context. It can be used for both individual leaders and teams of leaders; however, it is important that its role is clearly articulated within the leadership development process. Coaching should be viewed as a developmental rather than a remedial process.

- *Mentoring:* Mentoring can be a formal or an informal process in which a more senior person takes a vested interest in the personal and professional development of someone more junior, usually a professional colleague. Informal mentoring programmes tend to be more effective and receive more favourable responses than formal programmes (Megginson, 2006). Mentoring is very time-intensive for both parties and there may be insufficient numbers of qualified mentors. Mentoring may therefore be only used in targeted situations involving high-potential managers and senior-level executives. It may be more realistic to set up mentoring networks, in which employees are assisted in identifying existing helpful relationships and then trained in how to better use these relationships for their development.

- *Job assignments:* These are considered to be very effective tools in leadership development practice, especially those assignments that 'stretch' the thinking or other capabilities of the target leader (Ohlott, 2004). Leaders view their most potent development activities to be experiential, especially those that take place 'on the job'. Putting development leaders into 'stretch' job assignments is a valuable development tool. However, two fundamental questions need to be answered: How prepared should someone be for a stretch assignment? and What is the right assignment for a particular leader at this time? This judgement requires a detailed knowledge of the career goals, career paths and development readiness of a leader.

- *Action-learning projects:* This approach is based on the assumption from adult learning theory that people learn most effectively when working on organisational problems in real time (Leonard and Lang, 2010). Action learning typically takes place in project teams composed of people from diverse functions and locations working together for 6 to 12 months on an issue that is strategically important to the organisation. What makes or breaks action learning in terms of development is whether ongoing learning is valued as much as performing well. External coaches are often used to help facilitate team self-reflections and to enhance learning and development.

Many organisations accept that leadership development is a sound investment for organisations to make for their future; therefore the focus of any leadership development activity should be on ensuring the fit of leadership development with organisational goals. Organisations that invest in human capital development, which inevitably includes leadership development, will achieve significant advantages in terms of business performance. Leadership development is big business worldwide and the costs of leadership development continue to increase. However, many organisations have moved past questioning the worth of this investment to questioning which approach brings the best results and is most effective in impacting the bottom line. It is estimated that leadership development can have significant pay-off for organisations in terms of creating a sustained competitive advantage, as well as benefits for productivity and financial performance (Day *et al.*, 2009).

Leadership for a New Generation?

Apple, Amazon, Google, Twitter and a host of other companies based in Silicon Valley espouse a particular West Coast USA idealistic culture to the extent that they are often given the label 'new corporations'. These cultures portray a missionary-like sense of purpose that their work is changing the world for the better, and that it will solve many of society's problems. These organisations tend to highlight what they are *not* and how they are distinct from the supposedly narrow-minded organisations that have come before them. Apple implore you to 'Think differently', Google's motto is 'Don't be evil', while

Twitter claim to 'Defend and respect the user's voice'. But do the leaders of these companies actually act any differently from those who have gone before them?

Steve Jobs (1955–2011), former CEO of Apple, was an archetypal 21st-century leader in many aspects. Jobs is remembered for his capacity to create innovation and harness it into transformative product lines such as the iPod and iPhone, but his interactions with those who worked for him were by no means flawless. His influence is so great that the review of his career has become a bit of a battleground among thought leaders and practitioners seeking to draw lessons from it, with dozens of books dedicated to examining his legacy.

Jobs' leadership style was to commit to highly ambitious targets and drive his staff, however cruelly, to obtain these results. One Apple employee told Fred Vogelstein, author

Google founders Larry Page and Sergey Brin.

of *Dogfight: How Apple and Google went to war and started a revolution*, that Jobs 'mostly just looked at you and very directly said in a very loud and stern voice, "You are f*****g up my company" or "If we fail, it will be because of you"'. Vogelstein also describes how, prior to the launch of the first iPhone in 2007, Jobs' favouritism alternated between Scott Forstall, who was in charge of the iPhone's software development, and Tony Fadell, who managed the hardware production. Both individuals were considered to be potential successors to Jobs at Apple, and constantly vied for his approval. After months of showing his preference for Forstall, Jobs once made a point of openly ignoring him and talking instead to Fadell, much to Forstall's obvious dismay. Why? Because he could. Jobs also positioned himself with his back to Forstall so that Fadell and Forstall could see each other's faces while it was happening.

Jeff Bezos, founder and CEO of Amazon.com, has a similar way of motivating employees, often asking them 'Are you lazy or just incompetent?' Jack Dorsey, co-founder and co-creator of Twitter, idolised Jobs to such an extent that he began wearing Jobs' iconic rimless round glasses and adopting similar verbal cues. Of more concern was his allegedly ineffective leadership style, which led to his departure from the company in 2008. One Google executive gave his engineers a particularly ambitious deadline and suggested to them that 'If you can't get it done I'll fire you guys and hire a new team that can do it'.

Is leadership any different for 'new corporations'? Life for employees appears to differ little from life elsewhere, even if there are probably more free smoothies and sushi. As Steve Jobs (and later Jack Dorsey) was fond of saying, 'We're just humans running this company'.

Questions

1 What type of leadership styles might be demonstrated by these CEOs?
2 Debate the difference in styles between contemporary leaders and old-style corporate leadership.
3 Why do you think people like Steve Jobs are considered to be visionary leaders?

Source

Vogelstein, F. (2013). *Dogfight: How Apple and Google went to war and started a revolution*. New York: Farrar, Straus & Giroux.

 SUMMARY

 IN THE EBOOK, CLICK TO HEAR AN AUDIO SUMMARY

This chapter highlights the concept of leadership and the role that it plays in organisations. By looking at the differences between leadership and management, we can identify characteristics that distinguish effective leaders. It is important to understand the distinction between trait, behavioural and contingency-based theories of leadership so that we can place leaders in an appropriate position within the workplace. Selecting the right leaders for the right jobs can be strategic in achieving both short- and long-term goals for an organisation. Gender equality in terms of leadership offers significant benefits for organisations, not least in financial terms. Leadership strength represents an important source of competitive advantage and organisations can use a variety of leadership development strategies to develop this human resource pool. Investment in leadership development is driven by the belief that it confers significant benefits on both individual leaders and organisations.

CHAPTER REVIEW QUESTIONS

1 What do leaders do in an organisation?
2 Does management really differ from leadership?
3 Differentiate between trait and behavioural theories of leadership.
4 What are the main criticisms of trait theories of leadership?
5 What do you understand by leader-member exchange theory?
6 What is transformational leadership?
7 How can a manager become a leader?
8 What are the main approaches to developing leaders?

MULTIPLE CHOICE QUESTIONS

In your ebook, click to take a multiple choice quiz to test your understanding of this chapter.

FURTHER READING

Avolio, B.J., Walumbwa, F.O., and Weber, T.J. (2009) Leadership, current theories, research, and future directions, *Annual Review of Psychology*, 60, 421–449.

Billsberry, J. (2009) *Discovering Leadership*, Basingstoke: Palgrave Macmillan.

Kotter, J.P. (2001) What leaders really do, *Harvard Business Review*, 71(11), 3–11.

Sinek, S. (2014) *Leaders Eat Last: Why Some Teams Pull Together and Others Don't*, New York: Penguin.

USEFUL WEBSITES

www.ccl.org

Centre for Creative Leadership: A very useful website that provides interesting articles, white-papers and blogs on contemporary leadership development issues.

www.real-leaders.org/

The website of the Young Presidents' Organization's official leadership magazine. Intended to inspire better leaders for a better world, this site contains leadership editorial, CEO profiles, and topical case studies designed for CEOs by CEOs.

www.cebglobal.com

The Corporate Leadership Council website includes a variety of resources on contemporary leadership development topics.

www.I-L-M.com

The Institute of Leadership and Management site provides resources including education and publications on leadership topics.

9 POWER, POLITICS AND CONFLICT AT WORK

Christine Cross and Lorraine Ryan

LEARNING OUTCOMES

BY THE END OF THIS CHAPTER YOU SHOULD BE ABLE TO:

- Discuss the importance of power and politics in organisational life.
- Outline the different sources of power.
- Explain how people translate power into action (power tactics).
- Differentiate between power, authority and leadership.

- Identify the causes and consequences of conflict at work and explain the different conflict perspectives.
- Explain the approaches that can be taken to resolve conflict at work.

© ISTOCK.COM / ALEXBRYLOV

THIS CHAPTER DISCUSSES:

IN REALITY

We often think we have to fight for what we want; that it's the only option to get our way. But is it? Think of a situation in which two people have equal power and both are unwilling to compromise. For example, you want to watch a soap opera and your flatmate wants to watch the *X-Factor* final, but they are on at the same time and you only have one television. What do you do? Your first instinct is to fight over it! But that inevitably means one winner and one loser. Research indicates that the best solution is one in which both people get what they want. Sounds impossible? It's not. Achieving this outcome means both people have to take a problem-solving approach. Research from Fisher and Ury (1983) shows that the best possible solution can be achieved if both people make a significant effort not just to get what they want, but to help the other person get what they want too. You both need to find out *why* the other person wants what they want, rather than just take a stand on your own position. You could try and 'expand the pie' as a possible solution – maybe one of you has an iPad and could watch the programme on that. The person watching the *X Factor* final can't record it and watch it later in case they find out the result before they watch it, but the person watching the soap opera could record it and watch it after the *X Factor* final – meaning both people get what they want. One of them has compromised to some extent, so perhaps the other offers to wash the dishes for a week to repay the favour! This shows that in reality there are different options for resolving a conflict other than 'win-lose'.

INTRODUCTION

An analysis of power and politics is key to understanding the behaviour of individuals and groups within the organisation. Much of what happens in organisational life can be explained by the concept of power – who has it and how they use it. This chapter examines the linked concepts of power and politics in the workplace. The allocation of resources at work, including money and staff numbers, decisions over pay and rewards, and the interconnectedness of workflows are all subject to the exercise of power and politics. This chapter also includes an examination of the main factors involved in conflict at work, often caused by the expressions of power and politics. The differing needs, values and perspectives of individuals in the workplace naturally lead to the emergence of conflict and because of this we also examine conflict resolution. We begin by looking at what exactly it is that makes people in organisations powerful and where this power comes from. We will then explain how people use their power and discuss some of the complexities that surround the concept of power. We also describe how power differs from authority and leadership.

POWER IN ORGANISATIONS

Power is everywhere in organisations and people are concerned with it – those who have it want to keep it and those who don't have it often want to get it. Yet power is a difficult concept to identify and is often confused with other concepts such as authority and leadership. For example, a manager may find it difficult to get employees to do what he wants them to do, even though he is in a position of authority. Someone else in the organisation may easily persuade others to do as she wants, but is not 'the boss'. So, who has more power in these two situations? Where does power come from and why are some people in organisations powerful, while others aren't? How do people in organisations use their power? To answer these questions, we must first understand what power is.

DEFINING POWER

Dahl's (1957) famous definition of power asserts that it exists where person A can get person B to do something that B would not otherwise do. A closely related concept is influence. Power often refers to the *potential* of one person to cause another to act in accordance with their wishes, whereas influence refers to the *actual* behaviour of that person (Somech and Drach-Zahavy, 2001). Definitions of power typically assume that the person with power and the person subject to it have incompatible objectives; influence, however, can be exerted collaboratively where goals are not mutually exclusive (Tjosvold *et al.*, 1992). The essence of power therefore may be *control* over the *behaviour of others* or the ability to influence others. This may be achieved by bringing about change in others' beliefs or attitudes or by having the capacity to reward or punish others. In an organisational context, power can stem from those who have control over resources and the ability to make decisions around the allocation of those resources to others. Power can come in many different forms, but importantly, power is not absolute.

The extent of power is dependent on the amount of resistance to it. In other words, person A has more power over person B if he can get B to do something without B 'putting up a fight' or resisting doing it. The extent to which people will resist power or succumb to influence depends on a number of factors including personality ▶Chapter 2◀ and culture. The cultural values of a society have a tremendous impact on the extent to which people readily accept others in positions of power. Hofstede's (1991) well-known model of culture identified power distance ▶Chapter 12◀ as reflecting the extent to which employees welcome the idea that people in organisations rightfully have power. Japan typically has a high level of power distance meaning people readily accept the role of management as power holders. Western cultures tend to have lower power distance, meaning that they do not accept management power as readily and value individuality and diversity. This makes them less susceptible to power influence. Dependency is also very important when examining power relationships. The more dependent one party is on another, the more they may be influenced by them.

power exists where person A can get person B to do something that B would not otherwise do

 THIS...

Think about a person you would consider as a powerful leader, for example, Michael O'Leary, CEO of the airline Ryanair, or Barack Obama, President of the United States. What is it about them that makes them powerful?

SOURCES OF POWER

Where does power come from? There are a number of different sources of power in organisations and these can relate to the person as an individual (informal or personal power) or to the position a person holds within the organisation (formal power). Some sources of power may be negative; for example, an employee will do something because they feel they *have to*, while other sources may be positive; for example, the employee will do something because they *want to*. Which do you think would be more effective? Research has shown that positive sources of power are the most important to acquire (Robbins and Judge, 2012). One of the most commonly used classifications of power in organisational behaviour literature is French and Raven's (1959) model. They identify five power bases or sources of power: three which relate to the position a person holds (formal power) and two which relate to the person as an individual (informal or personal power).

Table 9.1 Sources of power

FORMAL POWER/POSITION POWER	
Reward power	Derives from individuals' control over resources and is dependent upon the ability of the power wielder to confer valued material rewards such as pay increases or promotions. The target of this power must value the rewards.
Coercive power	Refers to the power to punish or withhold rewards, the power to threaten and to use one's position to force others to take action. Again the target of the power must value the rewards and fear having them withheld.
Legitimate power	This is exercised in accordance with organisational rules and with the authority of the organisation.
INFORMAL POWER/PERSONAL POWER	
Referent power	Contingent upon the charisma, interpersonal skill and/or personal attraction of the individual. This is dependent on the target wishing to identify with the powerful individual, wanting to 'be like them'.
Expert power	Derives from know-how or expertise which sets the individual apart from others. This source of power is determined by the extent to which others attribute knowledge and expertise to the power seeker.

Source: Adapted from French and Raven (1959).

French and Raven's model remains relevant today, both within and outside organisations. Think of the power celebrities have over the way we dress and act because we want to be like them (Referent power). Or the power a car mechanic has over a customer who knows nothing about cars (Expert power). A parent may have power over a child by offering or withholding pocket money (Reward/Coercive power) and Mark Zuckerberg is powerful because he is the CEO of Facebook (Legitimate power). The strength of these sources of power depends on the characteristics of those the power holder is trying to influence. There are also limits to how many of these sources can be used at the same time. If, for example, a manager uses coercive power towards a group of workers they would be unlikely to identify closely with him, and so he would not expect to use referent power. Sources of power also depend on the perceptions of others. For example, you may be an expert in something but unless others perceive this expertise as important then this may not be a source of power. Power therefore is often 'in the eye of the beholder'.

Power in French and Raven's model is viewed as something that is dependent on relationships between individuals and groups in organisations. In other words, one party only holds power over another because of the relationship between them. If the relationship ends or changes, then so does the power. Other views see power as something that is possessed, something that you have or can accumulate. Pfeffer (1981) identified sources of power and, similarly to French and Raven's model, classified these into *structural* and *personal* sources of power. Structural sources of power include formal position and authority, access to and control over information and resources and being irreplaceable; for example, power as held by a manager. Personal sources of power include talent, energy, endurance and stamina, and emotional intelligence; for example, David Beckham. While power can be viewed as something that is possessed, something that relates to position or personal factors, or something dependent on relationships, power is also context dependent. A number of factors can shape or change sources of power and these include the structure of the organisation ▶ **Chapter 11 ◀**, formal and informal networks, factors in the external environment and sources of knowledge or information. Other theories can also provide insight into power in organisations. Negotiation theory tells us that power can come from having alternatives; that is, the more and better alternatives available to you, the less pressure you are under to agree to what's on the table and the more power you have to demand changes. Conversely, if you have little or no good alternatives then you have very little power to negotiate anything better than what is on offer (Lewicki *et al*, 2011).

BUILDING YOUR SKILLS

Identifying Sources of Power

Patrick is Financial Director of XYZ International. His father is the CEO. Patrick essentially controls the company finances and has overall responsibility for employee performance reward packages. He has qualifications from Harvard Business School in Economics and Finance and last year his quick thinking with regard to an important financial decision saved the company from losing $1million. He is very well-respected

(Continued)

Identifying Sources of Power (*Continued*)

by the other directors in the company. In addition to this, Patrick is a typical 'nice guy'. He is good-looking, very involved in charity work and is a family man. He is seen as being honest and trustworthy. Last year however, there were rumours of a 'rift' between Patrick and one of the accountants who didn't agree with some of his  financial decisions. The accountant resigned shortly afterwards. Some say this was because Patrick 'had a word in his father's ear' but nobody knows for sure what went on.

How many sources of power does Patrick have?

POWER IN ACTION – POWER TACTICS

Is power any good if you do not use it? There are some schools of thought that say the ultimate power is power that you do not even have to use. Margaret Thatcher (British Prime Minister from 1979 to 1990) once said, 'Being powerful is like being a lady … if you have to tell people you are, you aren't'. In other words, the ultimate form of power is one that others recognise implicitly, without question; you don't have to use it (or threaten to use it) and you don't have to explain it. Nonetheless, we can identify a number of different ways in which power is often used in organisations. Power tactics refer to the ways in which people use their power. Different power tactics may be combined and certain combinations work better together than others. Some examples of power tactics used in organisations are:

- *Friendliness* – using flattery, praise and ingratiation.
- *Rational persuasion* – presenting facts, data and rational arguments to show why someone should do what you want them to do.
- *Coalitions* – getting the support of others, particularly those in positions of authority, for your ideas.
- *Control of information* – includes withholding damaging information or using information to make yourself or others appear favourable.
- *Use of organisationally derived rewards and punishments.*
- *Creating obligations* – based on the principle of reciprocity ('You owe me one!')

power tactics the ways in which power bases are translated into actions

- *Bringing in outside experts* to provide support for your ideas.
- *Assertiveness* – use of a direct and forceful approach including demanding agreement with requests and orders.

Yukl *et al.* (1996) showed that people are more easily influenced by some requests than others. They identified content factors as being important in determining how people respond to influence attempts. Content factors relate to how important the requested action is for the work, and how interesting and enjoyable the requested action would be for the target person. These will affect whether the response will be commitment, compliance or resistance by the target person. That is, a person may respond positively and enthusiastically and display commitment to achieving the task (commitment); they may comply but only display minimal effort (compliance); or they may resist and try to avoid, refuse, argue or delay the requested action (resistance). Figure 9.1 shows the relationships between the power of a person (agent power), the influence tactics they use, the content factors and how these shape influence outcomes.

MANAGEMENT POWER

Of course, power is a fundamental part of the management process in organisations and is often viewed as a right of management, or a management prerogative. That is, management, as owners (or representatives of the owners) of capital, have a right to power and control over the resources within that organisation including human resources. Employment relations scholars have long emphasised the *imbalance of power* that exists between management and workers in capitalist organisations (Fox 1966; Salamon, 2000; Wallace *et al.*, 2013). Although management typically has more power than workers in an organisation, that is not to say that workers have no power. Workers do not usually have legitimate or position power over management, but they may have access to power sources of their own such as

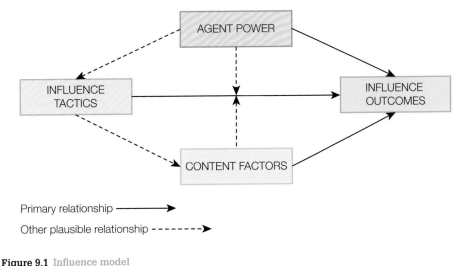

Figure 9.1 Influence model

Source: Yukl et al. (1996).

tacit knowledge of a work process: in other words only they know how something is done. There may also be powerful elements of moral persuasion around issues of fair treatment of workers in the workplace. That is, management should treat workers fairly because it is the right thing to do. A recent trend has been the use of 'zero-hours contracts' where employees are not guaranteed work but have to make themselves available in case the employer requires them. This use of management power may seem unusual, but it is used by such well-known organisations as McDonald's, Sports Direct and even Buckingham Palace! Because of the imbalance of power in this employer–employee relationship there is little employees can do to improve their working conditions. One way in which workers can try to increase their power is by joining trade unions to represent their interests and negotiate with management on their behalf, the principle being to gain 'power in numbers'.

THE DIRECTION OF POWER

We often think of power as being 'top-down'; that is, the power management has over workers. However, it is important to note that power can also be 'bottom-up', which is typically the power workers have over management, or lateral, which is the power workers have over other workers or management has over other managers. Many organisations are no longer characterised by typical hierarchical bureaucratic structures ▶Chapter 11◀. They have changed and become 'flatter', emphasising more lateral relationships. Power tactics depend on the direction of power; for example, management may use certain tactics to influence and/or control workers but workers may use different power tactics to influence management or other workers.

EMPOWERMENT

No discussion of power in modern-day life is complete without identifying the concept of empowerment. As a result of flatter organisational hierarchies there has been a move to transfer power to employees. There is an expectation in contemporary organisations that managers empower their employees and that those empowered employees make decisions without seeking supervision (Wilkinson, 1998). Kanter's (1977) structural theory of power in organisations identifies those structures that are important to the growth of empowerment as access to information, being provided with the appropriate resources and support to perform required tasks at a high level of achievement, and having access to programmes that will enable individuals to develop and enhance their work experience. This approach is grounded in trust, commitment and cooperation within and across self-organised units/teams.

empowerment a process whereby managers delegate power to employees who use it to make decisions affecting both themselves and their work

The goal in empowering employees is to create a work environment in which people have a degree of autonomy, are productive, contributing, motivated and happy, and in which the speed of decision-making is improved, all of which contribute to organisational success (Wilkinson, 1998). The philosophy behind empowerment is based on the idea that if employees are empowered to take control and make decisions, they feel more confident, capable and motivated to work more effectively and efficiently. As a result employees become more productive. Toyota has been associated with embracing the concept of employee empowerment. The company believes that every employee should take ownership of their work by identifying quality defects and ways to improve efficiency. This philosophy helped to establish the company as a quality champion and one of the world's largest car makers. Empowered employees engage in a number of behaviours, such as taking the initiative, applying critical thinking skills, offering judgements and identifying and acting on opportunities to improve systems.

It is worth noting here the differences in cultures in terms of perceptions of empowerment. In Scandinavian countries there is an expectation that managers will involve workers in decision-making processes. A directive manager would not be well accepted by workers in Scandinavian organisations. Yet, in countries such as India, Singapore and Hong Kong workers value the directive use of power, and they see a directive manager as powerful and a consultative one as having little power.

AUTHORITY AND LEADERSHIP

So far we have examined different sources of power and discussed how power is used in organisations. We have also reviewed the ethical issues surrounding the use of power. It is important to understand that power is closely linked with other concepts in organisational behaviour, particularly ideas around authority and leadership ▶Chapter 8◀. Although sometimes the terms power, authority and leadership are used to describe the same thing, there are differences between these concepts and it is important to be able to distinguish between them. Power and authority are closely linked in organisations. Authority relates to the concept of management's prerogative or right to manage. There is an expectation from those in authority that others will conform and there is generally acceptance from others that authority is legitimate. Authority is sometimes unquestioned by subordinates and obedience follows as a matter of course. In a now-famous experiment, Yale University psychologist Stanley Milgram showed just how much people were willing to obey those perceived to be in authority (Milgram, 1963). His experiment involved participants administering electric shocks to volunteers if they got answers to questions wrong (no shocks were actually administered but the participants did not know this and believed they were inflicting pain on another person). Although they expressed various levels of discomfort in administering the shocks,

authority typically refers to positional power and relies on the assumption that others are willing to obey

a surprisingly large number inflicted the highest voltage of shock because the person 'in authority' told them it was ok to do so. This was despite hearing sounds of distress from those they were administering electric shocks to!

Reading our definitions of power and leadership ▸ Chapter 8 ◂ we can identify similarities between them. Yet, not all those who have power are leaders and not all leaders use the same type of power. Robbins and Judge (2012) identify a number of key differences between leadership and power:

1   Power does not require goal compatibility, merely dependence. Leadership requires some connection between the goals of the leader and those of the ones being led.
2   Leadership typically refers to downward influence on followers whereas power can refer to different 'directions'.
3   Leadership research focuses on leadership style while research on power focuses on tactics to ensure compliance.
4   Leaders typically refer to individuals whereas groups as well as individuals can be powerful in organisations.

Think about a sports team you have been involved in. Have you ever seen a situation where the person providing the leadership for the team is not actually the captain? This player does not have formal authority, but has power, perhaps because they are the best player on the team. This allows them to provide leadership without necessarily having authority. Regardless of the situation within which people use their power there will be questions around whether their use of power is appropriate in the particular circumstances. This is related to the ethical dimension of power.

POWER AND ETHICS

Ethical behaviour refers to the extent to which it is seen as right or wrong to use power in any given situation. Ethics are codes that reflect our values and moral principles and drive our decisions and behaviours with respect to what is right and wrong, good and bad. Just because we can behave in a certain way, does it mean that we should? Typically, unethical behaviour in organisations might include accepting bribes, avoiding taxes or taking credit for work that is not yours. These actions usually relate to power in some way, either by those who have it or those who want it. For example, a manager with decision-making authority may be bribed to decide things a certain way. Colleagues fighting for a promotion which will increase their power may take credit for others' work to 'get ahead'. It is very difficult to identify hard and fast rules around ethics and ethical behaviour and it may be argued that whether or not a behaviour is ethical is strongly dependent on context, and that sometimes the end justifies

ethics codes that reflect our values and moral principles and drive our decisions and behaviours with respect to what is right and wrong, good and bad

the means. Do you think unethical behaviours can be more acceptable if 'everybody does it' or if 'you have to look out for number one'?

ETHICAL BEHAVIOUR AND POWER AND POLITICS

Every employee has a duty and a responsibility to act in an ethical manner. Yet the discussion above on political tactics may lead you to question the ethics of organisational politics. This is because the use of politics is often focused on gain for an individual rather than the good of the group or the organisation. The focus may be on achieving a promotion, or a bonus, regardless of the cost to others. Essentially, political behaviour is unethical when the political tactics do not serve the organisation's goals or the goals of a larger group of people than the single political actor, and when using power and political behaviour violates another person's rights. Although politics are a natural feature of organisational life, by definition, they promote individual self-interest. Deciding whether 'playing politics' is ethical can depend on whether 'the end justifies the means'. Having discussed the concepts of power and politics, we can see that much of people's behaviour in organisations stems from issues of conflict.

Nice Guys Don't Win

Why do so many workers end up frustrated at work, dreaming about leaving the workplace well before their retirement age? One possible answer could be found in a study on office politics by psychologist and broadcaster Oliver James. In his book, *Office Politics: How to thrive in a world of lying, backstabbing and dirty tricks* (2013), he identifies the existence of three well-known dysfunctional personality types among white-collar workers – the psychopath, the Machiavellian and the narcissist. He also identifies a fourth, which is a combination of all three – a person with psychopathic tendencies, Machiavellian cunning and narcissistic selfishness – a 'triadic'. He proposes that this dark triad of characteristics is very likely to be present in that person in your office who causes you so much trouble. Among James' examples of fictional 'triadics' are Walter White from *Breaking Bad* and Tony Soprano from *The Sopranos*.

There are many self-help books that offer useful suggestions on how to survive in the neurotic workplace. *The Rules of Work* by Richard Templar is one such book. For example, Templar advises his readers to 'learn how to switch off, relax, not take it too seriously, enjoy it more, put things into perspective'. Being able to switch off when one leaves the place of work is a skill that can help preserve one's sanity. This is even more important when one is employed in a workplace where toxic personalities abound.

You may be thinking now that the simplest thing is to

OB IN **THE NEWS**

© ISTOCK.COM/VIORIKA

(Continued)

Nice Guys Don't Win (*Continued*)

avoid office politics altogether. However, all the great management writers note the political realities of business life. Idealists and political avoiders, who believe you should get ahead only by following the rules and working harder, tend to have a lower impact in the workplace. The pragmatists and realists get involved in politics and have a higher impact. According to Adrian Furnham, Professor of Psychology at University College London, there are three factors you need to be aware of to become a 'savvy' manager:

1 *Networking*. Savvy managers really know who's who. They can work out the real structure within the organisation – those who truly hold power and influence. This is invaluable when you want to make things happen.

2 *Emotional intelligence*. Savvy people are good at summing up others, getting into their heads and understanding their motivations. They are attentive and insightful.

3 *Courage and risk-taking*. You have to be prepared to fail – often and in small ways – in order to learn how to succeed. Situations are not always clear; you are not always right; your intuition and judgement do not always guide you well, but if you take no risks, you get nothing done.

Questions

1 Have you ever worked in a place where you could recognise any one of the four toxic personality types? If so, what behaviours lead you to classify them as one of these types? And what was the effect of this on your behaviour at work?

2 Would you get involved in office politics? If not, why not and how would you use your power and influence if not in a political way?

3 Have you seen the 2011 film *Horrible Bosses*? How does office politics manifest itself in this film?

Sources:

www.dailymail.co.uk/news/article-2269154/Horrible-bosses-New-study-shows-modern-offices-reward-narcissism-psychopathic-behaviour.html#ixzz3GmMP8zkd (last accessed on 24 August 2015).

www.timesofmalta.com/articles/view/20130613/business-comment/Dealing-with-toxic-office-politics.473698 (last accessed on 24 August 2015).

www.thesundaytimes.co.uk/sto/public/Appointments/article1264043.ece (last accessed on 24 August 2015).

ORGANISATIONAL POLITICS

The concepts of power and politics are closely related in organisational life. Power is more than dominance; it is a capacity to get something done in an organisation and is a central feature of political behavior. Politics is about getting, developing, and using power to reach a desired result. Even if you have never worked in an organisation you can identify office politics from television programmes such as *House*, *Suits* and *The Office*. Politics often happen outside accepted channels of authority and is an unavoidable presence in organisational life. One of the most well-known definitions of organisational politics is that it 'involves those activities taken within organisations to acquire, develop and use power and other resources to obtain one's preferred outcome in a situation where there is uncertainty or dissensus about choices' (Pfeffer, 1981, p. 7). DuBrin (2001, p. 192) defined organisational politics as 'informal approaches to gaining power through means other than merit or luck'. Both of these definitions help us to identify that political activity in the workplace results from the conversion of power into action. When the use of power moves outside formal lines of authority, or when it is aimed at achieving goals not authorised by the organisation, it is seen to be political.

People use political behaviour for many reasons; for example, in order to affect decisions, to obtain scarce resources and to earn the cooperation of people outside their direct authority. Political behaviour is based on influence tactics used to further personal and/or organisational interests. Politics essentially acts as a mediator between power and influence. We often tend to think of politics as being associated with negative terms such as coercion, manipulation, 'behind closed doors' and 'cutthroat'. But politics can also have positive associations, particularly in the arena of change interventions, where it can be used to gain acceptance to change and to acquire the momentum to push through changes (Pfeffer, 1992) ▸**Chapter 13**◂.

A number of organisational and individual factors contribute to the use of political behaviour (DuBrin, 2001):

1 *A pyramid-shaped organisation structure.* Because this type of organisational structure concentrates power at the top of the pyramid, each layer has less power than the level above, meaning that those at the bottom are virtually powerless and that competition for power is intense.

2 *Environmental uncertainty and turbulence.* Where the environment is unpredictable and unstable people tend to behave politically in an effort to exert some control over the situation.

3 *Emotional insecurity.* If people lack confidence in their skills and abilities they can choose to engage in political tactics to create a favourable impression with those in positions of authority.

4 *Manipulative tendencies.* Some people engage in political behaviour because they want to manipulate others, sometimes for their own personal advantage. These include people with Machiavellian personality traits ▸**Chapter 2**◂.

5 *Subjective standards of performance.* Where people believe that the organisation does not have an objective or fair way of judging performance and suitability for promotion they often resort to political behaviour.

CONSIDER THIS...

There are many more male politicians than female, regardless of the country you examine. The global participation rate of women in national-level parliaments is just less than 20%. Why is this? How does gender impact politics?

In order to behave politically, a number of political tactics and techniques can be used to reach the desired goal. There are many tactics available (Elron and Vigoda-Gadot, 2006) and some of these include:

● *Building powerful coalitions.* This tactic is often used in advance of attending a meeting where your idea is being put forward. You lobby other decision makers in an effort to convince them, ensuring the decision goes your way on the day. This tactic also avoids you

political behaviour the conversion of power into action

facing an embarrassing defeat at the meeting if you know you have a majority before you publicly ask what people think about your idea.

- *Impression management.* Here you are concerned with ensuring you create a favourable impression on others. You may 'dress for success'; associate yourself with successful tasks and projects; ensure people know about your successes and positive characteristics. Also, being seen as an expert in an area is a useful tactic to employ to provide you with more power.
- *Ingratiation.* The use of flattery can create goodwill with another person and affect their behaviour positively towards you.
- *Using information and controlling it.* This tactic is related to the fact that in organisations information is viewed as power. This is especially true where a small number of people control access to information, making them more powerful. This tactic is about using information to gain a political advantage.
- *Threats, demands and intimidation.* The use of threats, demands and intimidation has long been used as a political tactic to allow those in possession of some limited power to achieve their goal. Blackmail is a tactic we all are familiar with, at least in fictional situations.
- *Use of favours and benefits.* This is the opposite of threats, demands and intimidation, and focuses on influencing another person by providing them with positive outcomes or the promise of positive outcomes.
- *Networking.* A common and more subtle form of political behaviour involves networking; that is, developing informal social contacts to enlist their cooperation and support when necessary. The 'old boy's network' is a well-known example of how networking operates. It is a male informal network through which men are believed to use their positions of influence to help other men who went to the same school/university or who share a similar background to 'get on' in business and in life.
- *Rational persuasion.* Using logical arguments and facts to persuade another that a desired result will occur.

Of course, some of these political tactics overlap with ways of increasing power as discussed earlier in the chapter, further illustrating how power and politics are linked in organisational life.

According to Schein (1977), the decision on which political tactics to use depends on three factors:

1 What the person hopes to achieve
2 The personal characteristics of the person – some people are more comfortable with using certain tactics than other people
3 The situation itself.

For example, if you were hoping to get promoted at work and you knew that those who were making the promotion decision were big fans of Manchester United, even if you don't follow that team you might learn as much as you could in order to appear knowledgeable to them and create a good impression. You might also start going to Manchester United football games in order to network with them. Your decision to use this tactic might depend on your personality type (you are more likely to choose this if you are extroverted or assertive). If you had access to tickets to a match they particularly wanted to go to you could give them to one of the decision makers in order to make them grateful for the favour and feel like they owed you.

Much of our academic knowledge of office politics is based on research conducted in the United States and thus impacts on our perceptions of office politics. The context in which we operate has a direct effect on the political tactics we might use. Given the effect of national level culture on how organisations operate we can see differences in the approaches to the use of power and politics in different countries. If people are going to be working in different countries, for example, as part of a multinational organisation, it is important to have an understanding on how power and politics are perceived within those cultures. For example, when negotiating business deals certain behaviours may be viewed differently depending on the context or culture within which they are occurring. In the West, someone negotiating a deal who claims that he needs to 'check with the boss' may be perceived by others as using a delaying tactic, because the person at the negotiating table usually has authority to conclude the deal. In countries such as Russia, however, it is common practice for the negotiator not to have the final decision-making power. In these countries there is much emphasis on trust and relationships rather than focusing on legal contracts, whereas in the US legal contracts are very important. An understanding of these types of differences in the way business is conducted in different countries helps people in organisations not to misinterpret behaviour as a political or power tactic becuause it may just be the way business in conducted is that national context ▶**Chapter 12**◀. One key difference between Eastern and Western cultures is the relative focus on the good-of-the-group (collectivism) in the East, versus the good-of-the-individual (individualism) in the West.

WHAT IS CONFLICT?

Conflict is a part of everyday life, both personally and professionally. Workplace conflict exists at all levels of the organisation, although it may be less visible among senior managers than among peers. This is not because it does not exist, but often because it is less obvious. Conflict exists where one person's objectives or motives regarding an issue or interest are incompatible or irreconcilable with that of others. It can be defined as 'an expressed struggle between at least two interdependent parties who perceive incompatible goals, scarce resources, and interference from others in achieving their goals' (Wilmot and Hocker, 2007, pp. 8–9).

conflict a difference of interests between two or more parties which exists when one person believes that another disagrees with them over an issue or interest

We usually refer to two different types of conflict. Firstly, there is the type of conflict which can occur when there is a 'personality clash', where two people essentially do not like each other, and this can be referred to as relational or emotional conflict. This type of conflict can destroy relationships between colleagues and can lead those involved to believe that it would be easier to leave the organisation than try to remedy the situation. Secondly, when people work together every day it is to be expected that they will have different perspectives and ideas about the work they are involved in and how it is to be accomplished. This is referred to as substantive conflict (Walton, 1969).

When we are involved in a conflict situation we move through four stages. Think of a time when you were really annoyed with someone over something. Initially we are *irritated* by the situation, issue or person, but we can often ignore this and the conflict does not move to the next stage. If the conflict is beginning to escalate, the next stage is *annoyance.* Here stress increases, we feel frustration but we are able to voice our emotions logically. The third stage is *anger*. This stage is characterised by strong feelings and hurt, and emotions are voiced. This is the stage we most often associate with conflict. The final stage is *violence,* which is not a feature of work-related conflict. In this stage we feel totally justified in taking physical action and we feel the need to win irrespective of the cost. We will not always go through all these stages but we can recognise how one stage can lead to the next if it is unresolved.

FUNCTIONAL AND DYSFUNCTIONAL CONFLICT

For many of us, conflict has negative connotations. If asked to think of words associated with conflict you might choose anger, fight, frustration, argue and clash. This is the traditional view of conflict and is referred to as dysfunctional conflict. It is normally identified as something to be avoided or eliminated as quickly as possible; something which can damage the organisation. If asked to think of workplace conflict you might first think of conflict between unions and management where union members go out on strike. This type of conflict negatively affects organisational productivity, reputation, targets and often profits, and is very visible to those outside the organisation. In reality, other expressions of conflict such as absentee-ism, turnover and low morale are more difficult to manage, and are much more prevalent in organisations than worker strikes.

There is, however, another view which identifies conflict as a positive situation, one which can actually create positive outcomes. Automatically assuming that conflict is nega-tive can shut down the possibilities and opportunities presented by a conflict situation. A positive view of conflict is referred to as functional conflict and can lead to benefits for the organisation. Functional conflict can be constructive and can improve organisational

dysfunctional conflict is normally identified as something negative which is to be avoided or resolved as quickly as possible, and as something which can damage the organisation

functional conflict can be constructive and can improve organisational performance

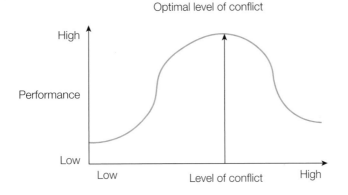

Figure 9.2 Functional and dysfunctional levels of conflict

performance. If managed correctly (see later in this chapter) it can act as a catalyst for change and can strengthen relationships. Conflict can be positive when it stimulates creativity and problem-solving, improves the quality of decision-making and creates a culture of self-evaluation and change (Jehn and Mannix, 2001). Given the inevitability of negative forms of conflict it is important that managers manage conflict effectively so that it does not damage the organisation. Figure 9.2 shows that an optimal level of conflict can be achieved that will create high levels of performance. In a group someone might play devil's advocate and challenge ideas in order to generate creative solutions. This can work up to a point and then conflict becomes dysfunctional and negatively affect's the group's performance.

CAUSES OF CONFLICT

As mentioned above, conflict is an inevitable feature of the workplace and thus we need to understand what causes it. There are six key sources of conflict at work which are discussed in turn below:

- The employment relationship.
- Different interests and values.
- Competition over scarce resources.
- Ambiguity over responsibility or authority.
- Interdependence.
- Poor communication.

THE EMPLOYMENT RELATIONSHIP

As many commentators highlight (see, for example, Wallace *et al.*, 2013), the employment relationship emphasises employer needs for productivity, change and cost-effectiveness, yet, these needs are often in competition with employee needs for job security, adequate rewards and development opportunities. It is this clash of interests which often leads to conflict in the workplace over issues such as pay and changes to pay and conditions of employment. You will often see or read media reports of industrial conflicts in which one group of employees (often represented by a union) is going to strike over an issue such as pay. This is a good example of the employment relationship as a cause of conflict at work.

DIFFERENT INTERESTS AND VALUES

The workplace is made up of individuals who see things from different perspectives. Conflict occurs when there is a lack of acceptance and understanding of these differences. Individual workers fighting for their personal goals and ignoring organisational goals and organisational well-being can also lead to conflict. One such example occurs when workers are looking for a wage increase but managers are saying that increasing wages will negatively affect profits and thus they cannot pay employees any more.

COMPETITION OVER SCARCE RESOURCES

Organisations operate within a set of limited resources and it is this aspect which often creates conflict. Often employees feel they have to compete for available resources in order to do their job. In an environment where resources are scarce this causes conflicts. For example, if the production department requires additional staff to complete an order, but the finance department stresses the need to remain within the allocated budget for production this can cause significant conflict.

AMBIGUITY OVER RESPONSIBILITY OR AUTHORITY

Role ambiguity in terms of both task responsibility and lines of authority is a major cause of conflict at work. Conflict occurs where there is a lack of clarity around the employee's expectations of their role. Often an employee's reporting lines are also unclear, an issue which is becoming more common in organisations because many employees are working on more than one task or project at a time, with different project leaders.

INTERDEPENDENCE

In the workplace we are rarely responsible for every aspect of a task. Organisational units are interdependent. When we have to wait for someone else to complete a task before we can begin ours, this can inevitably lead to conflict.

POOR COMMUNICATION

Unsurprisingly, poor communication causes much conflict at work. This can be as a result of inadequate communication methods, failure to communicate, interpersonal barriers, cultural barriers or lack of feedback ▶ Chapter 10 ◀.

BUILDING YOUR SKILLS

Conflict Resolution

Resolving conflict is an aspect of everyday life. Here we want you to put yourself in the shoes of the lecturer who has to deal with an issue between group members. You have included a group project for this module and each group of four is required to make a presentation and produce a report. You have chosen the group members alphabetically and are aware this can cause problems if students are regularly absent from class. This is particularly true for those who are apprehensive about the effect other group members in this assessment will have on their overall grade. At the end of the semester four students approach you with a problem which has arisen because one member of the group has not been pulling their weight in the group work. How do you resolve the situation?

PERSPECTIVES ON CONFLICT AT WORK

In trying to understand conflict at work it is useful to examine four well-known alternative perspectives on conflict (Fox, 1966). By examining these we can better understand the approach to conflict resolution taken by managers:

- *Unitarist:* In this perspective, conflict is viewed as abnormal and occurs because of a failure in the normal functioning of the organisation. Conflict is seen as both negative and damaging to the harmony which exists between management and employees and the emphasis is on conflict avoidance. This perspective is often found in organisations which do not recognise unions.
- *Pluralist:* In contrast, this perspective sees conflict as naturally occurring in the organisation due to the different perspectives and interests of the parties involved. Because it is an inevitable feature, management should plan to handle conflict effectively in order not to negatively affect the functioning of the organisation. The emphasis here is on the management of conflict rather than its elimination, and in these organisations there is an acceptance of union representation.
- *Interactionist:* This is perhaps a less common approach to conflict in which an acceptable level of conflict is seen as positive for the organisation, and thus it is initiated in order to stimulate innovation and creativity.

The fourth view is somewhat different from the others and is referred to as the:

- *Radical perspective:* This stems from the Marxist theory of capital society. Conflict arises from the unequal power distribution between employers and employees and is a symptom of the broader class conflict; hence it is inevitable. The inequalities in the power held by different classes of society are mirrored in work organisations between unequal groups, such as management and workers. The only way of eliminating conflict from the workplace is by eliminating conflict from society.

SPOTLIGHT ON SKILLS

Over their tea break, a group of workers is discussing their country's semi-final match in the World Cup next week. This is the first time the country has reached this stage of the competition for 20 years. The entire country will come to a standstill to see if the team might manage to beat Brazil and qualify for the final for the first time ever!! The game starts at 3pm and the workers are due to finish their shift at 4.30. They decide to approach management and see what the options are. There's no way any of them are going to miss the big game. Anyway, they've just finished a huge order for which they worked overtime and things have quietened down a bit now. Surely management will be reasonable, and anyway they'll probably be watching the match on the big screen they have in the company boardroom (this screen is used for presentations to clients and it is fantastic quality).

1 If you were in management's position, what approach would you use to resolve this issue and why choose that approach?

2 What do you think might be the benefits of the approach you choose?

3 What might be the disadvantages of adopting a different approach?

To help you answer these questions, in your ebook click the play button to watch the video of Declan Deegan at Milford Care Centre talking about conflict resolution.

RESOLVING CONFLICT: DUAL CONCERNS MODEL

Thomas' dual concerns model of conflict-handling styles is very useful in helping us to understand the approaches to resolving conflict which an individual can take (Thomas, 1976). The model suggests that 'concern about self' and 'concern about others' are what motivate individuals to choose between five conflict-handling strategies. In other words, individuals in conflict have two independent levels of concern – concern about their own outcomes, which makes them assertive, and concern about others' outcomes, which makes them more compliant. Figure 9.3 illustrates these concerns and places them on an axis with five possible conflict resolution strategies arising – competition, accommodation, avoidance, compromise and collaboration.

In the *competition* approach individuals are strongly interested in pursuing their own goals without having concern for what others want from the situation. This style is characterised by a desire to win at the other party's expense and is often referred to as a 'win-lose' approach.

	Low concern for others		High concern for others
High concern for self	Competing Dominating Contending Forcing		Collaborating Integrating Problem-solving
		Compromising	
Low concern for self	Avoiding Withdrawing		Accommodating Obliging Yielding Smoothing

Figure 9.3 Dual concerns model

Source: Adapted from Wallace et al. (2013).

There are situations where it may be appropriate, such as when a quick decisive action is required or when an unpopular action is needed.

The second approach is *accommodation* and is found on the opposite axis to the competition approach. It is also referred to as a 'lose-win' approach and is most appropriate when people find out that they are wrong about something, or when maintaining relationships is the overriding concern. This approach can be part of a long-term strategy because individuals using this style are often viewed favourably by others. However, they may also be viewed as weak or submissive. The third approach is the *avoiding* style and is used by someone who does not want to get involved in resolving a conflict situation. Often people using this approach hope that by ignoring the conflict it will just disappear by itself over time. Although this style may be useful in some situations, for example, if the issue is a minor one or there is not enough information to deal with the issue at the time, unresolved conflict can lead to detrimental outcomes for the organisation.

One of the most common approaches to resolving conflict is that of *compromising*. Here we try to achieve some of what we want while at the same time allowing the other side to get some of what they want. In effect it is a 'mini win-win' as both sides get part of what they want. This is often the easiest approach for people to take, especially when time constraints are an issue. It is also often used in order to achieve temporary settlements to complex issues.

The literature tells us that *collaboration* is the approach by which a 'win-win' can be achieved (Fisher and Ury, 1983). As you can see from Figure 9.3, taking a collaborative approach means you have a high interest in ensuring that both parties achieve their desired outcomes. This approach requires a problem-solving attitude and requires time, effort and creativity to come up with solutions that will satisfy both party's needs.

There is no single best way to handle every conflict. Each of the five conflict-handling modes has its own sets of benefits and costs. Each can be highly effective if used properly in the right circumstance. While much of our understanding of conflict in organisations stems from American and British research and culture, it is important to remember that different cultures, norms and behaviours in different countries add complexities to conflict and how it should be resolved. For example, certain cultural norms in the West, such as shaking hands and making eye contact, may be insulting to other cultures. Furthermore, certain accepted ways of handling the employment relationship in one country may cause conflict when international companies attempt to replicate that style in another country. Take, for example, the German company Volkswagen's base in the US. The US and Germany have different labour relations with regard to worker representation and trade unions. Workers in Germany contribute to decision-making through their works councils, but this was a source of conflict when Volkswagen officials based in Germany wanted workers in the US to have similar means of input to decision-making because it clashed with anti-union opinions and typical labour practices in the US.

EngCo.: Power, Politics and Conflict in Action

You are the CEO at EngCo, a multinational engineering company with a subsidiary based in the Middle East. A position has become vacant for a specialist engineer to work on an international project. This would be an excellent opportunity for the appointee to gain valuable experience in

a niche area and to network with senior engineers in other divisions of the company.

Everyone knows that positions like this are crucial in gaining a foot on the career promotion ladder and they very rarely arise. The engineering field is one of the most sex-segregated professions in the Middle East.

The job is advertised, in accordance with company policy, both internally and externally. EngCo is an equal opportunities employer. After shortlisting, a selection board is set up which consists of a HR Officer, an administrator and the Senior Engineer, James Wood, who is an American working with EngCo. James Wood is an outstanding engineer and is well-respected in his field. He is known, however, for being very forceful with his opinions and people rarely disagree with him. He is well-connected in the company and has a reputation for being able to 'make things happen'.

Adira is a graduate engineer with a first class Masters from King Saud University and her work is exceptional. Ever since she started out in her career, she has faced obstacles due to her gender. She has never directly been told she hasn't been picked for projects or promotions because she is female but she has a feeling that it has been a

© ISTOCK.COM/LISA-BLUE

key factor. This is particularly the case since she took maternity leave a year ago and missed out on finalising a project she had been working hard on for two years – Project X. Fareed is also a graduate engineer and works on a lot of the same projects as Adira. He has an engineering degree and a Diploma in Project Management. Although his work is of a very high standard, he does not have as much experience as Adira. He is seen as having been instrumental in finalising Project X because he took the lead in presenting the proposals to Senior Management. During this presentation, he took credit for a lot of Adira's ideas – after all, she wasn't there to contradict him! Fareed really wants this international position (there is a lot of extra money) and tells his father about it over dinner one evening. His father is good friends with James Wood; they went to university together. His father tells him he'll 'have a word with James and see what he can do'. He has a golf game organised with James that Saturday.

The interviews go ahead the following week and both Adira and Fareed are interviewed, along with other candidates. There is not a huge difference between their scores but Adira is the better candidate. James Wood is very clear, however, on 'who he wants working with him on this' and insists on Fareed being offered the position. He refuses to listen to the other two on the selection panel, who point out that Adira meets more of the criteria. At one point he claims, 'If you two really want to push this then you might be recruiting for a Senior Engineer next month as I have plenty of other options'. The panel appoints Fareed as the highest ranking candidate and he receives a phone call from James to offer him the position. Adira hasn't heard anything and as she is leaving work she bumps into Fareed who tells her 'Hard luck on the interview, I heard the competition was tough!' Adira is really upset that this is the way she finds out the outcome. She hears rumours the next day that there were 'issues' with the interview process. She speaks to the HR Officer who tells her that he 'wasn't sure who had

the final call on it' and felt under pressure to agree with James Wood. Now Adira is talking about leaving the company and you, as CEO, feel under pressure to sort the whole mess out. You do not want to lose Adira because there are few female engineers available in the labour market, and this is a source of competitive advantage for your firm, because many governments in the Middle East support organisations who recruit women and often allow them to access valuable resources.

Questions

1 What sources of conflict can you identify?
2 What sources of power does each of the individuals have?
3 What conflict handling style would you use to resolve the issues?
4 What political tactics have been used by the parties involved?
5 Put yourself in the position of the CEO and arrange a meeting with Adira. How will you approach this meeting to resolve the conflict and what information will you gather first?

🔊 SUMMARY

IN THE EBOOK,
CLICK TO HEAR
AN AUDIO SUMMARY

We have outlined and discussed the related concepts of power, politics and conflict in this chapter. The key sources of power in the workplace were identified as deriving from positional and personal bases. This power is then translated into action through the use of power tactics, including the use of information, building networks and reciprocity. Power is also dependent on the context in which it is used, both at an individual level and at an organisational level. We have seen in this chapter how power and authority are closely linked in organisations, and how people are expected to behave in a certain way regardless of whether they are leaders or followers. The ethics of using power and politics at work is also an area of concern. Although politics are a natural feature of organisational life, political tactics are usually focused on promoting individual self-interest. The concept of politics is about getting, developing and using power to achieve a desired result, and there are many ways in which political tactics can be used to gain advantage in the workplace. The use of power and political tactics can, however, result in the emergence of conflict. While there are many reasons for disagreement in the workplace, the employment relationship itself is often the greatest source of conflict. The fact that conflict can be a positive force in an organisation is often overlooked. While we mostly think of conflict in a negative light, a certain level of conflict can have a positive effect on organisational outcomes. There are a number of options for resolving conflict at work which are identified in the dual concern model. Each option will be more or less appropriate depending on the specific situation. The concepts of power, politics and conflict are complex but they are interrelated and an understanding of them is essential for effectively managing people in organisations.

CHAPTER REVIEW QUESTIONS

1   Why is it important to understand the concepts of power and politics in organisations?
2   Outline the different sources of power in organisations. What sources of power do you have?
3   Identify four different power tactics that people in organisations use and give an example of a work situation where each tactic might be most appropriate or effective.
4   Is there a difference between power, authority and leadership?
5   How do you feel about politics in the workplace? Would you engage in office politics? What would you do if a colleague used political tactics against you?
6   What are the possible negative outcomes of using political tactics in your job?
7   Describe a situation from your personal experience in which conflict between groups was dysfunctional. What conflict resolution strategies would you use if this situation arose again in the future?
8   What are the main sources of conflict in the workplace? Are they different from the sources of conflict in university life?

MULTIPLE CHOICE QUESTIONS

In your ebook, click to take a multiple choice quiz to test your understanding of this chapter.

FURTHER READING

Buchanan, D.A. and Badham, R.J. (2008) *Power, Politics and Organisational Change*, 2nd edn, London: Sage Publications.
Kotter, J.P. (2008) *Power and Influence: Beyond Formal Authority*, New York: The Free Press.

McConnon, S. and McConnon, M. (2010) *Managing Conflict in the Workplace*, 4th edn, Oxford: How To Books.

Pfeffer, J. (2010) *Power: Why Some People Have It and Others Don't*, New York: Harper Collins Publishers.

Vigoda-Gadot, E. and Drory, A. (eds) (2008) *Handbook of Organizational Politics*, Cheltenham: Edward Elgar Publishing.

USEFUL WEBSITES

www.crnhq.org

This conflict resolution network website contains a wealth of material to help better understand the causes of conflict and methods of conflict resolution. The free training material includes a 'CR Kit' containing a toolkit of 12 skills essential to resolve conflict.

www.mindtools.com

This website aims to help you learn the practical, straightforward skills you need to excel in your career. It has sections on managing conflict at work, negotiation, persuasion and influence, and understanding power.

www.managementstudyguide.com

Management study guide is an educational portal with the vision of providing students and corporate workforces worldwide with access to rich, easy to understand, frequently updated instruction on many management-related topics. There is a useful section on office politics.

www.hbr.org

The *Harvard Business Review* has many excellent articles on power, politics and conflict at work.

www.thenation.com/article/178696/can-germany-reform-american-labor-relations

This article identifies how German corporations respect worker rights and considers whether they may have an influence on future US developments.

10 COMMUNICATION IN THE WORKPLACE

Vivienne Byers

LEARNING OUTCOMES

BY THE END OF THIS CHAPTER YOU SHOULD BE ABLE TO:

- Understand the importance of communication in the workplace.
- Describe the process of communication, both verbal and non-verbal.
- Identify the different communication channels and barriers to effective communication.
- Demonstrate how changes in technology have affected communication within and between organisations and their employees.
- Explain how to overcome potential problems in inter-cultural communication.

© ISTOCK/SHIRONOSOV

THIS CHAPTER DISCUSSES:

IN REALITY

You may have read or heard that in face-to-face interactions most of the message is communicated through non-verbal gestures and tones rather than words – 93% of it! However, this statistic has long been debated. Commonly, it is reported that only 7% of a message is communicated by words with visual or non-verbal cues making up 55% and the other 38% conveyed by tone of voice. This handy calculator for communicating a message has been misrepresented for many years by communications consultants and trainers, as well as on websites and in books. It is referred to as the 'Mehrabian Myth' and is based on a single study into non-verbal communication carried out by Mehrabian in 1967. He and his co-workers asked participants to judge the meaning of or feelings conveyed by a speaker of one word (a positive, neutral or negative word) spoken in different tones which were positive, neutral or negative. The results showed that the listener frequently attributed an incorrect meaning when there was a discrepancy between the tone and the word. For example, a positive word such as 'love' spoken in a negative tone resulted in the total message being judged as negative. It was found across the experimental group that, when the message conveyed by words and tone contradicted each other, the participants determined the overall meaning by using visual clues 55% of the time and tone of voice 38% of the time (reported in Mehrabian, 2007). This study is clearly limited to situations in which verbal and non-verbal messages are in conflict, so it cannot be applied across the board to all communicative scenarios.

INTRODUCTION

All individuals, groups and organisations communicate by sharing 'meaning' between each other. This meaning is conveyed through information and ideas and by tone as outlined in the feature above. Communicating is not just about transferring this meaning, but it is a two-way process which is also about being understood and belonging to a group. The study of communication employs concepts which are basic to an understanding of human behaviour and, at the collective level, reflects on how an organisation works. Communication is a core organisational behaviour topic, which has become a specialist sub-discipline in its own right (Huczynski and Buchanan, 2014). Bringing people together with common goals in an organisation cannot be done without communication (Thompson, 2013). It is central to understanding organisational behaviour for a number of reasons, the main one being that it is rare for individuals to work alone. According to Boone and Kurtz (2010) managers themselves spend about 80% of their time in direct communication with others, whether on the phone, in meetings, via email or in individual conversations. Communication and organisational

communicating sharing or exchanging information

success are directly related. Good communication can have a positive and mobilising effect on employees. Poor communication can lead to strong negative consequences, such as the distortion of goals and objectives, conflict, loss of motivation and poor performance.

This chapter identifies the key factors involved in organisational communication and explains how changes in technology have affected communication within and between organisations and their employees.

WHAT IS THE PURPOSE OF COMMUNICATION?

People have always needed to communicate to live in social groups and to plan and coordinate activity. No group or organisation can exist without sharing meaning in some way between its members. When we communicate with others, we are usually trying to influence other people's understanding, behaviour or attitudes. Core to most organisational activity is an understanding of the process of communication and how the use of different communication channels can impact on the messages delivered and received.

HOW IMPORTANT IS COMMUNICATION IN THE WORKPLACE?

Mintzberg (1990a) describes the purpose of communication with others in the workplace as being able to inform, instruct, motivate or seek information. His seminal study of the work of senior managers points out that they don't often leave meetings or hang up the telephone to get back to work, because communication *is* their work. From a top management perspective, the purpose of organisational communication is to achieve coordinated action. The members of the organisation will have no focus if they are not involved in effective communication with one another. Employers expect employees to be effective communicators and rate them for their communicative performances. A study in the US reported that employers ranked communication skills among the top three most valued skills, but rated new graduates at all levels as largely deficient in this area (Association of American Colleges and Universities, 2013). However, many organisations see organisational communication as a problem. It has been cited as a key issue that impacts on planning effectiveness, organisational change ▶ Chapter 13 ◀ and implementation (Kotter, 1995; Jones *et al.*, 2004; Lewis and Seibold, 2012). How often do we hear 'What we need around here is good communication'? (Cai and Fink, 2009). It is pivotal to dealing with people and the workplace and is fundamental to organisational success. Therefore, it is important that managers and employees are aware of the systems and techniques of communication that are in place for their organisation and use them well.

HOW DOES THE COMMUNICATION PROCESS WORK?

Communication in organisations is crucial; it may be deliberate in terms of a verbal instruction, an email or a written report, it may be more casual in terms of a chat at lunch, or it may be unintentional in terms of body language observed at a meeting. The most basic

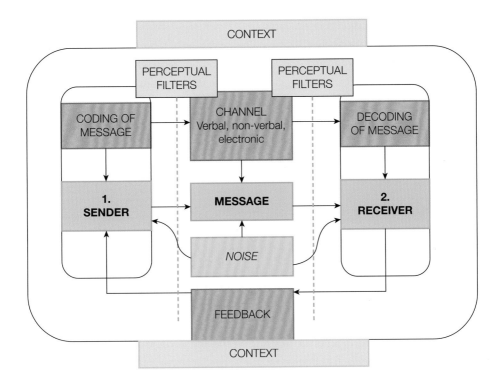

Figure 10.1 The communications process

Source: Developed and adapted from Shannon (1948) and Huczynski and Buchanan (2014).

form of human interpersonal communication can be described as a process by which ideas, information, opinions and attitudes – the message – are conveyed between one person or one group to another.

To explore this idea further we need to look at the key components in the communication process, which are illustrated in Figure 10.1. This model is adapted from the work of mathematician Claude Shannon (1948) whose original model was designed to accommodate any form of communication rather than just human interpersonal communication. However, the model of communication in Figure 10.1 includes a number of additions, including a feedback loop, perceptual filters and the context in which the communication takes place – all of which are very important in interpersonal human communication. The basic elements of the model include:

1 the source or sender (a person who is responsible for encoding an intended meaning into a specific message), and
2 the receiver (the person who decodes the message into a perceived meaning).

This process may appear to be very basic but it is not quite as simple as it looks. We need to examine it further to identify the other elements at work, their sequencing and the weaknesses and barriers that can arise and lead to communication problems or distortions.

Thus, the communication process commences with the encoding of the message to be transmitted or sent to the receiver. This requires selection of a message from a number of potential messages and composing it as a set of symbols or representations of the meaning that can be transmitted. For example, if the purpose of the communication is to instruct an employee on the details of a project, it is important that these instructions are clear and make sense to him or her. The next stage entails the selection of a channel for the transmission of this message, the medium through which the message is delivered: verbal, written or electronic. In the case of a project brief or for a student assignment or continuous assessment, communication will probably include verbal instructions as well as a written outline of what is required.

A carefully constructed email may make the instructions clear but a face-to-face meeting can utilise verbal and non-verbal channels not only to clarify the details but also to encourage and motivate the employee and to ensure they have received the message. Once it has been transmitted, the receiver needs to pick up the message, which will require decoding.

The signal or message can be affected by a number of factors including noise. If this is too strong the message may become garbled or fail to reach the receiver at all. This can be as simple as not being able to decode a telephone conversation due to a lot of external factors such as background noise in an office or static on the line. It could also refer to distractions caused by internal factors such as hunger, fatigue or headaches that affect how we process the message. The message can also be affected by perceptual filters ▶Chapter 3◀. For example, does the receiver perceive the message in a way that is consistent with the sender's intention? Misunderstandings may be due to cultural and language differences when the words themselves are not mutually understood. The message is also affected by the context. The communication style will vary if the boss and employee are in a very formal situation in the workplace, such as when the employee is called to the boss's office, as opposed to outside of the workplace in a social context. The context can also be affected by relations between both sender and receiver.

The model in Figure 10.1 allows for a feedback loop by which the receiver can send back what they have understood by the message. This can be done using non-verbal cues, such as a nod, or by requesting clarification verbally. Frequently, this feedback loop does not operate effectively and the sender may not be sure that the message has been received. Therefore, the process of communication is not as simple as you would think, because messages are not always perceived as intended (Kikoski, cited in Bowditch and Buono, 2005). Communication accuracy can be affected by the perceptual filters already mentioned, as they can play a large part in deciphering a message. People can associate different meanings with certain concepts

---

encoding the process of designing a message, represented as a set of symbols to be sent that makes sense to the receiver

decoding the process of deciphering and interpreting a received message in order to make sense of it

noise any factor, either external or internal that interferes with transmission of the message through creation of static or interference in the communication process

perceptual filters personal characteristics or perceptions that influence the way individuals take in and make sense of information which can interfere with transmitting or receiving messages and ideas because of their differing experiences and backgrounds, and these factors need to be taken into account when communicating with others. The process becomes even more complicated when working in a culturally diverse workplace (we will discuss this in more detail later). To recognise the errors that can occur in communication in the workplace we must consider six factors (adapted from O'Reilly and Pondy, cited in Bowditch and Buono, 2005):

1 Who is communicating to whom in terms of the roles they have in the organisation (for example, boss and subordinate)?

2 Are the language or symbols being used to communicate understood by both parties?

3 What communication channel is being used?

4 What is the content of the communication? (Is it familiar or unfamiliar information?)

5 What are the personal characteristics of the sender (for example, personality or appearance can lead to assumptions or judgements by the receiver based on experience) and what is the relationship between the sender and receiver (for example, do they trust one another)?

6 What is the context in which the message is being sent, such as the structure of the organisation, the physical space and social surroundings?

These factors mean that if you want to get your message across accurately, you need to consider:

- The message;
- The audience or receiver; and
- How the message is likely to be received.

This model also assumes that communication is intentional. However, in many cases our body language or non-verbal communication may transmit something that we never consciously meant to transmit. These non-verbal signals and communication will be dealt with later in the chapter.

INTERPERSONAL COMMUNICATION

A number of issues arise in attempting to communicate successfully with others. In the workplace it is crucial that we get our message across; whether it is in a job interview, a work presentation or instructing an employee about an important project or task. It is important to establish good open communication, not only through taking care to encode and deliver clear messages but also by being able to receive the messages that are returned and really take on board what the other person is saying. Effective usage of the feedback link in the communication process (see Figure 10.1) will help to ensure that the communication is successful. Listening is a large part of the communication process and its importance is often underestimated. How well you listen has a major impact on job effectiveness and on the quality of your relationships with others. It is not only used to receive the message and obtain the information, but also to understand it and to learn from it.

This can be achieved through active listening. Often we are only marginally listening; distracted, disinterested or already processing what we are going to say in response. This happens when you are introduced to a group of new people and you are too busy introducing yourself to actually keep track of their names, for example. Active listening in this case would require that you sense (receive the message – the name in an introduction), process (assign a meaning to the information transmitted) and then respond (clarifying what you have heard). In the case of introductions, that may simply be repeating the person's name, for example, 'Pleased to meet you, Mary'. Active listening means not only consciously engaging in listening and being encouraging but it also requires deferring judgement, letting the sender complete their point before asking questions. It is also appropriate to be respectful and understanding, because in that way you will get the best out of the communication exchange.

 **THIS…**

Do you think upward communication and questioning authority in the workplace is difficult? How important is it for management to listen to the opinions of employees? Research has shown that airlines from cultures that are typically more reluctant to question authority experience more crashes. Korean Air had a higher fatality rate than the average for a first-world airline until management realised that they had to facilitate upward communication from junior staff in the cockpit. They now have a superb safety record as they acknowledged the importance of upward communication as well as the influence of national culture on questioning authority.

COMMUNICATION CHANNELS

Looking again at the key components in the communication process (Figure 10.1) such as the choice of channel to communicate the message is very important in order to achieve under-standing. The organisation or workplace is a network of information and communication channels. There have always been formal and informal communication channels but the elec-tronic age has added a third category – quasiformal channels (French *et al.*, 2011). Managers now have tools such as intranets and web-based technologies to establish organisation-wide communication channels. All managers and employees should understand, and be able to use, each of the multiple channels for communication within their organisation.

active listening a process of making a conscious effort to sense, process and respond actively to a communicated message

FORMAL COMMUNICATION CHANNELS

These channels are officially defined pathways that follow the chain of command or hierarchy in organisations. These channels, being official and holding authority, are used to send letters, emails, policy statements or announcements. They are an important part of organisational life but they are only one element of a manager's communication skill set.

INFORMAL COMMUNICATION CHANNELS

These channels do not follow the chain of command. They are represented by interpersonal networks; for example, groups with similar interests form to exchange information. This networking cuts across chains of command and can come about, for example, when employees meet at the water cooler or in the canteen. Some managers use these informal networks to facilitate formal communication channels or to gather information. 'Management by walking around' (MBWA) (Peters and Waterman, 1982) can be seen as a way of cutting across the usual formal channels by visiting the staff as well as customers to find out what is happening at the front line. Managers who spend time walking around can reduce the 'distance' that might be perceived between themselves and their employees, and enable them to engage in more meaningful communication. It can result in better information and communication exchange. This intelligence will help to inform senior strategic decision-making, and the decisions will have more relevance for the front-line staff. However, the 'walking about' option needs to facilitate genuine engagement by senior managers rather than looking like an opportunity to check up on employees' activities.

Informal communication can take a number of forms, such as unofficial networks that supplement the formal channels and the grapevine. The grapevine functions as a major informal channel in organisations. Employees rely on it as an invaluable source of information. The grapevine arises from social interactions so it is as dynamic and varied as the people involved. There are some drawbacks to its use because information can become distorted along its pathways or channels and it can be used to spread rumour and negativity. However, it can also be used to disseminate important information along informal lines. Managers sometimes use the grapevine deliberately to transmit information that they may not wish to transmit formally or even to 'sound out' employees in respect of an initiative that they fear may be unpopular.

Van Hoye and Lievens (2009) showed that the grapevine and information communicated by peers had a strong influence on whether a potential applicant applied for a job in a company. A good manager should be aware of the information circulating in this unofficial communication channel and should take measures to prevent the flow of false information. In order to combat rumours in organisations it's important to promote healthy accurate communications and to avoid concealing bad news. It is also important to maintain open communication channels so that employees can voice their concerns and to encourage their ideas and suggestions.

grapevine informal communication networks in the organisation

Gossip is another informal source of information in an organisation. It is the idle talk or snippets of information about people and events that are passed along informal communication channels. It can be damaging and dangerous, but it can also fulfil a function as a source of socialising and developing group norms ▸ Chapter 12 ◂, as well as allowing employees to feel they belong to informal groupings and, thus, the organisation. In this way it can also be a morale booster, and a means to express employee concerns.

QUASIFORMAL CHANNELS

Quasiformal channels are planned communication connections between holders of various positions within the organisation. They are defined as being almost, or partly, formal, and they add additional channels between the formal and informal channels. Thus, managers can have access to information on an authorised basis and these channels can form a useful part of the company's overall management system. These communications, using structures such as project teams or product committees, are often used to help encourage innovation rather than through formal structures and communication processes. This approach has been extended by the information age, which has provided organisations with new opportunities to link managers effectively through email, intranet and other electronic media tools.

COMMUNICATION DIRECTION

Utilising the communication channels outlined above, one may assume that information is flowing both upwards from the employees and downwards from management. These flows of communication in an organisation are important, but communication must also be able to move laterally (see Figure 10.2).

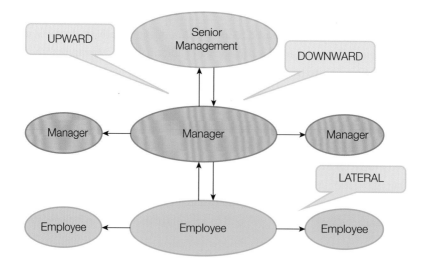

Figure 10.2 Direction of communication flows

DOWNWARD COMMUNICATION

Downward communication is used to implement plans and goals, explain policies and procedures, offer feedback on performance and give directions or instructions regarding job specifications and duties. Traditionally, this has been seen as the primary direction in terms of an organisation's information flow. It is important to gain employees' commitment, especially in times of organisational change, so that they are fully informed about the thinking behind any changes. There may be reasons why certain information is withheld, such as commercial sensitivities, but this has to be balanced with the need to involve and motivate employees ▶ Chapter 5 ◀. Another key issue in respect of effective communications is that of trust in management. If employees feel they are being left out of the information loop this can undermine their feelings of trust and belonging to the organisation and affect the psychological contract (Dries and De Gieter, 2014). They may even feel that management is out of touch and has no plan. Middle managers can also help in interpreting and explaining information coming from top management to lower-level staff (Floyd and Wooldridge, 1997). Neeley and Leonardi (2011) found that many managers repeated their communications a number of times to lower-level employees utilising different media, because this made the message more effective and ensured it was getting through. Blocks to downward communication can include managerial style, the organisational culture ▶ Chapter 12 ◀ which may be closed/secretive, and the organisation's tall or overly bureaucratic structure ▶ Chapter 11 ◀.

 THIS...

Are the communication skill sets that are required of you in the workplace today different from those required by managers and employees a decade ago? Many interviews and conference calls are carried out via videoconferencing or Skype. Computer screens display movements differently from normal face-to-face contact. Think about the skills that you require in managing your online behaviour. How careful do you have to be of the messages you are communicating?

UPWARD COMMUNICATION

Upward communication is used to provide information to management about what is happening at an operational level. It is important for a number of reasons: it facilitates

downward communication flows from a higher level of an organisation to a lower level

upward communication flows from a lower level of an organisation to a higher level

feedback regarding performance and progress of plans and goals, it notifies management of problems or potential problems and it passes on complaints. However, it is also important in providing a channel to facilitate ideas or suggestions. Upward communications from front-line and middle-level management have been found to be very important in terms of developing innovations and implementing change management (Floyd and Wooldridge, 2000). Middle managers can interpret and relate information from the front line to the organisation as a whole in what Swanson *et al.* (1997) describe as a communicative role. The story of the Post-it®, the self-attaching note that sticks, is an example of how Spencer Silver, its creator, used standard channels of communications both upwards and laterally to communicate his idea without success. It was only when he used informal channels to garner interest that he achieved a breakthrough (Glass and Hume, 2013). It is the staff who are experiencing the day-to-day real-ity of the organisation and its customers who are best-placed to provide feedback to senior management on what is working and what is not. Barriers to upward communication include a lack of facilitation of an upward communication channel and culture, as well as the employees' fear of admitting to mistakes or of finding that their ideas might be taken on board without due credit. Management can facilitate effective upward communications with an 'open door' policy and by enabling and acting on the receipt of feedback and information. See also the 'impact of technology' section later in this chapter for further details on communication flows.

LATERAL COMMUNICATION

Lateral communications are flows between members or employees in the same work group or department, or managers at the same level. They serve an important function in facilitating the coordination of the work undertaken. They also allow the sharing of information and ideas, as well as expertise and best practice. Barriers to lateral communication can be protect-ive self-interest of groups or departments, as well as increased specialisation and, hence, language problems such as 'jargon' that is not widely and easily understandable.

MODES OF INTERPERSONAL COMMUNICATION

How do members of an organisation communicate or transfer meaning between and among each other using the channels and information flows already described? Standard approaches are oral, written and non-verbal communication. With the development of multiple media tools there is an ever-expanding range of approaches that managers and employees can use. Some approaches can be more appropriate than others depending on the context.

ORAL COMMUNICATION

The main means by which we communicate with one another is through speaking. This can include conversations, group discussions and presentations, as well as using the grapevine to

lateral communications flows between members or employees in the same work group or department, or managers at the same level pass information by 'word of mouth'. Now thanks to communications technology, we can use video conferencing or voice-over-IP services such as Skype. The advantages of the oral communication approach are instant feedback and speed. You can gauge by body language whether or not your message has been understood, especially in a one-to-one situation. However, this can be more difficult with a wider audience and the message can be lost altogether if it becomes distorted as it is passed along the grapevine. To counteract any distortions or confusion, and to be effective in getting a message across, managers often repeat messages or instructions to employees by giving a verbal or oral message and backing it up with an email repeating the same instruction (Neeley and Leonardi, 2011).

Presentations are an important part of work life. They facilitate both upward and downward communication. If you are employed as a senior manager you will have to make presentations to your staff, to your shareholders and to potential clients. You may have to motivate your staff as you engage in an organisational change programme. Working as an employee you will need to be able to present results or progress in your own work or that of your team. You may have to be able to convince management about a new way of doing things or new ideas or concepts that you or your team has developed. According to Wertheim (2009) there are a number of basic steps to delivering an effective presentation. The first is to establish a *strategy*; that is, to understand your purpose and role and to formulate a plan for communicating with the specific audience. You then develop a *structure* to the presentation so that it flows, and put together the material with a good presentation *style*, making sure that you are aware of minimising distractions. Finally, you ensure that you can respond confidently to questions and challenges. It is important to remember that how you present is as important as the content that you present (McMahon, 2008).

BUILDING YOUR SKILLS

Successful Presentations

You have to make a presentation to senior management on behalf of your team. The thought of this makes you nervous. Many speakers lack the skills and confidence to deliver effective presentations. The last time you presented you knew the report and you had written down your ideas, but the presentation still didn't go well. This time you have to convince management  that the company needs to take an innovative approach to hiring new staff because you need more digital marketing experience in the team. Taking into account key features of a successful presentation, plan a strategy. How are you going to engage your audience? How will you deliver the speech? How will you convince them that the financial outlay will be worth it?

WRITTEN COMMUNICATION

Written communications include letters, emails, instant messaging, magazines or e-zines and notices (including those on electronic notice boards). A written communication can be useful to make sure the message is clear and verifiable. It can be stored and is available for reference. Taking time to draw up a concise yet detailed letter can help you to gather your thoughts clearly and carefully. Written communications can be given if the instructions required are complex and lengthy. They are used to transmit plans and strategies because they can be used as a continuous reference point by which to measure progress. The only drawback to the approach is that it can be time-consuming and lacks an immediate feedback mechanism.

SPOTLIGHT ON SKILLS

You have been selected as a communication consultant to support a restructuring of work teams in your organisation. This is part of an organisation-wide strategy to shake up people and develop innovation through teamwork. You need to put together an internal communications plan for this change initiative in your organisation.

1 What is your objective and how can communication help you to accomplish it?

2 How can you generate awareness, educate, inform, create action and drive behaviour change?

3 With whom do you need to communicate?

4 What tools do you use?

5 How do you make sure the correct information is getting through and being understood?

To help you answer these questions, in your ebook click the play buttons to watch the videos of Gina London, an international communications expert, and Philippa Brown, Global Internal Communications Manager at Springer Nature, talking about internal communication strategies.

NON-VERBAL COMMUNICATION

Verbal literally means 'in words'; therefore non-verbal communication is communication achieved without using words. It is the process of coding or conveying meaning through behaviours such as facial expressions, gestures and body posture. We can never 'not' communicate non-verbally because even an absence of response conveys some meaning. When we interact with others we are constantly sending and receiving messages via signs and gestures, and use of space, as well as vocal tone. This is often referred to as 'body language'. Body language can convey two important messages: the first is interest in another person and their views; and the second is the perceived status between sender and receiver. Body language can add to a verbal message or complicate it. If you use gestures that are encouraging and open, and smile when delivering praise to a colleague the message is augmented. If, in contrast, you are saying something positive but your facial gesture is negative this can cause confusion (see the In Reality feature at the start of the chapter).

BARRIERS TO EFFECTIVE COMMUNICATION

Communication is not always perfect. Earlier in the chapter we looked at the process of communicating and identified two barriers to communication: noise and perceptual filters. Noise is anything that interferes with the message, idea or information we are trying to convey in the process of communication. A number of factors can cause noise in the system, including tension or emotions, conflict, confusion, haste, cultural differences, gender differences or the setting itself (Thompson, 2013). The perceptual filters refer to the characteristics or perceptions of individuals that can interfere with transmitting or receiving messages, including filtering and selective perception ▸ Chapter 3 ◂. Filtering can mean purposely changing or manipulating information so that you present the best case possible and the receiver will respond positively. This can happen when you have made an error in the workplace and you want to explain it away in the most favourable light. Selective perception refers to how the receivers in the communication process will be influenced by their past experience, motivation, interest and expectations in decoding the message being conveyed by the sender. We all interpret reality in line with our experience and beliefs when we really need to actively listen and read and not be held back by preconceived beliefs and thoughts. A study reported in *BusinessWeek* in 2006 found that participants only correctly decoded the intent and tone of emails about 50% of the time (Brady, 2006).

Other barriers to communication include information overload. The developments in information and communications technology mean that communication is more frequent and faster, but it still needs management. For instance, the number of emails has increased exponentially; Brustein (2013) reported that 30% of all work time was spent reading and sifting through emails. Another barrier to effective communication is the use of language itself; there is no need to confuse your listener or receiver by using a lot of jargon, technical language or abbreviations. Finally, the problem of effective communication can involve the sender. Communication apprehension, or fear of communicating, is a major factor which inhibits a sender's willingness to communicate and thus affects their capability to develop effective communication skills. Byrne *et al.'s* (2012) study assessed first-year business students and showed varying levels of communication apprehension which were influenced by perceptions of peer evaluation, prior experiences of communicating with new people and how prepared they were.

BUILDING YOUR SKILLS

Understanding Information Overload

Many organisations use their communications channels to keep their employees up to date with developments. We now live in an 'information age' and that makes the process easier. The problem is that in the workplace there are piles of reports and other documents to read, in addition to a mounting number of emails to scan and the telephone is ringing constantly. The working day is longer due to easy access through smartphone, tablet or laptop. The perception of being overloaded is very real. This can lead to problems in which employees may not attend to important information because they may not be able to take important messages on board correctly. How would you develop a communications strategy within your organisation to help your employees prioritise and take notice of key information?

INTER-CULTURAL COMMUNICATION

Researchers have identified a number of language difficulties that can arise when people are communicating cross-culturally. The process of communication model in Figure 10.1 doesn't fully account for cultural differences between the sender and receiver, other than through perceptual filters. A study of cultural diversity in some of Toronto's major hotels found that language barriers made it difficult for managers to give non-English-speaking employees effective feedback (McShane, 2006). Some of these language barriers include:

- Semantics – differences in meanings of words to different people.
- Differences in non-verbal symbols and signals.
- Word connotations – words imply different things in different languages.
- Tone differences – in some cultures tone changes depending on context.
- Differences in perception – different world views.

As a manager you need to be sensitive to the fact that cross-cultural barriers may exist. You have to show respect for all workers. You should use language that is clear, without any clichés or colloquialisms and speak slowly and clearly. You should remain alert to cultural differences in customs and behaviours. Do not let style, accent or grammar affect your perceptions and interpretation of the communications you are involved in.

Working in multi-cultural teams requires good communications. Martha Maznevski has carried out extensive work on leading diverse teams globally (Maznevski, 2007). Her guide to building diverse teams provides invaluable insights into developing effective inter-cultural communication (see the video clip link in Useful Websites at the end of the chapter). She notes that diverse or multi-cultural teams need to do three things: mapping, bridging and integrating. Mapping requires drawing a picture of the similarities and differences in the team. This is a map of the differences in culture among different team members, as well as the differences in personality, and all of the different perspectives that people bring to the team. The second step is bridging: communicating effectively, taking those differences into account, speaking and listening to the other person. You need to decentre, or put yourself in the other person's place, and speak and listen from their point of view. Thereafter, you need to re-centre and find commonalities, develop common norms, common definitions of the situation and common objectives. The third part of the process is integrating, which involves using the differences to create new ideas to build on, to increase participation, to resolve conflicts and to foster innovation.

You can use the following link to complete a self-assessment of your communicative competence:

www.austincc.edu/colangelo/1318/interpersonalcommunicationcompetence.htm (last accessed 23 October 2015).

(Spitzberg, B.H and Cupach, W.R. (1984) *Interpersonal Communication Competence Self-Assessment*. Published by Sage Publications, 1984; Original from the University of Michigan.)

THE IMPACT OF TECHNOLOGY

As we have seen, a large amount of business communications is now being done electronically. The definition of communication technology is 'electronic systems used for communication between individuals or groups' (QFinance, 2011). A key purpose of communication technology is the facilitation of effective communications between individuals or groups that are physically distant from each other, as well as providing it by cheaper and more efficient means.

The ever-expanding development of communication technology has enabled new forms of working patterns to evolve, including working from home and other locations. Working from home is made possible because employees can communicate with their colleagues, managers and customers via the internet by emailing, Skype, instant messaging and other related technologies. PricewaterhouseCoopers, a large business consultancy, has adopted this practice. Bohlander and Snell (2009) cite significant cost savings for both company and employees as one of the main advantages of the practice, as well as increased levels of performance.

As information travels faster and faster and the barrier of distance disappears, organisations are outsourcing many jobs overseas. Outsourcing is the practice of hiring employees who work outside the company or remotely, even many thousands of miles away. Ernst & Young utilises cross-country teams to improve organisational performance, enabling remote working via video conferencing, emails, and company-specific communication technologies.

Video conferencing has proved very effective in terms of cost savings through cutting down on travel and other costs.

Instant messaging is seen as a key communication tool in the business world and will replace emails more and more over time because they are faster and allow for an instant response. Many companies, such as banks like NatWest in the UK, are using email as a primary means of communication with their customers. Email, though one of the 'older' of the new technologies, has had a major impact on personal communication because it has replaced the use of the phone and many personal conversations. In comparison to these modes of communication, email is unaffected by distance and time. It has also linked many people to leaders and senior managers directly through the simple click of the 'send' button. However, it has had another impact in that it encourages indiscriminate sending of often unimportant or unsolicited information. The volume of messages that managers as well as employees and customers receive has increased. Due to email always being accessible and not being regulated by business hours, a culture has been created whereby senders expect an instant response. At times that can mean that email responses are returned in the 'heat of the moment'. The French government introduced a labour agreement in April 2014 with an obligation to 'disconnect communications tools' after an employee has worked a 13-hour day.

THE IMPACT OF SOCIAL MEDIA

Social media is termed 'social' because it enables communication (King, 2012). Using social media tools by 'friending', 'liking', linking and following gives organisations direct access to their customers. Many large organisations such as Tesco, BP, Barclays and British American Tobacco maintain their own dedicated Facebook pages. Prospective and current customers of these businesses can 'Like' the company page on Facebook to receive status updates from the business. Marks & Spencer use Twitter to send messages to its followers which are used to market products, services and offers. As a result, companies have access to your email address, Facebook and Twitter accounts among others, and can utilise your preferences to monitor your buying, leisure and lifestyle habits to target you with specific ads online. A more recent development is access to free wifi. Companies such as Dublin-based wifi operator Bitbuzz increased its registered users by 81% to 2.08 million and recorded a 67% increase in logins in 2013. Now Bitbuzz facilitates faster log-in via Facebook or Twitter (Business & Leadership, 2014). All of these communications can be managed from your smartphone and will change the face of communication significantly in the future.

As a tool for communication, social media has a number of characteristics (Adler *et al.*, 2012). These include:

- *Message richness* – Messages transferred in face-to-face communication have traditionally been seen as rich due to the ability to use multiple cues (Cameron and Webster, 2005). Dennis *et al.* (2008) argue that the 'richest' medium is that which best provides the set of capabilities needed by the situation: the individuals, tasks and social contexts in which they interact. They conclude that online communication can be at times as 'rich' as face-to-face communication. The information or message transferred via social media can utilise text, chat, visual images and links to ensure communication success.

- *Hyperpersonal communication* – Text-based computer-mediated communication lacks physical and social cues, which may foster less inhibited behaviour as well as impeding the development of socio-emotional bonds (Sproull and Kiesler, 1991). Thus, Walther (1996) argues that the social media environment can create 'hyperpersonal' relationships in which the individual experiences a level of closeness above that gained in a face-to-face context because the absence of social cues enhances sharing and openness and idealisation of the other communicator. This idealisation can occur for both individuals in the dialogue because each sender can selectively self-represent by editing messages and images before sending. Then, through the feedback loop there can be an interplay of idealisation and, thus, the self-presentation becomes a dynamic process and creates a self-reinforcing cycle.

- *Asynchronous communication versus synchronous communication* – Synchrony refers to whether or not the sender and receiver are communicating in real time. Some media are used synchronously, so that all participants are communicating at the same time (for example, instant messaging, Skype, video conference, Snapchat). Others are used asynchronously so that participants do not communicate at the same time (for example, messages on Facebook). Some media can be used either synchronously or asynchronously depending upon how they are set up (for example, discussion forums) (Walther, 1996). During synchronous communication, multiple exchanges are completed in rapid succession. By contrast, asynchronous communication, such as posting messages, limits the process to only small portions of an exchange at any given time. Synchronous communication facilitates the 'give and take' that is required to understand each other and solve issues or problems (Moyer and Katz, 2007).

- *Permanence of digital messages* – Messages can be stored by both senders and receivers. Images, videos and tweets are transferrable and can go viral in the social media space. Removing an image from a social media account may be too late as it has already transferred beyond the creator's control. This happened with Snapchat, where images usually self-destruct after a short period of time, but were found to have been leaked to the internet and kept on a database (Grieg, 2013).

MEDIATED COMMUNICATION AND RELATIONAL QUALITY

Early studies suggested that mediated communication such as that through social media channels is less effective than other means of forming and sustaining strong social relationships (Cummings *et al.*, 2000). More recent research shows that, although using phrases such as 'online community', many social media users feel lonely and think that their social media use discourages community. A study examining the profiles and activity of 608 female Facebook users found that half described themselves as 'lonely' and as a result tended to overshare personal information (O'Callaghan, 2014). A study in 2013 by Ethan Kross and his colleagues of the University of Michigan concluded that, although on the surface Facebook provides an invaluable resource for fulfilling the basic human need for social connection and

The Impact of Social Media Communications on Obama's Landslide Victories

Barack Obama won the US presidency in a landslide victory in 2008 by transforming ordinary people into engaged and empowered volunteers, donors and advocates through social networks, email, text messaging and online video (Lutz, 2009). In 2012 he secured a second term by winning with over 51% of the popular vote yet again. The use of social media is revolutionising how organisations and teams work successfully in achieving their goals and communicating their message. Social media had been used by presidential candidates before, with Howard Dean's ground-breaking use of the internet in the 2004 election attracting a following, particularly among young voters. However, in 2008 social media was in a very different place and by 2012 it had become a means of targeting and responding to potential voters. Social media developed as a dominant

 **OB IN THE NEWS**

force during both elections, particularly on sites such as Facebook, Twitter and YouTube.

On Election Day in November 2008, Obama had almost 3 million Facebook fans, four times that of his opponent, and 23 times the number of Twitter followers (Vargas, 2008). By 2012 his Twitter account boasted 21 million followers and he had 32 million Facebook fans, compared to his opponent's 12 million fans (Burrus, 2012). What differentiated Barack Obama's use of social media in his communication campaigns was his website, Mybarackobama. com, or MyBO, to rally potential supporters and respond quickly to any negative publicity (via his 'Truth Team'). His second victory in 2012 was due to the team consolidating the data they had amassed in the 2008 campaign.

Lutz (2009) outlined a number of social media lessons gained from the Obama campaign,

which included starting early and innovating as well as channelling online enthusiasm and integrating online advocacy into every element of the campaign. He outlined a step-by-step approach using the metaphor of learning to crawl before walking and eventually taking off. It starts simply by establishing a website presence (crawl), then progresses on to developing podcasts and games (walk), then engaging online influencers through blogs and sponsorship (run), and finally to embracing the community through social networks and advocacy (fly). Barack Obama built upon these lessons before his subsequent re-election. His team created a single system to merge the information collected from pollsters, fundraisers and consumer databases as well as social media and mobile contacts with the main voter files (Scherer, 2012). The 2012 campaign then used data analytics to assemble a profile of voters. Thus, a national campaign was created in which the interests of individual voters were identified in detail and then all communication for every level of the campaign was informed by these findings (Issenberg, 2012).

These lessons have also been useful for Michelle Obama. She launched a campaign to eliminate childhood obesity in a generation with her 'Let's Move' initiative in February 2010. This was an ambitious goal to achieve, even within an extended timeframe. However, to communicate her message she used a number of

© GETTY IMAGES /ISTOCKPHOTO/THINKSTOCK IMAGES/TRILOKS

similar tools and techniques. These included deploying her leverage as an excellent role model for a healthier America and personally spearheading a campaign that more than 8 out of 10 Americans said they have heard of, according to a survey by the *Washington Post* and the Kaiser Family Foundation. This is all by design. Michelle Obama is a near-constant presence on cable's Nickelodeon channel, where her public service announcements are aired. She has engaged with key figures to push her message, having pop star Beyoncé write a song especially for the effort. She has also involved the big supermarket chains, including Walmart which has developed a nutrition charter. A recent study in the *Journal of the American Medical Association* found that obesity among children aged 2 to 5 had dropped from 14% ten years previously to 8% (Superville, 2014).

Questions:

1   How convinced are you that social media is driving how organisations and teams work, achieve their goals and get their message across?

2   Does social media generate as many negative messages as positive messages?

3   Do people believe and trust what they see and hear via social media?

Sources:

Lutz, M. (2009). The Social Pulpit: Barack Obama's Social Media Toolkit. Retrieved from http://cyber.law.harvard.edu/sites/cyber.law.harvard.edu/files/Social%20Pulpit%20-%20Barack%20Obamas%20Social%20Media%20Toolkit%201.09.pdf (last accessed on April 17th 2014).

Vargas, J.A. (2008) Obama's Wide Web. Washington Post. 20 August 2008. http://www.washingtonpost.com/wp-dyn/content/article/2008/08/19/AR2008081903186_pf.html (last accessed on April 17th 2014).

Burrus, D. (2012) Did Social Media Play a Role in Obama's Victory?

Huffington Post 11 September 2012 http://www.huffingtonpost.com/daniel-burrus/did-social-media-play-a-r_b_2094145.html (last accessed on October 31st 2014).

Scherer M. (2012) Inside the Secret World of the Data Crunchers Who Helped Obama Win. Time Magazine, 7 November 2012.

http://swampland.time.com/2012/11/07/inside-the-secret-world-of-quants-and-data-crunchers-who-helped-obama-win/ (last accessed on October 31st 2014).

Issenberg, S. (2012) How President Obama's campaign used big data to rally individual voters. MIT Technology Review 19 December, 2012. http://www.technologyreview.com/featuredstory/509026/how-obamas-team-used-big-data-to-rally-voters/ (last accessed on October 31st 2014).

Superville, D. (2014) Michelle Obama Praises Decline In Childhood Obesity. Huffington Post, 26 Feb 2014. http://www.huffingtonpost.com/2014/02/26/michelle-obama-childhood-obesity_n_4862663.html (last accessed on April 19th 2014).

communication, it may actually undermine rather than enhance well-being (Kross et al., 2013). Thus, communication can become less like an exchange and more like a passive observance of the lives of others.

In order to mitigate against the downside of social media use, Adler *et al.* (2012) suggest a number of strategies to employ in order to communicate competently. You should always be careful about what you post and be considerate of others in your online community. They warn you to keep your tone civil and watch for disinhibition. There is also a need to balance social mediated communication with face-to-face time. To conclude, social media can be used to enhance the communication experience by increasing opportunities, as well as improving connections. It has led to an overall facilitation of the communication experience in what McLuhan (1964) famously termed the 'global village' where he foresaw that members of every nation would be connected by communication technology.

The internet has become the most powerful driver of innovation the world has ever seen. One result has been to change the structure of the communications industry, shifting the focus of innovation toward young hothouses and start-ups. Another has been to drive forward communications technology at a formidable pace (Cairnross, 2001). Through the internet, new products can be developed and launched relatively inexpensively, potential customers and investors can be targeted, and markets can be quickly identified and tested. No other mechanism provides such instant communication links between investors and their customers.

Communications and Growth at Version 1

Version 1 is one of the fastest growing IT services companies in Western Europe. It has doubled both profitability and revenue over the last few years, while at the same time delivering consistent improvement in both customer satisfaction and world-class employee engagement. It has been in the Top 50 Best Workplaces in Europe since 2012 according to the Great Place to Work® survey and was in the top 3 Best Large Workplaces in Ireland (Great Place to Work® survey, 2014), as well as being a 'Best Managed' company (2014) in the Deloitte Best Managed Companies Awards Programme for the third consecutive year and winning the Tech Excellence award 2014 for business performance.

ACTIVE CASE STUDY

Its remit is to provide end-to-end IT consulting and managed services solutions across a number of areas. It was established in Dublin in 1996 by CEO Justin Keatinge and co-founder John Mullen. Version 1 has since grown through both organic growth and strategic acquisition to be a market leader in IT services in the UK and Ireland. From 2 employees and €60k in revenue in 1997, by 2014 Version 1 had more than 500 employees across the UK and Ireland and revenues of €60m. Version 1 has from day one invested heavily in communications, both internally and externally. The company sees its success as deriving from high-quality communications and communication strategies (with both its employees and wider stakeholders including the wider community).

Version 1's approach to success can be attributed to achieving equilibrium between vision, values, balance and rhythm. Their mission is to prove that IT can deliver real business benefits to their customers yet balance this with employee engagement and profitability. Therefore, core to the mission is the creation of a Great Workplace where core values are lived out. The company has created an environment that places employee engagement at the heart of everything they do and ensures that their culture is one in which people trust the people they work for, have pride in what they do and enjoy the people they work with.

Vision and values are crucial and underpin all work at Version 1. They are communicated to all members of the organisation itself, as well as to all the relevant stakeholders and the wider community. Version 1's culture is rooted in core values: honesty and integrity, personal commitment, no ego, customer first, excellence and drive.

According to Justin Keatinge, the vision for the company is to become the first €1 billion Irish services company. This is to be achieved through setting strong cultural foundations.

IMAGE SOURCE

With such a growth strategy the company encourages positive communications that enhance teamwork and build upon their open organisational culture. For all new acquisitions they have set a core objective of protecting and promoting their open, friendly, values-based culture as a priority across the organisation as a whole.

Preserving such an open culture can be difficult as Version 1 continues to expand in size and geographical spread. As with other multinational organisations, the danger in growth in size and scale is a parallel increase in formalisation and rules, and an expansion of corporate speak. It was decided to define and then maintain how employees in the organisation communicated with each other, in order to be able to sustain an easy open approach in which everyone has positive communication experiences. After some analysis Version 1 identified a consultancy (Greenline Conversations) specialising in communications and, in particular, conversations. This is based on the underlying belief that good human interaction enables businesses to run well and that conversation is the basic unit of currency. There are many conversations taking place in business each week and yet not all are created equal. By examining human interaction in terms of conversations, Greenline's approach offers understanding and skills development, resulting in better performance as well as better business and interpersonal outcomes. Common reasons why conversations can go bad (redline) or can go well (greenline) have been identified and then developed into prompt cards to be used as tools to keep all conversations 'greenline'. Some greenline principles that need to be bedded into every conversation include enquiring, hearing and reflecting as well as agreeing to next steps before completing the exchange. Although simple in principle, each conversation relies as much on listening and hearing as it does on talking, agreeing and reflecting. In addition, conversations are to be 'straight talking'. All Version 1 staff are trained in the Greenline approach to conversation and it is built into the organisation's cultural norms.

Other internal communications practices include quarterly briefings that not only confirm core values and mission, but also outline current strategy and thank and acknowledge employees. Included in these briefings are guest speakers who are invited to talk on their personal experiences, to inspire and to facilitate thinking outside 'comfort zones'. Practice briefings are used to promote company news and share information and knowledge. Another initiative is the company's use of a private social (Yammer®) that helps employees collaborate across departments and locations. Version 1 believes that the ability to listen is core to building up trust within and without an organisation. They ensure that all employees are listened to as well as facilitating them to ask questions, provide feedback and make suggestions. Version 1's positive internal communications focus is based on the belief that employees are core to creating the company brand, executing the strategy and building the business.

Question:

In your capacity as a communications consultant you have been asked to devise a plan to roll out a social media communications strategy to engage and recruit new graduates to Version 1. Keeping in mind the various social media tools on offer, the positives in terms of Version 1's communication culture and the grouping you need to engage with, what would your advice be? Visit the Version 1 website to inform your plan and draw up a report.

Sources:

www.version1.com/About-Version-1/Culture-Values#sthash.TlDwjLXm (last accessed 5th November 2015).

http://greenlineconversations.com/ (last accessed 5th November 2015).

www.ianmcclean.com/green_line.html (last accessed 5th November 2015).

www.yammer.com/ (last accessed 5th November 2015).

 SUMMARY

 IN THE EBOOK, CLICK TO HEAR AN AUDIO SUMMARY

This chapter described how understanding the process of communication is core to most organisational activity and how the use of different communication channels can impact on the way that messages are delivered and received. Also outlined in the chapter were the barriers that can arise in the communication process, such as noise, perception and information overload, and how they can be overcome. Later sections of the chapter explored the impact of communications technology and social media on communication in the workplace, including research into its effects on relations.

Communication is a central feature of organisations and people management. To be successful in our jobs we need to make the most of our communications skills. Communication isn't only about ourselves though; it's a careful balancing act requiring us to balance the needs of senders and receivers. When communicating in the workplace we need to take into account the content, manner and timing of our communications, as well as how to make the best use of the channels and modes of communication open to us.

CHAPTER REVIEW QUESTIONS

1   If communication is central to organisations, why do managers often fail to communicate effectively to their employees?
2   Are there advantages to face-to-face communication in modern organisations? Outline the key advantages and explain where this strategy could be best used.
3   What contribution can a competent communications strategy make to an organisation's sustained competitive advantage?
4   Identify and describe common barriers to effective communication.
5   Do technological advances in communication make it easier for members of an organisation to communicate with each other and with people outside the organisation?
6   You have been asked to address the issue of internal communication in your organisation because it is important for building a culture of transparency between management and employees and it can engage employees in an organisation's planning and priority setting. Outline the key features of your new internal communications programme.
7   Outline and describe the causes of potential problems in cross-cultural communication.
8   How can non-verbal communication techniques be used to enhance the delivery of important messages?

MULTIPLE CHOICE QUESTIONS

In your ebook, click to take a multiple choice quiz to test your understanding of this chapter.

📖 FURTHER READING

Bratton, J. (2015) *Introduction to Work and Organizational Behaviour*, 3rd edn, London: Palgrave.

Klein, S.M. (1996) A management communication strategy for change, *Journal of Organizational Change Management*, 9(2), 32–46.

McClave, H. (2008) *Communication for Busines.*, 4th edn, Dublin: Gill & Macmillan.

McMahon, G. (2008) Gift of the gab – How best to deliver your message in public, *The Irish Times*, 21 March, 24.

Mishra, K., Boynton, L. and Mishra, A. (2014) Driving employee engagement: The expanded role of internal communications. *International Journal of Business Communication*, 51(2), 183–202.

Neeley, T. and Leonardi, P. (2011) Effective managers say the same thing twice (or more). *Harvard Business Review*, May, 38–39.

Peyton, J., Caputo, J.M., Ford, E.A., Fu, R., Leibowitz, S.A., Liu, T., Polasik, S.S., Ghosh, P. and Wu, C. (2013) Investigating verbal workplace communication behaviors. *Journal of Business Communication* 50(2), 152–169.

Thompson, N. (2013) *People Management*. Basingstoke: Palgrave Macmillan.

🌐 USEFUL WEBSITES

www.shrm.org/

The Society for Human Resource Management (SHRM) has a lot of resources on their website for both students and managers in practice. Their research metrics section includes a well written article on how the US workforce is not prepared in the area of communication (oral and written) in the workplace. It also outlines strategies that organisations are employing to deal with these deficits.

http://video.ft.com/62063401001/IMD-Leading-diverse-teams/Management

The *Financial Times* website offers a business school section which presents video clips of experts discussing issues in management and communication. This is an interesting clip (IMD: Leading diverse teams Part 3) presented by Martha Maznevski on how to get the best performance from diverse teams through facilitating their communications.

www.greatplacetowork.com/

The Great Place to Work® Institute is a global research, consulting and training organisation that helps businesses to identify, create and sustain great workplaces through the development of high-trust workplace cultures. They work with businesses, non-profits and government agencies in 45 countries. This website has a host of material available which is very practitioner focused. Its best practices section is a useful resource to examine what developments in communication practices are taking place in exemplar companies.

www.hbr.com

https://hbr.org/2014/04/data-doesnt-speak-for-itself/

The *Harvard Business Review* website offers the visitor access to a number of blogs written by key thinkers, researchers and academics in the field. The blog highlighted here outlines the importance and responsibility for getting your message across and interesting tips for how to do so.

www.theguardian.com/theguardian/series/greatspeeches

A listing of some of the great speeches of the 20th century with background information put together by *The Guardian*.

www.melcrum.com/how-internal-communication-progressing-digital-workplace

www.melcrum.com/choosing-right-communication-channel-version-20

Melcrum is a platform set up to work with organisations globally to build skills and know-how in internal communication. Their website provides advice, analysis, tools and training to assist in connecting with people. These two brief but interesting articles look at the importance of using digital communications within the workplace and how to choose the right communication channel.

SECTION TWO CASE STUDY

Issues that arise in organisational life are often connected in ways that we do not anticipate. The actions of one organisational actor can create a vast array of unintended consequences for other stakeholders in an organisation. Decisions made in haste on one issue (even those intended to have positive outcomes) can result in negative employee perceptions across a whole range of matters. Take the example of MediCo, a medium sized company in the health sector in Australia. MediCo is a non-profit health care organisation employing 300 people, and is part-funded by the government. Those who work in MediCo range from doctors and nurses to groundkeepers, drivers and porters. The organisational culture was characterised by a clear philosophy about how business was to be conducted – one of a caring supportive approach, which was in keeping with the organisation's overall mission in the delivery of quality care. While there were a number of subcultures in some of the more administrative areas of the organisation, these were formed along functional differences but did not have any negative impact on organisational performance. In 2013 the organisation had to make changes as result of a projected 5% drop in funding from the government. However, it was how the situation was communicated to employees that created a series of unanticipated negative knock-on effects.

The decision was made by the CEO that the projected shortfall in revenue should be communicated to all staff as soon as possible. This was in part to highlight to staff the severity of the situation. The culture in the organisation was one where the CEO made wide-ranging decisions and his decision was final. It was difficult to change his mind about an issue once he had made a decision; indeed even in instances where a reversal of a decision made better sense his mantra was that of 'never go back'. He believed he would 'lose face' if he changed his mind once he had made a decision. In this case he wrote to all staff to communicate the reduction in government revenue for the coming year, and indicated a number of measures that would be put in place to reduce costs. This letter took the approach of telling employees how detrimental this cut would be to the organisation. Given the organisation's aim, the main priority was to maintain the base level of care provided, and therefore the impact of the cuts would be most widely felt in the staffing budgets which accounted for 70% of all MediCo's costs. One of the first measures the letter outlined was to put on hold all job recruitment that had already been given authorisation. The second measure was to end all fixed-term contracts, of which there were only four in total. This letter was written and communicated without consulting the HR manager, who could have anticipated the likely 'fall out' from such a letter. Indeed, the HR manager was not included in the consultation with the board of directors when the implementation of cuts and how to manage them were being discussed.

The immediate reaction among staff was one of hurt and outrage, particularly among those on fixed-term contracts and those who worked closely with them. While the letter outlined the main actions management intended to take, it did not elucidate any clear steps for line managers to take in putting these into action. The first issue was that the organisational culture developed into one of whispers and rumours. Corridor conversations became the source of information for employees. Yet, much of this grapevine produced inaccurate information. At the same time there was an increase in absenteeism of 5% with absence rates among nursing staff rising to 9%. There was a noticeable decrease in staff morale also, particularly in those departments where new resources had been promised and were now not going to materialise. Negativity became the dominant discourse. Staff began to worry whether more cuts to funding were planned and questions were raised about the viability of jobs and the organisation.

According to the HR manager the key lesson to be learned was the importance of communication, both in terms of the 'what' and the 'how'. It transpired that the reduction in government funding was only 3% rather than the anticipated 5%. The CEO had communicated the bad news before it was actually confirmed.

In an effort to address the negative culture that had been created over the three-month period in question, the HR manager began by organising a series of 'brown bag' lunches between employees and the CEO at which people could essentially vent their anger at what had happened and ask for information directly from the CEO. This had never been done before and the majority of employees attended. Anecdotal evidence indicated that they felt better after having had the chance to air their grievances and be listened to.

The process actually led to some positive initiatives being undertaken in the organisation. In an effort to address morale a 'well-being at work week' initiative was arranged, with talks from psychologists, fitness specialists and other health professionals. The HR manager also started a company newsletter which kept staff informed about what was going on in the company, and instigated a management development programme because it was clear that first-line managers had not been well equipped to deal with the negative consequences of the change in organisational culture.

Essentially the letter from the CEO was a catalyst for change in more ways than one.

QUESTIONS:

1   What impact did the CEO's method of communication have on the employees?
2   What could the CEO have done differently in order to communicate the information?
3   Show how the areas of communication, organisational culture and organisational change are connected in this case.
4   If this company had been based in Asia how would the CEO have communicated the information?

11 ORGANISATIONAL STRUCTURE

Paul McGrath

LEARNING OUTCOMES

BY THE END OF THIS CHAPTER YOU SHOULD BE ABLE TO:

- Understand the basic concepts of organisational structure.

- Be able to explain the impact that structure has on behaviour.

- Discuss the key differences between mechanistic and organic organisations.

- Identify and explain the key contingencies to be faced and design choices to be made by managers in choosing an organisational design.

- Be aware of current tendencies and debates in the area of organisational design.

© FOTOLIA/KURHAN

THIS CHAPTER DISCUSSES:

IN REALITY

The process of organisational structure and design is often viewed as a rational process, which is the outcome of careful situational analysis with a view to maximising efficiency and effectiveness. This view represents the dominant logic of how managers need to approach the challenge of designing the structure of the firm. However, in reality, research has shown that organisation design is frequently the outcome of a different, seemingly more irrational form of thinking.

One interesting alternative school of thought is that of institutional theory (Scott, 1995). This perspective focuses on explaining why some organisational design is driven by the need for legitimacy, rather than internal efficiency and effectiveness. Some organisations must meet the demands and expectations of their external environment, but in doing they may end up with a design that is not particularly internally efficient. The tendency to meet institutional demands (of the government, regulators and so on) can result in whole industries adopting very similar structures. The key point here is that the structural change is not introduced for efficiency concerns, but due to the need to be seen to meet the demands or expectations of their institutional environment. They need to look good to key players in the external world!

INTRODUCTION

The focus of this chapter is on organisational structure and design. We will explain what organisational structure is, why it is important, and how it is closely linked to the concept of organisational design. We will identify different types of structures and their core dimensions, and address the design challenges faced by managers in choosing one type of structure over another.

ORGANISATIONAL STRUCTURE AND DESIGN

The issues of organisational structure and organisational design need to be considered together because one does not exist without the other. When we use the term 'organisation structure' we typically refer to the formal infrastructure of an organisation. This concerns the formal reporting relationships (the chain of command – who reports to whom), how many levels there are in the hierarchy, the division of labour within the organisation, the width of the span of control of managers, how people are grouped into units and how these units

organisational structure the formal pattern of tasks and relationships within an organisation aimed at coordinating employees towards achieving organisational goals

organisational design a managerial process of deciding on and introducing a particular structural configuration

hierarchy the number of layers or levels of responsibility in an organisation

span of control how many people the manager has to supervise

are integrated. Put simply, structure distinguishes the different parts of an organisation and delineates the formal relationship between them.

Various definitions of organisational structure exist. Here are a few from some important reference texts in the field:

a 'The structure of an organization can be defined simply as the sum total of the ways in which it divides its labor into distinct tasks and then achieves coordination among them' (Mintzberg, 1979a, p. 2).

b 'The organizational structure determines where formal power and authority are located. It comprises the organizational components, their relationships, and hierarchy. It channels the energy of the organization and provides a "home" and identity for employees' (Galbraith *et al.*, 2002, p. 3).

c 'The formal system of task and authority relationships that control how people coordinate their actions and use resources to achieve organizational goals' (Jones, 2010, p. 29).

Organisation structure is difficult, and sometimes impossible, to see and so is normally represented in a formal organisational chart. This is a visual representation of the various parts of the organisation and shows how it ought to work. This graphical representation provides some insight into organisational functioning, but do bear in mind that the chart is a simplification of a complex entity and only provides a partial insight into some aspects of organisational functioning. In addition, the chart merely encourages its employees into particular types of relationship and interactions with a view to achieving organisational goals. Ultimately it is managerial and employee behaviour (for example, motivation, surveillance, sanction, commitment and so on) that will determine the successful implementation of the structure.

Figure 11.1 shows a typical organisational chart that you might find on a company website. The chart itself provides us with some basic information about the firm and its structure. First, it shows seven layers from top to bottom. It also shows grouping by function with all the finance, production, sales and marketing people grouped together in departments. As we will see later in this chapter, this structure would be classified as a functional structure with a relatively tall hierarchy. Put yourself somewhere in this structure and try to imagine how work and information might flow up, down and across the levels, how decisions might get made and what type of controls might exist to monitor and direct behaviour. How might the different departments try and coordinate their activities to ensure that they help each other out? The key issue to appreciate here is how the formal structure influences employee behaviour.

Organisation structure represents the basic skeleton or framework of an organisation. The related concept of organisational design is the process or dynamic which determines how the various elements of structure are combined. It is concerned with the construction and change of organisational structure. At this basic level, structure represents the component parts and design describes how these parts are assembled. The different combinations and permutations of parts give rise to different organisational forms or types. It is important to realise that organisational design is more than simply rearranging the boxes in an organisational chart.

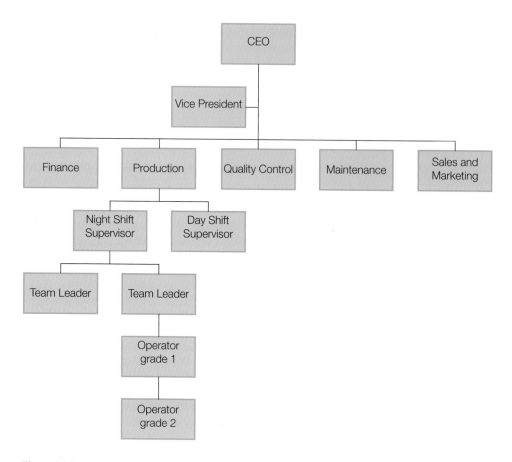

Figure 11.1 A sample organisational chart

It must also consider the integration between structure, organisational processes, incentive structures and people policies and practices (Galbraith *et al.*, 2002).

An interesting example of an organisational structure is that of Nike Inc., the well-known manufacturer and distributor of athletic footwear and apparel (Brenner *et al.*, 2013). The corporation is headquartered in the US and maintains operations (manufacturing facilities and stores) in more than 180 different countries around the world. It employs more than 33,000 people with revenues in excess of $20 billion per year. Nike's structure needs to be viewed at three levels – world headquarters (WHQ) (based in Beaverton, Oregon, USA), regional headquarters and individual subsidiaries.

WHQ controls global research and development and manages three of the corporation's four regional headquarters (the US, Americas and Asia Pacific). Regional headquarters adopt a matrix organisational form with managerial responsibility broken down into business units (Apparel, Equipment and Footwear) and business function.

integration how elements are linked together and interact
towards achieving a common purpose

With a view to reducing the complexity of its structure and enhancing transparency a new structural layer, European headquarters, was introduced, once again operating with a matrix type structure.

Regional headquarters in turn monitor and control the subsidiary companies within the corporation. The individual subsidiaries are allowed a certain level of operational flexibility to enable them to tailor their business to local needs.

WHY ARE ORGANISATIONAL STRUCTURE AND DESIGN IMPORTANT?

In order to compete and thrive in a competitive environment organisations need to be both efficient and effective (Daft, 2004). Organisation structure and design play an important but partial role in attaining both of these objectives. An effective structure will ensure good goal clarity and focus. Employees will know what they have to do, who they report to and how their effort and activities are integrated with others. An effective structure will ensure that appropriate and timely interactions happen across the organisation and that communications are clear and effectual. Think of organisation structure as the rails on which everything moves. Are these rails well designed, easy to follow and travel upon, or are they messy, poorly interconnected and confusing? Organisational design will influence the ability of the organisation to be creative and flexible in meeting the needs of its customers. In this way it may influence the organisation's ability to innovate ▶ **Chapter 13** ◀ and will influence the type and effectiveness of organisational, team and individual-level learning that will take place. It will determine the level and type of interactions that happen across the organisation and have a strong influence on the development of its culture ▶ **Chapter 12** ◀.

Structure and design can also have a strong influence on the behaviour and mind set of the employee or manager. It will have a socialising influence on employees and can encourage the display of a range of positive and negative behaviours. A good example of the somewhat negative influence of organisation structure on behaviour can be found in the work of Allinson (1984). He was interested in trying to understand the inflexibility and narrow-mindedness often displayed by employees of bureaucratic organisations (for example, hierarchical, procedural and rule-driven work arrangements much like a traditional public sector department). He suggested that these employees and managers do not come into these organisations with this rigid mind set but that it is the structural and ordered nature of the employing organisation that socialises or encourages the employees to behave in this way. The structure creates a certain work environment which in turn leads to the development of a characteristic pattern of negative attitudes and behaviours among the employees, particularly as regards to their interaction with customers. As an illustration of this tendency, think of what would happen if you went into McDonald's (a classic bureaucratic organisation) and asked for a medium-rare quarter pounder in a wrap with sweet chilli sauce. What do you think would be going on in the mind of the person serving you? While she or he might like to facilitate your order (the customer is always right!), the structure and system of work is highly unlikely to expedite them in meeting your request. Complaints by you about poor service are unlikely to produce positive effects; indeed they would be more likely to produce a clear refusal and your ejection from the premises. Thus the structure determines the behaviour of the employee.

PARTS OF AN ORGANISATION

A useful starting point in developing an understanding of organisational structure is to consider the parts of which it is made up. Here we draw on the work of Henry Mintzberg (1979b) who identifies five key parts of every organisation, as illustrated in Figure 11.2.

The **Strategic Apex** represents the senior management team. In more traditional organisations this part acts like the brain, taking in sensory data from a range of internal and external sources, deciding the strategy and goals of the organisation and then communicating these goals throughout the structure. The senior management team is responsible for the overall strategic performance of the organisation.

The **Middle Line** represents middle management. More recently, this part of the organisation has been the subject of much downsizing activity globally as organisations get rid of layers and try to flatten out their structures and eliminate what they see as 'non-contributing' positions. However, this layer plays a vital function. These employees are the conduit between senior management and the employees they manage in the operating core (see below). They translate and expedite the strategy and goals down the hierarchy and provide upward feedback to the senior team as to the effectiveness of their strategies.

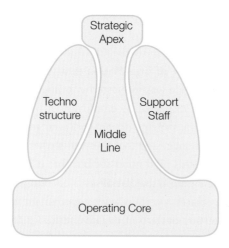

Figure 11.2 Mintzberg's model of organisational structure

Source: Mintzberg, Henry, Structuring of Organizations, 1st Ed., © 1979. Printed and electronically reproduced by permission of Pearson Education, Inc., New York.

The **Operating Core** is the heart of the organisation where employees perform the core operations. In here the basic functions of the organisation happen – sourcing inputs, turning inputs into outputs, distributing the outputs and getting feedback to evaluate efficiency and effectiveness levels.

The **Technostructure** represents the specialist staff charged with responsibility for introducing systems, processes and procedures designed to control and standardise the behaviour of the operating core. In this part of the organisation reside analysts – those employees concerned with operations research, quality control and risk management.

Support Services are the employees needed to keep the organisation functioning smoothly. These services support the core operations of the organisation but do not directly engage in manufacturing or service delivery. Included here are a wide diversity of activities from the canteen and mailroom services to research and development, public relations and legal support.

Bear in mind that the importance of each of the five parts will vary across different organisational designs and some may not be present at all. Indeed, some of these parts and their associated activities can now be outsourced to external parties and may no longer reside within the strict boundary of the organisation. What is useful about this categorisation is that it provides us with a concrete image or diagram to begin our exploration and conceptualisation of organisational structure and design.

BUILDING YOUR SKILLS

Understanding Organisational Structure

Try and categorise the various parts of the university where you are a student. Who are the key people in the strategic apex? What do they do and how do they interact and communicate with the rest of the organisation? Who would you include in the operating core? Academic departments and lecturing staff? What about research centres and the library? Who is occupying the technostructure? What do they do and what impact do they have on academic administrative staff? Do they impact on you? What support services have you used and what technical support is available to staff in carrying out their work?

DIMENSIONS OF STRUCTURE

Before a manager can make decisions about how to design the structure of the organisation he or she must be aware of and understand the various dimensions or elements that constitute organisation structure. These elements, along with the five parts described in the preceding section, provide us with a vocabulary to describe and compare different structures. What follows is a brief description of some of the core traditional dimensions of organisational structure.

Differentiation refers to the degree to which an organisation is divided up into different functional areas and levels. It has two aspects: horizontal and vertical. Horizontal differentiation measures the degree to which the organisation is broken up into specialised units or departments. Where high differentiation exists, the organisation will have many departments or units and many specialised tasks and staff categories. A small start-up organisation would have low levels of differentiation with few departments and staff getting involved in all the main activities. A general hospital would be a good example of an organisation with extremely high levels of differentiation – many highly specialised departments and staff. Differentiation thus aids specialisation (the development of very specific knowledge and expertise) and can improve efficiency. A highly specialised job has a very narrow range of skills and activities while a job low on specialisation will involve a wide range of activities and tasks that require a diversity of skills. Specialisation may be measured on a horizontal (involves a range of activities at the same level of responsibility) or a vertical (planning, execution and reviewing decisions) level. Excessive levels of differentiation may cause the development of a narrow 'silo mentality' where an employee's concerns focus exclusively on his or her own specific role and responsibilities to the detriment of the interests of the organisation as a whole.

The second type of differentiation is vertical differentiation and this reflects the number of layers between the strategic apex and the bottom of the operating core. The descriptive term frequently used here is 'hierarchy'. An organisation with many layers is referred to as a hierarchical organisation and has very high levels of vertical differentiation. Span of control (how many people you can effectively supervise) will determine how tall or flat any particular organisation might be.

Integration and coordination are necessary where organisations have high levels of differentiation (many specialised departments and potentially multiple layers of responsibility) to ensure that the various departments are working together to achieve the organisational goals. Differentiation and integration thus represent a balancing act undertaken by managers and are a huge managerial challenge. Integration may be carried out at and by the strategic apex or may be facilitated through activities such as goal-setting, scheduling and timetabling or through the use of structural mechanisms such as committees, cross-functional task forces or teamwork.

Formalisation concerns the degree to which the jobs within an organisation are standardised. An employee in McDonald's or in a call centre is typically in a highly formalised job with little or no discretion as to what is to be done, when and how it should be carried out. Where you have standardised work you typically see detailed job descriptions, rule books, extensive work manuals or standard operation procedures (SOPs). Standardisation is important

differentiation the extent to which the organisation is divided up into specialist parts and levels

formalisation the degree to which employee behaviour is governed by written rules, regulations and standardised procedures because it facilitates consistent output and reduces variability and risk. The downside of very high levels of formalisation is the demotivating impact this may have on employees. Consider what it must be like to repeat a simple boring task hour after hour, day after day. Think what it must be like to pack food cans on a supermarket shelf all day. All the cans must be straight, a maximum of three cans high and all have the labels facing out to the customer. Dull, repetitive tasks of this nature can lead to high levels of absenteeism (sickness levels) and turnover (employees leaving the firm) and can create a big gulf between management and ordinary employees ▶ **Chapter 5** ◀.

CONSIDER THIS…

Reflect back over your last week and consider the extent to which your behaviour was governed and occasionally restricted by rules as you went about your daily activities (attending university, travelling, shopping, eating and so on). List at least five rules that have regulated your behaviour or impacted upon you in some way. In what way do they help or hinder you and the organisation that created and implements them. Do they need to be improved?

Centralisation concerns the degree to which decision-making is controlled at a single point in an organisation. Where centralisation is high this typically means that decision-making is tightly controlled, normally by the managers in the strategic apex. If decision-making authority is dispersed throughout the organisation then the term 'decentralisation' is normally used to describe this situation. Centralisation can give rise to clear and concerted action but can also result in a slowness to respond to changing circumstances. In addition, the decision makers must have high-quality information upon which to make their decisions. Frequently, growing complexity means that senior managers must delegate decision-making to others down the hierarchy. This decentralisation can render the organisation more adaptive as decision-making can be speeded up. Decentralisation can also improve employee motivation as they are more involved in the operation of the organisation and can help in the training of junior managers ▶ **Chapter 5** ◀. A good example of a highly decentralised organisation would be the giant European industrial firm ABB. A global leader in power and automation technologies, its operations are organised into five global divisions with each composed of a number of specific business units. Each business unit is treated as a stand-alone profit centre and afforded a high level of autonomy as to how it wishes to run its operations (within fixed profit, cost, quality and ethical measures). This approach enables individual business units to manage their affairs and tailor their products and services in a manner that best suits their local requirements.

SPOTLIGHT ON SKILLS

You have been tasked with delivering a major organisational redesign in a large, traditional, publishing firm. The following questions will help you to reflect on how you might set about this task.

1 What type of impediments or problems might you anticipate?
2 How will you ensure that the redesign effort has a positive effect on organisation morale?
3 How would you know if the redesign effort has had a positive effect on the organisation overall? What measures might you use?

To help you answer these questions, in your ebook click the play button to watch the video of Jigna Patel from Springer Nature talking about organisational redesign.

ORGANISATION TYPES

The various dimensions of organisation structure may be arranged to give rise to different types of organisation. You need to bear in mind that these 'types' are rarely found in a pure form. In practice, most organisations are a mix of these different types – frequently referred to as hybrids. The list of types is rather open-ended and reflects the ongoing evolutionary development of organisational structures. Types of organisations may be described as categories around a range of criteria. For example, Mintzberg's categorisation of organisational types is premised around different methods of coordination. Most management and OB texts use a typology based around departmental groupings (Daft, 2004). In explaining this categorisation, this chapter will present an evolutionary story in which the structure and design change with the lifecycle of the firm. Do bear in mind that a firm does not have to follow this evolutionary cycle and we adopt this approach here merely for ease of explanation.

SIMPLE STRUCTURE

Imagine a small technology software start-up firm which sets up its operation in London. It has one owner-manager and three staff. Most start-ups never really grow to the extent that they develop any form of elaborate structure. The term used to describe this basic mode of organising is the simple structure (Mintzberg, 1979a). In the start-up all key decisions are made by the owner-manager (high centralisation), there are few rules and procedures other than 'Do what the owner-manager tells the members of staff to do' (low formalisation), the owner-manager exercises control through tight direct supervision, there are no specialist functions (low horizontal and vertical differentiation) and all staff join in on whatever needs to be done as required (low job specialisation).

FUNCTIONAL STRUCTURE

As the start-up experiences early commercial success it begins to hire extra staff and the owner-manager finds herself unable to supervise everyone effectively. Staff begin to specialise in specific tasks or areas of expertise (for example, software development, sales, marketing, HR, finance). Around these specialised areas of activity, groupings or departments begin to form. The owner-manager concentrates on strategic concerns focusing on expanding the firm and has to delegate responsibility for managing a range of day-to-day activities to other managers (so decentralisation increases). As each manager can only supervise a limited amount of employees a hierarchy may develop with staff appointed to different levels of responsibility (and pay) each with a specific span of control and line of responsibility. To aid efficiency and reduce costs a range of rules and standard operating procedures or methodologies are introduced (increased formalisation). Figure 11.3 shows this expanded entity.

Many firms adopt this type of structure, from universities and public sector departments to manufacturing companies. This organisational type is good at developing functional expertise which may increase efficiency, because employees concentrate on becoming an expert at one particular job rather than trying to be a 'jack of all trades', and ultimately both quality and productivity increase. Two primary dangers exist with this type of structure. As the organisation grows and develops specialist areas and a number of layers of responsibility it can become less responsive to change. This is because communication across units and up and down the layers of structure can become slower and more difficult. Also there is a tendency to become overly preoccupied with your own area of specialism (referred to as high sub-unit orientation) with a consequential loss of cross-organisational interaction and cooperation. Thus as differentiation increases (for example, specialist departments and jobs develop), there is a need to introduce mechanisms to aid integration. Normally in a functional

Figure 11.3 Typical functional structure

organisation this integration happens at the top (the strategic apex) but a range of other mechanisms exist. A good example of such a mechanism is a cross-departmental task force of employees from different areas who are brought together to work on a common problem. This can lead to improved 'joined-up' thinking, and action.

DIVISIONAL STRUCTURE

The firm continues to experience rapid growth in sales and employment and decides to open up substantial new operations in Dublin, Frankfurt and Barcelona to meet local demand, and to facilitate further expansion into new markets. Each division is a stand-alone unit with a full range of specialist functions. The original London operation develops as a headquarters location and while undertaking its own work also monitors and coordinates the activities of the other divisions. Divisional structures may be based on location (region or country) but can also reflect products or customer groups. While such structures enable the company to get closer to the local customer and develop strategies and practices in keeping with local realities, they can give rise to high costs due to excessive duplication of tasks and roles. A good example of an organisation with a divisional structure would be the huge supermarket chain Walmart. Have a look at the interactive map showing all 11,504 retail locations on Walmart's website (http://corporate.walmart.com/our-story/our-locations/: last accessed on 22 October 2015). Consider the challenge of trying to manage such a huge and dispersed global structure.

PROJECT-BASED ORGANISATION

The firm continues to experience great success but has now attracted a number of dynamic new competitors who are slowly stealing existing clients. The senior management team decide they need to up their game. If the company is to survive it will need to differentiate itself strategically in the marketplace and become significantly more adaptive and innovative. The senior managers thus undertake a large-scale organisational transformation change programme and re-orient the organisational structure towards a more project-based design. They focus on the London and Barcelona locations, and strip out the hierarchy and functional departments in order to de-differentiate the structure. In its place they create a team-based operation of highly-skilled and flexible employees. Teams are formed and re-formed to reflect the specific requirements of customers. There are only three layers in the firm, so it becomes a flat hierarchy. Employees are given considerable levels of discretion in dealing with clients (reflecting low formalisation and high decentralisation). Coordination takes place through face-to-face contact which is occasionally technologically-mediated given the dispersed locations. There are still some functional areas of specialism but these tend to be roles like HR, Finance and Quality Control which work to support the project teams in delivering their services. Examples of this type of structure would be management consulting and engineering and design firms.

Mechanistic   Organic

<--->

High levels of differentiation   High levels of integration

High levels of formalisation   Low levels of formalisation

Highly centralised decision-making   Decentralised decision-making

Highly standardised processes   High face-to-face interaction

Emphasis on position in the hierarchy   Emphasis on expertise

Figure 11.4 Dimensions of mechanistic and organic forms

Source: Based on information in Burns and Stalker (1966).

The list of organisational types continues to grow and evolve. Labels in current usage include the learning organisation, the customer-centric organisation, the hollow or donut organisation, the boundaryless organisation, the cellular organisation and the virtual organisation. We will return to a discussion of the virtual organisation later in the chapter. You need to be aware of the potentially faddish nature of some of these labels, with academics and consulting firms claiming falsely to have invented a new organisational form. In many instances these types are best captured under the broad label of 'organic form' (Burns and Stalker, 1966). Types exist along a continuum with mechanistic form (which is bureaucratic, functional and rule-driven) at one end and organic form (which is flat, flexible and team-based) at the other (see Figure 11.4).

Neither of the pure forms tends to exist in reality but an organisation's structure and design will orient itself somewhere along the continuum. Do also bear in mind that an organisation may mix both mechanistic and organic design principles with, for example, the accounts or production department organised differently from the R&D unit. In one department efficiency and procedural correctness are key while in the other creativity and experimentation are prioritised. Finally, the list of structural types will never be definitive because new ones will emerge as circumstances continue to change. It is to these changing circumstances and their connection to organisational structure and design that we now turn.

APPROACHES TO ORGANISATIONAL DESIGN

Approaches to organisational design have changed over time, as have the priorities that underpin them. At the turn of the 20th century Classical Management dominated managerial and organisational thinking. The concern here was with designing for maximum efficiency, controlling large numbers of people from the top, and having very clear and pure lines of authority and accountability. The relevant theorists included Henri Fayol, Max Weber and Chester Bernard. It is worth reading the early work of researchers of this period, particularly the fascinating sociological studies of bureaucracy and its nature by the likes of Alvin Gouldner and Robert Merton. The writings of Frederick Winslow Taylor on scientific management are

Efficiency-Driven Design?

For an excellent current example of the continuation of mechanistic and efficiency-driven design thinking and practice you should look at Hon Hai Precision – more commonly known by its trade name, Foxconn – the Taiwanese multinational manufacturing giant with massive plants across the globe. Foxconn manufactures products for Apple and many other leading electronic brands including Microsoft, Dell, Hewlett-Parkard, Sony and Lenovo. Foxconn now employs over 1.4 million workers in China and is expanding rapidly overseas as wage rates continue to rise in China and the firm tries to avoid costly import duties. The scale of some of its manufacturing operation is staggering. The Longhua campus in Shenzhen, Southern China, employs more than 240,000 people. Think of the management and organising challenges faced in operating such a complex. Foxconn operates on a reported net profit margin of 2% and is relentless in this regimented

OB IN THE NEWS

drive for efficiency and reliability. Complaints made against Foxconn include low pay, excessive overtime, long work hours, the use of child labour and poor health and safety standards. In 2010, 14 employees committed suicide by jumping off the factory buildings. In early 2012, 150 workers threatened mass suicide in protest at the working conditions within the firm.

Non-governmental agencies (NGOs) have targeted Apple and asked it to exert its influence to try and encourage Foxconn to improve working conditions in its plants. View the clips from YouTube on the companion website at www.palgrave.com/carbery-ob and see what it is like within a Foxconn facility and evaluate the efforts that are being made to improve matters. As you view the clips consider how work is organised within the plants, the level of supervision, the repetitive nature of the work and general working conditions. Would you like to work there? Are there alternatives to this system given the high demand for cheap and reliable manufacturing from wealthy Western firms?

In February 2015, Foxconn announced the closure of its Seiperumbudur manufacturing plant in Chennai, India following the exit of Nokia from manufacturing in the region. Nokia was the plant's main customer. Foxconn had moved to the region to take advantage of low wage rates in India. Workers' protests and a token hunger strike involving about 1,300 workers ensued, with demands to reopen the plant which had suspended manufacturing operations in December 2014. Ultimately, after weeks of negotiations involving unions, Indian governmental agencies and Foxconn, a compensation deal was reached with the workers and the plant shut down.

Questions:

1 How does the firm ensure maximum efficiency and productivity given the number of employees involved?

2 How can they ensure high quality while keeping costs very low?

3 What problems would you anticipate for the workforce operating in this type of work environment?

Sources:

www.ft.com/intl/cms/s/0/17af9b64-485d-11e2-a1c0-00144feab49a.html#axzz35YMjCBox (last accessed on 25 August 2015).

www.economist.com/news/business/21568384-can-foxconn-worlds-largest-contract-manufacturer-keep-growing-and-improve-its-margins-now (last accessed on 25 August 2015).

www.forbes.com/sites/connieguglielmo/2013/12/12/apples-labor-practices-in-china-scrutinized-after-foxconn-pegatron-reviewed/ (last accessed on 25 August 2015).

© GETTY IMAGES/ AFP/MIKE CLARKE

also important to read as they provide great insights into management thinking of the time. In many respects the guiding organisational model was that of the church and the army, and the message was clear – there is one best way to design your organisation (if it's big) and it's called bureaucracy. While managers and academics were aware of the behavioural dysfunctions associated with bureaucracy, and its inevitable functional approach to structure, there was not perceived to be any real structural alternative, particularly if you were concerned with accountability, efficiency and control – all core preoccupations of management. This preoccupation with linearity, hierarchy and bureaucracy dominated organisational thinking until the mid-1960s and still heavily influences global organisational design today.

The 1960s marked a new period in design thinking with the emergence of the Contingency School of organisational design and a growing typology of organisational structure. The **contingency approach**, which is best seen as a loose collection of ideas built around the central tenet that there is no one best way of organising rather than a clear theoretical model, has a simple normative message as regards structure and design – 'it depends'. This school of design is epitomised by the work of Henry Mintzberg (1979a) and his configurational approach. Central to the contingency perspective is the idea of fit or congruence. Partially derived from systems theory, this logic argues that if an organisation is to be effective its structural design must fit a range of internal and external contingencies. These contingencies are what causes the structure (the various parts and dimensions/elements) to be combined in a certain manner to produce an organisational type. The image portrayed here is like a jigsaw puzzle with the various contingencies determining in a rationalistic manner what design elements need to be put in place.

There are five key contingency determinants of design, as illustrated in Figure 11.5. These determinants are typically presented in the literature as 'imperatives' to which managers must respond or the organisation will go 'out of fit' and die. Nowadays these imperatives are seen

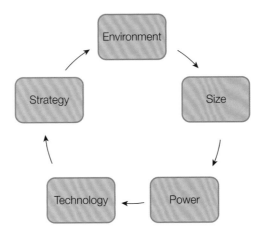

Figure 11.5 Key contingency variables

contingency approach an approach to organisational structure and design which argues that the choice of structure depends upon a range of contextual variables as overly deterministic and more recognition is afforded to the importance of the manager's agency (discretionary behaviour) in making key decisions to respond to these factors. We will now briefly examine each imperative in turn and explore their potential influence on the choice of design.

ENVIRONMENTAL IMPERATIVE

The organisational environment is typically regarded as the key determinant of organisational design. The environment is defined as the general forces or elements that exist outside the boundary of the organisation that may have an influence on its operation and survival. There is a huge array of external factors that may influence an organisation's survival and it would be impractical for a manager to be aware of and respond to these myriad factors. As such, managers tend to concentrate on the environmental elements with which the organisation most frequently interacts, such as suppliers, customers and external regulators. In a stable and simple environment organisations are able to adopt more mechanistic structures that maximise managerial control while ensuring consistent and standardised behaviour. The functional or bureaucratic types would be ideal here. However, as the domain becomes more complex, dynamic managers face increased uncertainty and need to introduce improved integration devices and boundary spanning and buffering activities (including introducing roles specifically designed to scan and respond to the changing demands of the environment). As environmental complexity continues to increase managers will typically adopt a more organic structural design in an attempt to better understand and respond to this growing complexity and uncertainty. In organic designs there will be higher levels of vertical and horizontal decentralisation as lower-level employees are afforded increased discretion to respond to changing local requirements. The classic study was that undertaken by Lawrence and Lorsch (1967). We recommend that you research and review this landmark study. Figure 11.6 shows a typical framework for categorising different types of external environments.

STRATEGY

This is the statement of the main goals and objectives of the organisation and is another key determinant of structure and design. An effective business strategy will clarify the direction of

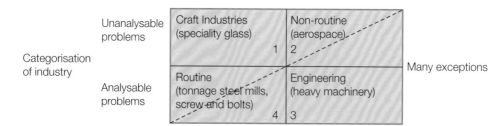

Figure 11.6 Categorising external environments

Source: Perrow (1967).

the organisation, explain how it will interact with the demands of the external environment and set down how it will organise its internal processes to best achieve its business goals and objectives. A firm pursuing a low-cost and/or low-differentiation strategy (few variations on its products or services) will tend to favour a more mechanistic design while an innovative firm will typically adopt a more organic design.

TECHNOLOGY

This refers to the tools, processes, methodologies, software, techniques and activities used within a firm to turn inputs into outputs. Different researchers have studied how structure needs to be aligned with the technology used within the firm. A good example of this research is the work of Charles Perrow (1967). Using two dimensions of task variability (How many unique problems do workers face?) and task analysability (How standardised are the tasks?) he suggested four types of technologies as shown in Figure 11.7. Routine technologies typically call for more functional or mechanistic structures while non-routine technologies require a more organic organisational design. At a broader level, technology, in particular advanced information and communication technologies (AICT), is seen as opening up huge new potential for new forms of organising. We will return to this issue later in the chapter.

SIZE

The size imperative (typically using the number of employees as a crude measure) suggests that the bigger the firm the greater the need for more mechanistic structures. Research suggests that as size increases there will be an associated increase in specialisation, formalisation, standardisation and hierarchy.

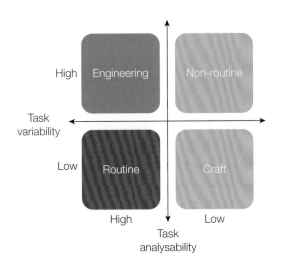

Figure 11.7 Types of technology

Source: Based on Perrow (1967).

POWER

This contingency element is a complex one and argues that it is power, and not a rational analysis of the diverse contingency variables, that will ultimately determine the structural design of a firm. The argument is that those in control in the organisation (typically the senior management team) will ultimately choose a structure that will maximise their continued control of the organisation. As an example, a firm may be facing an increasingly complex environment suggestive of the need for a more organic structure with project teams and delegated decision-making. However, those in power decide that they need to exercise tight control over the behaviour of employees and expenditure levels, and so continue to operate a traditional functional design with its clear overtones of authority.

BUILDING YOUR SKILLS

Contingency Analysis

Undertake a brief contingency analysis of 7-Eleven and Apple. Do a quick web search on each firm. How would you categorise the environment each firm is operating in? How would you describe or categorise their respective strategies? What technologies do they use? How big are they globally? What structural design would you recommend for each organisation? What future changes might you suggest and why?

Contingency Element	7-Eleven	Apple
Environment		
Strategy		
Technology		
Size		

Jones (2010) provides a useful summary of the key design challenges facing managers arising from a contingency perspective. They are:

1 Choosing the right degree of vertical and horizontal differentiation – how specialised and hierarchical do you want your organisation to be?

2 Getting the right balance between differentiation and integration – balancing specialisation and associated efficiencies with the need to work as one in concert.

3 Getting the right balance between centralisation and decentralisation.

4 Getting the right balance between mechanistic and organic structures – balancing the benefits of efficiency, focus, consistency, accountability and reliability that can come with a more mechanistic structure against the adaptability, flexibility and innovativeness of a more organic design.

While the contingency approach to organisational design is regarded as somewhat dated in terms of the very rationalistic, concrete and deterministic manner in which it portrays an organisation and its determinants, it remains an influential perspective in terms of management and consulting practice. A good illustration of the revitalisation of this 1970s perspective can be seen in the work of Goold and Campbell (2002a, b). They suggest that organisational structures tend to evolve in a very haphazard manner which is shaped more by politics than rational analysis. Frequently managers do not know how to assess the effectiveness of their organisation's design or how to undertake a redesign initiative, and even if they do, they tend to avoid addressing the problems because of their complexity and frequently divisive nature. Goold and Campbell's solution for confused executives trying to figure out whether they have a well-designed organisation is a practical framework of nine 'tests' to guide them through the complexities of organisational design.

Do bear in mind that Goold and Campbell's target audience comprises the CEOs of Fortune 500 US multinationals and that they are trying to achieve a balance between control and flexibility within these large and complex organisational arrangements. As you read through the nine tests try and relate them back to the contingency imperatives discussed above. Goold and Campbell refer to the first four tests as 'fit' tests. These ensure that the prospective design is compatible with the company's strategy, human resource pool and general situation. The remaining five tests are 'good design' tests designed to refine a prospective design to ensure that you establish the right amount of hierarchy, control and process to guarantee control and authority but not overly dampen creativity and flexibility.

TESTS 1 TO 4 – GETTING THE FIT RIGHT

- *Market advantage test:* Does your design fit and direct sufficient attention to (that is, is there clear responsibility for) each of your company's key market segments, and does it provide adequate support for each of your key sources of competitive advantage?
- *Parenting advantage test:* Does the design facilitate headquarters in providing necessary support and roles to the dispersed network of companies under its remit?
- *People test:* Is the design suited to the strengths, weaknesses and motivations of your employees? Does the design allocate appropriate responsibilities and good reporting relationships, and does it help in gaining employees' commitment to the organisation? Does the design disempower and demotivate certain groups in the organisation and how will you deal with this?
- *Feasibility test:* Have you identified and assessed internal or external constraints that may impede your design effort? For example, the existing culture of an organisation may act as a considerable impediment to a redesign change effort. External government regulation, such as that imposed on the Irish banking system following the 2008 financial crisis, may also restrict the desire to loosen up the structure to make it more flexible. These constraints need to be identified and assessed early in a redesign effort.

TESTS 5 TO 9 – REFINING THE DESIGN

- *Specialist cultures test:* Does your design afford adequate protection to organisational units that need to preserve distinctive cultures? For example, a research and development unit will typically have a different culture from that prevailing in a manufacturing department.

Managers need to make sure that the design preserves and protects these distinctive but important subcultures within its overall plan.

- *Difficult links test:* Does your design provide adequate coordination between key units in the organisation? Here the key questions are how specialised we want to make the organisation and how will we achieve coordination and integration between key parts of the organisation? If we envisage key problems arising between units then the design must be adapted to facilitate these difficult links or the incentive structure altered to encourage improved interaction and cooperation.
- *Redundant hierarchy test:* This test is designed to decide whether there are too many parent levels (layers in the hierarchy) in the design and whether the layers are adequately contributing to improving the performance of the units reporting to it. If the layer makes a poor or no contribution then it should be cut out. The design philosophy here is one of maximising decentralisation to the operating core in so far as is practical.
- *Accountability test:* Does your design ensure adequate and appropriate controls over the performance of each unit?
- *Flexibility test:* Does the design have sufficient flexibility to enable it to develop new strategies and adequately respond to change? The design should support or, at minimum, not actively impede the pursuit of new opportunities.

Goold and Campbell suggest that the tests need to be used in an iterative and systemic manner. As you change the design of one area of your organisation you may create unintended consequences in a different area. Managers should therefore take a broad view and as they work through the various steps become aware of and try to address the many trade-offs that will need to be faced as they make decisions on organisational design.

CURRENT TRENDS AND DEBATES

To provide a simple synopsis of current thinking on organisational design would be a very challenging task due to the growing diversity of perspectives on the topic. This is, in turn, a reflection of the growing complexity of our understanding of organisation itself. Much of the ongoing debate on organisational design hinges on the axis of mechanical design versus organic emergence – is design a mechanical process, an artifact of planned managerial control, calculation and imagination or is it a more organic, emergent, improvisational and unpredictable process that is reflective of the complex interplay of social and political forces that are not clearly controlled by anyone, particularly management? To try and give you a tentative feel for aspects of these complex debates, we will address two distinctive contributions. The first is from Anand and Daft (2007) and provides a useful historical overview of developments in organisational structure and design and leads us on to a basic insight into contemporary approaches to organisational design. The second view takes a retro-perspective on organisational design and re-examines the pre-modern model of the cooperative structure as a driver for new, more collaborative and sustainable approaches to organising.

Turning first to Anand and Daft (2007), they identify three distinctive design eras:

1   *Era 1 – Self-contained organisation design:* From the mid-1800s to the early 1970s the ideal organisation was self-contained with clear boundaries and high levels of internal control. This design would encompass the functional and divisional types discussed earlier. The image is one of a pyramid with hierarchy and high specialisation and formalisation.

2   *Era 2 – Horizontal organisational design with team- and process-based emphasis:* Starting in the mid-1980s this form concentrated on improving internal coordination and communication. The focus is on breaking down functional silos to try and make units work together more effectively with a distinctive horizontal and process (as opposed to task) mind set. Layers in the hierarchy disappear and cross-functional project teams proliferate.

3   *Era 3 – Organisational boundaries open up:* This era began to dominate design thinking from the mid-1990s onwards. It is closely associated with the rapid advancements in and adoption of information and communication technologies (ICTs) and the emergence of low-cost labour in countries such as China and India and outsourcing practices. Three types of organisation typify organisational design in this era.

    The first type is the 'hollow organisation' in which internal and external organisational boundaries begin to blur, with companies concentrating on issues of core strategic importance (such as design and marketing) while contracting out non-core activities (such as manufacturing and distribution where they did not retain a distinctive competency). Three principles govern the hollow organisation approach to design, namely the careful identification of core processes crucial to the success and survival of the firm, harnessing market forces to get remaining non-core processes undertaken as efficiently as possible (low cost but good quality); and writing an effective contract that aligns incentives between the parties but leaves some degree of flexibility to cover unforeseen contingencies. While this design can lower costs and improve overall flexibility (the core firm can increase or decrease activities quickly without the need to hire, train, select or possibly dismiss new staff), it can result in loss of key in-house expertise, reduced control over supply and a risk of being supplanted by the supplier.

    The second type is the 'modular organisation' in which decomposable product chunks or modules are provided by a range of internal and external sub-contractors. How the modular organisation differs from the hollow organisation is that the design is premised on products being broken into stand-alone modules rather than complete business processes. These modules are then carefully designed so that they will work together. Modules are manufactured internally or outsourced if they can be manufactured more efficiently by others. Final assembly is then completed internally. The example used by Anand and Daft is Nissan in the US where car frames, dashboard and seats are built by external contractors and then assembled by Nissan. This design excels where it is possible to break the company's product into self-contained modules that can then be seamlessly assembled. Its main disadvantage is the difficulty in rolling out innovation across the entire supply chain of collaborators. Every single one must simultaneously change, a process requiring high degrees of integration.

The final design type of this era is the 'virtual organisation'. This type is best conceived as a temporary form of organising involving a range of separate parties, each with a distinctive domain of excellence, which come together and collaborate to exploit an exceptional market opportunity. The virtual organisation is highly prevalent in the fast-moving high-technology sector and is only feasible due to the use of advanced ICTs and virtual products such as software for mobile phones and computers. The temporary organisation disbands once the opportunity has been exploited. The parties involved may re-form around a new opportunity or could revert to competing against each other. While this form can enable rapid and innovative response to a fleeting market opportunity it requires a very high level of communication to ensure that it operates effectively. Trust among the parties is also a major concern in this design approach.

Anand and Daft see the shift from Era 1 to Era 3 as having vastly expanded the organisational design choices available to managers. What we see here is a major realignment of design from one premised on vertical to horizontal thinking. While the evolution of Era 3 designs have brought about distinct gains, this more dispersed and collaborative approach presents many new challenges for managers, staff and organisational cultures. This design will only be effective if the still-prevailing top-down and control mentality changes and a new focus can be created around trust, influence and commitment.

CONSIDER THIS...

An interesting way to consider organisational structure and design and the role of the manager in the process is to compare and contrast the idea of constructing a jigsaw with that of playing with children's building blocks such as Lego. Mintzberg (1991) suggested this imagery as a useful way of considering the role of the manager in creating effective organisations. The

© ROYALTY-FREE/CORBIS

jigsaw is a rational activity – the various components only fit together in one way – so there is only one best way to construct it. In comparison, consider a young child with a large box of building blocks. There is no real master plan as to how the blocks should be assembled; the child may do as she pleases with the blocks. The only constraint is the imagination of the child, and possibly the limiting effects of gravity on the height of the design. A design following this logic is likely to be quite idiosyncratic and unique.

As a potential manager and designer of an organisation are you a jigsaw specialist or a creative Lego block constructor? Mintzberg suggests that the key challenge for a manager is to learn how to play with a jigsaw puzzle and building blocks simultaneously – no easy task.

COOPERATIVE FORMS OF ORGANISATIONAL STRUCTURE AND DESIGN

Finally in this section, we consider a form of organising that is typically neglected in the mainstream OB and management literature – the cooperative. With the rapid adoption of new technologies and networked modes of organising we have a tendency to look forward and neglect earlier successful modes of organising. The cooperative model in business has its roots in pre-industrial Europe. It is experiencing a global revival today as people become disillusioned with the crude capitalist market model and the associated tendency to treat employees as a mere factor of production, on a par with and as disposable as the machinery and plant within a firm. It is estimated that more than 500,000 people are employed in producer co-ops across Western Europe today and that this number is growing. The cooperative sector is particularly thriving in Italy, France and Germany.

The co-op model is designed to benefit the people who work for it or use its services. It is a voluntary association of people created to meet their common economic, social and cultural needs and aspirations and is seen as a viable egalitarian alternative to the structure and operation of the typical private firm. A co-op is not a slave to some disconnected external shareholder whose only concern is to maximise the return on her or his investment. It will normally operate on a one-person-one-vote basis, membership is typically open to all workers and has a value system focused on self-help, democracy, equity, ethics and social responsibility. The Rochdale Principles are a set of cooperative ideals developed by the Rochdale Society of Equitable Pioneers in 1844 that are often used as governing guidelines for co-ops around the world. The International Cooperative Alliance (ICA) provides an updated version of these principles:

1   Voluntary and open membership – non-discriminatory.
2   Democratic – controlled by the members themselves normally on a one-person-one-vote basis. Elected members or managers are directly responsible to the members.
3   Economic participation – members contribute equitably to and democratically control the capital of the co-op. Surpluses will be distributed for the benefit of the co-op and its members, normally in proportion to their transactions with the co-op.
4   Autonomy and independence – co-ops are autonomous and controlled by their members. Any collaborative arrangements with other organisations or capital raised from external sources must be under the control of the members and ensure that they maintain their autonomy.
5   Education, training and development – co-ops provide training and education to their members to ensure their personal development and that of the co-op.
6   Cooperation among cooperatives – co-ops should work towards strengthening the cooperative movement generally.
7   Concern for community – co-ops aim towards the sustainable development of their communities.

Many co-ops are small-scale social enterprises and tend to produce very positive work experiences for their members, such as improved involvement and control, higher self-esteem, better sense of identity and lower wage differentials among pay grades. However, they do tend to suffer common organisational problems, particularly low wages, long work hours, poor adoption of technologies, conservative approach to innovation, difficulties in raising capital on the open market and occasionally cumbersome decision-making processes. A classic example of an industrial scale cooperative is that of the Mondragon Group, set up in 1956 in the Basque area of Spain. This is a complex network of almost 300 businesses and employee-owned cooperatives employing more than 80,000 people. Visit their website and explore their principles and management arrangements at www.mondragon-corporation.com/eng/. Other examples of well-known cooperative organisations from around the world include CHS Inc. and Growmark Inc. in the US, Fonterra Group in New Zealand, Baywa Group in Germany, Zen-Noh in Japan, In Vivo in France, NH Nonghyup in South Korea and the Indian Farmers Fertiliser Co-operative Ltd.

Organisational Redesign at Novartis

Novartis AG is a Swiss multinational pharmaceutical company created by the merger of Ciba-Geigy and Sandoz in 1996. Novartis AG employs approximately 130,000 people and operates in more than 140 countries around the world. It had gross revenues of US$57.9 billion in 2013.

ACTIVE CASE STUDY

The strategic priorities of the company are to extend its lead in innovation, accelerate growth and drive productivity across its diversified portfolio in order to generate profits and increase shareholder return. Novartis AG operates a divisional structure with headquarters in Basel, Switzerland. Its existing six divisions are Pharmaceuticals, Alcon (eye care), Vaccines and Diagnostics, Sandoz (generic drugs), Consumer Health and Corporate. Novartis operates through subsidiaries in more than 140 countries, with each subsidiary falling under one of the core divisions.

In 2007 the company launched a major redesign initiative, 'Forward'. Its aim was to simplify organisational structures within the company, making it less bureaucratic and flatter, in order to accelerate and decentralise decision-making processes, redesign the way Novartis operates and increase productivity. The redesign initiative was also intended to bring about $1.6 billion in savings by 2010 and result in the elimination of 2,500 positions across the company. The cost of the initiative in the 2007 accounts was US$450 million. Impetus for the programme came from sluggish growth in the pharmaceutical industry at the time, declining operating income within the company, increasingly challenging industry conditions

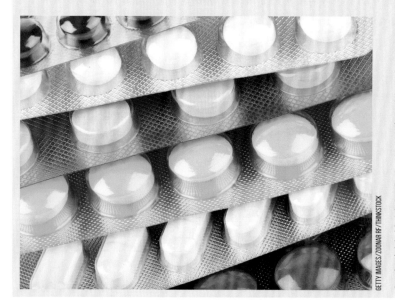

GETTY IMAGES/ZOONAR RF/THINKSTOCK

such as continuous price pressures on drugs, increasing R&D costs, a risk-averse regulatory environment and more aggressive competition from generic drug producers.

The redesign initiative was aimed at enhancing productivity by streamlining the organisation and changing the way it operated, making it more adaptive and customer-centric in focus. Implemented between 2007 and 2009, the programme contained the following elements:

- Organisational structures were streamlined in the Corporate division as well as in the Pharmaceuticals and Consumer Health divisions. Particular attention was aimed at reducing general management numbers and administrative areas.
- In the Pharmaceuticals division, the effectiveness of the worldwide sales force was improved with a more geographic-tailored marketing approach. Duplication

between global, regional and local activities was eliminated, while certain non-core support activities were outsourced.

- The Consumer Health division removed organisational layers to streamline processes and eliminate duplications, while some product supply chains were restructured to optimise capacity utilisation. In certain business units, regional management structures were modified in order to better focus resources on global or local activities.
- A range of initiatives were undertaken to capture savings from the creation of group-wide shared functions, including procurement and information technology, to provide greater economies of scale and leverage opportunities in low-cost countries.
- Novartis created a new cross-divisional operation to accelerate growth in small emerging markets, expand-

ing the presence of all Novartis products in regions that include Northern and Sub-Saharan Africa, Central Asia and parts of Southeast Asia.

Questions:

1 What do you think was the main driver of the redesign effort in this case?
2 Do you think some of the multiple outcomes Novartis was trying to achieve were somewhat contradictory? Explain why or why not.
3 Identify and justify an alternative direction for redesign that Novartis could have undertaken.

Sources:

www.novartis.com (last accessed on 25 August 2015).

www.firstwordpharma.com/node/75267#axzz35fIHBWXI (last accessed on 25 August 2015).

www.novartis.com/about-novartis/healthcare-portfolio/pharmaceuticals.shtml (last accessed on 25 August 2015).

 SUMMARY

IN THE EBOOK, CLICK TO HEAR AN AUDIO SUMMARY

In this chapter we have defined and explained the concepts of organisational structure and design. We identified the main parts of an organisational structure and the various dimensions or elements that are the building blocks of structure. Knowledge of the parts and dimensions of structure provided us with a vocabulary to describe and compare different types of structure that are the building blocks of the process of organisational design. We next explored how the parts and dimensions may be combined or designed in different ways to create different types of organisational structures. We discussed how thinking about organisational design has shifted from a classical approach which stressed a one-size-fits-all approach to design (that is, bureaucracy) to a contingency approach. Here we explored how the structure we design needs to reflect and respond to the demands of a range of external and internal demands or contingencies, such as the environment in which the firm is operating, the strategy it wishes to pursue, the technology it is using or its size. If the design does not match these contingencies then the argument is that the structure will not be effective. Finally we explored current trends and debates in the area of structure and design. We emphasised the growing role that new technology is playing in the creation of organisational forms and discussed the growing tendency towards horizontal and networked modes of organising. Finally we looked back to highlight the potential of cooperative structures and design principles as we move forward.

CHAPTER REVIEW QUESTIONS

1   Explain both the difference and interconnection between organisational structure and design.
2   Why is it important for a manager to understand organisational structure and design?
3   Illustrate how the nature of the business environment a firm is facing can influence the type of structure it should have.
4   How does the technology a firm uses influence its structural design?
5   Explain the connection between the strategy a firm uses and the structure it needs to adopt.
6   Describe the advantages and disadvantages that an organic organisational design may have over a more traditional mechanistic design.
7   Under what circumstances might a mechanistic organisational structure be more effective than an organic design?
8   Explain how a firm adopting the classic principles of cooperative design differs from one following a normal business/managerial logic.

MULTIPLE CHOICE QUESTIONS

In your ebook, click to take a multiple choice quiz to test your understanding of this chapter.

FURTHER READING

Daft, R. (2004) *Organization Theory and Design*. Thomson.

Galbraith, J., Downey, D. and Kates, A. (2002) *Designing dynamic organizations*. New York: American Management Association.

Lawrence P. and Lorsch, J.W. (1968) *Organization and Environment: Managing Differentiation and Integration*. Boston, MA: Harvard Business School Press.

Miles, R., Snow, C., Fjeldstad, O., Miles, G. and Lettl, C. (2010) 'Designing organizations to meet 21st century opportunities and challenges', *Organizational Dynamics*, 39(2): 93–103.

Mintzberg, H. (1990) *Structure in Fives*. Prentice Hall (see Chapters 9 and 10).

www USEFUL WEBSITES

http://organizationalphysics.com/2012/01/09/the-5-classic-mistakes-in-organizational-structure-or-how-to-design-your-organization-the-right-way/

A management consultancy website exploring some of the classic mistakes in organisational design.

http://education-portal.com/academy/topic/organizational-design-structure.html

An interesting educational portal with a number of animations explaining the basic elements of structure and design.

www.mckinsey.com/insights/organization/taking_organizational_redesigns_from_plan_to_practice_mckinsey_global_survey_results

For guidance on what managers actually do when redesigning their organisations, visit this website from McKinsey & Company (a major global management consultancy firm). This link reports on a survey they undertook with executives asking why they redesigned, what challenges they faced, what tactics they used and how the redesign affected employee morale and shareholder value.

12 UNDERSTANDING ORGANISATIONAL CULTURE

Jean McCarthy and Caroline Murphy

LEARNING OUTCOMES

BY THE END OF THIS CHAPTER YOU SHOULD BE ABLE TO:

- Understand the concept of organisational culture and explain the nature of culture within an organisational context.

- Identify and discuss both the visible and invisible elements of organisational culture.

- Understand how organisational culture is formed, transmitted, reinforced and changed by management, groups and individuals.

- Outline the linkage between organisational culture and organisational type.

- Demonstrate the benefits and drawbacks of strong organisational cultures.

- Describe the interplay between organisational culture and work performance.

© ISTOCK/RAWPIXEL

THIS CHAPTER DISCUSSES:

IN REALITY

Organisational culture may strike some people as a 'nice thing to have' if it can be achieved without costing a business any significant financial outlay. In reality, however, culture is no accident in high-performing organisations. For decades, researchers have recognised the link between organisational culture and productivity (Kopelman *et al.*, 1990) and organisational culture and employee job performance (Sheridan, 1992; Shahzad *et al.*, 2013). Many organisations are willing to go to extreme lengths to create and protect their culture, even when this incurs heavy financial costs. Take for example, the shoe retail giant, Zappos, which actively encourages those employees who do not embrace the culture of their organisation to leave by offering incentivised cash payments of $2000. The company explains the rationale by stating that, 'We really want everyone at Zappos to be here because they want to be, and because they believe in the culture. If they know they don't quite mesh with our culture, we don't want them to feel stuck here, so we give them an option.' Zappos reports that fewer than 2% of all employees take up the offer. The thinking underlying their policy is that individuals who do not share the ethos and values of the organisation will take the money and leave, which in the long term is better for the organisation than allowing their culture to be damaged by recruits who do not fit in.

Source:

www.hcamag.com/hr-news/cultivate-culture-by-paying-new-employees-to-leave-186075.aspx (last accessed on 2 April 2014).

INTRODUCTION

When you walk into a department store, what do you notice? When you visit your local library, gym or coffee shop, what do you see? What does the environment look like? Is it colourful, comfortable, friendly or otherwise? How are people dressed? Is the atmosphere formal or informal? What kinds of behaviour do you observe? What kind of behaviour is expected of you? What signs or signals do you receive to tell you to behave in this way? Think of an organisation that you visited recently, and answer these questions. Your answers will highlight aspects of this organisation's culture. Just as you notice and observe aspects of the national culture when you visit a different country, you notice and observe aspects of organisational culture when you visit an organisation.

Culture is part of everyday life, evident in the people we meet and the places we go. It can be viewed as a pattern of learned assumptions about our thoughts, behaviour and actions, which are shared and transmitted among individuals in society. Just as cultures vary across different countries, organisational cultures vary across different organisations. Cultural processes underlie much of what happens in modern organisations, prescribing some forms of behaviour while discouraging others. The values, beliefs and norms adopted by members of an organisation have an impact on the behaviour of individuals and groups at work. An organisation's culture, therefore, has a significant impact on those working in the organisation, as well as on those who interact with the organisation, such as customers, clients, suppliers and other stakeholders.

This chapter explores the ways in which organisational culture is formed and transmitted, and its impact on organisational performance. It also addresses how an organisation might go about changing its culture.

WHAT IS ORGANISATIONAL CULTURE?

The concept of 'culture' is difficult to define. It is derived from the field of anthropology (the study of humans), and broadly represents the transmission of the beliefs and behaviours of one group, or generation, to another. From an anthropological perspective, culture is seen as something which individuals are either consciously aware of, or which exists without their recognition, but that impacts on their behaviour and actions regardless. When we look to the concept of 'culture' from an organisational perspective, we define organisational culture as the basic pattern of shared assumptions, values, beliefs, and practices that govern behaviour in an organisation; they are transmitted (and sometimes adapted) from one generation of employees to the next, and observed by all new organisational members. The notion of culture in organisations is derived from interpretations of the anthropological concept of culture, applied to organisations. Organisations were seen as entities characterised by a particular system of collective values, beliefs and symbols which were transmitted throughout the organisation, and which governed the behaviour of those within it. The term 'organisational culture' (also 'organisation culture' and 'corporate culture') became popular in the 1980s, when a number of managerial, practitioner-orientated books were published on the topic. What followed was a burgeoning interest among academics in organisational culture as a way of understanding and explaining collective behaviour in organisations, as well as a tool for examining the ways in which organisations operated differently and were distinct from one another. Perhaps the most familiar writer on the topic is Edgar Schein, who defined organisational culture as a set of beliefs, values, and assumptions that are shared by members of an organisation (1985). Another common definition still utilised by many practitioners is, simply, 'the way we do things around here' (Deal and Kennedy, 1982, p. 4). Table 12.1 presents the various ways in which culture has been defined through the years.

---

values and beliefs basic convictions or ideals about desirable behaviour and outcomes

norms standards of behaviour that are considered acceptable within and among members of a group

organisational culture the basic pattern of shared assumptions, values, beliefs, and practices that govern behaviour in an organisation; they are transmitted (and sometimes adapted) from one generation of employees to the next, and observed by all new organisational members

Table 12.1 Definitions of culture

'a set of beliefs, values, and assumptions that are shared by members of an organisation' – Schein, 1985
'the way we do things around here' – Deal and Kennedy, 1982
'the collective programming of the mind which distinguishes the members of one group or category of people from another' – Hofstede, 1980
'the set of attitudes, values, beliefs, and behaviors shared by a group of people, but different for each individual, communicated from one generation to the next' – Matsumoto 1996
'Although there are a variety of meanings and connotations about organizational culture (Ostroff, Kinicki, & Tamkins, 2003), researchers conceptualize organizational culture as being shared among members (Glisson & James, 2002), existing at multiple levels (e.g., group and organizational levels; Detert, Schroeder, & Mauriel, 2000), influencing employees' attitudes and behaviors (Smircich, 1983), and consisting of collective values, beliefs, and assumptions (Schein, 2004)' – Hartnell *et al.*, 2011

ORGANISATIONAL CULTURE AND CLIMATE

The terms organisational culture and organisational climate have come to be used inter-changeably by some. However, subtle differences exist between the two. Organisational culture refers to 'the way' in which tasks are completed and organisational climate relates to 'how it feels' to work in that organisation. Interpersonal relationships between employees and between employees and managers are core to the development of an organisation's climate. Given the impact of interpersonal relations on climate, it is prone to more variability across the organisation with climate varying between different subsidiaries, departments or units. It is also therefore viewed more subjectively by employees. Both culture and climate affect employee behaviour at work through their impact on the context, environment and social interactions in the workplace. Organisational culture envelopes the ethos, values and behavioural norms of the organisation and often takes years of tradition to cultivate and refine, which is why it is considered to be very difficult to change in a short period of time. Organisational climate, however, is viewed as more malleable and immediate in terms of its impact on employees because it is defined by current situations, performance and group interactions. Since organisational climate has a more immediate impact on employees and is something which can be adjusted more easily than organisational culture, an understanding of employees' perceptions of their own organisational climate is a valuable tool for organ-isational leaders and managers. An analysis of employee perceptions of their work setting through, for example, a survey or focus group is referred to as a 'climate study'.

Just as culture impacts on employees and organisational performance so too does climate. A healthy organisational climate is one in which support, cooperation and democratic decision-making are strong contributors towards greater work effectiveness. In contrast, stressful organisational climates are characterised by limited participation in

organisational climate relates to 'how it feels' to work in that organisation

decisions, use of punishments, conflict avoidance and non-supportive group and leader relations (Rousseau, 2011).

A variety of dimensions have been found to impact on employees' perceptions of organisational climate, including:

- *Support* – the perception of the degree to which superiors in the organisation value their contribution and care about their well-being.
- *Fairness* – the perception of the degree to which organisational policies are non-arbitrary and are operated on a fair and equitable basis.
- *Autonomy* – the perception of the degree to which individuals can assume control over their work.
- *Recognition* – the perception of the degree to which employees' contributions to the organisation are acknowledged.
- *Trust* – the perception of the degree to which the organisation communicates with integrity with its employees and takes decisions in the best interests of all.

SCHEIN'S MODEL OF CULTURE

In 1985 Schein wrote that:

> Organisation culture is the pattern of basic assumptions which a group has invented, discovered and developed in learning to cope with its problems of external adaption and integration, which have worked well enough to be considered valid, and therefore to be taught to new members as the correct way to perceive, think and feel in relation to problems...culture is not the overt behaviour or visible artefacts that one might observe if one were to visit the company. It is not even the philosophy or value system which the founder may articulate or write down in various 'charters'. Rather it is the assumptions which lie behind the values and which determine the behaviour patterns and the visible artefacts such as architecture, office lay out, dress codes and so on. (1985, p. 14)

Schein proposed that there are three 'layers' or 'levels' of organisational culture: first, there is the visible layer, what he termed 'surface manifestations'; second, there are 'organisation values and beliefs', located beneath the surface, and although this level is not visible, individuals in the organisation can be made aware of it; third, there are the 'basic assumptions' which underpin both the first and second layers, which are invisible, but are what Schein sees as true organisational culture. This model is explicated in Figure 12.1.

Some have likened Schein's model to an apple. The first layer, the surface-level manifestations, is the skin, which you can see. The second layer, the organisation's values and beliefs, is the pulp – visible once the skin has been peeled away. The final layer, the basic assumptions, are the core which holds the apple together, but needs to be deeply rooted out in order to be observed. Other people have attempted to explain Schein's model by using an iceberg as a metaphor. The tip of the iceberg (the visible part) represents the surface-level manifestations of culture while the organisational values and beliefs, and the basic assumptions, lie beneath the water and are large and deep.

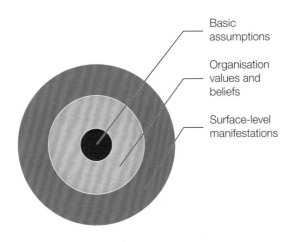

Figure 12.1 Schein's model of organisational culture

Source: Adapted from Schein (1985).

LAYER 1 – SURFACE-LEVEL MANIFESTATIONS

Surface-level manifestations in Schein's model are the visible elements of an organisation's culture. Schein does not view these elements as organisational culture itself; rather, he sees them as manifestations of the culture including:

1 *Artefacts:* These are physical, tangible manifestations of an organisation's culture such as furniture, appliances, tools and clothing. Some examples include McDonald's 'Ronald McDonald' statues and the new uniforms provided to staff at Zara, a large European clothing retailer, every season to display their new fashions.

2 *Symbols:* These are the visuals that represent the organisation, usually in the form of company logos. Some examples include Nike's swoosh, McDonald's golden arches and Apple's bitten apple. Symbols can be used to convey a message about the company; for example, the FedEx logo contains a horizontal arrow between the 'E' and the 'x' to represent precision, while the logo of the broadcasting company, NBC, displays a peacock with six feathers to represent the six divisions of the organisation.

3 *Norms:* These are expected behaviours that are demonstrated by members of the organisation; for example, employees greeting each other on arrival at the office in the morning, employees having lunch together, and the style of dress adopted by organisational members.

4 *Ceremonials and rituals:* Activities that express and reinforce the values and assumptions of an organisation's culture. Examples would be the concept of 'casual Fridays' when employees dress more informally, which often reflects an organisation which values creativity, autonomy and flexibility; annual award ceremonies, which reflect the value an organisation places on hard work and good performance; family days, which reinforce an organisation's belief in work–life balance; and charity events, which instil the importance of corporate social responsibility

5 *Language:* This can refer to e-jargon or more technical vocabulary which is used to express and reinforce an organisation's culture. For example, McDonald's staff are known as 'crew', not employees, reflecting the value placed on teamwork; and Google's staff are known as 'googlers' to instil a sense of identity with the organisation and to reflect what the organisation does

6 *Mottos and slogans:* These are phrases used in organisations that manifest an organisation's culture. For example, McDonald's 'I'm lovin' it', Nike's 'Just do it' and Pepsi Max's 'Live life to the max'.

7 *Stories:* These are narratives which can contain elements of both truth and fiction, and are based on real-life events that may have shaped the organisation or decisions made by individuals which helped to steer the success of the organisation (often referred to as 'heroes'). For example, there is a story that the founders of Snapchat (a popular photo messaging app) turned down an offer of $3 billion from Facebook to sell the company so that they could retain creative control aligned with their vision. Obviously, the Snapchat founders value commitment to their ideals.

8 *Physical layout:* This is the way in which an organisation chooses to organise its office space, floor space or store space and is another manifestation of its culture. For example, in every Subway the service starts at the ordering station with choosing a bread, then a meat, then salads and sauce, before finally reaching the cash register. This is a surface-level manifestation of the culture aligned with Subway's basic assumptions about how they make their product.

LAYER 2 – ORGANISATIONAL VALUES AND BELIEFS

Schein believes that surface-level manifestations are underpinned by the organisation's values and beliefs, and while values and beliefs are intangible and invisible, organisational members can be made aware of them. The values and beliefs usually hold meaning to the founders or senior management, and are typically based on moral principles (Huczynski and Buchanan, 2001). Just like surface-level manifestations, Schein does not believe the organisation values and beliefs are the organisational culture itself, rather they are manifestations which can be articulated and transmitted throughout the organisation. They are often presented in an organisation's mission statement or values statement, and can be incorporated into employee handbooks, company policies and procedures, as well as employee induction programmes and other forms of organisational training and development. For example, Accenture, an international consultancy firm, which in 2013 was ranked among the top 50 companies in the world for valuing diversity, include the following statement in their employee handbook and on their website: 'Inclusion and diversity are fundamental to our culture and core values, fostering an innovative, collaborative and high-energy work environment. Having a diverse workforce of people with different capabilities, cultures, and experiences enables Accenture to compete effectively in the global marketplace' (www.accenture.com/ie-en/Careers/team-culture-diversity.aspx, last accessed on 25 August 2015).

CONSIDER THIS...

Every educational institution, college or university has its own unique culture. Think about the culture where you study. Complete the following template to assess the culture in this institution.

Alone, or in groups, list the surface-level manifestations of culture, the values and beliefs, and the basic assumptions present in your institution/organisation.

1 Surface-level manifestations of culture (e.g. artefacts, stories, mottos, physical layout etc.)	2 Values and beliefs (e.g. what values and beliefs are contained in the mission statement and the strategy statement of your institution?)	3 Basic assumptions (taken for granted understandings about behaviour)

This exercise has been used to successfully measure culture in many organisations (Schein, 1990).

LAYER 3 – BASIC ASSUMPTIONS

In Schein's view, true organisational culture lies within the basic assumptions that individuals hold about the organisation and how it should function. Huczynski and Buchanan describe basic assumptions as 'invisible, preconscious and "taken for granted" understandings held by individuals with respect to aspects of human behaviour, and the nature of reality' (2001, p. 633). Indeed, the strength of an organisation's culture is based on how homogeneous the basic assumptions of all organisational members are. For example, in a hospital setting, the overall objective of the organisation is to provide high-quality patient care; therefore if the basic assumptions and behaviour of all health care staff match this belief, then the organisational culture can be said to be strong.

HOW IS ORGANISATIONAL CULTURE FORMED?

Now that we know what organisational culture is, we move on to explain how it comes to be. The formation of an organisation's culture begins with its founders. The personal assumptions, beliefs and values of the organisational founder(s) shape the development of organisational culture. As an organisation grows in size, these assumptions, values and beliefs, are passed on to every new employee. This process may be conscious or unconscious. Founders and senior-level management may consciously set out to 'design' an organisation's culture, or it may form organically as a response to the business environment. Some organisations train their employees on 'the way we do things around here', draw up extensive mission and value statements, and pay particular attention to the surface-level manifestations of the espoused basic assumptions held by senior-level management. Later in this chapter, we will consider how different types of organisational culture can exist, and how they can vary from each other.

SOCIALISATION

Socialisation is the process through which organisational culture is reinforced among employees. The term is used to 'describe the process in which an individual acquires the attitudes, behaviors and knowledge needed to successfully participate as an organizational member' (Wesson and Gogus, 2005, p. 1018). Induction and socialisation are also typically referred to as assimilation, transition, orientation, alignment, organisational entry, integration and onboarding. It has also been suggested by Schneider and Rentsch (1988) that a socialisation process can be considered effective when newcomers understand and accept the organisation's key values, goals and practices. Ashkanasy et al. (2000) suggests that if socialisation is implemented correctly within an organisation it can ensure that both the organisation's and the newcomer's expectations are met. Van Maanen and Schein's (1979) work on socialisation theorised about the tactics organisations employ to socialise employees and defined them as ways in which the experiences of individuals in transition from one role to another are structured for them by the organisation.

According to Feldman (1976), three phases occur during socialisation: the anticipatory phase, the entry/encounter phase and the change/metamorphosis phase. At the anticipatory stage the organisation should have created a realistic set of expectations for the individual before they take up a role there. This can be achieved through, for example, a comprehensive job description in recruitment and a realistic job preview in selection. The individual, on accepting the position, then enters the encounter phase, which really represents their initial induction period, the formal process of placing an individual in a new role. The final stage of change/metamorphosis focuses on the ability of the new employee to master tasks, resolve problems and 'fit in' with the organisational culture as well as sustain working relationships.

When it comes to filling a vacant position, many organisations will look at their internal candidates first. According to Werner and DeSimone (2006) an existing employee may have some advantages over new external hires. These include:

● Accurate expectations of the organisation, its culture, staff and reward systems.
● An existing knowledge-base of products/services that the organisation provides, knowledge of internal systems and even minor items such as locations and directions.
● Relationships with others in the company that can be built on to form internal synergies.

socialisation is the process through which organisational culture is reinforced among employees

TYPES OF ORGANISATIONAL CULTURE

As stated earlier, culture varies from one organisation to another. In some organisations, the culture has a significant influence on the manner in which employees complete their tasks; in other organisations, the impact of culture is less obviously felt. A strong organisational culture is viewed as one in which widespread agreement with the core elements of the culture exists, making it possible for culture to exert major influences on the way people behave (Greenberg, 2011). In a strong organisational culture, members exhibit greater levels of commitment to the core values of the organisation, which in turn impacts on everyday behaviour. In the long term this has the effect of reducing employee turnover through building cohesiveness and loyalty (Robbins and Judge, 2010). In contrast, a weak organisational culture is defined as one in which there is limited agreement with respect to the core elements of the organisation's culture, and where the culture as a whole has little impact on the way people behave (Greenberg, 2011). Maintaining a strong organisational culture becomes increasingly difficult as organisations grow and expand. This is mainly due to the diffusion of culture across larger organisations with greater numbers of employees. A further issue in larger organisations is that the leadership and values of the original founder are less widely felt by employees who are in daily contact with management teams rather than the person who initiated the culture and ethos ▸ **Chapter 8** ◂. Indeed some organisations, for example Walmart, have taken steps to ensure that the values and ethos of the original founder, Sam Walton, continue to be understood by employees today by instilling 'the Walmart way' of doing business. (You can read more about this in the Further Reading section at the end of this chapter.)

Table 12.2 Characteristics of strong and weak organisational cultures

Strong culture	Weak culture
A clear philosophy with regard to how the business is operated	No clear philosophy exists to guide how the business should operate
Emphasis on the communication of core values and beliefs of the organisation	Core values are not clearly defined or well communicated
The existence of statements, symbols and traditions which explicitly describe the values of the organisation	Few if any indicators of the values and traditions of the organisation
A shared sense of values and norms of behaviour exists among members	Only limited or no evidence of alignment between the way things are done and the espoused values of the organisation
Attention is paid to the importance of maintaining organisational culture when recruiting new employees, for example selection of new members involves screening to ensure they fit with the culture	No efforts are made to retain organisational culture and there is a greater need for procedures and policies in order to achieve desired results

Source: Based on information in Greenberg (2011).

strong organisational culture one in which the company values are widely held and felt by all members of the organisation

weak organisational culture one in which the values of the company are not widely held by members of the organisation

SUBCULTURES

In addition to an overarching organisational culture, a number of subcultures can also exist beyond that system of shared meaning held by all organisational members. Subcultures tend to develop in different sections of the organisation, for example different departments or geographic locations, and reflect common issues faced by members of those sections. As discussed earlier, the larger an organisation grows, the more diffused the culture becomes and this typically results in more subcultures. Within a large organisation that values promotion based on performance, an example of a subculture would be a department in which a manager promotes members of his team based on seniority rather than performance, and this is accepted as the norm in that particular department.

What's Really at the Core of Apple?

OB IN THE NEWS

Apple Inc. is an American multinational corporation which designs, develops and sells computer software, personal computers and consumer electronic goods all over the world. It is widely recognised as one of the most successful organisations of the 21st century, with *Forbes Magazine* naming it the world's 'Most Admired Company' every year from 2008 to 2014. Since its beginnings in 1976, Apple has credited its success with its focus on creating a culture of innovation within the company. On their official website, Apple states that: 'We expect creative thinking and solutions from everyone here, no matter what their responsibilities are. Innovation takes many forms, and our people seem to find new ones every day. Ask anyone here. It's hard work. It means forever asking, "Why is it this way?" and "How can it be better?" It means rethinking every customer experience until the clutter has fallen away — until all that remains is what's essential, useful, and beautiful'. Indeed, Apple's culture of innovation has been described as being 'as distinct as its products are ground-breaking' (Business Insider, 2011). Speaking at a Goldman Sachs Conference in 2013, Tim Cook, CEO of Apple, stated that Apple's culture of innovation has 'never been stronger. Innovation is so deeply embedded in Apple's culture... There's that word "limit." We don't have that in Apple's vocabulary... The boldness, ambition, belief there aren't limits, a desire to make the very best products in the world. It's the strongest ever.

It's in the DNA of the company' (appleinsider, 2013).

But what is it really like inside the apple? Here's what some former employees had to say to MacDailyNews:

'Apple is a pretty divided mix of typical corporate red tape and politics mixed in with start-up level urgency when the direction comes from Steve [former CEO, Steve Jobs]. If you have a project that Steve is not involved in, it will take months of meetings to move things forward. If Steve wants it done, it's done faster than anyone thinks is humanly possible. The best way to get any cross-departmental work done was to say it's for Steve and you'd probably have it the same day.'

'Paranoid management, disrespect, constant tension, and long hours sum up most of the real culture in operations... Most of the people in SDM [supply demand management] see it as something they need to suck

subcultures hold the core assumptions of the dominant culture, as well as supplementary assumptions unique to members of that particular section of the organisation

up for a few painful years after b-school so they can move on to a better gig with the Apple brand on their resume. Like the investment banking of tech. Culture here is strictly top down: any attempt to streamline, impact change, or even discuss a better way to do anything is strictly frowned upon when it comes from the bottom. Work

longer/harder, don't complain or try to fix any of the myriad broken systems or processes, and don't forget that there are 10 people lined up outside to take your spot (your manager won't forget). Work here at your own risk. On the upside, cafe food is pretty good and dress is casual.'

© PHOTODISC/GETTY IMAGES

Questions

1   Compare and contrast what Tim Cook says about Apple's organisational culture with those of the employees quoted above.

2   What issues do you think might arise when the espoused organisational culture is different from reality? Do you think this often happens in organisations? Can you think of any examples?

3   Whose perceptions of organisational culture matter most, the senior-level managers' or the employees'? Provide a reason for your answer.

Sources:

www.apple.com (last accessed on 25 August 2015).

http://money.cnn.com/magazines/fortune/most-admired (last accessed on 25 August 2015).

www.businessinsider.com/10-ways-to-think-different-inside-apples-cult-like-culture-2011-3 (last accessed on 25 August 2015).

http://appleinsider.com/articles/13/02/12/cook-apples-culture-of-innovation-refuses-to-recognize-limits (last accessed on 25 August 2015).

www.businessinsider.com/what-apple-employees-say-about-the-companys-internal-corporate-culture-2013-10 (last accessed on 25 August 2015).

FORMS OF ORGANISATIONAL CULTURE: THE COMPETING VALUES FRAMEWORK

The Competing Values Framework (CVF) developed by Cameron and Quinn (1999) provides a tool for identifying and comparing cultures across organisations. The basic premise of the CVF is that organisational cultures differ with regard to two sets of values, namely organisational focus, as represented in a contrast between internal and external focus, and organisational structure, as represented in a contrast between an interest in flexibility and change or an interest in stability and control. Figure 12.2 presents this framework in which four unique types of organisational culture can be identified: hierarchy, market, clan and adhocracy.

HIERARCHY CULTURE

Organisations which have a hierarchy culture are characterised by formalisation, structures, policies and procedures. Effective leaders within such a culture are those who display strong

hierarchy culture present in organisations which have an internal focus, and demonstrate a strong interest in maintaining stability and control

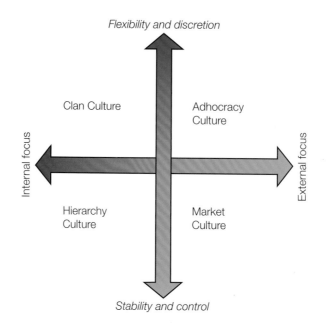

Figure 12.2 The competing values framework

Source: Adapted from Cameron and Quinn (1999).

coordination and organisational skills. This type of culture is highly associated with a bureau-cratic structure. Public sector bodies, government agencies and very large organisations often fall into this category. Advantages of this type of culture are the existence of clear reporting relationships, clear communication channels and recognition of authority. Disadvantages include a potential lack of innovation and creativity, as well as resistance to change given the formalised nature of this type of culture.

MARKET CULTURE

The core assumptions of an organisation with a market culture are competitiveness and productivity. These assumptions result in a strong emphasis on external positioning and control. Leaders in this type of culture tend to be goal-oriented and emphasise the achieve-ment of measurable targets. ▶ **Chapter 8** ◀. A good example of an organisation with a market culture would be the European low-cost airline, Ryanair.

CLAN CULTURE

Typical characteristics of an organisation with a clan culture are teamwork, employee involvement programmes and corporate commitment to the employee. These organisations are usually paternalistic environments in which the leaders or heads of the organisation are viewed as mentors. Loyalty, tradition and emphasis on development are strong.

ADHOCRACY CULTURE

The major goal of an adhocracy culture is to foster adaptability, flexibility and creativity so as to produce innovative products and services and adapt quickly to new opportunities. Leaders in this type of culture are considered to be risk takers ▶Chapter 8◀. For example, Richard Branson's Virgin Group is widely recognised as one which responds quickly to market changes and adapts its products and services to meet market preferences.

 THIS...

Having considered the competing values framework, which of the four types of organisational culture – hierarchy, market, clan or adhocracy – do you think would best suit the business needs of a digital marketing start-up company employing 100 people? Provide a justification for your answer.

IMPACT OF CULTURE ON ORGANISATIONAL PERFORMANCE

As we have seen above, there are many different types of organisational culture and organisations often go to great lengths to form and preserve their culture. But why is it so important? The culture of any organisation affects the performance of that organisation through its impact on individuals and teams at work. Maintaining a positive organisational culture is therefore an important aspect of sustaining strong organisational performance over time. Sustained business success has as much to do with company values and vision as with market forces, competitive positioning and resources. Siehl and Martin (1990) state that organisational culture influences employee attitudes ▶Chapter 6◀ and these attitudes, in turn, impact organisational effectiveness. Organisational culture should guide employees to form attitudes and consequently behave in ways that are consistent with the organisation's values and beliefs. In addition to impacting on employee attitudes and behaviour, research indicates that organisational culture also affects overall organisational performance and profitability. For example, Kotter and Heskett (1992) conducted research detailing the corporate cultures of 200 companies to determine how each company's culture affected its long-term economic performance. They found that strong corporate cultures facilitated change (which we discuss later in the chapter) and were associated with strong positive financial results. A common feature of the strongest performing companies was a culture that encouraged leadership but also empowered everyone in the organisation, thus facilitating change and adopting new practices to meet new needs

The Society for Human Resource Management (SHRM) outlines four major cultural traits that correspond to high performance and overall organisational effectiveness: involvement, consistency, adaptability and mission. These traits were identified in research by Denison and

Mishra (1995) which studied 764 organisations. Their results found that involvement and adaptability are indicators of flexibility, openness, responsiveness, and are strong predictors of growth in organisations. Consistency and mission were found to be indicators of integration and profitability. All four of the traits were shown to significantly predict other effectiveness criteria such as quality, employee satisfaction and overall performance. While this research shows that a link exists between culture and performance, there has been debate as to the nature of this causal link; that is, whether culture causes performance or if indeed performance causes culture. Studies by Sackmann (2011) and Boyce et al. (2015) indicate that culture 'comes first, with performance levels to follow'.

However, while a positive organisational culture can enhance business performance it can never supersede the effects of a flawed business model (Stanford, 2010; Mullins, 2013). Moreover, according to Sørensen (2002) who examined the relationship between the strength of organisational culture and business performance, strong cultures contributed to successful business strategy in a stable operating environment, but in scenarios where market or economic conditions were volatile, businesses with strong cultures tended to be *less* successful. Sørensen suggested that strong cultures, which tend to be stable over time, were less adaptable in a rapidly-changing environment. In a strong culture, members exhibit greater levels of commitment to the core values of the organisation, which results in very well-established ways of behaving that are hard to change.

PROMOTING CREATIVITY AND INNOVATION

As you have seen in the example of Apple, creating an environment in which an employee can nurture and develop their own creative ideas makes sense from a business perspective as it can help foster innovation. There are risks, however, associated with high levels of innovation. For one, innovation can prove costly when technology and expertise are required to refine a good before it can be produced cost effectively. Secondly, there is a greater risk of failure involved in developing new ideas, for example that they will not be well received by consumers. Nonetheless, Ekvall (1996) found a positive relationship between climates or cultures emphasising creativity and innovation, and their overall profitability. So, how do organisations develop a culture of innovation and creativity? Oldham and Cummings (1996) identify a number of conditions which organisations can create in order to foster an environment which is conducive to innovation. These are:

- *Autonomy:* employees are more likely to display creative qualities when they are given a degree of freedom over the way in which they work, rather than feeling as though they are being constantly micromanaged by a supervisor.
- *Empowerment:* enabling workers to set their own goals and take responsibility for problem-solving liberates employees and allows creativity to flourish.

innovation in business refers to the process of developing inventions or ideas into marketable goods, services or processes that customers want

- *Encouraging diversity:* organisations employing people from diverse ethnic and cultural backgrounds benefit from the existence of a greater range of viewpoints and ideas about how to solve problems and create new products/services.
- *Top level support for creativity:* encouragement from managers, leaders and top executives is a fundamental part of an innovative culture. Employees are far less likely to exercise their creative flair and risk failure if they fear criticism and reprisal from superiors for doing so.
- *Making tasks intrinsically motivating:* individuals will be more creative and put more effort into tasks that they actually *want* to be involved in. This may occur because the individual has a personal interest in the task or because they find it interesting or even fun to be involved in.
- *Resources:* innovation and creativity usually require time and finances; if organisations are to develop a culture of innovation employees cannot be expected to operate in a vacuum without the necessary resources to bring their ideas to fruition.

SPOTLIGHT ON SKILLS

Mergers and acquisitions are a staple part of business life across all industries in the modern, globalised marketplace. A merger happens when two or more companies come together to form a new company, while an acquisition occurs when one company purchases another company. What aspects of business operations and functions could contribute to a potential 'culture clash' during a merger or an acquisition? How can an organisation manage this issue, or indeed, avoid it altogether? How can management ensure a uniform culture is created and maintained once an acquisition or merger has occurred?

To help you answer these questions, in your ebook click the play button to watch the video of Micheál Clancy from Kerry Group talking about his experience of 'culture clash' during mergers and acquisitions.

CULTURE CHANGE

Most theorists agree that organisational culture is difficult to change, or at the very least, that cultural change takes a long time to achieve. The previous section explored the interplay between organisational culture and performance. A performance enhancing culture is unlikely to be in need of change; however a culture which is toxic or unethical and therefore

cultural change the process of changing mind sets, behaviour and practices in an organisation is a long process which cannot be achieved effectively in a short timeframe

damaging to either the organisation's performance or reputation does need to be altered. Similarly, an organisation which may have been highly successful may need to change to adapt to market conditions, new competitors, and technological, political or social changes in the external environment

Mergers, the joining of two companies on a relatively level footing, and acquisitions, the purchase of one organisation by another, are two key drivers of organisational cultural change. The respective cultures of each organisation tend to be ignored during the initial merging or takeover process; however internal cultural differences often emerge quite quickly as one of the major obstacles to successful business functioning afterwards. This process is referred to as 'culture clash'. Kotter (2008) outlines that cultural change at this level is extremely challenging 'because group members are often not even aware of the values that bind them together'.

The dynamic nature of both organisational culture and organisational change ▸ Chapter 13 ◂ means that the two concepts are inextricably interlinked. Naylor (2004) points out that, while organisational changes affect the culture of the organisation, the existing culture also affects or constrains the process and impact of any changes.

As discussed at the beginning of this chapter, culture is developed, transmitted and reinforced through a system of rituals, communications, symbols and values ▸ Chapter 10 ◂. These facets of an organisation are deep rooted and therefore require enormous effort to change. Meek (1988) argues that culture is not something an organisation 'has' but rather culture is what it 'is'. Indeed so strong is the belief of some theorists in the prevailing strength of organisational culture that they argue organisations should adopt market strategies to match existing culture rather than attempt to alter their values and ethos (Schwartz and Davis, 1981). Take, for example, Apple's long-established culture of innovation. While the mobile phone development trend was towards smaller, lighter handsets, Apple pursued its own strategy and launched the iPhone in 2007 which subsequently revolutionised the market. However, not all organisations take such an approach to maintaining their ethos and cultures. Some organisations have opted, or been forced to change their organisational culture in reaction to market forces or to combat internal problems. A number of approaches they have taken to achieve this are outlined below.

APPROACHES TO CULTURE CHANGE

Ashleigh and Mansi (2012) have identified the following different approaches to achieving cultural change in an organisation:

1 *Changing employees' values and beliefs* – achieved through development, such as training, education and effective communication of the organisation's new mission and values.

2 *Altering the composition of the workforce* – achieved through recruitment, selection and human resource interventions to retain only those employees who share the new values and beliefs of the organisation.

3 *Altering the organisational climate* – achieved through changes in policies, procedures and routines which result in changes in employee behaviour.

4 *Behaviour change* – achieved through organisational restructuring where, through new roles, responsibilities and relationships, employees are compelled to learn new behaviours. Altered beliefs, values and attitudes follow from a change in behaviour

Hope and Hendry (1995) compared a range of different approaches to culture change and found behaviour change to be the most effective.

EMPLOYEE RESPONSES TO CULTURAL CHANGE

Piderit (2000) outlines three types of negative response to cultural change: affective (where employees become emotional or anxious about the impact of change), cognitive (feelings of resentment toward management with regard to how the change was introduced) and behavioural (collective industrial action, reduction in performance, damaging the organisation in some way). Achieving employee 'buy in' and commitment to new practices and new ways of doing things can be one of the most challenging aspects of an organisational change process. Even when top-level managers are dedicated to introducing a cultural change they may inadvertently revert to old patterns of behaviour because the existing culture is so engrained. For example, in attempting to introduce a culture that is more environmentally aware, a manager produces a glossy report that is distributed to each member of the organisation. For a more in-depth review of the management of organisational change ▶ Chapter 13 ◀.

BUILDING YOUR SKILLS

Communicating Organisational Culture to Employees

Reinforcing and communicating organisational culture is a critical requirement of management. You are the director of a financial services organisation in a large city. You've recently hired a new employee whose work, so far, has been to a high standard. Recently, however, you've noticed that other employees have expressed their dissatisfaction with this individual's time-keeping. Although the stipulated hours of work are 9am–5:30pm, employees usually stay until around 7pm on a number of evenings a week in order to manage international clients in different time zones. The new employee rarely, if ever, remains in the office past 5.30pm. How would you deal with this situation?

© PHOTOALTO

NATIONAL AND INTERNATIONAL CULTURES

Values, language, education, political and legal systems vary widely from country to country, and these practices in turn impact on the culture within organisations. It is important to recognise that even in the initial design of an organisation's structure, national culture plays a role ▶Chapter 11◀. For example, basic theories on how work should be organised reflects the different cultural backgrounds of the theorists: Frederick Taylor's principles of scientific management are regarded as reflecting an American work ethic and culture; the bureaucratic model of work espoused by Max Weber is considered to fit with the norms of German society; and Henri Fayol's administrative model is viewed as mirroring a French approach to work organisation.

An appreciation of cultural difference is imperative in international business for understanding how best to accomplish organisational goals effectively. Hofstede's cultural dimensions theory describes the effects of a society's culture on the values of its members, and how these values relate to behaviour. Hofstede's work was based on the results of a world-wide survey of IBM employees' values in the 1960s and 1970s. The cultural dimensions theory was one of the first to explain observed differences between cultures. Hofstede's original theory proposed four dimensions along which cultural values could be analysed: individualism–collectivism; uncertainty avoidance; power distance, and masculinity–femininity.

- *Individualism–collectivism:* this relates to the extent to which societies reflect an individualistic or a collective ethic. In individualistic societies, great importance is placed upon personal achievement, competition and individual rights; in contrast a collectivist society is one which prefers its members to act in a cohesive fashion. The US, Britain, Canada, France and Spain are all considered to be highly individualistic societies, in contrast with India, Hong Kong, Portugal, Greece and much of Latin America which hold more collectivist values.
- *Uncertainty avoidance:* this dimension reflects how members of a society cope with ambiguity. It examines the extent to which members attempt to minimise or avoid uncertain situations. Societies with high uncertainty avoidance tend to exhibit more rules, laws and regulations in order to carefully plan their way through changes. France, Spain, Germany and Latin America display high uncertainty avoidance. In contrast, low uncertainty avoidance countries tend to have fewer laws and often cope with change more easily; the Netherlands and Scandinavia are examples of low uncertainty avoidance.
- *Power distance:* this relates to the extent to which members of society (or within organisations) accept that power is distributed unequally, and this manifests in individuals' interactions with hierarchy and management. Cultures that endorse low power distance demonstrate social relations that are more consultative or democratic in nature; examples are Germany, Australia and the United States.
- *Masculinity–femininity:* this dimension refers to a continuum between characteristics assumed to be masculine in nature such as assertiveness and competition at one end and characteristics assumed to be feminine such as care and concern at the other. In masculine

cultures, the differences between gender roles are more dramatic than in feminine cultures. Scandinavia and the Netherlands reflected feminine cultures whereas the United States, Germany and Britain were found by Hofstede to have more masculine cultures.

Hofstede's work has been extremely influential in the organisational behaviour field. With regard to the interaction between national culture and organisational cultures, however, Hofstede's work has been questioned with regard to its applicability across cultures because it explores only national-level characteristics and ignores variations that may exist at regional level, which can be quite significant in some countries. Furthermore, some theorists question whether the findings have the same relevance in today's society because many nations have experienced significant changes, in particular with regard to the individualist–collectivist dimension. More recently, Project GLOBE has become established in discussions about national culture. GLOBE is a long-term research effort designed to explore the complex effects of culture on leadership, organisational effectiveness and the economic competitiveness of societies (House *et al.*, 2004). Extending Hofstede's work (Shi and Wang, 2011), Project GLOBE developed nine cultural dimensions that make it possible to capture the similarities and/or differences in norms, values, beliefs and practices among societies (Table 12.3).

Table 12.3 Project GLOBE

Dimensions	Definitions
Power distance	Degree to which members of an organisation or society expect and agree that power should be shared unequally.
Uncertainty avoidance	Extent to which members of collectives seek orderliness, consistency, structure, formalised procedures and laws to cover situations in their daily lives.
Institutional collectivism	Level at which a society values and rewards collective action and resource distribution.
In-group collectivism	Level at which a society values cohesiveness, loyalty and pride in their families and organisations.
Humane orientation	Ideas, values and prescriptions for behaviour associated with the dimension of culture at which a society values and rewards altruism, caring, fairness, friendliness, generosity and kindness.
Performance orientation	Level at which a society values and rewards individual performance and excellence.
Assertiveness	A set of social skills or a style of responding amenable to training or as a facet of personality.
Gender egalitarianism	Level at which a society values gender equality and lessens role differences based on gender.
Future orientation	The extent to which members of a society or an organisation believe that their current actions will influence their future, focus on investment in their future, believe that they will have a future that matters, believe in planning for developing their future, and look far into the future for assessing the effects of their current actions.

Source: Adapted from House et al. (2004) and Shi and Wang (2011).

BUILDING YOUR

Appreciating National Cultural Diversity

In the globalised economy, managers are increasingly expected to work in varied international settings. A key competency for today's manager, therefore, is the ability to recognise and appreciate national cultural diversity. National cultures impact strongly on organisational cultures. Imagine you are the CEO of a multinational organisation with worksites operating in Ireland, Japan and the United States. How would you ensure that a 'dominant' organisational culture is created and maintained across each worksite despite the differing national cultures?

Trouble Brewing?

The Kabuki Brewery is a niche brewery located in a small town just outside of Osaka, Japan, and specialising in the production of craft beers. It was founded in 1999 by Norio Yamada, who grew up in Osaka. The Kabuki Brewery specialises in environmentally friendly technologies and practices, and operates an energy-efficient brewing process. In 2010, the organisation became the first independent brewery in Japan to sustain its operations purely through natural energy sources (solar and wind power). In 2012, it generated a US$1.8 million profit. This year, Kabuki exported products to Australia, Southeast Asia and ten European countries. Its signature beer Kuro Ku won *Beer of the Year* at the world's largest international craft beer festival in Germany.

Kabuki Brewery has become a tourist magnet in the small town where it is situated. The main brewery is open to the public four days per week, and visitors can tour the facilities with an employee who provides a history of the company and walks the visitors through the brewing process while they sample beers. In addition, local artists display their work for sale in the brewery lobby. The revenue generated from these visits has been significant to both the brewery and the rest

© IMAGESOURCE

of the town, because visitors stay in local accommodation and spend their money in local stores.

As a young man, Norio Yamada worked part-time in his father's hospitality business in Osaka, before moving to Tokyo to attend college. Upon completing his engineering degree, Norio took a job on an energy project with a multinational engineering company in Hong Kong. Although he enjoyed his work, he was dissatisfied with the lack of autonomy, and knew that he would prefer to work for himself in a role that matched his technical skills and experience. Pursuing his passion for renewable energy, Norio completed a Master's degree in the field at a university in the US where he met his future wife, Kate, a marketing executive. Whilst on honeymoon in Europe in the mid-1990s, the couple visited a number of small craft breweries and vineyards, and it was during this time that the idea for the Kabuki brewery originated. Norio noticed that some of the breweries they visited were not held in high regard in their local communities. Residents complained about the over-production of barley and hops, and the resulting negative effects on the land.

Subsequently on their return to Japan, the couple set about establishing the Kabuki Brewery. The company mission was 'to operate a profitable business which is environmentally responsible, and that produces high quality alcohol product unique to the market'. Given the nature of the industry, with strong competition from existing large-scale producers and high start-up costs with regard to equipment and licensing, getting the business off the ground was challenging. Through a mix of personal savings, small loans and help from other local businesses (including low rent of a vacant building and supplies sold to him by local producers at a reduced rate), Norio successfully brought to market a small quantity of his signature beer, Kuro Ku, in 2001. Norio secured a small business loan in 2002 allowing him to grow the business by opening his brewery to the public, expanding production and exporting internationally.

Cognisant of the local support he had received, in 2004 Norio decided to redevelop a small military base which had been left vacant since the 1960s as the company headquarters. The building was converted into a modern brewery utilising local tradesmen wherever possible. The use of local talent and produce is something the company places strong value on today. Norio invested seed capital in a local business which manufactured packaging products, and purchased crates and boxes for his goods from them. Local artists were employed to develop the branding and promotional displays for the business, all of which are based on the Osaka landscape and feature familiar symbols such as the Ginkgo tree. Locals in the community are hugely proud that a product which has achieved international success originated in their town.

Norio places a high value in ensuring that customers, suppliers, and employees are satisfied. The organisation's motto – 'Satisfying, sustaining, sharing – it's all in the beer' – was developed by Kate to reflect the core values: an interest in achieving customer and employee satisfaction through great products; producing in a sustainable way so that ethical consumers have confidence that the environment is not being damaged; and creating a product designed to be shared and enjoyed, not only by family and friends, but also the staff and the local community, who share in the success of this business.

Norio encourages teamwork and autonomy in decision-making at all levels. He still works on site, and tours the company each morning to discuss issues with the production manager. The brewery offers discounts for staff on goods and a *Free Beer Friday* policy, whereby staff are given a case of beer every Friday. A special summer family BBQ is held each year, with suppliers and trade customers invited also. In addition, to promote its environmental values, instead of the usual corporate gifts associated with length of service, the company issues employees with a bicycle to mark one year's service. Further, Norio personally sponsors scholarships in the nearby

(Continued)

Trouble Brewing? (*Continued*)

university in Osaka each year in the areas of food science and production management. Although raw materials for the product could be sourced more cost efficiently elsewhere, Norio still purchases 70% of production materials from local sources. In addition, he heavily discounts the price of his product in local pubs, which has had a positive impact on tourism.

The company has gained increasing interest from food and gourmet magazines, in which chefs and food critics have heaped praise on the products. With this has come the interest of a group of American business people who already own shares in a spirit producing company in Tokyo. They contacted Norio, asking if they could come and talk to him about his business model. The export sales of the whiskey product this consortium are involved with doubled after their buy-in, so Norio was well aware of the potential value of their involvement. Following a visit last September, the consortium expressed concern

at what they deemed to be 'inefficiencies' with regard to sourcing products and the production process itself, and also in 'giving away' profits to others (largely indicated towards the discounted sale of the beer to local publicans). Nonetheless, they seem willing to invest. However, Norio is worried that they will force him to change many of his business practices if they do invest. While he would love to take his products global, and believes it is possible to do so with the right backing, he is worried that attempting such a venture could damage much of what he has already achieved.

Questions

1 Imagine you are Norio Yamada. You have been asked by the American investment consortium to prepare a report about the development of the current business model. You are aware that they are not yet convinced of the value of some of your practices and the level of engagement with both external and internal groups.

In your report, you want to highlight:

a The purpose that the current organisational culture at Kabuki serves.
b The factors that influenced the development of the organisational culture at the Kabuki brewery.
c How the culture is transmitted in the organisation.
d How you believe changing the business model, as suggested by the potential investors, might impact on the organisational culture and the organisation's success.

2 In groups of 3 or 4, assume the role of employees at the Kabuki Brewery. From an employee perspective, what concerns do you have about this potential business deal with the American consortium? What do you think are the key aspects of organisational culture that employees value, and would not want to see changed?

 SUMMARY

 IN THE EBOOK, CLICK TO HEAR AN AUDIO SUMMARY

The focus of this chapter has been on the nature of organisational culture, something which has an impact on individuals who work in an organisation, or those who interact with an organisation, either consciously or unconsciously. We have discussed the emergence of organisational culture as a concept within the field of management. Moreover, we have outlined how organisational culture, in reality, is formed, transmitted and reinforced by organisations. We have examined the differences that exist between organisational culture and organisational climate, and we have also looked at how a subculture can differ from an organisation's dominant culture. Throughout the chapter we have shown how organisational culture can impact on both employee and organisational performance; the types of organisational culture that exist can impact on this profoundly. Further we have discussed the issue of cultural change and varying national cultures. We have also discussed the important question of whether organisational culture impacts on organisational performance, a question which most managers continually seek to answer.

CHAPTER REVIEW QUESTIONS

1 What is organisational culture?
2 Does organisational culture have a purpose?
3 How is organisational culture formed, transmitted and reinforced?
4 Discuss the visible and invisible aspects of organisational culture.
5 Does culture impact on organisational performance?
6 How can we tell if an organisation has a strong culture?
7 Are there different types of cultures in organisations?
8 Describe how organisational culture can be changed.

MULTIPLE CHOICE QUESTIONS

In your ebook, click to take a multiple choice quiz to test your understanding of this chapter.

FURTHER READING

Barney, J.B. (1986). 'Organizational culture: can it be a source of sustained competitive advantage?' *Academy of Management Review*, 11(3), 656–665.

Koss, L. (2012). 'The impact of Recession on Culture: And What it Means for Organizations and Leaders', ONTOS Global, available online: http://ontosglobal.com/2012/04/the-impact-of-recession-on-culture-and-what-it-means-for-organizations-and-leaders/

Levering, R. (2010). *Transforming Workplace Cultures: Insights from Great Place to Work Institute's first 25 years*. Primavera Editorial.

Lok, P. and Crawford, J. (2004). 'The effect of organisational culture and leadership style on job satisfaction and organisational commitment: A cross-national comparison'. *Journal of Management Development*, 23(4), 321–338.

Naranjo-Valencia, J.C., Jiménez-Jiménez, D. and Sanz-Valle, R. (2011). 'Innovation or imitation? The role of organizational culture'. *Management Decision*, 49(1), 55–72.

Rafaeli, A. and Pratt, M.G. (Eds.). (2013). *Artifacts and organizations: Beyond mere symbolism*. Psychology Press.

Schneider, B. and Barbera, K.M. (Eds.). (2014). *The Oxford Handbook of Organizational Climate and Culture*. Oxford University Press.

Soderquist, D. (2005). *The Walmart-Way*. Nashville, TN: Thomas Nelson Inc.

 USEFUL WEBSITES

www.greatplacetowork.ie

Great Place to Work Institute is a global research, consulting and training organisation which focuses on helping organisations identify, create and sustain high-trust organisational cultures. Their website's publication and events section contains lots of interesting information on their work and their research findings.

www.worldatwork.org

This is a non-profit human resources association for professionals. The website's 'resource center' has lots of stimulating information for anyone interested in learning more about organisational culture, and people management more generally.

www.kotterinternational.com

Kotter International was founded by Harvard Business School professor, John Kotter. It's an organisation focused on helping organisations manage change, including cultural change. Professor Kotter has published widely on the process of organisational change, and Kotter International's website provides a step-by-step guide to managing change in organisations, located in the 'Our principles' section. It also publishes lots of interesting articles, and free resources on managing change (including cultural change) in organisations.

www.ted.com/conversations/topics/organizational%20culture

TED is a non-profit organisation 'devoted to spreading ideas' from experts around the globe. This is a link to 'TED conversations' which focuses on discussions about organisational culture.

www.huffingtonpost.com/vala-afshar/100-tweetable-business-cu_b_3575595.html

Go to this link from the Huffington Post blog to read '100 Tweetable Business Culture Quotes from Brilliant Executives', and see what top business executives have to say about organisational culture.

13 MANAGING ORGANISATIONAL CHANGE

Gráinne Kelly

LEARNING OUTCOMES

BY THE END OF THIS CHAPTER YOU SHOULD BE ABLE TO:

- Demonstrate an understanding of the nature of organisational change.

- Explain the forces of organisational change.

- Discuss the planned approach to change management.

- Identify why employees resist change and recognise strategies for overcoming resistance.

- Explain the role of leadership in organisational change.

- Discuss the field of organisational development (OD) critically.

© ISTOCK/JOSHBLAKE

THIS CHAPTER DISCUSSES:

IN REALITY

'A change is as good as a rest', or so the saying goes. We all generally associate change with something welcome, a fresh start or a new challenge. In contemporary business environments managers have to consider many factors involved in a complex and dynamic situations before making decisions about implementing changes that will positively influence the effectiveness, efficiency and ultimately the sustainability of their organisations. Yet, does it not depend on what the change is, the size of the change effort, the actual and perceived changes(s) and who the change affects? Some people may be more deeply affected than others by the change. Dahl's (1957) research illuminates the potentially negative outcomes of change at the level of the employee. His study of 92,860 employees working in 1,517 of the largest Danish organisations found that organisational changes are associated with significant risks of employee health problems. Change has been equated with high levels of stress among employees. During periods of constant change employees may encounter stress when they don't have sufficient time to adjust to the change. ACAS (2012) recommends that employees' emotional well-being is taken into account when managing change by including the following within every change process:

- Create a vision.
- Lead the change.
- Consult with employees.
- Engage employees.
- Reflect on the change process.

INTRODUCTION

Organisational change is an inevitable consequence of organisational life. Almost every organisation must adjust to a global marketplace, demographic changes, immigration and technological advances. An empirical study with 800 managers from around the world indicated that half of the participants expected their organisations to undertake more merger and acquisition activities in the next 12 months than they had in the previous 12 months (Uhlaner and West, 2011) in response to these external pressures. Continued deregulation of markets through the removal of state regulations means that organisations have to continually adjust product and marketing strategies to operate in increasingly competitive markets. This complexity requires organisations to make moderate to major changes every couple of years. Although large-scale organisational change efforts occur with increasing frequency, the efforts often fail to deliver the desired results on a variety of outcomes, including cost reduction, employee attitudes, productivity and revenue (Seo et al., 2012). In this chapter we will learn about the nature of organisational change and discuss which forces act as simulants to change. We will describe what factors contribute to and influence employees' resistance to change. We will also learn about the planned approaches to change management and outline the key insights to effective implementation offered by the field of organisational development (OD).

THE NATURE OF ORGANISATIONAL CHANGE

Organisational change occurs when a company makes a transition from its current state to some desired future state. Change management can be described as an integral part of all managerial work that '(a) copes with the changing patterns of resource input and knowledge available to work organisations and the shifting demands made by the parties with which they deal, and (b) initiates change that managers perceive to be in the interests of those who employ them' (Watson, 2002, p. 418). Today's business environment requires companies to undergo changes frequently if they are to remain competitive. Factors such as the internationalisation of markets and growth in technology force businesses to be proactive in order to survive.

Theories of change have a long history and draw on organisational behaviour concepts, including learning theory, motivation theory, organisational culture theory and theories of leadership and strategy. In order to understand organisational change, it is important to remember that there are many types and levels of change. Such changes may be relatively minor – as in the case of installing a new software program or removing a major section or practice – or quite major – as in the case of refocusing an overall production strategy. Change also occurs when an organisation evolves through various lifecycles. In organisational settings, change is often understood in terms of specific techniques to manage it, but change can also occur at a broader level and be less structured if it is unplanned or the result of unforeseen events. When this happens, organisations often use a discrete piecemeal approach in order to respond to the change as it emerges.

TYPES OF ORGANISATIONAL CHANGE

Change can be categorised as planned, unplanned, emergent, incremental or quantum. Lewin (1951), who we will discuss further in this chapter, first made the distinction between planned change and unplanned or emergent change. Child (2005) provides a useful framework for differentiating between incremental and quantum or radical change. Incremental change is usually targeted at fixing specific departments of the organisation, or specific problems such as changes agreed in staff performance plans, while quantum or radical change involves a more generic organisation-wide change programme, such as business process engineering (BPR). By its very nature, planned change is likely to be either quantum or incremental while unplanned change is more likely to be emergent.

planned change change that an organisation consciously thinks about and decides to engage in, which is designed to specifically change organisational outcomes

unplanned or emergent change change that the organisation did not initiate or had no control over planning

incremental change a small change aimed at achieving certain goals

quantum or radical change change that affects the entire organisation

Yet despite this emphasis on the need for change, for a number of organisations change is not part of their strategic plan and, in some cases, change is not even something that is viewed as desirable. In these cases, change is occurring as an unplanned response to external or internal events beyond the control of the organisation that make it necessary for organisation survival. As an illustration, we can consider organisational changes following the 9/11 terrorist attacks in the US, when, among other things, the travel industry experienced a decline in business. At this point, airlines and hotels across the US and Europe were forced to engage in unplanned, incremental and emergent change, including lay-offs, as they looked for ways to cope with the crisis. We can also see an example of quantum change at airports, which had to introduce new security regulations and train staff in safety procedures to combat further terrorist attacks.

CONSIDER THIS...

Are certain types of individuals likely to resist change? Have you heard people saying that older workers are more likely to resist change than younger workers, or men are more likely to resist change than women? What do you think are the reasons for this? Is there evidence to back up these claims?

LEVELS OF ORGANISATIONAL CHANGE

As well as the type of change, it is important to understand the different levels within the organisation where change can occur. At the broadest organisational level change usually centres on restructuring and reorganising. This can mean the introduction of new policies and rules that affect the entire organisation. At this level, different strategies can be planned, which are then transformed into two other levels which are more specific and detailed. We can take the example of Total Quality Management (TQM), which is a management approach that centres on quality and customer satisfaction, based on the participation and commitment of an organisation's workforce. At the group level, change is aimed at altering work processes, including the introduction of new technologies to accomplish the work. This would be the stage at which entire work processes would be changed by implementing TQM initiatives. Finally, at the individual level, changes attempt to alter the behaviours, attitudes, norms and perceptions of the employees in the organisation to bring them in line with the new values and cultural context ▶ Chapter 12 ◀.

CONTENT-DRIVEN CHANGE

While it may be assumed that all organisational change occurs at various levels, it is useful to explore patterns of change in terms of content and process-driven types. Content-driven change is a programmatic change in which specific interventions are used as the driver for change. Examples include lean manufacturing, which seeks to eliminate activities that do not add value from the perspective of the customer, and agile development, which consists of a process for product development based on collaborative cross-functional team effort. To help understand content-driven change, we can identify a set of characteristics that are common across particular change efforts:

- Serves as the building block for stimulating change throughout the company unit or department.
- Is directed by top management.
- Relies on standardised, off the shelf solutions.
- Is practised in a uniform manner across the organisation.

PROCESS-DRIVEN CHANGE

A process-driven approach to change works from the opposite direction to content-driven change. Process-driven change emphasises the methods of conceiving, introducing and institutionalising new behaviours, and uses content as a reinforcer rather than a driver of new behaviours. An example involves the use of a process model for developing new applications. Process-driven change seeks to foster a cultural context and climate in which employees at all levels of the organisation engage in a mutually collaborative way to achieve the strategic goals of the organisation. It is clear from the literature that there are various types and levels of organisational change. However, ultimately the type of change an organisation engages in is dependent on forces that are both within and beyond its control. It is to these forces that we now turn.

FORCES FOR CHANGE

External and internal forces have been responsible for driving change in relation to work for centuries, with one of the most significant examples being the Industrial Revolution which changed the nature of work. Internal forces for change include employee dissatisfaction and industrial conflict, both of which are important factors in highly collectivised environments characterised by a strong trade union presence. Other internal forces are new leadership, new strategy, new structures, the redesign of jobs and the installation of new technology. External forces for change include the growth in the knowledge economy which has stimulated the increasingly knowledge-intensive nature of work (Kase *et al.*, 2009) and the need for more autonomous and collaborative work designs (Foss *et al.*, 2009). In addition, since the 1990s societal and political pressures such as the fall of communism, increased global competition, privatisation and deregulation and the growing influence of EU directives on employment relations have played a role in the changing nature of the organisational environment. Below we identify some of the major external forces of change:

- *Technological innovations:* Organisations are being transformed by the presence of faster, cheaper and more mobile computers, the growth of social media and rise in e-commerce.
- *Socio-economic forces:* Since 2008 the housing and financial sectors have experienced economic shocks and organisations have had to cope with a recessionary climate.
- *Market competition:* Competition now occurs on a global scale.

- *Social trends:* Organisations must constantly adjust product and market strategies in light of changing social trends. For example, in 2015 Apple faced a growing number of competitors in the sale of the tablet computers due to the new social demand for these devices. As a result Apple needed to continually update and innovate to keep ahead of market competitors such as Samsung, and aimed to achieve this through a focus on the attraction and retention of a talented staff.
- *Global politics:* There is ongoing growth in the interdependency of economies and opening of trade with the introduction of the BRIC countries (Brazil, Russia and India).

These elements do not occur in an isolated manner. Rather, the changes to any one of the external or internal elements of an organisation's system will cause changes to other elements. We will now discuss two frameworks that provide insight into the interaction between the external and internal organisational environments affecting change events. The first model by Kotter (1980) is presented in Figure 13.1.

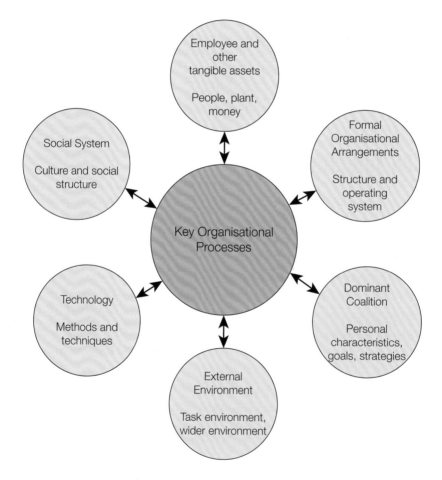

Figure 13.1 Kotter's integrative model of organisational dynamics

Source: Adapted from Kotter (1980).

The primary organisational processes in Kotter's framework consist of information gathering, communication and decision-making. More specific processes include the market research process, the product development process and the manufacturing process. Kotter's framework describes six structural dimensions:

- The external environment involving the political and government systems.
- Employees and other tangible assets such as buildings, plant and inventories.
- Formal structure, job design and operating systems.
- Social systems involving organisational culture and social structure.
- Technology.
- Dominant coalition embracing the objectives and strategies of those who control policy-making.

Kotter's process perspective on change management provides a useful framework for managers leading a change and highlights, in terms of leadership, what needs to be done to ensure success for each element. For instance, an organisational leader needs to identify and remove obstacles that can prevent employees acting to implement the organisational vision. Some of these obstacles might include organisational process, such as reward systems that penalise valued behaviour, restrictive rules and regulations or inflexible organisational structures.

THE MCKINSEY 7S FRAMEWORK

The McKinsey framework was developed in the early 1980s by Peters and Waterman, two consultants working at the McKinsey & Company consulting firm. The basic premise of the model is that there are seven internal aspects of an organisation that need to be aligned if it is to be successful with a change event. The McKinsey 7S model involves seven interdependent factors which are categorised as either 'hard' or 'soft' elements. Hard elements are easier to define or identify and management can directly influence or direct them through strategy statements, organisation charts and reporting lines, and formal processes and IT systems. Soft elements are less tangible and more influenced by culture, and include employee skills and shared values. The model in Figure 13.2 depicts the interdependency of the elements and indicates how a change in one area affects all the others.

We can illustrate this interdependency with the example of the introduction of digital technology into an organisation. The modification of organisation structure to support digital business may require cross-functional teams or steering groups and decisions around insourcing or outsourcing. The development of specific systems, processes and information technology to support digital business could consist of the choice of internal or external integrated technology solutions. Staff considerations involve those around recruitment and training and development, and exploring employee skills in specific areas such as project management or e-marketing campaigns. Managerial style focuses on the manager's vision for the introduction of the technology in light of achieving the organisational objectives. Shared values are at the core of the framework and they involve the leader fostering perceptions of the importance and effectiveness of digital business among senior managers and staff. These beliefs and assumptions underpin the development of a climate in which people believe in the value of their roles and are confident that they have the support of senior staff to make changes.

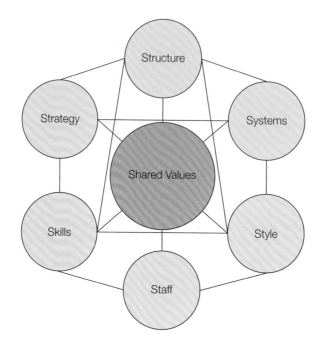

Figure 13.2 The McKinsey 7S framework

Source: Adapted from Peters and Waterman (2004).

The elements of the model can be explained as follows:

- *Strategy:* the plan devised to maintain and build competitive advantage over the competition.
- *Structure:* the way the organisation is structured and who reports to whom.
- *Systems:* the daily activities and procedures that staff members engage in to get the job done.
- *Shared values:* the core values of the company that are evidenced in the corporate culture and the general work ethic.
- *Style:* the style of leadership adopted.
- *Staff:* the employees and their general capabilities.
- *Skills:* the actual skills and competencies of the employees working for the company.

Peters and Waterman's (1982) research emphasises the management of culture ▸ **Chapter 12** ◂ and employee behaviour as critical interventions for sustaining organisational capability to manage long-term change and improve performance. For example, it emphasises the importance of training and developing people using organisational learning methods to develop the skills they need to carry out their new roles.

THE PLANNED CHANGE PROCESS

At some point in time all organisations have desired to change some facet of how they operate and have taken deliberate, planned rational steps to accommodate this change. Leaders seeking to implement organisational change are often surprised by the degree of complacency and lack of interest they face from their employees. They are perplexed as to why their employees want to retain the status quo and continue with the same behaviours – often even in the face of declining organisational performance. How can managers overcome this? Some adopt a strategy whereby they announce the need for change and present a rational argument around the importance of the change for improving organisational performance. They tell employees how they need to adjust their behaviours and work together in new ways in the interests of the organisation. However, studies indicate that this will not motivate behavioural change and often weak organisational performance will not create an urgent need to change within an organisation. An explanation for this was provided by Kurt Lewin who suggested the need for an approach which would 'unfreeze' the existing situation. The planned approach to organisational change assumes that change strategies are intentional and rational processes which rely on analysis, forecasting and planning, thus resulting in the logical and rational implementation of change within the organisation (Hayes, 2014). An example of the planned approach was provided by Kotter and is illustrated in Table 13.1.

We have highlighted the planned nature of change events in organisations. In the next section we will study a seminal approach by Lewin in the field of organisational change.

Table 13.1 Kotter's 8-step process

Steps	Transformation suggestions
1. Increase urgency	• Examine market and competitive realities • Identify and discuss crisis, potential crisis or major opportunities • Provide evidence from outside the organisation that change is necessary
2. Build the guiding team	• Assemble a group with enough power to lead the change effort • Attract key change leaders by showing enthusiasm and commitment • Encourage the group to work together as a team
3. Get the vision right	• Create a vision to help direct the change effort • Develop strategies for achieving that vision
4. Communicate for buy-in	• Build alignment and engagement through stories • Use every vehicle possible to communicate the new vision and strategies • Keep communication simple and heartfelt • Teach new behaviours by the example of the guiding coalition
5. Empowering action	• Remove obstacles to the change • Change systems and/or structures that work against the vision
6. Create short-term wins	• Plan for and achieve visible performance improvements • Recognise and reward those involved in bringing the improvements to life
7. Do not let up	• Plan for and create visible performance improvements • Recognise and reward personnel involved in the improvements • Reinforce the behaviours that led to the improvements
8. Make change stick	• Articulate the connections between the new behaviours and the improvements

Source: Adapted from Kotter (1995).

ASDA's Planned Strategic Change in Northern Ireland

In 2005, Britain's second-biggest supermarket, Asda, bought 12 Safeway supermarket stores in Northern Ireland from Morrisons for £73.6 million. Asda is owned by the US retail organisation Walmart. Asda's leaders formulated a new strategy which involved changing perceptions of Safeway as a discount store targeting working-class customers to marketing itself to wealthier shoppers. However, one of the key problems with this strategy was that it was led by senior management who failed to draw upon the store managers' knowledge that existing customers were no longer visiting the stores, resulting in huge losses for the organisation.

OB IN THE NEWS

Asda's executives learned that, for change implementation to stay on track, knowledge of whether interventions were working must be communicated upward and shared in a timely way with top management.

Other issues that the company faced involved the local community's fears about the implications of this change for indigenous farmers and producers.

Asda reassured customers and promised to collaborate with all of Safeway's existing Northern Irish product suppliers. It also offered prices which mirrored those of its stores in the rest of the UK. Its prices were very competitive and resulted in savings for customers and significant investment in Northern Ireland through job creation which initially amounted to 250 new jobs. After undergoing a successful change process, Asda's business went from strength to strength with a growing number of stores in Northern Ireland. The company also expanded its range of products to include books, movies, electronics, flowers, furniture, mobile phones, and insurance, photo and travel services.

Questions

1   Consider what has happened in the retail industry since Asda came to Northern Ireland.
2   What other major changes have occurred since 2005, and what was the nature of these changes?

Source:

http://news.bbc.co.uk/1/hi/northern_ireland/4612591.stm (last accesssed on 26 August 2015).

© ROYALTY-FREE/CORBIS

LEWIN'S CHANGE MODEL

In the mid-20th century, psychologist Kurt Lewin identified three stages of change that are the basis of contemporary approaches to change management. In the aftermath of the Second World War, Lewin published two essays, 'Behaviour and Development as a Function of the Total Situation' (1946) and 'Frontiers in Group Dynamics' (1947) (see Lewin, 1951), which made important contributions to our understanding of organisational change and

Figure 13.3 Three-step model of change

Source: Adapted from Lewin (1997).

development. First, he highlighted the role that context plays in shaping individual behaviours. Second, he argued that the only way to motivate an individual to change his or her pattern of behaviour is to create a sense of disequilibrium or dissatisfaction with the status quo within the individual. Lewin suggested that successful change requires a three-step procedure that involves the stages of unfreezing, moving and refreezing (see Figure 13.3).

- *Unfreezing* is the first stage of the change process and consists of unlearning past behaviour. Lewin emphasised that announcing the need for change or presenting a rational argument for how the changes will improve performance will not motivate behavioural change among employees. This is because existing behaviours are often ingrained in shared expectations or norms of how organisational members ought to behave. Organisational membership instils a positive sense of belonging to members and a shared understanding; they like being part of the group, accept the group's norms, and are pleased with what the group has been able to achieve in the past as a result of a collective effort. The literature suggests that the more individuals assign positive value to group membership and group norms, the greater the resistance on the part of the individual group members to any change in those norms ▸ **Chapter 7** ◂. To break the social habits that support existing patterns of behaviour, a leader needs to initiate unfreezing or create dissatisfaction with the status quo by alerting organisational members to the need for change. This is brought about by the leader creating a vision of the future desirable state and communicating this vision, which instils a sense of urgency and reduces any restraining forces.

- *Moving* is where the change actually occurs and the organisation moves to a desired state. During this stage, new policies, procedures, structures, behaviours and attitudes are developed. A key part of Lewin's model is the notion that change, even at the psychological level, is a journey that unfolds over time rather than a single event. Employees must be involved and participate in the change process. Old customs and norms that reinforce the old ways of doing things must be replaced with norms that reinforce the new ways. For example, if the organisation is developing teams and moving away from functional departments, then teamwork across departmental boundaries should be emphasised and a suitable team-based reward structure should be considered to reinforce the moving process.

- *Refreezing* is the final stage of the change process and involves reinforcing and measuring behavioural change. Once change has been implemented, in order to be successful, the new situation must be refrozen so it can be sustained over time. Without this last step, change is likely to be a brief event and employees will attempt to revert to the previous equilibrium state. Here it is critical that the appropriate organisational systems such as reward structures and social support are implemented to strengthen the development of new behaviours. Training must be provided to ensure that employees understand and can perform their roles in the change process. After the training requirements are defined, the reward system, reporting relationships, performance management and development systems need to be adjusted. These aspects are critical to help people and the organisation internalise or institutionalise the changes.

BUILDING YOUR SKILLS

Understanding Resistance to Change

Your organisation has decided to introduce a new performance management system. As a section manager you have been asked for your views on likely employee attitudes for and against this change initiative. What are the likely impacts of this type of change in the organisation? How can these be anticipated and planned for?

An example of what these three stages might look like when put into practice is that of an insurance company which has been receiving poor customer evaluations over the last three months. The organisation realises that good customer service is essential for success in the industry and wishes to become more customer focused. New competitors are emerging and the company is concerned over losing its market share. Managers in the firm survey its customers and the findings suggest that customers feel disengaged from the agents they speak with on the telephone and that the waiting time to speak to a representative is quite long.

The application of Lewin's three-step model of change might look like the following:

- *Unfreezing:* Managers hold a meeting with all telephone representatives. During the meeting, the customer survey results are presented and discussed. Additionally, lost customer estimates are translated into financial terms so that telephone representatives can see how poor customer service results in overall poor company performance.
- *Moving:* After the meeting, telephone representatives are provided with customer service training that involves role-playing, group discussions and peer-based learning. This allows them to experience poor versus good service. Representatives are instructed to take their time with calls and to exhibit active listening techniques. In addition, more staff are trained and moved into the customer service section to provide feedback and support.
- *Refreezing:* The organisation needs to examine its existing compensation system which rewarded representatives based on the quantity of calls made per hour. To support the desired behavioural changes representatives will be paid an hourly rate and can receive a bonus based on improvements in customer satisfaction surveys.

Several researchers have built on Lewin's model. Lippitt *et al.* (1958) have expanded the moving stage in relation to managing change for people, groups, organisations and communities. They differentiate three dimensions which are important to achieving the change:

- Clarification or diagnosis of the problem.
- Examination of alternative routes and goals, and the establishment of goals and intentions for action.
- Transformation of intentions into actual change efforts.

Research by Egan (1996) focused on both the unfreezing and moving stages of Lewin's model. He identified the importance of the assessment of the current scenario (diagnosis), mapping out the preferred scenario (visioning) and the movement from the current to the preferred scenario (planning for change). The dimensions of each of these three stages can be described as:

- *The current scenario*: assessing problems and opportunities, developing new perspectives, and choosing high-impact problems or opportunities for attention.
- *The preferred scenario*: developing a range of possible futures, evaluating alternative possibilities to establish a viable agenda for change, and gaining commitment to the new agenda.
- *Strategies and plans for moving to the preferred scenario*: brainstorming strategies for getting there, choosing the best strategy or best-fit package of strategies, and turning these strategies into a viable plan.

To summarise the planned change approach, it is apparent that change requires significant individual and organisational commitment before, during and after the change event. Lewin's model considers the organisation's environment in a holistic manner, and recognises the need for employee receptiveness to change before it occurs and support for change by management once it has occurred. In addition Lewin's model suggests that the most effective way to manage behavioural change among employees is to devote attention on changing the group's norms ▶ Chapter 7 ◀ before adjusting individual behaviours. Surprisingly, the literature suggests that organisations frequently neglect to focus on these areas when attempting to implement change initiatives. Employees are often asked to accept change initiatives without a clear understanding of the need for the change or any involvement in the decision-making processes. In addition, employees often don't receive the support they need to maintain the change, aspects which are explored further in the next section.

EMPLOYEE RESISTANCE TO CHANGE

As mentioned in the In Reality box at the start of this chapter, individuals can undergo a traumatic experience when they are personally confronted with major organisational change. It is suggested in the literature that most employees go through four phases: initial denial, resistance, gradual exploration and eventual commitment. In this section we will focus on resistance. Resistance occurs along a continuum, ranging from passive withdrawal from change initiatives to actively sabotaging them to make them fail (Bacharach and Bamberger, 2007). Each of these reactions to change shapes the behaviour of individuals and, ultimately, the success of the change event. Resistance is a natural part of the change process and occurs because change involves going from the known to the uncertain. Change appears threatening to many people, which makes it difficult to gain their support and commitment to implementing changes. Resistance to change can have a significant impact and influence upon the success of an organisational change project. The results of a survey of 1,536 executives

resistance refers to action, overt or covert, exerted on behalf of maintaining the status quo

involved in a wide variety of minor and substantial change initiatives indicated that only 38% had accepted these initiatives and deemed them to be successful and just 30% thought they had contributed to the sustained improvement of their organisations (Isern and Pung, 2007).

A study by Meaney and Pung (2008) also reported employee resistance as the most common problem faced by management in implementing change. Given that resistance to change can be a very real problem for those leading change, focus has been directed in the literature around change attitudes and in particular individual and organisational change readiness (Bouckenooghe, 2010). Individual change readiness reflects an individual's beliefs, attitudes and intentions regarding the extent to which changes are needed, and the organisation's capacity to successfully undertake those changes (Armenakis *et al.*, 1993).

According to Jones *et al.* (2005) the reasons why employees resist change include the following:

- Satisfaction with the status quo.
- Perception of change as a personal threat.
- Viewing the cost of change as outweighing the benefits.
- Belief that management is mishandling the process.
- Belief that the change effort is not likely to succeed.

A useful framework for gaining a broader understanding of why the resistance is happening was proposed by Dijk and Dick (2009). They discuss two individual sources of resistance to change. The first, person-orientated resistance to change, involves an employee's fear of a loss of status, loss of pay or concern that the change has or will have a negative impact on their job security. The second source, principle-orientated resistance, centres on employee beliefs that the proposed or enacted change carries more costs than it does benefits for the organisation. By studying these elements, we can see how often employee resistance can be understood in part as a natural and expected outcome of implementation. Given the issues just explained, we will now outline some strategies for managing resistance to change.

IMPROVING EMPLOYEE REACTIONS TO CHANGE

Although it appears that employee resistance to change is inevitable, managers need to understand whether change interventions are being implemented as intended and are producing the desired outcomes. Just as management practices have a powerful effect on employees' work experiences and performance, the way changes are managed can influence employees' attitudes towards the change and their level of receptiveness and commitment ▶Chapter 6◀. According to Kotter and Schlesinger (1979) there are six methods that managers can draw upon to facilitate change and overcome resistance, and we look at these in turn below.

EDUCATION AND COMMUNICATION

It has been argued that the reason so many change efforts encounter resistance can be traced back to the absence of any attempt by the organisation to communicate with employees at

SPOTLIGHT ON SKILLS

You are working as a manager in Novetal, an organisation which is a privately-owned worldwide manufacturer of metal cans, operating in 21 countries, with 8,000 employees and turnover of €1.6 billion in 2006. The corporate culture centres on trust, transparency and teamwork. Novetal is based in the Netherlands but has a head office in Paris, and operates primarily throughout Europe. Its strategy is to be one of the best metal-can manufacturers as opposed to the most profitable or biggest, and it places great emphasis on values surrounding operational excellence. The company is considering an acquisition strategy in order to meet company objectives.

1 Assess how the company could approach the change using Kotter's checklist.

2 Consider whether the leadership of change always happens from the top of the organisation.

To help you answer these questions, in your ebook click the play button to watch the video of Simon Shaw at Eurostar talking about organisational change.

---

both individual and team levels (Alas and Sharifi, 2002). As a result some literature has pointed to understanding change readiness at the collective level involving the individual and group change processes. According to Weiner (2009) the concept of organisational change readiness refers to organisational members' change commitment and self-efficacy to implement organisational change. Kim *et al.* (2011) define change supportive behaviours in this context as actions employees participate in which facilitate and contribute to a planned change initiated by the organisation. They state that trust and social support are integral to good employee relations and maintaining the outcomes of change initiatives. Empirical research has indicated that high communication increases acceptance, openness, and commitment to change (for example, Bordia *et al.*, 2004; Jones *et al.*, 2005) ▸Chapter 10◂. Individuals need to know what is happening, why it is happening and how it will impact them. Indeed as we discussed earlier, one of the reasons for a failed change event is that management invests in the planned change strategy but fails to communicate, train and follow up with staff as the change process progresses.

PARTICIPATION AND INVOLVEMENT

Employees are unlikely to resist a change decision in which they have participated. Their participation is critical for obtaining commitment and increasing the quality of the change decision. The success of implementing change is generally associated with those who facilitate the change process. It is thus important to view the change process through the eyes of the participants who are most critical to the process – that is, the managers themselves, the people who establish priorities, devise strategies, control resources, and manage performance ▸ Chapter 3 ◂. In this respect, managers constitute internal change agents who shape the conditions for change. A change agent is generally a person from inside or outside the organisation who helps an organisation transform itself by focusing on such matters as organisational effectiveness, improvement and development. Such change agents may be senior line managers or those specifically charged with managing the processes of organisational development and cultural change in the organisation. They act as a champion for employees, representing employee concerns to senior management and working to increase employee commitment to the organisation and their ability to deliver business results.

NEGOTIATION AND AGREEMENT

Literature on the management of change has frequently indicated that the first step to achieving lasting organisational change is to deal with the resistance; that is, to identify resistance as an obstacle to be overcome and to select a change strategy that will minimise or eliminate it. However, this underplays the political dimensions which shape organisations' and their members' decisions and conduct ▸ Chapter 9 ◂. Indeed, the change agent has to find a balance between being the technical expert (the person assumed to have the answers on all matters relating to the change) and the process facilitator (the person with the techniques to allow the organisation to find its own answers). This is challenging given the diversity of values and interests, politicised and value-driven decision-making processes and the subjective interpretation of information in change efforts. In addition, some employees see change programmes as just another task to do in addition to the tasks which are central to their individual roles.

MANIPULATION AND CO-OPTATION

Manipulation refers to covert ways of influence employees. For example, if management threatens to close a plant where employees are resisting an across-the-board pay cut, but the threat is actually untrue, management are using manipulation. In contrast, co-optation combines manipulation and participation. It strives to pay off the leaders of a resistance group by giving them a key role, seeking their advice to get their approval and emphasising the value placed on their opinions.

change agent a manager who seeks to reconfigure an organisation's roles, responsibilities, structures, outputs, processes, systems, technology or other resources in the light of improving organisational effectiveness

THIS...

You have just taken over as the new Student Union president. You are aware that many students are not engaged with the activities of the SU so you need to make changes in order to make the SU more relevant to all students. What steps would you take to make the changes?

SELECTING PEOPLE TO LEAD CHANGE

The literature suggests that proactive, open-minded managers embrace change willingly as additional opportunities to help their organisations grow, to generate more sales and deliver more value to customers. Models of change have been critiqued for implying a top-down approach to initiation and implementation of change. However as we have discussed, employee involvement and participation are critical for ensuring employee commitment to and ownership of the change process.

EXPLICIT AND IMPLICIT COERCION

Kotter and Schlesinger (1979) define coercion as the application of direct threats or force on the resisters. Examples of this strategy include threats of transfer, loss of promotions, negative performance evaluations and a poor letter of recommendation.

LEARNING HOW EMPLOYEES RESPOND TO THE CHANGE

One way in which the organisation can review the success of a change event is by studying employee perceptions of the way the changes were managed and the effect it had on their experience of work. A useful framework in this regard is the change management indicator proposed by Hayes and Hyde (1998) which provides managers with an insight into employee attitudes towards the change and the issues they encounter. This is presented in Figure 13.4.

This diagnostic change tool can be used by management to promote an open discursive culture around the change initiative. It can also be used to capture employees' opinions over time and to assess employee experiences in different departments, functions and organisational levels. Managing change involves helping an individual, group or organisation to change their existing behaviour and providing feedback that signals the effectiveness of new behaviours with incentives that reward new levels of performance to help embed new practices.

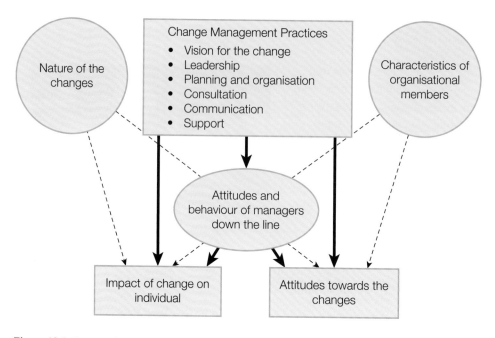

Figure 13.4 Factors affecting employee responses to change

Source: Adapted from Hayes (2010).

LEADERSHIP AND ORGANISATIONAL CHANGE

Leadership is widely regarded as the primary enabler of the change process in which a strong vision can make a valuable contribution to the success of an initiative. Reflecting on the role of the leader as a critical change agent is a central theme in the literature on change processes. Leadership can be understood as a set of activities or behaviours that mobilise adaptive behaviours on the part of members of the organisation.

Within the literature, focus has been directed on differentiating between transactional and transformational types of leadership ▶ **Chapter 8** ◀. The Ohio State studies, Fielder's model, and path-goal theory describe transactional leaders who guide their followers towards established goals by clarifying role and task requirements. Transformational leaders inspire followers to transcend their self-interest for the good of the organisation and can have an extraordinary effect on their followers.

CHARACTERISTICS OF TRANSACTIONAL AND TRANSFORMATIONAL LEADERS

According to Bass (1999), and discussed in more detail in Chapter 8, transformational leaders can be differentiated from transactional leaders as follows:

BUILDING YOUR SKILLS

Change Management Skills

Change is an inevitable feature of working in an organisation. Because of this, you will most likely be involved in managing a change project at some point – be it a simple change to the way your organisation deals with customer orders or a major change in organisational strategy. Most change management projects involve changing the way that people work. To achieve successful change, therefore, you must first understand how people react to change. Using the information in this chapter identify the change management approach you would use to introduce a new customer complaint system into a retail clothing shop with 40 employees.

© GETTY IMAGES/ISTOCKPHOTO/THINKSTOCK/YAHOR PIASKOUSKI

Transactional leader

- Contingent reward: emphasises the exchange of rewards for effort; promises remuneration for good performance; recognises accomplishments.
- Management by exception (active): watches and searches for deviations from rules and standards; takes corrective action.
- Management by exception (passive): intervenes only if standards are not met.
- Laissez-faire: abdicates responsibilities; avoids making decisions.

Transformational leader

- Idealised influence: provides vision and sense of mission; instils pride; gains respect and trust.
- Inspirational motivation: communicates high expectations; uses symbols to focus efforts; and expresses important purposes in simple ways.
- Intellectual stimulation: promotes intelligence, rationality, and careful problem-solving.
- Individualised consideration: gives personal attention; treats each employee individually; coaches and advises.

KOTTER'S CHANGE MODEL AND LEADERSHIP

John P. Kotter is a Harvard Business School professor and leading thinker and author on organisational change management. Kotter believes that organisational change can be managed by a leader using a dynamic, non-linear 8-step approach. Each stage acknowledges a key principle identified by Kotter relating to people's response and approach to change. Kotter's 8-step change model is summarised below.

1 Establish a sense of urgency by creating a compelling reason for why change is needed.
2 Form a coalition with enough power to lead the change. Kotter indicates that unless those who recognise the need for change can build a team to direct the process, the change event is unlikely to build momentum.
3 Create a new vision to direct the change and strategies for achieving the vision. Kotter (1996) identifies six criteria for an effective vision: imaginable (conveys a picture of what the future will look like); desirable (appeals to the long-term interests of employees, customers and stakeholders); feasible (comprises realistic, attainable goals); focused (is clear enough to provide guidance in decision-making); flexible (is general enough to allow individual initiatives and alternative responses in light of changing conditions); communicable (is easy to communicate).
4 Communicate the vision throughout the organisation.
5 Empower others to act on the vision by removing barriers to change and encouraging risk-taking and creative problem-solving.
6 Plan for, create and reward short-term wins that move the organisation toward the new vision.
7 Consolidate improvements, reassess changes, and make necessary adjustments in the new programmes.
8 Reinforce the changes by demonstrating the relationship between new behaviours and organisational success.

Kotter (1996) organises each of these steps into three distinct phases. The first phase, creating a climate for change, includes steps 1, 2, and 3. The second phase, engaging and enabling the whole organisation, consists of steps 4, 5, and 6. The final phase, implementing and sustaining the change, encompasses steps 7 and 8.

ORGANISATIONAL DEVELOPMENT

In the last section we learned that leading change is a form of management control through the application of techniques that involves assisting employees to achieve a desired future with defined performance outcomes in line with the organisational strategy. Organisational development (OD) is an approach to organisational effectiveness that draws on behavioural and social sciences for understanding planned change efforts. French and Bell (1978) described organisational development as the long-term effort to improve an organisation's problem-solving and renewal processes. This improvement should occur through fostering

organisational development the concern for the vitalising, energising, actualising, activating, and renewing of organisations through technical and human resources the development of a more collaborative organisation culture characterised by team working arrangements and supported by a change agent and the use of applied behavioural sciences, including action research. OD offers a systematic framework on how and why people behave and organisations operate. Below we identify ten key perspectives and assumptions that underpin the field:

1   *Systems perspective:* Outstanding performance depends on interactions between and among the multiple elements of the organisation; between the people, processes, structure and values of the organisation, and between the organisation and its external environment.

2   *Alignment perspective:* The effectiveness of organisations will be determined by a state of congruence between people, process, structure, values and environment.

3   *Participation perspective:* People will become more committed to implementing solutions if they have been involved in the problem-solving process.

4   *Social-capital perspective:* To achieve outstanding performance, organisational leaders seek to create a network of interdependent relationships that provides the basis for trust, cooperation and collective action.

5   *Teamwork perspective:* Accepting a shared purpose and responsibility for interdependent tasks enhances coordination, commitment and creativity, and supports outstanding performance.

6   *Multiple stakeholder perspective:* Outstanding performance requires the organisational leaders to balance the expectations of multiple stakeholders: shareholders, employees, customers, suppliers, host community, labour unions, trade associations, governments and so on.

7   *Problem-solving perspective:* Conflicts over task issues can increase the quality of decisions if they occur in an environment of collaboration and trust.

8   *Open communications perspective:* Open and candid communication, especially upward in the hierarchy, creates the opportunity for learning and development while building trust and collaboration.

9   *Evolution/revolution perspective:* Organisations must develop competencies to engage in both incremental (evolutionary) and fundamental (revolutionary) change.

10 *Process facilitation perspective:* Individuals who reside outside of the organisational hierarchy can become both facilitators and teachers of effective implementation processes in partnership with organisational members.

DEFINING AND EXPLAINING ORGANISATIONAL DEVELOPMENT

French and Bell (1978) identified several characteristics that differentiate OD from more traditional change interventions. These consist of an emphasis on group and organisational processes, the work team as the key unit for learning more effective modes of organisation, the collaborative management of work-team culture, the use of employees as change agents and a view of the change effort as an ongoing process. French and Bell (1978) also indicated the key assumptions of OD. These centred on assumptions that employees are motivated if provided with an environment that is both supportive and challenging. In addition it supposes that employees wish to be accepted and to interact cooperatively and that the interplay of the dynamics of work teams has a powerful effect on the attitudes and behaviours of people. In particular the leadership style and the climate of the team are powerful in the change effort. Finally, organisational development efforts need to be sustained by corresponding changes in the appropriate compensation, training, staffing, task and communications system.

Organisations can draw on a number of OD techniques or interventions for bringing about change. We will outline three of these.

1 *Survey feedback approach.* This tool assesses the attitudes possessed by organisational members. For this approach employees are usually asked to complete a questionnaire about their perceptions and attitudes on a range of topics. Such topics include decision-making practices, communication effectiveness, coordination among units and satisfaction with the organisation, job, peers, and immediate supervisor.

2 *Team building.* Team building is an approach which focuses on goal-setting, the development of interpersonal relations among team members, role analysis to clarify each member's role and responsibilities and team process analysis to increase trust, improve coordinative efforts and accomplish work tasks.

3 *Appreciative inquiry.* This approach seeks to identify the unique qualities and special strengths of the organisation, which members can build on to improve performance. The approach consists of four steps: discovery, which sets out to identify what people think are the organisation's strengths; dreaming, where employees use information from the discovery phase to speculate on possible futures; design, where participants find a common vision of how the organisation will be in the future; and destiny, which involves writing action plans and developing implementation strategies.

Change at PharmaChem

You are a HR manager for an international organisation, PharmaChem, which distributes pharmaceutical products throughout Europe, the Middle East and recently in Indonesia. Despite a long history of growth through acquisition, some of the company's recent acquisitions, which have been led by a relatively new top team, have not delivered the anticipated level of benefit. The company faces increased external pressures from changes in the legal, technological and economic environments in which it operates. The CEO has turned to you for advice about the management of the current acquisition.

As part of a strategy to grow its share of the specialist pharmaceuticals market in Asia, the company has recently finalised a deal to acquire a local distributor, Pharmaceutical Solutions, which dominates the pharmaceuticals market in large parts of Asia.

This acquisition will involve operating in a completely foreign business environment characterised by poor infrastructure due to a lack of public infrastructure investment and endemically high levels of corruption. In addition, approximately 80 per cent of the population count themselves as Muslims, but it is also one of the most ethnically diverse. More than 500 languages are spoken in the country, and separatists are active in a number of provinces.

Pharmaceutical Solutions has four distribution depots

the acquisition will centre on consolidating existing sales and jointly developing new products and services to secure future business.

Questions:

Imagine that you have been asked as part of your role as HR Manager to advise PharmaChem about how to manage the integration of Pharmaceutical Solutions in Asia.

1 Outline what you see as issues which may act as barriers to the change process.
2 What advice would you give to the CEO regarding strategies to tackle the issues?
3 Which theories and concepts of managing change would inform the advice you would offer?

in the country and two of these depots will have to be closed to ensure operational efficiencies. This will result in a reduction in the number of depot staff. In addition there will be some overcapacity of middle managers. The focus after

 SUMMARY

 IN THE EBOOK, CLICK TO HEAR AN AUDIO SUMMARY

The purpose of this chapter has been to bring to your attention the area of change management, commencing with the nature of organisational change. We considered the key forces driving organisations to adjust their strategies and examined factors such as globalisation, technology and economic instability which have underpinned research aimed at understanding what makes change processes work. We also explained the three key phases of the planned change theory of Kurt Lewin. We highlighted that the success rate of major change initiatives within organisations has been less than expected. To understand this issue we focused on the question of why employees resist change in their organisations, and discussed the ways in which organisations can manage this resistance. We drew attention to the importance of a leader who develops a vision for change. We emphasised the central role of management practices involving communication, participation and consultation, planning and organisation, and an awareness of the personality types of the people involved and their level of receptivity towards the change. Finally, we presented the key assumptions and themes characterising the field of organisational development.

CHAPTER REVIEW QUESTIONS

1 Outline the different types of organisational change.
2 How can a manager analyse the change context?

3   What are the considerations for organisations when deciding upon the nature and type of change, and how change should take place?

4   What are some of the potential forces acting for and against a change initiative? Use Lewin's model as a guide.

5   How can organisational development (OD) improve organisational performance through managing change?

6   A significant feature of Kotter's model is the role of leadership in the management of change. Discuss this statement.

7   To what extent can the HR function act as a change agent during the change process?

8   Why do employees resist change efforts?

☑ MULTIPLE CHOICE QUESTIONS

In your ebook, click to take a multiple choice quiz to test your understanding of this chapter.

📖 FURTHER READING

Black, S. (2014). *It Starts With One: Changing Individuals Changes Organizations*, 3rd edn, New Jersey: Pearson.

Buchanan, D., Fitzgerald, L. and Ketley, D. (2007). *The Sustainability and Spread of Organizational Change*, London: Routledge.

Burke, W. (2002). *Organization Change: Theory and Practice*, Thousand Oaks, CA: Sage.

Clegg, C. and Walsh, S. (2004) Change Management: Time for Change? *European Journal of Work and Organizational Psychology*, 13(2): 217–29.

Hayes, J. (2014). *The Theory and Practice of Change Management*, 4th ed, Basingstoke: Palgrave.

Rafferty, A. and Restubog, S. (2010). The Impact of Change Process ad Context on Change Reactions and Turnover During a Merger, *Journal of Management*, 36(5): 1309–1338.

🌐 USEFUL WEBSITES

www.shrm.org

The Society for Human Resource Management provides relevant and current information on HR topics such as managing organisational change.

http://www.cipd.co.uk/pm/peoplemanagement/b/weblog/archive/2013/01/29/abridgetoofar-2005-08.aspx

A bridge too far by Lucie Carrington, 11 August 2005.

www.cipd.co.uk/pm/peoplemanagement/b/weblog/archive/2007/02/88/drillinspection-2007-02.aspx

Drill inspection by Bruce Tulgan, 22 February 2007.

These two CIPD factsheets concern the changing nature of the business environment in two different organisational scenarios – the US military and professional service firms.

GLOSSARY

Active listening is the process of making a conscious effort to sense, process and respond actively to a communicated message.

Affect describes the automatic and mainly non-conscious responses to stimuli.

Anticipated emotions are experienced when one imagines how one will feel in the future once certain desirable or undesirable future events have occurred.

Attitudes are evaluative judgements relating to people, events or objects.

Authority typically refers to positional power and relies on the assumption that others are willing to obey.

Change agents are managers who seek to reconfigure an organisation's roles, responsibilities, structures, outputs, processes, systems, technology or other resources in the light of improving organisational effectiveness.

Citizenship behaviour is discretionary behaviour that is often not formally recognised or rewarded by organisations but benefits the organisation and/or its members.

Classical conditioning is the process by which, through repeated association, a formerly neutral stimulus can elicit a reaction that was previously elicited only by another stimulus.

Cognitive dissonance is an unpleasant cognitive state that motivates an individual to resolve perceived conflict among beliefs, attitudes and behaviours.

Cognitive response refers to a thought created in response to persuasive communication.

Cognitive scripts are predetermined steps in our mind that tell us how to behave in a certain situation.

Command groups are permanent formal groups that are formed as a result of organisational structures.

Communicating is the sharing or exchanging of information.

Competencies describe the practical application of the knowledge, skills, attitudes, motivation, values, beliefs, cognitive style and personality that enable an individual to work effectively and autonomously in a clearly defined context.

Confirmation bias is a tendency to seek out information that is in line with expectations and existing knowledge.

Conflict describes a difference of interests between two or more parties which exists when one person believes that another disagrees with them over an issue or interest.

Content theories focus on the needs that motivate people. The internal drive that motivates specific behaviours in an attempt to fulfil the needs.

Contingency approach is an approach to organisational structure and design which argues that the choice of structure depends upon a range of contextual variables.

Contingency theories present a belief that there is no best way to lead.

Core affect momentary, elementary feelings of pleasure or displeasure and of activation or deactivation.

Counterfactual thinking is a human tendency to create possible alternatives to events that have already occurred; for example, by asking 'What if…?' or lamenting 'If only I had…'.

Counterproductive work behaviour is any intentional behaviour by an employee that is seen to be contrary to the organisation's interests.

Cross-functional teams have members from a range of functional departments within the organisation working towards a common goal.

CSE is a broad trait indicator that includes four more specific traits: internal locus of control, emotional stability, self-esteem and generalised self-efficacy.

Cultural change is the process of changing mind sets, behaviour and practices in an organisation; it is a long process which cannot be achieved effectively in a short timeframe.

Decoding is the process of deciphering and interpreting a received message in order to make sense of it.

Deep acting involves efforts to change the actual experience of an emotion in order to display this emotion in the workplace.

Deviant behaviours are those that are counterproductive to an organisation.

Differentiation is the extent to which the organisation is divided up into specialist parts and levels.

Discretionary effort is the level of effort people could give if they wanted to, but above and beyond the minimum required.

Discrimination is a negative action towards members of a specific group.

Distributed leadership is the idea that leadership of an organisation should not rest with a single individual, but should be shared or 'distributed' among those with the relevant skills.

Downward communication describes flows from one level of an organisation to a lower level.

Dysfunctional conflict is normally identified as something negative which is to be avoided or resolved as quickly as possible, and as something which can damage the organisation.

Emotional labour describes any job that requires the management of feeling to create a publicly observable facial and bodily display, including tone of voice.

Emotion regulation refers to the processes by which people manage their emotional states.

Emotions describe a conscious state which occurs briefly in response to a specific stimulus and is accompanied by bodily arousal and they make themselves observable through expression and behaviour.

Employee engagement is the degree to which an individual is attentive and absorbed in the performance of their role.

Empowerment is the process by which managers delegate power to employees who use it to make decisions affecting both themselves and their work.

Encoding is the process of designing a message, represented as a set of symbols to be sent, that makes sense to the receiver.

Equity theory is a process-based motivational theory that focuses on how individuals compare their circumstances to those of others and attempts to explain how such comparisons may motivate certain kinds of behaviour.

Ethics are codes that reflect our values and moral principles and drive our decisions and behaviours with respect to what is right and wrong, good and bad.

Evidence-based practice grounds decisions on the best presented scientific evidence.

Expectancy theory is a process-based theory of motivation that focuses on the thought processes people use when choosing between alternative courses of action and their anticipated consequences.

External 'pull' forces are motivational forces which come from the environment that surrounds the person.

Extinction is the absence of positive consequences in an effort to decrease undesirable behaviour.

Extrinsic rewards are tangible or physically given to an individual for accomplishing a task.

Formal groups are officially established, usually as a result of the organisation's structure, with a specific purpose.

Formalisation is the degree to which employee behaviour is governed by written rules, regulations and standardised procedures.

Functional conflict can be constructive and improve organisational performance.

Fundamental attribution error occurs when individuals attribute external causes to their own behaviour, and internal causes to the behaviour of others.

Goal-setting theory emphasises the importance of conscious goals and intentions in directing human behaviour.

Grapevine describes the informal communication networks in the organisation.

Group cohesiveness is the force that binds a group together.

Group conformity is the tendency of group members to consciously or unconsciously align their beliefs and behaviours with the apparent beliefs and behaviours of the group.

Group roles describe the pattern of behaviour expected of each group member.

Groups are two or more people who interact together to achieve a common objective and who are interdependent.

Groupthink occurs when maintaining group conformity is more important than critically evaluating alternative viewpoints, even if it means actively discouraging dissenting opinions.

Hierarchy describes the number of layers or levels of responsibility in an organisation.

Hierarchy cultures are present in organisations which have an internal focus, and demonstrate a strong interest in maintaining stability and control.

Hindsight bias refers to the tendency, after an event has occurred, to overestimate our ability to have foreseen the outcome.

Hygiene factors focus on lower-order needs and involve the presence or absence of job dissatisfiers, such as working conditions and pay.

Incremental change is a small change aimed at achieving certain goals.

Idiographic refers to an approach which describes personality in terms that are unique to the individual.

Individual differences are psychological ways in which people differ from each other and include factors such as intelligence, personality, and emotionality, and mean we can describe people according to their different personality characteristics.

Informal groups develop naturally in the workplace in response to a need for belonging.

In-group bias is the process whereby members of a group favour members of their own group over members of other groups.

In-groups are social groups to which an individual believes he or she belongs. In contrast, out-groups are social groups to which the individual believes he or she does not belong.

Innovation in business refers to the process of developing inventions or ideas into marketable goods, services or processes that customers want.

Integration describes how elements are linked together and interact towards achieving a common purpose.

Internal 'push' forces are motivational forces which come from the person.

Intrinsic rewards refer to outcomes that give an individual personal satisfaction, such as that derived from a job well done.

Job enrichment involves increasing the complexity of a job to provide a greater sense of responsibility, accomplishment and achievement.

Job involvement is the extent to which an employee psychologically identifies with their job.

Job satisfaction is a positive emotional state which exists as a consequence of appraising one's job and job experience.

Lateral communication flows between members or employees in the same work group or department, or managers at the same level.

Leadership is the ability to lead, guide and inspire a group of followers.

Leadership development comprises activities and practices that enhance the ability of leaders to work as part of a team to develop relationships with organisational stakeholders.

Management teams consist of individuals with managerial roles in different areas of the organisation who coordinate the work of their respective teams.

Mood is a long-term objectiveless affective response.

Motivation is a set of forces that make people behave in certain ways.

Motivators influence job satisfaction based on fulfilling higher-level needs such as achievement, recognition, responsibility.

Negative affectivity is a dispositional tendency to experience negative moods such as nervousness, annoyance and hostility.

Negative reinforcement occurs when an undesirable consequence decreases the likelihood of an individual engaging in an undesirable behaviour again.

Noise describes any factor, either external or internal, that interferes with transmission of a message through the creation of static or interference in the communication process.

Nomothetic refers to an approach which describes personality in terms of specific dimensions that vary across people.

Norms are the unwritten and unspoken rules and expectations of behaviour that apply to the members of a group.

Objective career success can be assessed by a third party and is usually measured by hierarchical level reached, the salary attained and/or the number of promotions received.

Organisational behaviour is a field of study which seeks to understand and improve organisational effectiveness by examining factors such as individuals, teams, and organisational culture and structure and the way they interact.

Organisational citizenship behaviour (OCB) is voluntary behaviour from the employee that is likely to have positive consequences for the organisation.

Organisational climate relates to 'how it feels' to work in an organisation, in contrast to organisational culture which refers to 'the way' in which tasks are completed.

Organisational commitment is an individual's comparative strength of identification and involvement with an organisation.

Organisational culture is the basic pattern of shared assumptions, values, beliefs, and practices that govern behaviour in an organisation. They are transmitted (and sometimes adapted) from one generation of employees to the next, and observed by all new organisational members.

Organisational design is a managerial process of deciding on and introducing a particular structural configuration.

Organisational development is the concern for the vitalising, energising, actualising, activating, and renewing of organisations through technical and human resources.

Organisational structure describes the formal pattern of tasks and relationships within an organisation aimed at coordinating employees towards achieving organisational goals.

Out-groups are social groups to which an individual believes he or she does not belong.

Perception comes from the Latin 'perceptio' and means 'comprehension' or literally 'a taking in'.

Perceptual defence occurs when an individual discounts information in order to defend his or her existing perception.

Perceptual distortions are the errors that people make in their perception of others and events.

Perceptual filters are personal characteristics or perceptions that influence the way individuals take in and make sense of information which can interfere with transmitting or receiving messages.

Perceptual set describes the set of internal factors which influence what stimuli we select and pay attention to.

Personality is typically defined as the relatively stable set of psychological characteristics that can distinguish one individual from another and can provide generalised predictions about a person's behaviour.

Planned change is change that an organisation consciously thinks about and decides to engage in, which is designed to specifically change organisational outcomes.

Political behaviour describes the conversion of power into action.

Positive affectivity is a dispositional tendency to experience pleasant moods such as enthusiasm and excitement.

Positive discrimination is the preferential treatment of members of a minority group over a majority group.

Positive reinforcements are desirable consequences that follow a behaviour and are likely to increase the chances of that behaviour being repeated in the future.

Power exists where person A can get person B to do something that B would not otherwise do.

Power tactics are the ways in which power bases are translated into actions.

Predictive validity is the extent to which a measurement tool accurately predicts future job behaviour or performance.

Prejudice is a negative attitude towards members of a specific group and can be either explicit or implicit.

Presenteeism is attendance at work while suffering with illness.

Problem-solving teams are formed specifically to find a solution to an existing problem.

Process of perception is the process of how we attend to, organise, interpret and react to stimuli.

Process theories focus on how people decide what actions to choose in order to meet their needs and how they decide whether these actions were successful.

Pro-social behaviours are those that benefit another party.

Punishments are unwanted consequences following an undesirable behaviour that are intended to decrease the likelihood of that behaviour being repeated.

Quantum or radical change is change that affects the entire organisation.

Relational interdependence is the degree of mutuality or give and take within a group.

Reliability is the extent to which a measure is consistent or repeatable.

Repression is a defensive mechanism by which anxiety-producing thoughts are pushed into the unconscious.

Resistance to change refers to action, overt or covert, exerted on behalf of maintaining the status quo.

Schema is a unique mental representation of the world around us and is based on information from our memories.

Scientific research is the systematic study of phenomena according to scientific principles.

Selective attention is the process through which we attend to certain stimuli and select out others.

Self-actualisation refers to a person's desire to reach their full potential, to grow and develop to achieve your absolute potential and to use your abilities to the greatest extent.

Self-managed work teams (SMWT) consist of a small number of employees who have been given autonomy to plan and manage their team's day-to-day activities with relatively little supervision.

SMART goal-setting identifies goals which are specific, measurable, achievable, realistic and time-bound.

Socialisation is the process of learning how to think, feel and behave by conforming to and imitating influential others within social settings.

Social loafing refers to a team member who benefits from team membership but does not actively participate in, or contribute to, the team's work.

Span of control describes how many people a manager has to supervise.

Stereotyping is the tendency to assign a set of characteristics to a group of people or to an individual.

Strong organisational cultures are those in which the company values are widely held and felt by all members of the organisation.

Strong situations are those in which the rules and expectations of the social context control the behaviour of people regardless of their personality.

Subcultures hold the core assumptions of the dominant culture, as well as supplementary assumptions unique to members of particular sections of the organisation.

Surface acting is displaying an emotion that is not felt.

Synergy occurs when the effect of combining efforts leads to more creative or effective outcomes than would have been achieved had each individual operated alone.

Systems thinking is an approach that considers the organisation as a system made of different parts that affect and are affected by one another. Similarly the organisation interacts with its larger environment.

Task groups are temporary groups designed to deal with specific issues and are dismantled once the task is complete.

Task interdependence is the degree of mutual reliance and reciprocity within the group.

Team motivation arises when there is agreed collective effort on the part of a group of people aimed at achieving a common goal.

Team role refers to a pattern of behaviour or set of characteristics that is displayed in the way one team member interacts with another when serving to progress the performance of the team towards its aims.

Teams are groups of people working together with a defined purpose in order to achieve a common goal.

Theories are collections of assertions that specify how and why variables are related, as well as the circumstances in which they should and should not be related.

Trait affectivity describes people's tendency to experience pleasant or unpleasant emotional states.

Trait theories describe people in terms of enduring personality characteristics.

Transactional leadership is a leadership style that focuses on managing and supervising employees.

Transformational leadership is a leadership style that can inspire positive changes in those who follow.

Turnover intentions are an employee's self-reported intentions to leave their job.

Type theories place individuals into predetermined categories, thereby identifying them as a particular personality type.

Unplanned or emergent change is change that the organisation did not initiate or had no control over planning.

Upward communication flows from a lower level of an organisation to a higher level.

Valence is the extent to which an individual values a particular outcome.

Validity is the extent to which a measurement tool measures what it purports to measure.

Values and beliefs can be defined as basic convictions or ideals about desirable behaviour and outcomes.

Virtual teams comprise team members who are dispersed geographically, and communicate and collaborate together through the use of a variety of electronic systems.

Weak organisational cultures are those in which the values of the company are not widely held by members of the organisation.

Work values are the general and relatively stable goals that people try to reach through work.

BIBLIOGRAPHY

ACAS (2012) How to manage change. Available at: www. acas.org.uk/media/pdf/k/m/Acas-How-to-manage-change-advisory-booklet.pdf (accessed 22 October 2015).

Adler, R.B, Rosenfeld, L.B. and Proctor, R.F. (2012) *Interplay: The process of interpersonal communication*, 12th edn. New York: Oxford University Press.

Ajzen, I. (1991) The theory of planned behavior. *Organizational Behavior and Human Decision Processes*, 50(2), 179–211.

Alas, R. and Sharifi, S. (2002) Organizational learning and resistance to change in Estonian companies, *Human Resource Development International*, 5(3), 313–331.

Allen, N.J. and Meyer, J.P. (1990) The measurement and antecedents of affective, continuance and normative commitment to the organization. *Journal of Occupational Psychology*, 63(1), 1–18.

Allinson, C.W. (1984) *Bureaucratic Personality and Organizational Structure*. Aldershot: Gower.

Allport, G.W. (1935) *Attitudes: A Handbook of Social Psychology*. Worcester, MA: Clark University Press.

Allport, G.W. (1954) *The Nature of Prejudice*. Reading, MA: Addison-Wesley.

Allport, G.W. and Odbert, H.S. (1936) Trait-names: A psycho-lexical study. *Psychological Monographs* 47(1), i–171.

Anand, N. and Daft, R. (2007) 'What is the right organization design?' *Organizational Dynamics*, 36(4): 329–344.

Armenakis, A., Harris, S. and Mossholder, K. (1993) Creating readiness for organizational change, *Human Relations*, 46(6), 81–703.

Aronson, E. (2007) *The Social Animal*, 10th edn. New York and Oxford: Freeman.

Arvey, R.D., Harpaz, I. and Liao, H. (1996) Work centrality and post-award work behavior of lottery winners. *The Journal of Psychology*, 138(5), 404–420.

Asch, S.E. (1951) *Social Psychology*. New York: Prentice-Hall.

Ashforth, B.E. and Humphrey, R.H. (1993) Emotional labor in service roles: The influence of identity. *Academy of Management Review*, 18, 88–115.

Ashkanasy, N., Wilderom, C. and Peterson, M. (eds) (2000) *Handbook of Organizational Culture and Climate*. Thousand Oaks, CA: Sage.

Ashleigh, M.J. and Mansi, A. (2012) *The Psychology of People in Organisations*. Harlow: Pearson.

Ashton-Jones, C.E. and Ashkanasy, N.M. (2008) Affective events theory: A strategic perspective. In W.J. Zerbe, C.E.J. Hartel and N.M. Ashkanasy (eds), *Emotions, Ethics and Decision-making*. Bingley: JAI Press.

Association of American Colleges and Universities (2013) *It Takes More Than a Major: Employer priorities for college learning and student success*. Washington: Hart Research Associates.

Bacharach, S. and Bamberger, P. (2007) 9/11 and New York City firefighters' post hoc unit support and control climates: A context theory of the consequences of involvement in traumatic work-related events, *Academy of Management Journal*, 50(4), 849–868.

Bagozzi, R.P., Baumgartner, H. and Pieters, R. (1998) Goal-directed emotions. *Cognition & Emotion*, 12, 1–26.

Bagozzi, R.P., Dholakia, U.M. and Basuroy, S. (2003) How effortful decisions get enacted: The motivating role of decision processes, desires, and anticipated emotions. *Journal of Behavioral Decision Making*, 16, 273–295.

Baker, W.K. (2004) Antecedents and consequences of job satisfaction: Testing a comprehensive model using integrated methodology. *Journal of Applied Business Research*, 20(3), 31–43.

Bakker, A., Demerouti, E. and Schaufeli, W. (2003) Dual processes at work in a call centre: An application of the job demands–resources model. *European Journal of Work and Organizational Psychology*, 12(4), 393–417.

Bakker, A.B. and Oerlemans, W. (2011) Subjective well-being in organizations. In K.S. Cameron and G.M. Spreitzer (eds), *The Oxford Handbook of Positive Organizational Scholarship*. New York: Oxford University Press.

Bandura, A. (1986) *Social Foundations of Thought and Action: A social-cognitive view*. Englewood Cliffs, NJ: Prentice-Hall.

Barrick, M.R., Mount, M.K. and Judge, T.A. (2001) Personality and performance at the beginning of the new millennium: What do we know and where do we go next? *International Journal of Selection and Assessment*, 9(1–2), 9–30.

Barrick, M.R., Patton, G.K. and Haugland, S.N. (2000), Accuracy of interviewer judgments of job applicant personality traits. Personnel Psychology, 53: 925–951.

Barsade, S.G. and Gibson, D.E. (2007) Why does affect matter in organizations? *Academy of Management Perspectives*, 21, 36–59.

Barsade, S., Brief, A. and Spataro, S. (2003) The affective revolution in organizational behavior: The emergence of a paradigm. In J. Greenberg (ed.), *Organizational Behavior: The State of the Science*. Mahwah, NJ: Lawrence Erlbaum Associates.

Bass, B.M. (1985) *Leadership and Performance Beyond Expectations*. New York: Free Press.

Bass, B.M. (1990) *Bass & Stogdill's Handbook of Leadership*, 3rd edn. New York: Free Press.

Bass, B. (1999) Two decades of research and development in transformational leadership, *European Journal of Work and Organizational Psychology*, 8(1), 9–32.

Batenburg, R., Walbeek, W. van, Maur, W. in der (2013) Belbin role diversity and team performance: Is there a relationship? *Journal of Management Development*, 32(8), 901–913.

Baumeister, R.F., Dewall, C.N. and Zhang, L. (2007a) Do emotions improve or hinder the decision making process? In K.D. Vohs, R.F. Baumeister and G. Loewenstein (eds), *Do Emotions Help or Hurt Decision Making? A hedgefoxian perspective*. New York: Russell Sage Foundation.

Baumeister, R.F., Vohs, K.D., Dewall, C.N. and Zhang, L. (2007b) How emotion shapes behavior: Feedback, anticipation, and reflection, rather than direct causation. *Personality and Social Psychology Review*, 11, 167–203.

Beal, D.J., Cohen, R., Burke, M.J. and McLendon, C.L. (2003) Cohesion and performance in groups: A meta-analytic clarification of construct relation. *Journal of Applied Psychology*, 88, 989–1004.

Beal, D.J., Trougakos, J.P., Weiss, H.M. and Green, S.G. (2006) Episodic processes in emotional labor: Perceptions of affective delivery and regulation strategies. *Journal of Applied Psychology*, 91, 1053–1065.

Belbin, R.M. (1993a). A reply to the Belbin team-role self-perception inventory by Furnham, Steele and Pendleton. *Journal of Occupational and Organizational Psychology*, 66(3), 259–260.

Belbin, R.M. (1993b) *Team Roles at Work*. Oxford: Butterworth-Heinemann.

Belbin, R.M. (2012) *Team Roles at Work*. Routledge.

Bendersky, C. and Shah, N.P. (2013) The downfall of extroverts and rise of neurotics: The dynamic process of status allocation in task groups. *Academy of Management Journal*, 56(2), 387–406.

Benne, K.D. and Sheats, P. (1948) Functional Roles of Group Members. *Journal of Social Issues*, 4, 41–49.

Bennis, W.G. (1959) Leadership theory and administrative behavior: The problem of authority. *Administrative Science Quarterly*, 259–301.

Bennis, W. and Nanus, B. (2003) *Leaders: Strategies for taking charge*. New York: HarperCollins.

Bertalanffy, von, L. (1968) *General System Theory: Essays on its foundation and development*, rev. edn. New York: George Braziller.

Blake, R.R. and Mouton, J.S. (1962) *Managerial Grid*. Advanced Management-Office Executive.

Blenko, M.W., Mankins M.C. and Rogers P. (2009) Decide & deliver: 5 steps to breakthrough performance in your organization, *Harvard Business Review*, hbr.org/2010/01/stat-watch/ar/1.

Bohlander, G. and Snell, S. (2009) *Managing Human Resource Management*. Cengage Learning.

Bolden, R., Petrov, G. and Gosling, J. (2008) Tensions in higher education leadership: Towards a multi-level model of leadership practice, *Higher Education Quarterly*, 62(4), 358–76.

Bolger, N. and Zuckerman, A. (1995) A framework fo studying personality in the stress process. *Journal of Personality and Social Psychology*, 69, 890–902.

Boone, L.E. and Kurtz, D.L. (2010) *Contemporary Business*. Chichester: Wiley.

Bordia, P., Hobman, E., Joes, E., Gallois, C. and Callan, V. (2004) Uncertainty during organizational change: Types, consequences, and management strategies, *Journal of Business and Psychology*, 18(4), 507–532.

Bouckenooghe, D. (2010) Positioning change recipients' attitudes towards change in the organizational change literature, *Journal of Applied Behavioural Science*, 46(4), 500–531.

Bowditch, J.L. and Buono, A.F. (2005) *A Primer on Organizational Behavior*, 6th edn. Hoboken, NJ: John Wiley.

Boyce, A.S., Nieminen, L.R.G., Gillespie, M.A., Ryan, A.M. and Denison, D.R. (2015) Which comes first, organizational culture or performance? A longitudinal study of causal priority with automobile dealerships, *Journal of Organizational Behaviour*, 36(3), 339–359.

Boydell, T., Burgoyne, J. and Pedler, M. (2004) Suggested development. *People Management*, 10(4), 32–34

Brady, D. (2006) #?@ the e-mail. Can we talk? *BusinessWeek* (December 4).

Branson, R. (2014) *The Virgin Way: Everything I know about leadership*. London: Portfolio.

Bratton, J. (2015) *Introduction to Work and Organizational Behaviour*, 3rd edn. London: Palgrave.

Brenner, B., Schlegelmilch, B.B. and Ambos, B. (2013) Inside the NIKE matrix. Available at: http://epub.wu.ac.at/3791/1/Nike__WU-CaseSeries.pdf (accessed 31 August 2015).

Brief, A.P. and Weiss, H.M. (2002) Organizational behavior: Affect in the workplace. *Annual Review of Psychology*, 53, 279–307.

Briner, R.B. (1999) The neglect and importance of emotion at work. *European Journal of Work and Organizational Psychology*, 8, 323–346.

Britt, T.W. (2003) Black Hawk Down at work. *Harvard Business Review*, 81(1), 16–17.

Broucek, W.G. and Randell, G. (1996) An Assessment of the construct validity of the Belbin self-perception inventory and observer's assessment from the perspective of the five-factor model. *Journal of Occupational and Organizational Psychology* 69, 389–405

Brown, S.P. (1996) A meta-analysis and review of organizational research on job involvement. *Psychological Bulletin*, 120(2), 235–255.

Brustein, J. (2013) How to cope with e-mail overload at work, *Bloomberg BusinessWeek*, 19 December 2013. Available at: www.bloomberg.com/bw/articles/2013–12–19/asanas-justin-rosenstein-on-e-mail-overload (accessed 27 April 2014).

Burns, J.M. (1978) *Leadership*. New York: Harper & Row.

Burns, T. and Stalker, G.M. (1966) *The Management of Innovation*, London: Tavistock.

Burrus, D. (2012) Did social media play a role in Obama's victory? *Huffington Post*, 11 September 2012. Available at: www.huffingtonpost.com/daniel-burrus/did-social-media-play-a-r_b_2094145.html (accessed 31 October 2014).

Business & Leadership (2014) Bitbuzz registered user numbers up 81pc in 2013. *Business and Leadership*, 6 January.

Butler, E.A. and Gross, J.J. (2009) Emotion and emotion regulation: Integrating individual and social levels of analysis. *Emotion Review*, 1, 86–87.

Byrne, M., Flood, B. and Shanahan, D. (2012) A qualitative exploration of oral communication apprehension. *Accounting Education: An International Journal*, 21(6), 565–581.

Cai, D.A. and Fink, E.L. (2009) Communicate successfully by seeking balance. In E.A. Locke *Handbook of Principles of Organizational Behaviour: Indispensable knowledge for evidence-based management*. Chichester: Wiley.

Cairnross, F. (2001) *The Death of Distance: How the communications revolution is changing our lives*. Cambridge, MA: Harvard University Press.

Cameron, A.F. and Webster, J. (2005) Unintended consequences of emerging communication technologies: Instant messaging in the workplace. *Computers in Human Behavior*, 21, 85–103.

Cameron, K.S. and Quinn, R.E. (1999) *Diagnosing and Changing Organizational Culture Based on the Competing Values Framework*. Reading, MA: Addison-Wesley.

Carron, A.V., Bray, S.R. and Eys, M.A. (2002) Team cohesion and team success in sport. *Journal of Sports Sciences*, 20(2), 119–127.

Carver, C.S. (2001) Affect and the functional bases of behavior: On the dimensional structure of affective experience. *Personality and Social Psychology Review*, 5, 345–356.

Carver, C.S. and Scheier, M.F. (2008) Feedback processes in the simultaneous regulation of action and affect. In J. Shah and W.L. Gardner (eds), *Handbook of Motivation Science*. New York: Guilford Press.

Cascio, W.F. (2000) Managing a Virtual Workplace, *Academy of Management Executive*, 14(3), 81–90.

Catalyst (2004) Women and men in U.S. corporate leadership. Same workplace, different realities? Available at: www.catalyst.org/system/files/Women%20and_Men_in_U.S._Corporate_Leadership_Same_Workplace_Different_Realities.pdf (accessed 10 April 2015).

Cattell, R.B. (1965) *The Scientific Analysis of Personality*. Baltimore: Penguin Books.

Child, J. (2005) *Organization. Contemporary principles and practices*. Oxford, Blackwell Publishing.

CIPD (2002) Variations on a team. People Management editorial, 7 February. Available at: www.cipd.co.uk/pm/peoplemanagement/b/weblog/archive/2013/01/29/6143a-2002-02.aspx (accessed 7 September 2015).

Clark, R.E. (2003) Fostering the work motivation of individuals and teams. *Performance Improvement*, 42(3), 21–29.

Clark, R.E. and Estes, F. (2002) *Turning Research into Results: A guide to selecting the right performance solutions*. Atlanta, GA: CEP Press.

Clore, G.L., Gaspar, K. and Garvin, E. (2001) Affect as information. In J.P. Forgas (ed.), *Handbook of Affect and Social Cognition*. Mahwah, NJ: Erlbaum.

Connell, R.W. (1972) Political socialization in the American family: The evidence re-examined. *Public Opinion Quarterly*, 36(3), 323–333.

Conte, J.M. (2005) A review and critique of emotional intelligence measures. *Journal of Organizational Behavior*, 26, 433–440.

Cordery, J.L., Mueller, W.S. and Smith, L.M. (1991) Attitudinal and behavioral effects of autonomous group working: A longitudinal field study. *Academy of Management Journal*, 34, 464–476.

Correll, S.J., Benard, S. and Paik, I. (2007) Getting a job: Is there a motherhood penalty? *American Journal of Sociology*, 112, 1297–1339.

Cuddy, A.J.C., Fiske, S.T. and Glick, P. (2004) When professionals become mothers, warmth doesn't cut the ice. *Journal of Social Issues*, 60, 701–718.

Cummings, J.N., Butler, B. and Kraut, R. (2000) The quality of online social relationships. *Communications of the ACM*, 45(2), 103–8. Available at: http://citeseerx.ist.psu.edu (accessed 31 October 2014).

Cunningham, I. (1986) Self-managed learning. In A. Mumford (ed.), *Handbook of Management Development*. Aldershot: Gower.

Daft, R. (2004) *Organization Theory and Design*, 8th edn. Mason, OH: South-Western.

Dahl, R.A. (1957) The Concept of Power. *Behavioural Science*, 2(3), 201–215.

Davies, B. (2011) *Leading the Strategically Focused School: Success and sustainability*. Sage.

Day, D.V., Harrison, M.M. and Halpin, S.M. (2009) *An Integrative Approach to Leader Development: Connecting adult development, identity, and expertise* New York: Routledge.

De Hauw, S. and De Vos, A. (2010) Millennials' career perspective and psychological contract expectations: does the recession lead to lowered expectations? *Journal of Business and Psychology*, 25(2), 293–302.

De Neve, J.E., Mikhaylov, S., Dawes, C.T., Christakis, N.A. and Fowler, J.H. (2013) Born to lead? A twin design and genetic association study of leadership role occupancy. *The Leadership Quarterly*, 24(1), 45–60.

De Vos, A., Buyens, D. and Schalk, R. (2005) Making sense of a new employment relationship: psychological contract-related information seeking and the role of work values and locus of control. *International Journal of Selection and Assessment*, 13(1), 41–52.

Deal T.E. and Kennedy, A.A. (1982) *Corporate Cultures: The rites and rituals of corporate life*. Harmondsworth: Penguin.

Delarue, A., Van Hootegem, G., Procter, S. and Burridge, M. (2008) Teamworking and organizational performance: A review of survey-based research. *International Journal of Management Reviews* 10(2), 127–148.

Deloitte (2014) *The Corporate Learning Factbook 2014: Benchmarks, trends, and analysis of the U.S. training market*. New York: Deloitte Development LLC.

Denison, D.R. and Mishra, A.K. (1995) Toward a theory of organizational culture and effectiveness. *Organization Science*, 6(2), 204–223.

Dennis, A.R., Fuller, R.M. and Valacich, J.S. (2008) Media, tasks, and communication processes: A theory of media synchronicity. *MIS Quarterly*, 32, 575–600.

Detert, J.R., Schroeder, R.G. and Mauriel, J.J. (2000) A framework for linking culture and improvement initiatives in organizations. *Academy of Management Review*, 25, 850–863.

Deutsch, M. and Collins, M.E. (1951) *Interracial Housing: A psychological evaluation of a social experiment*. University of Minnesota Press.

Development Dimensions International (2009) *Holding Women Back: Troubling discoveries – and best practices for helping women leaders succeed*. DDI Consulting.

Dijk, R. and Dick, R. (2009) Navigating organizational change: Change leaders, employee resistance and work based identities. *Journal of Change Management*, 9(2), 143–163.

Dijkstra, M.T.M., Van Dierendonck, D., Evers, A. and De Dreu, C.K.W. (2004) Conflict and well-being at work: The moderating role of personality. *Journal of Managerial Psychology*, 20(2), 87–104.

Dries, N. and De Gieter, S. (2014), Information asymmetry in high potential programs. *Personnel Review,* 43(1), 136–162.

Drucker, P.F. (2011) *Managing the Non-profit Organization.* New York: Routledge.

DuBrin, A.J. (2001) *Leadership,* 3rd edn. New York: Houghton Mifflin.

Dunn, B. (2012) When should I listen to my heart? In P. Totterdell and K. Niven (eds), *Should I Strap a Battery to my Head? (and Other Questions about Emotion).* Self-published.

Eagly, A.H. (2013) Sex Differences in Social Behavior: A social-role interpretation. Lawrence Earlbaum Associates, London.

Egan, G. (1996) *Change Agent Skills: Managing innovation and change,* Englewood Cliffs, NJ: Prentice Hall.

Egan, T.M., Yang, B. and Bartlett, K.R. (2004) The effects of organizational learning culture and job satisfaction on motivation to transfer learning and turnover intention. *Human Resource Development Quarterly,* 15(3), 279–301.

Ekman, P. (1984) Expression and the nature of emotion. In K. Scherer and P. Ekman (eds), *Approaches to Emotion* (Vol. 3). Hillsdale, NJ: Erlbaum.

Ekvall, G. (1996) Organizational climate for creativity and innovation. *European Journal of Work and Organizational Psychology,* 5(1), 105–123.

Ellinger, A.D. and Kim, S. (2014) Coaching and human resource development: Examining relevant theories, coaching genres, and scales to advance research and practice. *Advances in Developing Human Resources,* 16(2), 127–138.

Elron, E. and Vigoda-Gadot, E. (2006) Influence and political processes in cyberspace: case of global virtual teams. *International Journal of Cross-Cultural Management,* 6(3), 295–317.

Ely, R.J., Ibarra, H. and Kolb, D.M. (2011) Taking gender into account: Theory and design for women's leadership development programs. *Academy of Management Learning & Education,* 10(3), 474–493.

Engel, D., Woolley, A.W., Jing, L.X., Chabris, C.F. and Malone, T.W. (2014) *Reading the Mind in the Eyes or Reading between the Lines? Theory of mind predicts collective intelligence equally well online and face-to-face.* PLoS ONE 9(12): e115212.

Erez, M. and Earley, P.C. (1993) *Culture, Self-identity, and Work.* New York: Oxford University Press.

Evans, C.R. and Dion, K.L. (1991) Group cohesion and performance: A meta-analysis. *Small Group Research,* 22, 175–186.

Eysenck, H. (1965) *Fact and Fiction in Psychology.* Penguin.

Feldman Barrett, L., and Russell, J. A. (1998). Independence and bipolarity in the structure of current affect. *Journal of Personality and Social Psychology,* 74(4), 967–984.

Feldman, D.C. (1976) Contingency theory of socialization. *Administrative Science Quarterly,* 21(3), 433–452.

Feldman, D.C. (1981) The multiple socialization of organization members. *Academy of Management Review,* 6(2), 309–318.

Feldman, D.C. (1984) The development and emergence of group norms. *Academy of Management Review,* 9, 47–53.

Festinger, L. (1957) *A Theory of Cognitive Dissonance.* Evanston, Ill: Row Peterson.

Fiedler, F.E. (1971) *Personality and situational determinants of leader behavior* (Technical Report), Seattle: University of Washington, Department of Psychology.

Fiedler, F.E. and Chemers, M.M. (1974) *Leadership and Effective Management.* Glenview, IL: Scott, Foresman.

Fisher, C.D. and Ashkanasy, N.M. (2000) The emerging role of emotions in work life: An introduction. *Journal of Organizational Behavior,* 21, 123–129.

Fisher, R. and Ury, W. (1983) *Getting to Yes: Negotiating agreement without giving in.* New York: Penguin.

Floyd, W.S. and Wooldridge, B. (1997) Middle management's strategic influence and organisational performance. *Journal of Management Studies,* 34, 465–485.

Floyd, W.S. and Wooldridge, B. (2000) *Building Strategy from the Middle: Reconceptualizing the strategy process.* Thousand Oaks, CA: Sage.

Forgas, J.P. et al. (2007) When sad is better than happy: Negative affect can improve the quality and effectiveness of persuasive messages and social influence strategies. *Journal of Experimental Social Psychology,* 43(4), 513–528.

Forgas, J.P. (2008) The role of affect in attitudes and attitude change. In W.D. Crano and R. Prislin (eds), *Attitudes and Attitude Change.* New York: Psychology Press.

Forgas, J.P. and George, J.M. (2001) Affective influences on judgments and behavior in organizations: An information processing perspective. *Organizational Behavior and Human Decision Processes,* 86, 3–34.

Foss, N.J., Minbaeva, D., Pederseon, T. and Reinholt, M. (2009) The impact of autonomy, task identity, and feedback on employee motivation to share knowledge. *Human Resource Management,* 48(1), 871–893.

Fox, A. (1966) *Industrial Sociology and Industrial Relations, Research Paper No 3 to the Royal Commission on Trade Unions and Employers' Associations*. London, HMSO.

Franzoi, S. (2009) *Social Psychology*, 5th edn. New York: McGraw-Hill.

Fredrickson, B.L. (1998) What good are positive emotions? *Review of General Psychology*, 2, 300–319.

Fredrickson, B.L. and Cohn, M.A. (2008) Positive emotions. In M. Lewis, J.M. Haviland-Jones and L. Feldman Barrett (eds), *Handbook of Emotions*. New York: Guilford Press.

French, W. and Bell, C. (1978) *Organizational Development: Behavioural science interventions for organization improvement*, 2nd edn. Englewood Cliffs, NJ: Prentice.

French, J.R.P. and Raven, B. (1959) The Bases of Social Power. In D Cartwright (ed.), *Studies in Social Power*. Ann Arbor, MI: Institute for Social Research.

French, R., Rayner, C., Rees, G. and Rumbles, S. (2011) *Organizational Behaviour*, 2nd edn. Chichester: Wiley.

Frenkel-Brunswik, E. and Sanford, R.N. (1945) Some personality factors in anti-Semitism. *The Journal of Psychology*, 20(2), 271–291.

Frijda, N.H. (1986) *The Emotions*. New York: Cambridge University Press.

Frijda, N.H. (2008) The psychologists' point of view. In M. Lewis, J.M. Haviland-Jones and L. Feldman Barrett (eds), *Handbook of Emotions*. New York: Guilford Press.

Fulmer, I.S., Gerhart, B. and Scott, K.S. (2003) Are the 100 Best better? An empirical investigation of the relationship between being a 'Great Place to Work' and firm performance *Personnel Psychology*, 56, 965–993.

Galbraith, J., Downey, D. and Kates, A. (2002) *Designing Dynamic Organizations*. New York: American Management Association.

Gambrel, P.A. and Cianci, R. (2003) Maslow's hierarchy of needs: Does it apply in a collectivist culture. *Journal of Applied Management and Entrepreneurship*, 8(3), 143–161.

George, J.M. (1989) Mood and absence. *Journal of Applied Psychology*, 74, 317–324.

George, J.M. (1991) State or trait: Effects of positive mood on prosocial behaviors at work. *Journal of Applied Psychology*, 76, 299–307.

Gibb, C.A. (1947) The principles and traits of leadership *The Journal of Abnormal and Social Psychology*, 42(3), 267.

Glass, N. and Hume, T. (2013) The 'hallelujah moment' behind the invention of the Post-it note. CNN, 4 April 2013. Available at: http://edition.cnn.com/2013/04/04/tech/post-it-note-history/ (accessed 17 April 2014).

Glick, P. and Fiske, S.T. (2001) Ambivalent stereotypes as legitimizing ideologies: Differentiating paternalistic and envious prejudice. In J. Jost and B. Major (eds), *The Psychology of Legitimacy*. Cambridge: Cambridge University Press.

Glisson, C. and James, L.R. (2002) The cross-level effects of culture and climate in human service teams. *Journal of Organizational Behavior*, 23, 767–794.

Goette, L. and Huffman, D. (2007) Affect and cognition as a source of motivation: A new model and evidence from natural experiments. In K.D. Vohs, R.F. Baumeister and G. Loewenstein (eds), *Do Emotions Help or Hurt Decision Making? A hedgefoxian perspective*. New York: Russell Sage Foundation.

Gökçen, E., Furnham, A., Mavroveli, S. and Petrides, K. (2014) A cross-cultural investigation of trait emotional intelligence in Hong Kong and the UK. *Personality and Individual Differences*, 65, 30–35.

Goleman, D. (1995) *Emotional Intelligence: Why it can matter more than IQ*. New York: Bantam Books.

Goleman, D. (1998) *Working with Emotional Intelligence*. New York: Random House LLC.

Goold, M. and Campbell, A. (2002a) *Designing Effective Organizations*. San Francisco: Jossey-Bass.

Goold, M. and Campbell, A. (2002b) Do you have a well-designed organization? *Harvard Business Review*, March, 117–124.

Gooty, J., Gavin, M. and Ashkanasy, N.M. (2009) Emotions research in OB: The challenges that lie ahead. *Journal of Organizational Behavior*, 30, 833–838.

Gosling, S.D., Rentfrow, P.J. and Swann Jr., W.B. (2003) A very brief measure of the Big-Five personality domains. *Journal of Research in Personality*, 37, 504–528.

Graen, G.B. and Uhl-Bien, M. (1995) Relationship-based approach to leadership: Development of leader-member exchange (LMX) theory of leadership over 25 years: Applying a multi-level multi-domain perspective. *The Leadership Quarterly*, 6(2), 219–247.

Greenberg, J. (2011) *Behaviour in Organizations*, 10th edn. Harlow: Pearson.

Greenwald, A.G. (1968) Cognitive learning, cognitive response to persuasion, and attitude change. *Psychological Foundations of Attitudes*, 1, 147–170.

Grieg, A. (2013) All the lonely Facebook friends: Study shows social media makes us MORE lonely and unhappy and LESS sociable. Available at: www.dailymail.co.uk/news/article-2419419/All-lonely-Facebook-friends-Study-shows-social-media-

makes-MORE-lonely-unhappy-LESS-sociable.
html#ixzz33U3nWSHm (accessed 20 May 2014).

Griffin, M.A., Patterson, M.G. and West, M.A. (2001) Job satisfaction and teamwork: The role of supervisor support. *Journal of Organizational Behavior*, 22(5), 537–550.

Griffin, R.W. (2014) *Fundamentals of Management*. Mason, OH: South-Western Cengage Learning.

Gross, J.J. (1998) Antecedent- and response-focused emotion regulation: Divergent consequences for experience, expression, and physiology. *Journal of Personality and Social Psychology*, 74, 224–237.

Gross, J.J. (1999) Emotion regulation: Past, present, future. *Cognition & Emotion*, 13, 551–573.

Gross, J.J. and John, O.P. (2003) Individual differences in two emotion regulation processes: Implications for affect, relationships, and well-being. *Journal of Personality and Social Psychology*, 85, 348–362.

Gross, J.J. and Thompson, R.A. (2007) Emotion regulation: Conceptual foundations. In J.J. Gross (ed.), *Handbook of Emotion Regulation*. New York: Guilford Press.

Guest, D.E. (2004) The psychology of the employment relationship: An analysis based on the psychological contract. *Applied Psychology*, 53(4), 541–555.

Hackman, J.R. and Oldham, G.R. (1976) Motivation through the design of work: Test of a theory. *Organizational Behavior and Human Performance*, 16, 256.

Hallberg, U.E. and Schaufeli, W.B. (2006) 'Same same' but different? Can work engagement be discriminated from job involvement and organizational commitment? *European Psychologist*, 11(2), 119.

Hannah, S.T., Balthazard, P.A., Waldman, D.A., Jennings, P L. and Thatcher, R.W. (2013) The psychological and neurological bases of leader self-complexity and effects on adaptive decision-making. *Journal of Applied Psychology*, 98, 393–411.

Harrison, D.A., Newman, D.A. and Roth, P.L. (2006) How important are job attitudes? Meta-analytic comparisons of integrative behavioral outcomes and time sequences. *Academy of Management Journal*, 49(2), 305–325.

Harrison, M.S. and Thomas, K.M. (2009), The hidden prejudice in selection: A research investigation on skin color bias. *Journal of Applied Social Psychology*, 39, 134–168.

Hart, E. (1996) Top Teams, *Management Review*, February, 43–47.

Harter, J.K., Schmidt, F.L. and Hayes, T.L. (2002) Business-unit-level relationship between employee satisfaction, employee engagement, and business outcomes: A meta-analysis. *Journal of Applied Psychology*, 87(2), pp. 268.

Hartnell, C., Ou, A. and Kinicki, A. (2011) Organizational culture and organizational effectiveness: A meta-analytic investigation of the competing values framework's theoretical suppositions. *Journal of Applied Psychology*, 96(4), 677–694

Hayes, J. (2014) *The Theory and Practice of Change Management*, 4th edn. Basingstoke: Palgrave.

Hayes, J. and Hyde, P. (1998) *Managing the Merger: A Change Management Simulation*. Novi, MI: Organizational Learning Tools.

Heider, F. (1958) *The Psychology of Interpersonal Relations*. New York: Wiley.

Heimler, R., Rosenberg, S. and Morote, E.S. (2012) Predicting career advancement with structural equation modelling. *Education + Training*, 54(2), 85–94.

Heine, S.J. and Buchtel, E.E. (2009) Personality: The universal and the culturally specific. *Annual Review of Psychology*, 60, 369–394.

Hermann, A. and Rammal, H.G. (2010) The grounding of the 'flying bank'. *Management Decision*, 48(7), 1051.

Hersey, P. and Blanchard, K.H. (1969) Life cycle theory of leadership. *Training and Development Journal*, 23(2), 26–34.

Hersey, P. and Blanchard, K.H. (1982) *Management of organization behaviour: Utilizing human resources*, 4th edn. Englewood Cliffs, NJ: Prentice Hall.

Herzberg, F. (1966) Work and the Nature of Man. Cleveland: World Publishing.

Hitt, M.A., Black, S.J. and Porter, L.W. (2012) *Management*, 3rd edn. New Jersey: Pearson.

Hochschild, A.R. (1983) *The Managed Heart: Commercialization of human feeling*. Berkeley, CA: University of California Press.

Hoffman, M.L. (2008) Empathy and prosocial behavior. In M. Lewis, J.M. Haviland-Jones and L. Feldman Barrett (eds), *Handbook of Emotions*. New York: Guilford Press.

Hofstede, G. (1980) *Culture's Consequences: International differences in work related values*. Thousand Oaks, CA: Sage.

Hofstede, G. (1991) *Cultures and Organizations*. London: McGraw-Hill.

Hofstede, G. (1991) *Cultures and Organizations: Software of the mind*. London: HarperCollinsBusiness.

Hofstede, G., Hofstede G.J. and Minkov, M. (2010) *Cultures and Organisations: Software of the Mind*, 3rd edn. New York: McGraw-Hill.

Hogan, J., Barrett, P. and Hogan, R. (2007) Personality measurement, faking, and employment selection. *Journal of Applied Psychology*, 92, 1270–1285.

Hope, V. and Hendry, J. (1995) Corporate cultural change – Is it relevant for the organisations of the 1990s? *Human Resource Management Journal*, 5, 61–73.

House, R.J. (1971) A path goal theory of leader effectiveness. *Administrative Science Quarterly*, 16(3), 321–338.

House, R.J. and Mitchell, T.R. (1974) *Path-goal theory of leadership* (No. TR-75–67). Washington University Seattle Department of Psychology.

House, R.J., Hanges, P.J., Javidan, M. et al. (2004) Culture, Leadership, and Organizations: The GLOBE study of 62 societies. Thousand Oaks, CA: Sage.

Hovland, C.I., Janis, I.L. and Kelley, H.H. (1953) *Communication and Persuasion: Psychological studies of obvious change*. New Haven, CT: Greenwood Press.

Howard and Howard (2001) *The Owner's Manual for Personality at Work: How the Big Five Personality Traits affect your performance, communication, teamwork, leadership, and sales*. USA: Bard Press.

Huczynski, A. and Buchanan, D. (2001) *Organizational Behaviour: An introductory text*. Harlow: Pearson Education.

Huczynski, A. and Buchanan, D. (2014) *Organizational Behaviour: An introductory text*, 8th edn. New Jersey: Prentice Hall.

Hughes, L.A. and Short, J.F. Jr (2005) Disputes involving youth street gang members: Micro-social contexts. *Criminology*, 43(1).

Isern, J. and Pung, C. (2007) Harnessing energy to drive organizational change. *The McKinsey Quarterly*, 1, 1–4.

Issenberg, S. (2012) How President Obama's campaign used big data to rally individual voters. *MIT Technology Review*, 19 December 2012. Available at: www.technologyreview.com/featuredstory/509026/how-obamas-team-used-big-data-to-rally-voters/ (accessed 31 October 2014).

Izard, C.E. (2009) Emotion theory and research: Highlights, unanswered questions, and emerging issues. *Annual Review of Psychology*, 60, 1–25.

Jack, R.E., Caldara, R. and Schyns, P.G. (2012) Internal representations reveal cultural diversity in expectations of facial expressions of emotion. *Journal of Experimental Psychology: General*, 141(1), 19.

James, L.A. and James, L.R. (1989) Integrating work environment perceptions: Explorations into the measurement of meaning. *Journal of Applied Psychology*, 74, 739–751.

James, O. (2013) *Office Politics: How to thrive in a world of lying, backstabbing and dirty tricks*. London: Vermilion.

Jamieson, J.P., Mendes, W.B. and Nock, M.K. (2013) Improving acute stress responses the power of reappraisal. *Current Directions in Psychological Science*, 22, 51–56.

Janis, I. (1972) *Victims of Groupthink*. New York: Houghton Mifflin.

Jehn, K.A. and Mannix, E.A. (2001) The Dynamic Nature of Conflict: A longitudinal study of intragroup conflict and group performance. *Academy of Management Journal*, April, 238–251.

Johns, G. (2010) Presenteeism in the workplace: A review and research agenda. *Journal of Organizational Behavior*, 31(4), 519–542.

Jones, E., Watson, B., Gardner, J. and Gallois, C. (2004) Organization communication: Challenges for the new century. *Journal of Communication*, 54(4), 722–750.

Jones, G. (2010) *Organizational Theory, Design and Change*, 6th edn. New Jersey: Pearson.

Jones, R., Jimmieson, N. and Griffiths, A. (2005) The impact of organizational culture and reshaping capabilities on change implementation success: The mediating role of readiness for change. *Journal of Management Studies*, 42(2), 31–386.

Judge, T.A. and Bono, J.E. (2000) Five-factor model of personality and transformational leadership. *Journal of Applied Psychology*, 85, 751–765.

Judge, T.A. and Bono, J.E. (2001) Relationship of core self-evaluations traits – self-esteem, generalized self-efficacy, locus of control, and emotional stability – with job satisfaction and job performance: A meta-analysis. *Journal of Applied Psychology*, 86(1), 80–92.

Judge, T.A., Bono, J.E. and Thoresen, C.J. (2003) The core self-evaluation scale: Development of a measure. *Personnel Psychology*, 56, 303–331.

Judge, T.A., Heller, D. and Mount, M.K. (2002) Five-factor model of personality and job satisfaction: A meta-analysis. *Journal of Applied Psychology*, 87(3), 530–541.

Judge, T.A., Klinger, R., Simon, L.S. and Yang, I.W.F. (2008) The contributions of personality to organizational behavior and psychology: Findings, criticisms, and future research directions. *Social and Personality Psychology Compass*, 2(5), 1982–2000.

Judge, T. A., Lepine, J. A. and Rich, B. I. (2006) The narcissistic personality: Relationship with inflated self-ratings of leadership with task and contextual performance. *Journal of Applied Psychology*, 91(4), 762–776.

Judge, T.A., Piccolo, R.F. and Kosalka, T. (2009) The bright and dark sides of leader traits: A review and theoretical extension of the leader trait paradigm. *The Leadership Quarterly*, 20(6), 855–875.

Judge, T.A., Thoresen, C.J., Bono, J.E. and Patton, G.K. (2001) The job satisfaction–job performance relationship: A qualitative and quantitative review. *Psychological Bulletin*, 127(3), 376–407.

Kacmar, K.M., Collins, B.J., Harris, K.J. and Judge, T.A. (2009) Core self-evaluations and job performance: The role of the perceived work environment. *Journal of Applied Psychology*, 94(6), 1572–1580.

Kanter, R.M. (1977) *Men and Women on the Corporation*. New York: Basic Books.

Kanungo, R.N. (1982) Measurement of job and work involvement. *Journal of Applied Psychology*, 67(3), 341–349.

Kapp, K.M. and O'Driscoll, T. (2010) *Learning in 3D: Adding a new dimension to enterprise learning and collaboration*. John Wiley.

Karau, S.J. and Williams, K.D. (1993) Social loafing: A meta-analytic review and theoretical integration. *Journal of Personality and Social Psychology*, 65(4), 681–706

Kase, R., Paauwe, J. and Zupan, N. (2009) HR practices, interpersonal relationships and intra-firm knowledge transfer in knowledge-intensive firms: a social network perspective. *Human Resource Management*, 48(4), 615–639.

Kast, F.E. and Rosenzweig, J.E. (1972) General systems theory: Application for organizational and management. *Academy of Management Journal*, 15, 447–465.

Katzenbach, J.R. and Smith, D.K. (2005) The discipline of teams, *Harvard Business Review*, July.

Keith, N. and Frese, M. (2005) Self-regulation in error management training: Emotion control and metacognition as mediators of performance effects. *Journal of Applied Psychology*, 90, 677–691.

Kelley, H.H. (1973) The process of causal attribution. *American Psychologist*, 28(2), 107–128.

Kim, T., Hornung, S. and Rousseau, D. (2011) Change-supportive employee behavior: Antecedents and the moderating role of time. *Journal of Management*, 37(6), 1664–1693.

King, D.L. (2012) Social Media. *Library Technology Reports*, 48(6): 23–27.

Kinnunen, U., Mauno, S., Nätti, J. and Happonen, M. 1999. Perceived job insecurity: A longitudinal study among Finnish employees. *European Journal of Work and Organizational Psychology*, 8: 243–260.

Klein, S.M. (1996) A management communication strategy for change. *Journal of Organizational Change Management*, 9(2), 32–46.

Koole, S.L. (2009a) Does emotion regulation help or hurt self-regulation? . In J.P. Forgas, R.F. Baumeister and D.M. Tice (eds), *Psychology of Self-regulation: Cognitive, affective and motivational processes*. New York: Psychology Press.

Koole, S.L. (2009b) The psychology of emotion regulation: An integrative review. *Cognition & Emotion*, 23, 4–41.

Kopelman, R.E., Brief, A.P. and Guzzo, R.A. (1990) *The Role of Climate and Culture in Productivity*. San Francisco: Jossey-Bass.

Kotter, J. (1980) An integrative model of organizational dynamics. In E. Lawler, D. Nadler and C. Cammann (eds), *Organizational Assessment*. New York: Wiley.

Kotter, J.P. (1988) *The Leadership Factor*. New York: The Free Press.

Kotter, J.P. (1995) Leading change: Why transformation efforts fail. *Harvard Business Review*, 73(2), 59–67.

Kotter, J. (1996) *Leading Change*. Boston, MA: Harvard Business School Press.

Kotter, J. (1998) Cultures and coalitions. In R. Gibson (ed.), *Rethinking the Future: Rethinking business, principles, competition, control & complexity, leadership, markets and the world*. London: Nicholas Brealey.

Kotter, J.P. (2008) *Corporate Culture and Performance*. New York: Simon & Schuster.

Kotter, J.P. and Heskett, J.L. (1992) *Corporate Culture and Performance*, New York: Free Press.

Kotter, J. and Schlesinger, L. (1979) Choosing strategies for change. *Harvard Business Review*, 57(March/April), 106–114.

Kramer, A.D., Guillory, J.E. and Hancock, J.T. (2014) Experimental evidence of massive-scale emotional contagion through social networks. *Proceedings of the National Academy of Sciences*, 201320040.

Kross, E., Verduyn, P., Demiralp, E., Park, J., Lee, D.S., Lin, N., Shablack, H., Jonides, J. and Ybarra, O. (2013) Facebook use predicts declines in subjective well-being in young adults. *PLoS One*. 8(8): e69841. Available at: www.ncbi.nlm.nih.gov/pmc/articles/PMC3743827/ (accessed 18 March 2014).

Lambert, N.M., Gwinn, A.M., Baumeister, R.F., Strachman, A., Washburn, I.J., Gable, S.L. and Fincham, F.D. (2013)

A boost of positive affect: The perks of sharing positive experiences. *Journal of Social and Personal Relationships,* 30, 24–43.

Latane, B., Williams, K. and Harkins, S. (1979) Many hands make light the work: The causes and consequences of social loafing. *Journal of Personality and Social Psychology,* 37, 822–832.

Lawrence, P. and Lorsch, J.W. (1967) *Organization and Environment: Managing differentiation and integration.* Boston, MA: Harvard Business School Press.

Lazarus, R.S. (1991a) Cognition and motivation in emotion. *American Psychologist,* 46, 352–367.

Lazarus, R.S. (1991b) *Emotion and adaptation.* Oxford University Press.

Le, H., Oh, I.-S., Robbins, S.B., Ilies, R., Holland, E. and Westrick, P. (2011) Too much of a good thing: Curvilinear relationship between personality traits and job performance. *Journal of Applied Psychology,* 96(1), 113–133.

Lee, L., Frederick S. and Ariely D. (2006) Try it you'll like it: The influence of expectation, consumption and revelation on preference for beer. *Psychological Science,* 17(12), 1054–1058.

Leonard, H.S. and Lang, F. (2010) Leadership development via action learning. *Advances in Developing Human Resources,* 12(2), 225–240.

Levesque, M.J. and Kenny, D.A. (1993) Accuracy of behavioral predictions at zero acquaintance: A social relations analysis. *Journal of Personality and Social Psychology,* 65, 1178–1187.

Lewicki, R.J., Saunders, D.M. and Minton, J.W. (2011) *Essentials of Negotiation,* 5th edn. Boston: McGraw-Hill.

Lewin, K. (1948) *Resolving Social Conflicts.* New York: Harper & Row.

Lewin, K. (1951) *Field Theory in Social Science: Selected theoretical papers.* New York: Harper & Row.

Lewis, L.K. and Seibold, D.R. (2012) Reconceptualizing organizational change implementation as a communication problem: a review of literature and research agenda. In M.E. Roloff (ed.), *Communication Yearbook 21.* New York: Routledge.

Likert, R. (1932) A technique for the measurement of attitudes. *Archives of Psychology,* 22, 1–55

Likert, R. (1961) *New Patterns of Management.* New York: McGraw-Hill.

Lippitt, R., Watson, J. and Westley, B. (1958) *The Dynamics of Planned Change.* New York: Harcourt, Brace and World.

Locke, E.A. (1968) Toward a theory of task performance and incentives. *Organizational Behavior and Human Performance,* 3, 157–189.

Locke, E.A. (1976) The nature and causes of job satisfaction. *Handbook of Industrial and Organizational Psychology,* 1, 1297–1343.

Locke, E.A. and Latham, G.P. (1990) *A Theory of Goal Setting and Task Performance.* Upper Saddle River, NJ: Prentice Hall.

Locke, E.A. and Latham, G.P. (2002) Building a practically useful theory of goal setting and task motivation. *American Psychologist,* 57(9), 705–717.

Loehlin, J.C. (1992) *Genes and Environment in Personality Development.* Newbury Park, CA: Sage.

Lok, P. and Crawford, J. (2004) The effect of organisational culture and leadership style on job satisfaction and organisational commitment: A cross-national comparison. *Journal of Management Development,* 23(4), 321–338.

Lutz, M. (2009) The Social Pulpit: Barack Obama's Social Media Toolkit. Available at: http://cyber.law.harvard.edu/sites/cyber.law.harvard.edu/files/Social%20Pulpit%20-%20Barack%20Obamas%20Social%20Media%20Toolkit%201.09.pdf (accessed 17 April 2014).

Lyness, K.S. and Heilman, M.E. (2006) When fit is fundamental: Performance evaluations and promotions of upper-level female and male managers. *Journal of Applied Psychology,* 91(4), 777–785.

Lyubomirsky, S., King, L. and Diener, E. (2005) The benefits of frequent positive affect: Does happiness lead to success? *Psychological Bulletin,* 131, 803–855.

MacDuffie, J.P. (1995) Human resource bundles and manufacturing performance: Organizational logic and flexible production systems in the world auto industry. *Industrial & Labor Relations Review,* 48(2), 197–221.

Mann, S. (2013) Trust in virtual teams. *Leadership & Organization Development Journal,* 34(8), 805–806.

Martins, A., Ramalho, N. and Morin, E. (2010) A comprehensive meta-analysis of the relationship between emotional intelligence and health. *Personality and Individual Differences,* 49, 554–564.

Maslow, A.H. (1943) A theory of human motivation. *Psychological Review,* 50(4), 370–96.

Matsumoto, D. (1996) *Culture and Psychology.* Pacific Grove, CA: Brooks/Cole.

Maznevski, M. (2007) *IMD: Leading diverse teams Part 3.* Available at: http://video.ft.com/62063401001/IMD-Leading-diverse-teams/Management (accessed 2 June 2014).

McCall, M.W. and Lombardo, M.M. (1983) *Off the Track: Why and how successful executives get derailed* (No. 21). Center for Creative Leadership.

McCarthy, A. and Garavan, T. (2006) Postfeedback development perceptions: Applying the theory of planned behavior. *Human Resource Development Quarterly*, 17(3), 245–267.

McClelland, D.C. (1971) *Assessing Human Motivation*. Morristown, NJ: General Learning Corporation.

McClelland, D.C. (1985) *Human Motivation*. Glenview: Scott, Foresman.

McCrae, R.R. and Costa, P.T. Jr. (1987) Validation of the five-factor model of personality across instruments and observers. *Journal of Personality and Social Psychology*, 52, 81–90.

McCrae, R.R., Terracciano, A. and Members of the Personality Profiles of Cultures Project (2005) Personality profiles of cultures: Aggregate personality traits. *Journal of Personality and Social Psychology*, 89(3), 407–425.

McLuhan, M. (1964) *Understanding Media: The extensions of man*. New York: Signet Books.

McMahon, G. (2008) Gift of the gab – how best to deliver your message in public. *The Irish Times*, 21 March.

McShane, S.L. (2006) *Canadian Organizational Behaviour*, 6th edn. Boston, MA: McGraw Hill.

Meaney, M. and Pung, C. (2008) McKinsey global results: Creating organizational transformations. *The McKinsey Quarterly*, August, 1–7.

Meek, V.L. (1988) Organizational culture: origins and weaknesses. *Organization Studies*, 9(4), 453–473.

Megginson, D. (2006) *Mentoring in Action: A practical guide*. London: Kogan Page.

Mehrabian, A. (2007) *Nonverbal Communication*. Piscataway, NJ: Transaction Publishers.

Mehrabian, A. and Wiener, M. (1967) Decoding of inconsistent communications. *Journal of Personality and Social Psychology*, 6, 109–114.

Merton, R.K. (1948) The Self Fulfilling Prophecy. *Antioch Review*, 8(2, Summer), 193–210.

Miles, R., Snow, C., Fjeldstad, O., Miles, G. and Lettl, C. (2010) Designing organizations to meet 21st century opportunities and challenges. *Organizational Dynamics*, 39(2), 93–103.

Milgram, S. (1963) Behavioral Study of Obedience. *Journal of Abnormal and Social Psychology*, 67(4), 371–378.

Milgram, S. (1974) *Obedience to Authority: An Experimental View*. New York: HarperCollins.

Milne, P. (2007) Motivation, incentives and organisational culture. *Journal of Knowledge Management*, 11(6), 28–38.

Mintzberg, H. (1979a) *The Structuring of Organizations*. Englewood Cliffs, NJ: Prentice-Hall.

Mintzberg H. (1979b) The structuring of organizations: A synthesis of the research. University of Illinois at Urbana-Champaign's Academy for Entrepreneurial Leadership Historical Research Reference in Entrepreneurship.

Mintzberg, H. (1990a) *Mintzberg on Management: Inside our strange world of organizations*. London: Free Press, Macmillan.

Mintzberg, H. (1991) The effective organization: Forces and forms. *Sloan Management Review*, Winter, 54–67.

Mishra, K, Boynton, L. and Mishra, A. (2014) Driving employee engagement: The expanded role of internal communications. *International Journal of Business Communication*, 51(2), 183–202.

Mor Barak, M.E. (2014) *Managing Diversity: Towards a globally inclusive workforce*, 3rd edn. Thousand Oaks, CA: Sage.

Morrison, E.W. (1993) Newcomer information seeking: Exploring types, modes, sources, and outcomes. *Academy of Management Journal*, 36(3), 557–589.

Mowday, R.T., Porter, L.W. and Steers, R.M. (1982) *Employee–Organization Linkages: The psychology of commitment, absenteeism and turnover*. London: Academic Press.

Mowday, R.T., Steers, R.M. and Porter, L.W. (1979) The measurement of organizational commitment. *Journal of Vocational Behavior*, 14(2), 224–247.

Moyer, C.A. and Katz, K. (2007) Online patient-provider communication: How will it fit? *The Electronic Journal of Communication*, 17(3–4), 1–14.

Mullins, L.J. (2007) *Management and Organisational Behaviour*. Harlow: Pearson Education.

Mullins, L.J. (2013) *Management and Organisational Behaviour*, 10th edn. Harlow: Pearson.

Naylor, J. (2004) *Management*, 2nd edn. Harlow: Financial Times, Prentice Hall.

Neeley, T. and Leonardi, P. (2011) Effective managers say the same thing twice (or more). *Harvard Business Review*, May, 38–39.

Nelson, B. (2010) Creating high-performing teams: Characteristics of an effective team and team recognition tips. *Healthcare Registration*, 19(9), 10–13.

Nettleton, S., Burrows, R. and Watt, I. (2008) How do you feel doctor? An analysis of emotional aspects of routine professional medical work. *Social Theory & Health*, 6, 18–36.

Nicholson, N. (2003) How to motivate your problem people. *Harvard Business Review*, 81(1), 56–58.

Nicholson, N. and Johns, G. (1985) The absence culture and psychological contract—Who's in control of absence? *Academy of Management Review*, 10(3), 397–407.

Niedenthal, P.M., Krauth-Gruber, S. and Ric, F. (2006) *Psychology of Emotion: Interpersonal, experiential, and cognitive approaches*. New York: Psychology Press.

Noe, A.R. (2010) *Employee Training and Development*, 5th edn. New York: McGraw-Hill.

Northcraft, G.B., Polzer, J.T., Neale, M.A. and Kramer.R. (1995) Productivity in cross-functional teams: Diversity, social identity, and performance. In S.E. Jackson and M.N. Ruderman (eds), *Diversity in Work Teams: Research paradigms for a changing world*. Washington, DC: APA Publications.

O'Callaghan, J. (2014) The unsocial network? Facebook users who say they are 'lonely' are more likely to overshare personal information. Available at: www.dailymail.co.uk/sciencetech/article-2640390/The-unsocial-network-Facebook-users-say-lonely-likely-overshare-personal-information.html (accessed 2 June 2014).

Ofri, D. (2013) *What Doctors Feel: How emotion affects the practice of medicine*. Boston: Beacon Press.

Ohlott, P.J. (2004) Job assignments. *The Center for Creative Leadership Handbook of Leadership Development*, 2, 151–182.

Oldham, G.R. and Cummings, A. (1996) Employee creativity: Personal and contextual factors at work. *Academy of Management Journal*, 39, 607–634.

O'Reilly, C. (1989) Corporations, culture and commitment: Motivation and social control in organizations. *California Management Review*, 31, 9–25.

Organ, D.W. (1997) Organizational citizenship behavior: It's construct clean-up time. *Human Performance*, 10(2), 85–97.

Orsburn, J.D., Moran, L., Musselwhite, E. and Zenger, J.H. (1990) *Self-Directed Work Teams: The new American challenge*. Homewood, IL: Business One Irwin.

Ostroff, C., Kinicki, A.J. and Tamkins, M.M. (2003) Organizational culture and climate. In W.C. Borman, D.R. Ilgen, R.J. Klimoski and I. Weiner (eds), *Handbook of Psychology, Vol. 12*. Hoboken, NJ: Wiley.

Palmer, J.K. and Loveland, J. (2008) The influence of group discussion on performance judgments: Rating accuracy, contrast effects, and halo. *The Journal of Psychology*, 142(2) 117–130.

Parker, G.M. (1990) *Team Players and Teamwork*. San Francisco, Jossey-Bass.

Parker, S.K., Bindl, U.K. and Strauss, K. (2010) Making things happen: A model of proactive motivation. *Journal of Management*, 36, 827–856.

Paulhus, D.L. and Williams, K.M. (2002) The dark triad of personality: Narcissism, Machiavellianism, and psychopathy. *Journal of Research in Personality*, 36(6), 556–563.

Paulhus, P.B., Dzindolet, M.T., Poletes, G. and Camacho, L.M. (1993) Perception of performance in group brainstorming: The illusion of group productivity. *Personality and Social Psychology Bulletin*, 19(1), 78–89.

Pekrun, R. (2006) The control-value theory of achievement emotions: Assumptions, corollaries, and implications for educational research and practice. *Educational Psychology Review*, 18, 315–341.

Perrow, C. (1967) A framework for the comparative analysis of organizations. *American Sociological Review*, 32, 194–208.

Peters, T. and Waterman, R. (1982) *In Search of Excellence – Lessons from America's best-run companies*. London: HarperCollins Publishers.

Petrides, K. (2011) Ability and trait emotional intelligence. *The Wiley-Blackwell Handbook of Individual Differences*. Chichester: John Wiley.

Petrides, K.V. and Furnham, A. (2003) Trait emotional intelligence: Behavioural validation in two studies of emotion recognition and reactivity to mood induction. *European Journal of Personality*, 17, 39–57.

Petty, R.E. and Cacioppo, J.T. (1986) The elaboration likelihood model of persuasion. *Advances in Experimental Social Psychology*, 19, 123–205.

Peyton, J., Caputo, J.M., Ford, E.A., Fu, R., Leibowitz, S.A., Liu, T., Polasik, S.S., Ghosh, P. and Wu, C. (2013) Investigating verbal workplace communication behaviors. *Journal of Business Communication* 50(2), 152–169.

Pfeffer, J. (1981) *Power in Organisations*. London: HarperCollins.

Pfeffer, J. (1992) *Managing with Power: Politics and influence in organisations*. Boston: Harvard Business School Press.

Piderit, S.K. (2000) Rethinking resistance and recognizing ambivalence: A multidimensional view of attitudes toward an organizational change. *Academy of Management Review*, 25(4), 783–794.

Pink, D.H. (2011) *Drive: The surprising truth about what motivates us.* London: Cannongate.

Podsakoff, P.M. and Williams, L.J. (1986) The relationship between job performance and job satisfaction. In E.A. Locke (ed.), *Generalizing from Laboratory to Field Settings.* Lexington, MA: Lexington Books.

Polley, D. and Ribbens, B. (1998) Sustaining self-managed teams: A process approach to team wellness. *Team Performance Management*, 4(1), 3–21.

Popovich, P. and Wanous, J.P. (1982) The realistic job preview as a persuasive communication. *Academy of Management Review*, 7(4), 570–578.

Proença, T. (2010) Self-managed work teams: An enabling or coercive nature. *The International Journal of Human Resource Management*, 21(3), 337–354.

Purcell, J., Kinnie, N., Hutchinson, S., Rayton, B. and Swart, J. (2003) *Understanding the People and Performance Link: Unlocking the black box.* London, CIPD.

Quinn, R.E., Faerman, S.R., Thompson, M.P. and McGrath, M.R. (2003) *Becoming a Master Manager: A competency framework*, 3rd edn. New York: John Wiley.

Quoidbach, J., Berry, E.V., Hansenne, M. and Mikolajczak, M. (2010) Positive emotion regulation and well-being: Comparing the impact of eight savoring and dampening strategies. *Personality and Individual Differences*, 49, 368–373.

Reich, B. and Adcock, C. (1976) *Values, Attitudes and Behaviour Change.* London: Methuen.

Rentsch, J.R. and McEwen, A.H. (2002) Comparing personality characteristics, values, and goals as antecedents of organizational attractiveness. *International Journal of Selection and Assessment*, 10(3), 225–234.

Rich, B.L., Lepine, J.A. and Crawford, E.R. (2010) Job engagement: Antecedents and effects on job performance. *Academy of Management Journal*, 53(3), 617–635.

Riketta, M. (2008) The causal relation between job attitudes and performance: A meta-analysis of panel studies. *Journal of Applied Psychology*, 93(2), 472–481.

Robbins, S.P. and Judge, T.A. (2010) *Essentials of Organizational Behavior.* 10th edn. New Jersey: Pearson.

Robbins, S.P. and Judge, T.A. (2012) *Essentials of Organizational Behavior*, global edn. Harlow: Pearson.

Roberson, L. and Kulik, C.T. (2007) Stereotype threat at work. *Academy of Management Perspectives*, 21(2), 24–40.

Roberts, B.W., Walton, K.E. and Viechtbauer, W. (2006) Patterns of mean-level change in personality traits across the life course: A meta-analysis of longitudinal studies. *Psychological Bulletin*, 132, 1–25.

Robinson, M.D. and Barrett, L.F. (2010) Belief and feeling in self-reports of emotion: Evidence for semantic infusion based on self-esteem. *Self and Identity*, 9, 87–111.

Roethlisberger, F.J and Dickson, W.J. (1939) *Management and the Worker.* Cambridge, MA: Harvard University Press.

Rosenberg, S., Heimler, R. and Morote, E.S. (2012) Basic employability skills: a triangular design approach. *Education + Training*, 54(1), 7–20.

Ross, L. and Nisbett, R.E. (1991) *The Person and the Situation: Perspectives of social psychology.* Philadelphia: Temple University Press.

Rouse, K.A.G. (2004) Beyond Maslow's hierarchy of needs what do people strive for? *Performance Improvement*, 43, 27–31.

Rousseau, D.M. (1995) *Psychological Contracts in Organizations: Understanding written and unwritten agreements.* Thousand Oaks, CA: Sage.

Rousseau, D.M. (2006) Is there such a thing as 'evidence-based management'? *Academy of Management Review*, 31(2), 256–269.

Rousseau, D.M. (2011) Organisational climate and culture. In J. Mager Stellman (ed.), *Encyclopedia of Occupational Health and Safety.* Geneva: International Labor Organization. Available at: www.ilo.org/oshenc/part-v/psychosocial-and-organizational-factors/macro-organizational-factors/item/29-organizational-climate-and-culture?tmpl=component&print=1 (accessed 12 July 2014).

Russell, J.A. (2003) Core affect and the psychological construction of emotion. *Psychological Review*, 110, 145–172.

Russell, J.A. and Barrett, L.F. (1999) Core affect, prototypical emotional episodes, and other things called emotion: Dissecting the elephant. *Journal of Personality and Social Psychology*, 76, 805–819.

Sackett, S. J. (1998). Career counseling as an aid to self-actualization. *Journal of Career Development*, 24(3), 235–244.

Sackmann, S.A. (2011) Culture and performance. In N. Ashkanasy, C. Wilderom and M. Peterson (eds), *The Handbook of Organizational Culture and Climate*, 2nd edn. Thousand Oaks, CA: Sage.

Saks, A.M. (2008) The meaning and bleeding of employee engagement: How muddy is the water? *Industrial and Organizational Psychology*, 1(1), 40–43.

Salamon, M.W. (2000) *Industrial Relations: Theory and practice*, 4th edn. Harlow: Financial Times Prentice Hall.

Salancik, G.R. and Pfeffer, J. (1978) A social information processing approach to job attitudes and task design. *Administrative Science Quarterly*, 23, 224–253.

Salovey, P. and Mayer, J.D. (1990) Emotional intelligence. *Imagination, Cognition and Personality*, 9, 185–211.

Salovey, P., Hsee, C. and Mayer, J.D. (1993) Emotional intelligence and the self-regulation of affect. In D.M. Wegner and J.W. Pennebaker (eds), *Handbook of Mental Control*. Englewood Cliffs, NJ: Prentice-Hall.

Sandberg, S. (2013) *Lean In: Women, work, and the will to lead*. New York: Alfred A. Knopf.

Saucier, G. (1994) Mini-markers: A brief version of Goldberg's unipolar Big-Five markers. *Journal of Personality Assessment*, 63(3), 506–516.

Schein, E.H. (1980) *Organizational Psychology*, 3rd edn. Englewood Cliffs, NJ: Prentice Hall.

Schein, E.H. (1985) *Organizational Culture and Leadership: A dynamic view*. San Francisco: Jossey-Bass.

Schein, E.H. (1990) Organizational culture. *American Psychologist*, 45, 109-119.

Schein, E.H. (2004) *Organizational Culture and Leadership*. San Francisco: Jossey-Bass.

Schein, V.E. (1977) Individual power and political behaviors in organizations: An inadequately explored reality. *Academy of Management Review*, 2, 64–72.

Scherer, M. (2012) Inside the secret world of the data crunchers who helped Obama win. *Time Magazine*, 7 November 2012. Available at: http://swampland.time.com/2012/11/07/inside-the-secret-world-of-quants-and-data-crunchers-who-helped-obama-win/ (accessed 31 October 2014).

Schneider, B. and Rentsch, J. (1988) Managing climates and cultures: a future perspective. In J. Hage (ed.), *Futures of Organizations*. Lexington, MA: Lexington Books.

Schonfeld, I.S. (2000) Short research paper: An updated look at depressive symptoms and job satisfaction in first-year women teachers. *Journal of Occupational and Organizational Psychology*, 73(3), 363–371.

Schutte, N.S., Malouff, J.M., Thorsteinsson, E.B., Bhullar, N. and Rooke, S.E. (2007) A meta-analytic investigation of the relationship between emotional intelligence and health. *Personality and Individual Differences*, 42, 921–933.

Schwartz, H. and Davis, D. (1981) *Matching Corporate Culture and Strategy*. Cambridge, MA: MAP Concept Paper.

Schwarz, N. (2001) Feelings as information: Implications for affective influences on information processing. In L. Martin and G. Clore (eds), *Theories of Mood and Cognition: A user's guidebook*. Mahwah, NJ: Lawrence Erlbaum Associates.

Schwarz, N. and Clore, G.L. (2003) Mood as information: 20 years later. *Psychological Inquiry*, 14, 296–303.

Scott, W.R. (1995) *Institutions and Organizations*. Thousand Oaks, CA: Sage.

Seibert, S.E. and Kraimer, M.L. (2001) The five-factor model of personality and career success. *Journal of Vocational Behavior*, 58(1), 1–21.

Seijts, G.H. and Latham, G.P. (2001) The effect of learning, outcome, and proximal goals on a moderately complex task. *Journal of Organizational Behavior*, 22, 291–307.

Seo, M.G. and Barrett, L.F. (2007) Being emotional during decision making – good or bad? An empirical investigation. *Academy of Management Journal*, 50, 923–940.

Seo, M.G., Barrett, L.F. and Bartunek, J.M. (2004) The role of affective experience in work motivation. *Academy of Management Review*, 29, 423–439.

Seo, M., Taylor, M., Hill, N., Zhang, X., Tesluk, P. and Lorinkova, N. (2012) The role of affect and leadership during organizational change. *Personnel Psychology*, 65(1), 121–165.

Shahzad, F., Iqbal, Z. and Gulzar, M. (2013) Impact of organizational culture on employees job performance: An empirical study of software houses in Pakistan. *Journal of Business Studies Quarterly*, 5(2), 55–64.

Shannon, C.E. (1948) A mathematical theory of communication. *The Bell System Technical Journal*, 27(3).

Sheridan, J.E. (1992) Organizational culture and employee retention. *Academy of Management Journal*, 35, 1036–1056.

Sherman, L.W. (2002) Evidence-based policing: Social organization of information for social control. In E. Warring and D. Weisburd (eds), *Crime and Social Organization*. New Brunswick, NJ: Transaction.

Shi, X. and Wang, J. (2011) Interpreting Hofstede Model and GLOBE Model: Which way to go for cross-cultural research? *International Journal of Business and Management*, 6(5), 93–99.

Siehl, C. and Martin, J. (1990) Organizational culture: A key to financial performance? In B. Schneider (ed.) *Organizational Climate and Culture*. San Francisco: Jossey-Bass.

Simmons, B.L., Nelson, D.L. and Neal, L.J. (2001) A comparison of the positive and negative work attitudes of home health care and hospital nurses. *Health Care Management Review*, 26(3), 63–74.

Skarbek, D. (2012) Prison gangs, norms, and organizations. *Journal of Economic Behavior & Organization* 82(1), 96–109.

Smircich, L. (1983) Concepts of culture and organizational analysis. *Administrative Science Quarterly*, 28, 339–358.

Sobek II, D.K., Liker, J.K. and Ward, A.C. (1998) Another look at how Toyota integrates product development. *Harvard Business Review*, 76(4), 36–47.

Society for Human Resource Management (2010) Workplace diversity practices: How has diversity and inclusion changed over time? Alexandria, Va: SHRM. Available at: www.thehrgroupinc.net/assets/galleries/Events/Diversity-Leadership-Conf-2010/PowerPoint-presentations/Workplace-Diversity-Practices-Change-Over-Time.pdf (accessed 24 August 2015)

Solinger, O.N., Van Olffen, W. and Roe, R.A. (2008) Beyond the three-component model of organizational commitment. *Journal of Applied Psychology*, 93(1), 70–83.

Somech, A. and Drach-Zahavy, A. (2001), Relative power and influence strategy: The effects of agent/target organizational power on superiors' choices of influence strategies. *Journal of Organizational Behavior*, 23, 167–179.

Sørensen, J.B. (2002) The strength of corporate culture and the reliability of firm performance. *Administrative Science Quarterly*, 47(1), 70–91.

Spain, S.M., Harms, P. and LeBreton, J.M. (2014) The dark side of personality at work. *Journal of Organizational Behavior*, 35(S1), S41–S60.

Spillane, J.P. and Diamond, J.B. (2007) *Distributed Leadership in Practice*. New York: Teachers College Press.

Spitzer, D. (1995) *SuperMotivation*. New York: AMACOM Books.

Sproull, L. and Kiesler, S. (1991) *Connections: New ways of working in the networked organization*. Cambridge, MA: MIT Press.

Stahl, G.K., Maznevski, M.L., Voigt, A. and Jonsen, K. (2010) Unraveling the effects of cultural diversity in teams: A meta-analysis of research on multicultural work groups. *Journal of International Business Studies*, 41(4), 690–709.

Stajkovic, A.D. and Luthans, F. (1997) A meta-analysis of the effects of organizational behavior modification on task performance, 1975–95. *Academy of Management Journal*, 40(5), 1122–1149.

Stanford, N. (2010) Organisation culture: Getting it right. *The Economist*. London: Profile Books.

Staw, B.M., Sutton, R.I. and Pelled, L.H. (1994) Employee positive emotion and favorable outcomes at the workplace. *Organization Science*, 5, 51–71.

Steele, C.M. and Aronson, J. (1995) Stereotype threat and the intellectual test performance of African Americans. *Journal of Personality and Social Psychology*, 69(5), 797–811.

Steers, R.M., Bigley, G.A. and Porter, L.W. (2002) *Motivation and Leadership at Work*, 7th edn. New York: McGraw-Hill.

Stewart, G.L. and Carson, K.P. (1995) Personality dimensions and domains of service performance: A field investigation. *Journal of Business and Psychology*, 9, 365–378.

Stogdill, R.M. (1974) *Handbook of Leadership*. Chicago: Free Press.

Stogdill, R.M. and Coons A.E. (1957) *Leader behavior: Its description and measurement*. Columbus: Ohio State University, Bureau of Business Research.

Super, D.E. and Sverko, B. (1995) *Life Roles, Values, and Careers*. San Franciso: Jossey-Bass.

Superville, D. (2014) Michelle Obama praises decline in childhood obesity. *Huffington Post*, 26 February 2014. Available at: www.huffingtonpost.com/2014/02/26/michelle-obama-childhood-obesity_n_4862663.html (accessed 19 April 2014).

Suri, G. and Gross, J.J. (2012) What good are emotions anyway? In P. Totterdell and K. Niven (eds), *Should I Strap a Battery to my Head? (and Other Questions about Emotion)*. Self-published.

Swanson, S. R., Kelley, S.W. and Dorsch, M. J. (1997) Inter-organizational ethical perceptions and buyer-seller relationships. *Journal of Business-to-Business Marketing*, 4: 3–31.

Swiercz, P.M. and Lydon, S.R. (2002) Entrepreneurial leadership in high-tech firms: a field study. *Leadership & Organization Development Journal*, 23(7), 380–389.

Tajfel, H. (1974) Social identity and intergroup behaviour. *Social Science Information*, 13, 65–93.

Tamir, M. and Ford, B.Q. (2009) Choosing to be afraid: Preferences for fear as a function of goal pursuit. *Emotion*, 9, 488–497.

Tamir, M. and Ford, B.Q. (2012) When feeling bad is expected to be good: Emotion regulation and outcome expectancies in social conflicts. *Emotion*, 12, 807–816.

Templar, R. (2012) *The Rules of Work*. Harlow: Pearson Education.

Thomas, H.D. and Anderson, N. (1998) Changes in newcomers' psychological contracts during organizational socialization: A study of recruits entering the British Army. *Journal of Organizational Behavior*, 19(s1), 745–767.

Thomas, K.W. (1976) Conflict and conflict management. In M.D. Dunnette (ed.), *Handbook of Industrial and Organizational Psychology*. Chicago: Rand-McNally.

Thompson, L. (2003) Improving the creativity of organizational work groups. *Academy of Management Executive*, 17, 96–109.

Thompson, N. (2013) *People Management*. Basingstoke: Palgrave Macmillan.

Thoresen, C.J., Kaplan, S.A., Barsky, A.P., Warren, C.R. and de Chermont, K. (2003) The affective underpinnings of job perceptions and attitudes: A meta-analytic review and integration. *Psychological Bulletin*, 129, 914–945.

Thurstone, L.L. (1928) Attitudes can be measured. *American Journal of Sociology*, 33(4) 529–554.

Thurstone, L.L. (1931) The measurement of social attitudes. *The Journal of Abnormal and Social Psychology*, 26(3), 249–269.

Tice, D.M. (2009) How emotions affect self-regulation. In J.P. Forgas, R.F. Baumeister and D.M. Tice (eds), *Psychology of Self-regulation: Cognitive, affective and motivational processes*. New York: Psychology Press.

Tjosvold, D., Andrews, I.R. and Struthers, J.T. (1992) Leadership influence: Goal interdependence and power, *Journal of Social Psychology*, 132(1), 39–50.

Tuckman, B. (1965) Developmental sequence in small groups. *Psychological Bulletin*, 63(6), 384–399.

Tuckman, B.W. and Jensen, M.A. (1977) Stages in small group development revisited. *Group and Organisation Studies*, 2, 419–427

Turnipseed, L. (2002) Are good soldiers good? Exploring the link between organization citizenship behavior and personal ethics. *Journal of Business Research*, 55(1), 1–15.

Uhlaner, R. and West, A. (2011) McKinsey global survey results: Organizing for M&A. *The McKinsey Quarterly*, December, 1–8.

Van Der Lowe, I. (2012) Do emotions lead me to make dumb decisions? In P. Totterdell and K. Niven (eds), *Should I Strap a Battery to my Head? (and Other Questions about Emotion)*. Self-published.

Van Hoye, G. and Lievens, F. (2009) Tapping the grapevine: A closer look at word-of-mouth as a recruitment source. *Journal of Applied Psychology*, 94(2), 341–352.

Van Maanen, J (1978) People Processing: Strategies of organizational socialization. *Organizational Dynamics*, Summer 1978, 19–36.

Van Maanen, J. and Schein, E.H. (1979) Toward a theory of organizational socialization. *Research in Organizational Behavior*, (1) 209–264.

Vargas, J.A. (2008) Obama's Wide Web. *Washington Post*. 20 August 2008. Available at: www.washingtonpost.com/wp-dyn/content/article/2008/08/19/AR2008081903186_pf.html (accessed 17 April 2014).

Vigil, J.M. (2010) Political leanings vary with facial expression processing and psychosocial functioning. *Group Processes & Intergroup Relations*, 13, 547–558.

Vroom, V.H. (1964) *Work and Motivation*. New York: Wiley.

Wahba, M.A. and Bridwell, L.G. (1976) Maslow reconsidered: A review of research on the need hierarchy theory. *Organizational Behavior and Human Performance*, 15, 212-240.

Wallace, J., Gunnigle, P., McMahon, G. and O'Sullivan, M. (2013) *Industrial Relations in Ireland*, 4th edn. Dublin: Gill & Macmillan.

Walther, J.B. (1996) Computer-mediated communication – impersonal, interpersonal, and hyperpersonal interaction. *Human Communication Research*, 23(1), 3–43.

Walton, R.E. (1969) *Interpersonal Peace-making: Confrontation and third-party consultation*. Reading, MA: Addison-Wesley.

Wasti, S.A. and Can, Ö. (2008) Affective and normative commitment to organization, supervisor, and coworkers: Do collectivist values matter? *Journal of Vocational Behavior*, 73(3), 404–413.

Watson, D. and Clark, L.A. (1984) Negative affectivity: The disposition to experience aversive emotional states. *Psychological Bulletin*, 96, 465–490.

Watson, D. and Naragon, K. (2009) Positive affectivity: The disposition to experience positive emotional states. In S.J. Lopez and C.R. Snyder (eds), *The Oxford Handbook of Positive Psychology*, 2nd edn. Oxford: Oxford University Press.

Watson, D., Clark, L.A. and Tellegen, A. (1988) Development and validation of brief measures of positive and negative affect: The panas scales. *Journal of Personality and Social Psychology*, 54, 1063–1070.

Watson, T. (2002) *Organising and Managing Work*. Harlow: Prentice Hall.

Weber, M. (1947) *The Theory of Social and Economic Organization*. New York: Oxford University Press.

Weiner, B. (2009) A theory of organizational readiness for change. *Implementation Science*, 4(1), 67–75.

Werner, J.M. and DeSimone, R.L. (2006) *Human Resource Development*, 4th edn. Mason, OH: Thomson South-Western.

Wertheim, E.G. (2009) *Making Effective Oral Presentations*. Northeastern University, College of Business Administration. Available at: www.honors.vcu.edu/pdfs/MakingEffectiveOralPresentations.doc (accessed 21 April 2014).

Wertheimer, M. (1958) Principle of perceptual organization. In D.C. Beardslee and M. Wertheimer (eds), *Readings in Perception*. Princeton, NJ: Van Nostrand Co., Inc.

Wesson, M.G. and Gogus, C.I. (2005) Shaking hands with a computer: an examination of two methods of organizational newcomer orientation. *Journal of Applied Psychology*, 90(5), 1018–1026.

Wey Smola, K. and Sutton, C.D. (2002) Generational differences: Revisiting generational work values for the new millennium. *Journal of Organizational Behavior*, 23(4), 363–382.

Wilkinson, A. (1998) Empowerment: theory and practice. *Personnel Review*, 27(1), 40–56

Wilmot, W.W. and Hocker, J.L. (2007) *Interpersonal Conflict*. New York: McGraw Hill.

Wright, P., Dunford, B. and Snell, S. (2001) Human resources and the resource based view of the firm. *Journal of Management*, 27(6), 701–721.

Wu, J. and LeBreton, J.M. (2011) Reconsidering the dispositional basis of counterproductive work behavior: The role of aberrant personality traits. *Personnel Psychology*, 64, 593–626.

Yukl, G., Kim, H. and Falbe, C.M. (1996) Antecedents of influence outcomes. *Journal of Applied Psychology*, 81(3), 309–317.

Zeidner, M., Matthews, G. and Roberts, R.D. (2004) Emotional intelligence in the workplace: A critical review. *Applied Psychology*, 53, 371–399.

INDEX

Page numbers in **bold** refer to tables and in *italic* refer to figures.